The Essential Elements of Public Speaking

Joseph A. DeVito

Hunter College of the
City University of New York

PEARSON

Boston   New York   San Francisco
Mexico City   Montreal   Toronto   London   Madrid   Munich   Paris
Hong Kong   Singapore   Tokyo   Cape Town   Sydney

Executive Editor: Karon Bowers
Series Editor: Brian Wheel
Series Editorial Assistant: Heather Hawkins
Senior Marketing Manager: Mandee Eckersley
Editorial Production Service: Nesbitt Graphics
Composition Buyer: Linda Cox
Manufacturing Buyer: JoAnne Sweeney
Electronic Composition: Nesbitt Graphics
Interior Design: Nesbitt Graphics
Photo Researcher: Julie Tesser
Cover Administrator: Joel Gendron

For related titles and support materials, visit our online catalog at www.ablongman.com.

Between the time website information is gathered and then published, it is not unusual for some sites to have closed. Also, the transcription of URLs can result in typographical errors. The publisher would appreciate notification where these errors occur so that they may be corrected in subsequent editions.

Library of Congress Cataloging -in-Publication Data

DeVito, Joseph A.,
    The essential elements of public speaking/Joseph A. DeVito.—2nd ed.
       p. cm.
    Includes bibliographical references and index.
    ISBN 0-205-42381-7
       1. Public speaking. I. Title.

PN4129.15.D48 2005
808.5'1—dc22   2005041118

Credits appear on page 320, which constitutes on extension of the copyright page.

Printed in the United States of America

10 9 8 7 6 5 4 3 2 1 VHP 09 08 07 06 05

Detailed Contents

Specialized Contents

Critical Listening/Thinking Links

These boxes highlight the skills of critical listening and critical thinking that you need to apply in public speaking. Each of these links ends with a "Getting Critical" section that asks you to apply the content of the box to your own experiences.

Research Links

The Research Links explain the principles of effective and efficient research and identify lots of resource materials that you'll find useful in researching your speeches as well as throughout your college and professional career. Each of these links ends with a "Research Activity" that asks you to explore the principles of research and some of the most valuable research resources available.

Test Yourself

In every chapter a self-test headed "Test Yourself" asks you to pause and reflect on your thoughts and behaviors. In working with these tests, focus on the statements in the test, on the issues they raise, and on the thoughts they help generate. The number you get "right" or "wrong" or the score you get (some tests yield scores for comparison purposes) is far less important. These self-assessment instruments will help you personalize the material in the text and apply it to your own public speaking, listening, and criticizing.

A Case of Ethics

These ethics boxes explain principles of ethics, present you with ethical dilemmas, and ask what you would do in various situations.

Speeches

A variety of sample speeches will help you see what a poor speech looks like (the speeches in Chapters 2 and 3 are purposely poor examples) and what excellent speeches look like (all the remaining speeches in the text are models of effectiveness) —and will clarify the principles that make the difference.

Welcome to *The Essential Elements of Public Speaking*

The Essential Elements of Public Speaking will guide you through one of the most important courses you'll take in your entire college career: a course that will prove exciting, challenging, and immensely practical. The book will help you master the skills you'll need to give effective informative, persuasive, and special occasion speeches, as well as to listen more critically to the speeches of others. It will also help you increase your social and workplace communication abilities and enhance a wide variety of academic and professional skills such as organization, research, and language usage.

This text was designed to help you develop effective public speaking skills as efficiently as possible. Despite its relatively brief length, *The Essential Elements of Public Speaking* is a complete learning package and covers the entire range of topics in public speaking. It just does so without a lot of fluff.

Main Features of *The Essential Elements of Public Speaking*

Among the main features of this text are:

1. an initial concise overview of the steps in public speaking
2. critical listening/thinking links
3. research links
4. ethics cases
5. using technology suggestions
6. strategy development probes
7. self-appraisal tests
8. an emphasis on the cultural dimensions of public speaking

In addition, each chapter includes a summary, a vocabulary quiz, a section identifying Web experiences, and exercises to help you learn and internalize the material presented throughout this text and in your public speaking course.

Brief Overview of the Steps in Public Speaking

The first chapter presents the **10 steps for preparing a public speech** so that you can begin delivering speeches almost immediately. Here you'll learn to:

1. select your topic and purpose
2. analyze your audience
3. research your topic
4. develop your thesis and main points
5. support your main points
6. organize your speech materials
7. word your speech
8. construct your introduction, conclusion, and transitions
9. rehearse your speech
10. deliver your speech

The remaining chapters elaborate on these steps and will help you to gradually refine and perfect your public speaking skills.

Critical Listening/Thinking Links

Public speaking is a two-way process: Not only is it important to learn to develop and deliver public speeches, but it's also important to develop critical listening and critical thinking skills for your role as a receiver of public messages. Because of this, 16 **Critical Listening/Thinking Links** throughout the text highlight the skills for critically evaluating what you hear. Notable among the changes in these boxes is an expanded emphasis on fallacies; three Critical Listening/Thinking boxes focus on fallacies (fallacies of language in Chapter 7 and fallacies of personal attacks and of pseudo-argument, both in Chapter 10). A complete list of these Critical Listening/Thinking Links appears in the Specialized Contents.

In addition, a 25-question guide to listening and criticism appears on the inside back cover. Use this as a ready reference to help you check your own speeches and to help you formulate and express criticism of the speeches of others.

Research Links

Research is essential to an effective public speech and, of course, to your entire college and professional career. So knowing how to conduct research and knowing how to evaluate it are crucial skills. Rather than

presenting research in a traditional dense chapter, this book intersperses discussions of research throughout the text in 22 **Research Links**—about 2 per chapter. These Research Links progress from general research principles in early chapters to more specialized skills in later chapters. This approach will help you digest the information and will let you gradually practice research strategies. By the end of the course, you'll have mastered an arsenal of specific research techniques that will help you not only in public speaking but also throughout your college courses and into your professional life. A complete list of these Research Links appears in the Specialized Contents.

A Case of Ethics

Because public speaking is a powerful medium that can have enormous consequences, it has important moral implications. In each chapter of this book a box titled **A Case of Ethics** describes a situation that raises an ethical issue and asks how you would respond. By the end of the text, you should have formulated a clear and defensible ethical standard to govern your own public speaking. A complete list of these A Case of Ethics boxes appears in the Specialized Contents.

Using Technology

We're living in a time when technology dominates just about every aspect of our lives—and public speaking is no exception. Therefore, technology is discussed throughout the text. In addition, several **Using Technology** suggestions appear in the margins of each chapter. These items ask you to use the Internet to discover more about the topic or to uncover a variety of specific information. By the end of the course, you should feel comfortable researching just about any topic, using the latest and most efficient research tools.

When using the Internet, keep two cautions in mind. First, the Internet is constantly changing. URLs that are popular today may be shut down when you go to access them again later. This is simply one of the problems with such a huge and volatile system. Part of the art of Internet research is to work around these problems and to locate the same or similar information on other websites. Second, information on the Internet varies from the most scientifically accurate to the downright wrong and purposely misleading. Throughout this text you'll find suggestions for evaluating Internet information—useful tools that will help you distinguish the reliable from the worthless.

Developing Strategies

In all your public speaking experiences, you'll be confronted with choice points at which you'll have to make decisions as to what to say or how to say it. To help you in this essential process, **Developing Strategies** items appear in the margins of each chapter. As you seek to weigh the various options and the evidence and argument bearing on each, you'll fine-tune the skills you need for preparing and presenting effective speeches.

Test Yourself

Twelve **Test Yourself** features are interspersed throughout the text. These self-tests will promote active learning and personalize the material. They'll help you assess those qualities that you need to master speaking in public. For example, these tests will give you opportunities to explore your own level of communication apprehension (Chapter 1); your openness to intercultural communication (Chapter 4); your credibility (Chapter 10); and, in a new test, your leadership style (Chapter 12).

Culture

The effectiveness of public speaking principles will vary from one culture to another. Not all cultures respond to speakers in the same way. For example, in some cultures audiences will respond very positively to a speaker who is modest and appears unassuming; in other cultures audiences will see this speaker as weak and lacking in confidence. A direct style will prove clear and persuasive in some cultures but may appear invasive and inappropriate in others. As a result of the tremendous variations from one culture to another in the way in which people respond to public speakers and speeches, every chapter integrates cultural insights into its discussions. Among the issues covered are variations in how members of different cultures give and respond to public criticism (Chapter 2), cultural factors to consider in analyzing different audiences (Chapter 4), and the cultural differences in emotional and credibility appeals (Chapter 10).

Summary of Concepts and Skills

Each chapter ends with a series of summary statements to help you fix in your mind the key concepts of the chapter. You may find it helpful to look over these summary statements *before* reading the chapter so as to get a fairly detailed overview of what's covered in the chapter; then read the chapter, and then reread the summary.

Vocabulary Quiz

Because knowing the specialized vocabulary of a discipline will help you think about and talk about the material more effectively, each chapter ends with a 10-item quiz asking you to match the vocabulary terms with their definitions.

Public Speaking Exercises

Each chapter ends with two or more exercises. In nine of the chapters the final exercise is **Analyzing a Speech,** which offers a complete speech plus annotations and questions. Most of these speeches are presented as models of effectiveness and will show you what excellent speeches look like. (The exceptions are models of what not to do when making a public speech.) The annotations

will help guide you through the essential elements of public speaking. The other chapter-end exercises will help you work actively with the material covered in the text.

Emphasis on Technology

Throughout *The Essential Elements of Public Speaking,* you'll find an emphasis on using the latest technology. Some examples:

◆ *Research Links* cover research strategies and resources and emphasize using the latest technology, especially online sources. Thus, researching with online encyclopedias, almanacs, academic research articles, government publications, and museum collections is considered in detail. Similarly, researching through the World Wide Web, e-mail, listservs, newsgroups, and chat groups is thoroughly explored.

◆ *Using Technology* marginal notes offer suggestions for online research.

◆ Several *Critical Listening/Thinking Links* focus on technological research, offering suggestions for evaluating materials found on the Internet, where anyone can publish.

◆ *PowerPoint technology* is featured in Chapter 5. The discussion highlights the values of computer-assisted presentations in public speaking and offers suggestions for preparing slides and presenting them to an audience. A complete slide show speech (prepared in PowerPoint) is presented as an example. In addition, the chapter provides samples of speaker's notes and handouts prepared from the PowerPoint presentation.

◆ *Sample web pages,* presented throughout the text, visually stress the importance of Internet materials and showcase some of the best websites for learning more about public speaking and for research.

Technology Integration

One of the most exciting developments in textbooks is the integration of the textbook with technology. *The Essential Elements of Public Speaking* comes with extensive technology support that complements the material presented in this text and in the typical Introduction to Public Speaking course. As you'll see, this text's Companion Website, Allyn & Bacon's public speaking website, Research Navigator, MySpeechLab, and Video Workshop CD-ROM provide robust content, learning experiences, and guides to additional resources. Of course, it is not intended that every student should read the complete website in addition to the text. The textbook includes the essential information needed by all students for preparing and presenting a wide variety of speeches. But the available technology-based ancillaries offer extra avenues for pursuing topics raised in the text. Different students are likely to seek out different types of additional resources; some are likely to consult the exercises most, others the guides for research, others the videos of actual speakers, and so on. More complete descriptions of these supplements are provided below under "Ancillaries/Supplementary Materials."

What's New in This Second Edition?

Each of the chapters has been revised for added clarity, to include materials instructors using the text requested, and to incorporate new research and updated examples.

General Changes

This edition places special emphasis on the value of public speaking and on the importance of the material covered in each chapter. Students have a right to know the value of what they study and the reasons why they should do what instructors (and textbook authors) ask them to do. Following this basic belief, this edition now includes a discussion of "The Benefits of Public Speaking" in Chapter 1, and each chapter now begins with a brief section that answers the very legitimate question, "Why Read This Chapter?" At the same time, this feature helps provide an orientation and focus to the chapter contents.

Another significant change is in the new progression of the sample speeches presented in the text. Chapter 1 presents a brief sample annotated speech of introduction. Chapters 2 and 3 present an informative and a persuasive speech that were purposely poorly constructed—to illustrate the pitfalls to avoid and to complement the chapters' discussions of effective public speaking principles. The remaining sample speeches are all models of excellence and include both informative and persuasive speech examples on a variety of significant issues.

The organization of the chapters also has been changed a bit. In this edition the chapter on "Analyzing and Adapting to Your Audience" now comes before the chapter on "Using Supporting Materials and Presentation Aids."

All of the box materials have been revised extensively and now focus more clearly on the development of practical public speaking skills. All Research Link boxes now include a "Research Activity," which provides directions for using the material discussed in the box.

New speech excerpts appear throughout the text, and especially in Chapters 6 ("Organizing Your Speech") and 11 ("Speaking on Special Occasions"). New photos and captions, new cartoons, and new websites and captions have been added to this edition. Two new speeches, one informative and one persuasive, have been added to Chapters 4 and 10.

Chapter-by-Chapter Changes

Chapter 1 ("Introducing Public Speaking") revisions include new discussions of the roots of public speaking and expanded discussions of the benefits of public speaking and of ways to reduce apprehension. Also included is the NCA credo on ethical communication.

Chapter 2 ("Listening and Criticism") revisions include new discussions of the benefits of listening and guides to listening ethically as well as a new exercise on barriers to listening.

Chapter 3 ("Selecting Your Topic, Purpose, and Thesis") includes an expanded discussion of taboo topics and a new exercise on cultural beliefs.

Chapter 4 ("Analyzing and Adapting to Your Audience"), which was Chapter 5 in the previous edition, now includes discussions of audience assumptions, cultural factors, affectional orientation, and persons with disabilities.

Chapter 5 ("Using Supporting Materials and Presentation Aids"), which was Chapter 4 in the previous edition, now features a special box on plagiarism—what it is, why it's unacceptable, and how it can be avoided—as well as a revised section on statistics, new PowerPoint slides illustrating the slide show speech, and two new exercises on amplification and testimony.

Chapter 6 ("Organizing Your Speech") now includes a more extended illustration of how cultural differences can be reflected in organizational patterns and a detailed annotated outline using the motivated sequence.

Chapter 7 ("Wording Your Speech") includes discussions of ageist language, language relating to persons with disabilities, and ethnic expressions, as well as a box on fallacies of reasoning centering on language.

Chapter 8 ("Delivering Your Speech") offers advice for before and after the speech and a new exercise on communicating with paralanguage.

Chapter 9 ("Informing Your Audience") has a new section on alternate classifications of information speeches and a discussion of how to make your speech more memorable.

Chapter 10 ("Persuading Your Audience") now includes an introductory section on the goals of persuasion, two boxes on fallacies (personal attacks and pseudo-arguments), a summary of the motivated sequence as a persuasive strategy, and a focus on three types of persuasive speeches—speeches on questions of fact, questions of value, and questions of policy.

Chapter 11 ("Speaking on Special Occasions") now includes a farewell speech by Cal Ripken Jr.

Chapter 12 ("Speaking in Small Groups") now includes a new self-test on leadership that clarifies the four approaches to leadership; in addition, two new exercises deal with responding to individual roles and combating groupthink.

Ancillaries/Supplementary Materials

Instructor Supplements

Print Supplements

◆ **Instructor's Manual/Test Bank** by James Benjamin of the University of Toledo. This Instructor's Manual/Test Bank includes chapter overviews, learning objectives, a wealth of valuable classroom activities, and suggestions for further reading. The Test Bank contains hundreds of challenging multiple-choice, true-false, short answer, and essay questions, along with an answer key. The questions closely follow the text units and are cross-referenced with corresponding page numbers.

◆ **A Guide for New Public Speaking Teachers: Building toward Success,** 3/e, by Calvin L. Troup, Duquesne University. This guide is designed to help new teachers prepare their introductory public speaking course effectively by covering such topics as preparation for the term, planning and structuring the course, evaluating speeches, using the textbook, and integrating technology into the classroom. The third edition includes a brief guide on teaching students for whom English is a second language.

◆ **The ESL Guide for Public Speaking** by Debra Gonsher Vinik, Bronx Community College of the City University of New York. This guide provides strategies and resources for instructors teaching in a bilingual or multilingual classroom. It also includes suggestions for further reading and a list of related Web sites.

◆ **Allyn & Bacon Public Speaking Transparency Package** This set, produced using PowerPoint, includes 100 full-color transparencies that provide visual support for classroom lectures and discussions.

◆ **Great Ideas for Teaching Speech (GIFTS),** 13/e, by Raymond Zeuschner, California Polytechnic State University. This book provides descriptions of and guidelines for assignments successfully used by experienced public speaking instructors in their classrooms.

Electronic Supplements

◆ **VideoWorkshop for Public Speaking, Version 2.0,** by Tasha Van Horn of Citrus College and Marilyn Reineck of Concordia University–St. Paul, includes quality video footage on an easy-to-use CD-ROM plus an Instructor's Teaching Guide and a Student Learning Guide with textbook-specific Correlation Grids. *VideoWorkshop* brings textbook concepts to life with ease and helps students understand, analyze, and apply the objectives of the course.

◆ **Computerized Test Bank** The printed Test Bank is also available electronically through Allyn & Bacon's computerized testing system, TestGen EQ. The fully networkable test-generating software is now available on a multiplatform CD-ROM. The user-friendly interface allows instructors to view, edit, and add questions; transfer questions to tests; and print tests in a variety of fonts. Search and sort features allow instructors to locate questions quickly and arrange them in a preferred order.

◆ **Allyn & Bacon Digital Media Archive for Communication, Version** 3.0 This CD-ROM contains electronic images of charts, graphs, maps, tables, and figures, along with media elements such as video, audio clips, and related weblinks. These media assets are fully customizable to use with our preformatted PowerPoint outlines or to import into instructors' own lectures (Windows and Mac).

◆ **PowerPoint Presentation Package for *The Essential Elements of Public Speaking,*** 2/e (available on the Web) by Dan Cavanaugh. This text-specific package consists of a collection of lecture outlines and graphic images keyed to every chapter in the text.

◆ **Allyn & Bacon PowerPoint Presentation for Public Speaking** (available on the Web). This PowerPoint presentation includes approximately 125 slides that cover a range of public speaking topics as well as a brief User's Guide.

◆ **Allyn & Bacon Student Speeches Video Library** Instructors have their choice of seven videos from a collection that includes three 2-hour American Forensic Association videos of award-winning student speeches and four videos with a range of student speeches delivered in the classroom. Contact your Allyn & Bacon representative for ordering information. Some restrictions apply.

◆ **Allyn & Bacon Public Speaking Key Topics Video Library** This library contains three videos that address core topics covered in the classroom: Critiquing Student Speeches, Speaker Apprehension, and Addressing Your Audience. Contact your Allyn & Bacon representative for ordering information. Some restrictions apply.

◆ **Allyn & Bacon Public Speaking Video** This video includes excerpts of classic and contemporary public speeches and student speeches to illustrate the public speaking process. One speech is delivered two times under different circumstances by the same person to illustrate the difference between effective and noneffective delivery based on appearance and nonverbal and verbal style. Contact your Allyn & Bacon representative for ordering information. Some restrictions apply.

◆ **Allyn & Bacon Student Speeches Video III** This video includes student speeches covering a variety of topics that illustrate informative, persuasive, after-dinner, and special occasion topics. Contact your Allyn & Bacon representative for ordering information. Some restrictions apply.

◆ **Allyn & Bacon Interpersonal Communication Videos** Allyn & Bacon offers three Interpersonal Videos ranging from 30 to 50 minutes that contain scenarios illustrating key concepts in interpersonal communication. Accompanying user guides feature transcripts, teaching activities, and class discussion questions for the episodes. Contact your Allyn & Bacon representative for ordering information. Some restrictions apply.

◆ **Interpersonal Movie Library** This collection contains popular feature films dealing with a range of interpersonal topics. Contact your Allyn & Bacon representative for ordering information. Some restrictions apply.

◆ **Allyn & Bacon Communication Video Library** This library is a collection of communication videos produced by Films for the Humanities and Sciences. Topics include, but are not limited to: Business Presentations, Great American Speeches, and Conflict Resolution. Contact your local Allyn & Bacon sales representative for ordering information. Some restrictions apply.

◆ **CourseCompass for Public Speaking,** powered by Blackboard and hosted nationally, is the most flexible online course management system on the market today. By using this powerful suite of online tools in conjunction with Allyn & Bacon's preloaded textbook and testing content, you can create an online presence for your course in under 30 minutes. The Public Speaking course features preloaded content such as quiz questions, video clips, instructor's manuals, PowerPoint presentations, still images, course preparation and instruction materials, *VideoWorkshop for Public Speaking*, weblinks, and much more! Log on to www.coursecompass.com to access this dynamic teaching resource. The content is also compatible with Blackboard and WebCT.

◆ **CourseCompass for Public Speaking, Professional Development Edition,** is a collection of helpful instructional materials that feature public speaking teaching strategies, resources, and video examples that you can access on the Internet using CourseCompass. For course coordinators working with adjuncts and/or teaching assistants, our *CourseCompass Public Speaking, Professional Development Edition*, helps you to provide training materials to your instructors—on or off campus. You can access our preloaded instruction materials, add your own materials, and make the resulting combination available to other instructors for their own instructional development and for the continued benefit of their students. Log on at www.coursecompass.com for more information.

◆ **Allyn & Bacon Classic and Contemporary Speeches DVD** This DVD presents a collection of over 120 minutes of video footage in an easy-to-use format. Each speech is accompanied by a biographical and historical summary that helps students to understand the context and motivation behind each speech. Contact your Allyn & Bacon sales representative for additional details and ordering information.

Student Supplements

Print Supplements

◆ *Interviewing and Human Communication,* by Joseph A. DeVito. This booklet introduces students to the process of interviewing, including the job résumé and the letters that are an essential part of the entire interview process. It also provides worksheets for preparing for both the information-gathering interview and the employment interview. Listening, ethical, and power issues as they relate to interviewing are included in boxes, as are skill development exercises to help students work actively with the concepts discussed here. Skills topics include practicing interviewing skills, displaying communication confidence in the employment interview, and responding to unlawful questions. Scenarios asking students to apply their interview skills in different situations, quotations to highlight different perspectives, ideas for exploring online materials, and invitations to use Allyn & Bacon's online Research Navigator tool to learn more about interviewing are included in the margins. In addition, to make it easier for students to use the interviewing preparation guides in the booklet, these guides are also available on the website at www.ablongman.com/devito and may be downloaded for students to complete and submit to their instructor, or to keep in their personal records. This product is available FREE when packaged with this text. Contact your Allyn & Bacon representative for ordering information. Some restrictions apply.

- **Preparing Visual Aids for Presentations,** 4/e, by Dan Cavanaugh. This visual booklet provides ideas to improve presentations, including suggestions for planning a presentation, guidelines for designing visual aids, storyboarding, and a PowerPoint presentation walk-through.
- **Research Navigator Guide for Speech Communication,** by Terrence Doyle, Northern Virginia Community College, and Linda R. Barr, University of the Virgin Islands. This resource guide is designed to teach students how to conduct high-quality online research and document it properly. The guide provides access to Research Navigator (www.researchnavigator.com), which contains exclusive databases of credible and reliable source material, including EBSCO's ContentSelect Academic Journal Database and the New York Times Search by Subject Archive. This product is available FREE when packaged with this text. Contact your Allyn & Bacon sales representative for ordering information. Some restrictions apply.
- **Public Speaking in the Multicultural Environment,** 2/e, by Devorah A. Lieberman, Portland State University. This booklet helps students learn to analyze cultural diversity within their audiences and adapt their presentations accordingly. Contact your Allyn & Bacon representative for ordering information. Some restrictions apply.
- **Speech Preparation Workbook** by Jennifer Dreyer and Gregory H. Patton, San Diego State University. This workbook takes students through the various stages of speech creation—from audience analysis to writing the speech—and provides supplementary assignments and tear-out forms. Contact your Allyn & Bacon representative for ordering information. Some restrictions apply.
- **Outlining Workbook** by Reeze L. Hanson and Sharon Condon, Haskell Indian Nations University. This workbook includes activities, exercises, and answers to help students develop and master the critical skill of outlining. Contact your Allyn & Bacon representative for ordering information. Some restrictions apply.
- **Brainstorms** by Joseph A. DeVito. This is a guide to thinking more creatively about communication, or anything else. Students will find 19 practical, easy-to-use creative thinking techniques along with insights into the creative thinking process. Contact your Allyn & Bacon representative for ordering information. Some restrictions apply.
- **Studying Communication** by Joseph A. DeVito. This guide helps students learn how to conduct research and get the most out of the communication classroom—whether attending a lecture, taking notes, reading a textbook, taking a test, or writing a research paper.

Electronic Supplements

- **VideoWorkshop for Public Speaking, Version 2.0,** by Tasha Van Horn of Citrus College and Marilyn Reineck of Concordia University–St. Paul, includes quality video footage on an easy-to-use CD-ROM plus a Student Learning Guide with textbook-specific Correlation Grids. *VideoWorkshop* brings textbook concepts to life with ease and helps students understand, analyze, and apply the objectives of the course.
- **Interactive Speechwriter Software, Version 1.1 (Windows and Mac)** by Martin R. Cox. This interactive software package for student purchase provides supplemental material, writing templates (for the informative, persuasive, and

motivated sequence speeches, as well as for outlines), sample student speeches (text only), and more! This program enhances students' understanding of key concepts discussed in the text and is available for Windows and Mac. Contact your Allyn & Bacon representative for ordering information. Some restrictions apply.

◆ **Speech Writer's Workshop CD-ROM 2.0** This interactive software will assist students with speech preparation and will enable them to write better speeches. The software includes four separate features: (1) a speech handbook with tips for researching and preparing speeches, plus information about grammar, usage, and syntax; (2) a speech workshop that guides students through the speech writing process and includes a series of questions at each stage; (3) a topics dictionary containing hundreds of speech ideas—all divided into subcategories to help students with outlining and organization; and (4) a citation database that formats bibliographic entries in MLA and APA style. Contact your Allyn & Bacon representative for ordering information. Some restrictions apply.

◆ **Companion Website Plus with Online Practice Tests** http://www.ablongman.com/devito by Joseph A. DeVito and Diana Murphy. This site includes unit objectives, self-tests, skill building exercises, and extensions and elaborations on the text. The website also includes an online study guide with practice tests and weblinks.

◆ **Allyn & Bacon Communication Studies Website,** by Terrence Doyle, Northern Virginia Community College, and Tim Borchers, Minnesota State University at Moorhead, and **Allyn & Bacon Public Speaking Website,** by Nan Peck, Northern Virginia Community College. These websites contain modules built with enrichment materials, weblinks, and interactive activities designed to enhance students' understanding of key concepts. The Communication Studies Website includes interpersonal, small group communication, and public speaking topics. Access this site at www.ablongman.com/commstudies. The Public Speaking Website, updated for 2004, helps students build, organize, and research speeches while learning about the process of public speaking. Access this website at www.ablongman.com/pubspeak.

◆ **Communication Tutor Center (access code required),** www.aw.com/tutorcenter. The Tutor Center provides students with free, one-on-one interactive tutoring from qualified public speaking instructors on all material in the text. The Tutor Center offers students help with understanding major communication principles as well as methods for study. In addition, students have the option of submitting self-taped speeches for review and critique by Tutor Center instructors to help prepare for and improve their speech assignments. Tutoring assistance is offered by phone, fax, Internet, and e-mail during Tutor Center hours. For more details and ordering information, contact your Allyn & Bacon sales representative.

◆ **Allyn & Bacon Classic and Contemporary Speeches DVD** This DVD presents a collection of over 120 minutes of video footage in an easy-to-use format. Each speech is accompanied by a biographical and historical summary that helps students to understand the context and motivation behind each speech. Contact your local Allyn & Bacon sales representative for additional details and ordering information.

Acknowledgments

I want to thank the many people who contributed to the development of the text you now hold. Thank you Brian Wheel, editor; Kristen Desmond LeFevre, developmental editor; Heather Hawkins, editorial assistant; Mandee Eckersley, marketing manager; Julie Tesser, photo researcher; Jay Howland, copy editor; and Susan McIntyre of Nesbitt Graphics, project manager.

I also want to thank the reviewers who shared their experiences and insights with me; thank you Bruce Ardinger, Columbus State Community College; Robert Arend, Miramer College; Valerie Belew, Nashville State; Ellen R. Cohn, University of Pittsburgh; John R. Foster, Northwestern State University; Fred Garbowitz, Grand Rapids Community College; Victoria Leonard, College of the Canyons; Ken Sherwood, Los Angeles City College; Anita Tate, Weatherford College; and Chérie C. White, Muskingum Area Technical College.

Joseph A. DeVito
jadevito@earthlink.net

1 Introducing Public Speaking

Why Read This Chapter?

It introduces one of the most practical and empowering subjects you will study in your entire college career and will help you to:

❖ understand some of the personal, social, academic, and career benefits you'll get from studying public speaking

❖ manage your stage fright by explaining techniques you can use to feel more comfortable giving a speech in front of an audience

❖ start giving speeches early in the semester by presenting 10 steps for public speaking preparation and delivery

> " If all my possessions were taken from me with one exception, I would choose to keep the power of speech, for by it I would soon regain all the rest. "
>
> —Daniel Webster

Public speaking is both a very old and a very new art. It's likely that public speaking principles were developed soon after our species began to talk. Much of contemporary public speaking—at least the Western tradition of public speaking—is based on the works of the ancient Greeks and Romans, who articulated an especially insightful system of rhetoric or public speaking. This tradition has been enriched by the experiments, surveys, field studies, and historical studies that have been done since classical times and that continue to be done to this day.

Aristotle's *Rhetoric*, written some 2,300 years ago in ancient Greece, was one of the earliest systematic studies of public speaking. It was in this work that the three kinds of persuasive appeals—*logos* (or logical proof), *pathos* (emotional appeals), and *ethos* (appeals based on the character of the speaker)—were introduced. This three-part division is still followed today; Chapter 10 discusses these in more detail.

Roman rhetoricians added to the work of the Greeks. Quintilian, who taught in Rome during the first century, built an entire educational system—from childhood through adulthood—based on the development of the effective and responsible orator. Over the following 2,000 years, the study of public speaking continued to grow and develop.

Contemporary public speaking builds on this classical heritage and also incorporates insights from the humanities; the social and behavioral sciences; and, most recently, computer science and technology. Likewise, perspectives from different cultures are being integrated into our present study of public speaking. Table 1.1 shows some of the contributors to contemporary public speaking and illustrates the wide research and theory base from which the principles of this discipline are drawn.

Studying Public Speaking

A good way to begin your study of public speaking is to examine your own beliefs about public speaking and public speakers. Compare some common beliefs with the research and theory that bear on these beliefs:

Belief: Good public speakers are born, not made.
Research finds: Actually, effective public speaking is a learned skill. To be sure, some people are born brighter or more extroverted—characteristics that do help in public speaking. But all people can improve their abilities and become more effective public speakers.

Belief: The more speeches you give, the better you'll become at it.
Research finds: This is true only if you practice effective skills. If you practice bad habits, you're likely to grow less effective rather than more effective; consequently, it's important to learn and follow the principles of effectiveness.

Belief: You'll never be a good public speaker if you're nervous giving speeches.
Research finds: Most speakers are nervous; the goal is managing, not eliminating, the fear. You can become effective regardless of your current level of fear. In fact, your fear may actually energize you and encourage you to prepare more thoroughly and to practice more often, and this extra effort will contribute to more effective speaking.

TABLE 1.1	Growth and Development of Public Speaking
Here are just a few of the academic roots of public speaking and some of the contributions from these disciplines.	

ACADEMIC ROOTS	CONTRIBUTIONS TO CONTEMPORARY PUBLIC SPEAKING
Classical rhetoric	Emphasis on substance; ethical responsibilities of the speaker; use of a combination of logical, ethical, and emotional appeals; the strategies of organization
Literary and rhetorical criticism	Approaches to and standards for evaluation; insights into style and language
Philosophy	Emphasis on the logical validity of arguments; continuing contribution to ethics
Public address	Insights into how famous speakers dealt with varied purposes and audiences to achieve desired effects
Psychology	How language is made easier to understand and remember; theories and findings on attitude change; emphasis on speech effects
General Semantics	Emphasis on using language to describe reality accurately; techniques for avoiding common thinking errors that faulty language usage creates
Communication theory	Insights on information transmission; the importance of viewing the whole of the communication act; the understanding of such concepts as feedback, noise, channel, and message
Computer science	The virtual audience; design, outlining, and presentation software; search tools for research; easily accessed databases
Interpersonal communication	Transactionalism; emphasis on mutual influence of speaker and audience
Sociology	Data on audiences' attitudes, values, opinions, and beliefs and how these influence exposure to and responses to messages
Anthropology	Insights into the attitudes, beliefs, and values of different cultures and how these influence communication in general and public speaking in particular

Belief: It's best to memorize your speech, especially if you're fearful.
Research finds: This belief, if acted on, is likely to be detrimental. Memorizing your speech is one of the worst things you can do; there are easier ways to deal with fear.

Belief: The skills of public speaking are similar throughout the world.
Research finds: They aren't. The techniques of public speaking are culture specific; for example, what proves effective with an Asian audience may not work with audiences in the United States or in Latin America.

The Benefits of Public Speaking

Fair questions to ask of any course or textbook are *"What will I get out of this?"* and *"How will the effort and time I put into this class and this textbook benefit me?"* Here are just a few of the benefits you'll derive from this text and from your course work in public speaking.

Enhanced Personal and Social Abilities

Public speaking provides training in a variety of personal and social competencies. For example, in the pages that follow we cover such skills as developing self-awareness, building self-confidence, and dealing with the fear of communicating. These certainly are skills that you'll apply in public speaking. But they also

Companion Website

(www.ablongman.com/devito)
As you progress through your study of and experiences with public speaking, you'll find the Companion Website for this text a great help. The home page shown here will give you an idea of the varied topics this website covers. Suggestions for you to consult certain sections and thus expand on the areas you're interested in appear at the end of each chapter in the Web Explorations section. For now just browse this website, making note of topics to which you'll want to return.

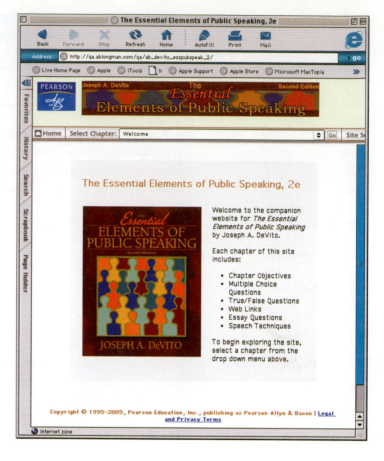

will prove valuable in all of your social interactions. It's relevant to note that students from varied cultures studying in the United States see public speaking as a method for climbing up the socioeconomic ladder (Collier & Powell, 1990).

Improved Academic and Career Skills

As you learn public speaking, you'll also learn a wide variety of academic and career skills. These skills are central to public speaking but are essential in many other areas as well. For example, you will learn to:

◆ conduct research efficiently and effectively

◆ explain complex concepts clearly

◆ support an argument with all the available means of persuasion

◆ understand human motivation and make effective use of your insights in persuasive encounters

◆ organize a variety of messages for clarity and persuasiveness

◆ present yourself to others with confidence and self-assurance

◆ analyze and evaluate the validity of persuasive appeals

Refined General Communication Abilities

Public speaking also will develop and refine your general communication abilities. For example, it will help you to:

- develop a more effective communication style
- adjust messages to specific listeners
- give and respond appropriately to criticism
- develop logical and emotional appeals
- communicate your credibility
- improve your listening skills
- organize extended messages
- refine your delivery skills

Improved Public Speaking Abilities

Speakers aren't born; they're made. Through instruction, exposure to different speeches, experience with diverse audiences, feedback on your own speeches, and individual learning experiences, you can become an effective speaker. Regardless of your present level of competence, you can improve through proper training—hence this course and this book.

At the end of this course, you'll be a more competent, confident, and effective public speaker. You'll also be a more effective listener—more open yet more critical, more empathic yet more discriminating. And you'll emerge a more competent and discerning critic of public communication.

❖ **CONSIDER** the benefits of skill in public speaking in the profession you're now preparing yourself to enter. What types of public speeches are you most likely to give during your professional career?

RESEARCH Link

Research in Public Speaking

Throughout the process of preparing your public speeches, you'll need to find information to use as source material in your speech. This is done through research. Through research you'll find examples, illustrations, and definitions to help you inform your listeners; testimony, statistics, and arguments to support your major ideas; personal anecdotes, quotations, and stories to help you bring your topics to life.

Research, however, also serves another important function: It helps you persuade your listeners and makes you appear more believable. For example, if your listeners feel you've examined lots of research, they'll be more apt to see you as competent and knowledgeable and therefore more apt to believe

what you say. And, of course, the content of the research itself can be convincing. When you present solid research to your listeners, you give them the very reasons they need to draw conclusions or to decide on a course of action.

Because of these dual roles that research plays in public speaking, it's crucial to conduct and critically evaluate research on your speech topic *and* to integrate this research into your speeches. To help you in these tasks, this book covers research in depth (but in small pieces) in Research Link boxes positioned throughout the text. Early boxes cover basic principles of research and suggest some useful general resources; later boxes deal with more specialized resources.

Research Activity. Additional resources for learning how to conduct research and a large number of databases to search are provided on Research Navigator, a powerful research library consisting of research guides, style manuals, archives for the *New York Times* and *Financial Times,* websites of interest to a wide variety of disciplines, and extensive databases of scholarly and popular articles in different disciplines. The home page for Research Navigator appears on page 6. If you have access, log on to Research Navigator (www.researchnavigator.com), take the tour, and then read the section "Help: A Guide for Students." Together, the tour and printed guide will help you get the most out of this powerful research tool.

Research Navigator

(www.researchnavigator.com)
As you can see from this home page, Research Navigator offers you a wealth of insights into the nature of research and provides guidance for conducting and evaluating research effectively and efficiently.

As a leader (and in many ways you can look at this course as training in leadership skills) you'll need the skills of effective communication to help preserve a free and open society. As a speaker who wants your message understood and accepted, as a listener who needs to evaluate and critically analyze ideas and arguments before making decisions, and as a critic who needs to evaluate and judge the thousands of public communications you hear every day, you will draw on the skills you'll learn in this course.

The Essential Elements of Public Speaking

In **public speaking** *a speaker presents a relatively continuous message to a relatively large audience in a unique context* (see Figure 1.1). Like all communication, public speaking is a transactional process, a process whose elements are *interdependent* (Watzlawick, 1978; Watzlawick, Beavin, & Jackson, 1967). In other words, each element in the public speaking process depends on and interacts with all other elements. For example, the way in which you organize a speech will depend on such factors as your speech topic, your audience, the purpose you hope to achieve, and a host of other variables—all of which are explained in the remainder of this chapter and in the chapters to follow.

Especially important to appreciate is the mutual interaction and influence between speaker and audience. True, when you give a public speech you do most of the speaking and the audience does most of the listening. The audience, however, also sends messages in the form of feedback—such as applause, bored looks, nods of agreement or disagreement, or attentive glances. The audience also influences how you'll prepare and present your speech. It influences your arguments, language, method of organization, and every other choice you make. You would not, for example, present the same speech on saving money to high school students as you would to senior citizens.

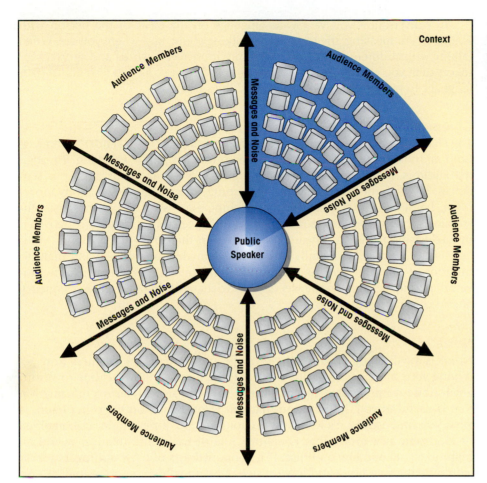

❖ **FIGURE 1.1**

The Essential Elements of the Public Speaking Transaction

This diagram is intended to illustrate the interplay of elements in the public speaking process and to emphasize (1) that you as the speaker are the center of the public speaking process and (2) that the audience for a public speech does not consist merely of the listeners in front of you. The physical setup that you'll face in most of your public speaking would better resemble the shaded area of the diagram, however. How would you diagram the process of public speaking?

Let's now consider the eight essential elements of public speaking: speaker, message, channels, noise, audience, context, delivery, and ethics.

⤳ Speaker

In conversation the speaker's role occurs in short spurts; Pat says something to which Chris replies to which Pat responds and so on. In public speaking you deliver a relatively long speech and usually are not interrupted. As the public speaker you're the center of the transaction; you and your speech are the reason for the gathering.

⤳ Message

Messages conveyed in public speaking include both verbal and nonverbal signals. In both conversation and public speaking, your message has a purpose. For example, in conversation you might want to tell a friend about what happened at a recent basketball game. In this case your purpose would be to inform. Or you might want to convince a coworker to switch vacation schedules with you. Here your purpose would be to persuade. And in public speaking, too, you communicate with a purpose.

Generally in conversation you don't give any real thought to how you're going to organize your message. In public speaking, however, organization is crucial, because it adds clarity to your message and therefore makes it easier for listeners to understand and to remember what you're saying.

In conversation you vary your language on the basis of the person with whom you're speaking, the topic you're talking about, and where you are. When talking with children, for example, you might use easier words and shorter sentences than you would with classmates. In public speaking you also adjust your language to your audience, the topic, and the situation.

Channels

The **channel** is the medium that carries message signals from sender to receiver. Both auditory and visual channels are significant in public speaking. Through the auditory channel you send spoken messages—your words and your sentences. Through the visual channel—eye contact (or the lack of it), body movement, hand and facial gestures, and clothing—you send visual messages. Increasingly, public speaking is mediated; public speeches are frequently delivered in a television studio and heard by millions in their own living rooms. Similarly, speeches may be digitally recorded and made available day and night to millions of Internet users. As video and sound capabilities become more universal, public speaking on the Net is likely to increase dramatically in frequency and in cultural significance.

Noise

Noise is anything that distorts the message and prevents the listeners from receiving your message as you intended it to be received. It's revealing to distinguish noise from "signal." In this context the term *signal* refers to information that is useful to you, information that you want. Noise, on the other hand, is what you find useless; it's what you do not want. So, for example, an e-mail list or electronic newsgroup that contained lots of useful information would be high on signal and low on noise; if it contained lots of useless information, it would be high on noise and low on signal. Spam is high on noise and low on signal, as is static on the radio, television, or telephone. Noise may be physical (others talking loudly, cars honking, illegible handwriting, "garbage" on your computer screen), physiological (hearing or visual impairment, articulation disorders), psychological (preconceived ideas, wandering thoughts), or semantic (misunderstood meanings).

Public speaking involves visual as well as spoken messages, so it's important to realize that noise also may be visual. Sunglasses that concealed the non-verbal messages from your eyes would be considered noise, as would dark print on a dark background in your slides.

All public speaking situations involve noise. You won't be able to totally eliminate it, but you can try to reduce its effects. Making your language more precise, organizing your thoughts more logically, and reinforcing your ideas with visual aids are some ways to combat the influence of noise.

Audience

In conversation the "audience" is often one listener or perhaps a few. The **audience** in public speaking is relatively "large," ranging from groups of perhaps 10 or 12 to hundreds of thousands, even millions.

In some public speaking situations—say, when you're addressing work colleagues—you may know your audience quite well. In other situations, however, you will not know your audience quite so well and will have to analyze them: to discover what they already know (so you don't repeat old news), to learn

DEVELOPING STRATEGIES

Apprehension. This is Linda's first experience with public speaking, and she's very nervous. She's afraid she'll forget her speech or stumble somehow, so she's wondering if it would be a good idea to alert the audience to her nervousness. What would you advise Linda to do if her audience was your public speaking class?

what their attitudes are (so you don't waste time persuading them of something they already believe), and so on.

But public speaking isn't just the art of adjusting messages to listeners, it also involves active involvement by the listeners. The listener plays a role in encouraging or discouraging the speaker, in offering constructive criticism, in evaluating public messages, and in performing a wide variety of other functions. Because listening is so important (and so often neglected) in public speaking, it is covered in two ways. First, a complete discussion of listening (see Chapter 2) explains the nature of listening, the forms of listening, and suggestions for improving your listening effectiveness. Second, a series of Critical Listening/Thinking Link boxes are distributed throughout the text. These boxes relate critical listening and thinking to the topic of the chapter and serve as frequent reminders that listening and thinking critically are essential parts of the public speaking act.

Context

Speaker and listeners operate in a physical, socio-psychological, temporal, and cultural **context.** The context influences you as the speaker, the audience, the speech, and the effects of the speech. The *physical context* is the actual place in which you give your speech (the room, hallway, park, or auditorium). A presentation in a small intimate room needs to be very different from an address in a sports arena.

The *socio-psychological context* includes, for example, the relationship between speaker and audience: Is a supervisor speaking to workers or a worker speaking to supervisors? A principal addressing teachers or a parent addressing principals? This socio-psychological context also includes the audience's attitudes toward and knowledge of you and your subject. A speech endeavoring to influence a supportive audience will employ very different strategies than would a speech delivered to a hostile audience.

The *temporal context* includes factors such as the time of day and, more importantly, where your speech fits into the sequence of events. For example, does your speech follow another presentation that has taken an opposing position? Is your speech the sixth in a series exploring the same topic?

The *cultural context* refers to the beliefs, lifestyles, values, and behaviors that the speaker and the audience bring with them and that bear on the topic and purpose of the speech. Appealing to "competitive spirit" and "financial gain" may prove effective with Wall Street executives but ineffective with people who are more comfortable with socialist or communist economic systems and beliefs.

Delivery

In conversation you normally don't think of how you'd deliver or present your message; you don't concern yourself with how to stand or gesture or how to raise or lower your vocal volume. In public speaking, however, the situation is different. Because public speaking is a relatively new experience and you'll probably feel uncomfortable and self-conscious at first, you may wonder what to do with your hands or whether you should move about. With time and experience, you'll find that your delivery will follow naturally from what you're saying, just as it does in conversation. Perhaps the best advice at this time is to view public speaking as "enlarged conversation" and not to worry about delivery just yet. In your early efforts it's better to concentrate on content; as you gain confidence, you can direct your attention to refining and polishing your delivery skills.

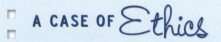

A CASE OF Ethics

Using Research

You recently read an excellent summary of research on aging and memory in a magazine article. The magazine is a particularly respectable publication, and so it's reasonable to assume that this research is thoroughly reliable.

Would it be ethical to use this research and to cite the original research studies but not to mention that you got the sources from a magazine summary? If not, how might you ethically use this material? More generally, what ethical obligations should govern the use of material written by others?

Ethics

Because your speech will have an effect on your audience, you have an obligation to consider **ethics**—issues of right and wrong, or the moral implication of your message. When you develop your topic, present your research, create the persuasive appeals, and do any of the other tasks related to public speaking, there are ethical issues to be considered (Bok, 1978; Jaksa & Pritchard, 1994; Johannesen, 1996; Thompson, 2000). You also have ethical obligations in your roles as listener and as critic. Because of the central importance of ethics, each chapter's A Case of Ethics box presents a specific situation that raises an ethical issue and asks how you would respond. In addition, consider the accompanying "Credo for Ethical Communication," an attempt by one communication association to identify clearly the principles that should govern morally responsible communication.

Culture, Gender, and Public Speaking

As we've seen, the cultural context is an essential element of public speaking. Let's look a little more closely at culture's impact. A walk through any large city, many small towns, or just about any college campus will convince you that the United States is largely a collection of different cultures, coexisting somewhat separately but also influencing one another. As demonstrated throughout this text, cultural differences span the entire public speaking spectrum—from the way you use eye contact to the way you develop an argument or present criticism (Chang & Holt, 1996).

Culture is the collection of beliefs, attitudes, values, and ways of behaving that are shared by a group of people and passed down from one generation to the next through communication rather than through genes. Thus, the term *culture* does not refer to genetic traits such as color of skin or shape of eyes. Culture does include beliefs in a supreme being, attitudes toward family, and the values people place on friendship or money.

Even though culture is not synonymous with race or nationality, members of a particular race are often enculturated into a similar set of beliefs, attitudes, and values. Similarly, members living in the same country are often taught similar beliefs, attitudes, and values. Thus, we often speak of "Hispanic culture" or

CREDO FOR ETHICAL COMMUNICATION

Preamble

Questions of right and wrong arise whenever people communicate. Ethical communication is fundamental to responsible thinking, decision making, and the development of relationships and communities within and across contexts, cultures, channels, and media. Moreover, ethical communication enhances human worth and dignity by fostering truthfulness, fairness, responsibility, personal integrity, and respect for self and others. We believe that unethical communication threatens the quality of all communication and consequently the well-being of individuals and the society in which we live. Therefore we, the members of the National Communication Association, endorse and are committed to practicing the following principles of ethical communication:

Principles

- *We advocate truthfulness, accuracy, honesty, and reason as essential to the integrity of communication.*
- *We endorse freedom of expression, diversity of perspective, and tolerance of dissent to achieve the informed and responsible decision making fundamental to a civil society.*
- *We strive to understand and respect other communicators before evaluating and responding to their messages.*
- *We promote access to communication resources and opportunities as necessary to fulfill human potential and contribute to the well-being of families, communities, and society.*
- *We promote communication climates of caring and mutual understanding that respect the unique needs and characteristics of individual communicators.*
- *We condemn communication that degrades individuals and humanity through distortion, intimidation, coercion, and violence, and through the expression of intolerance and hatred.*
- *We are committed to the courageous expression of personal convictions in pursuit of fairness and justice.*
- *We advocate sharing information, opinions, and feelings when facing significant choices while also respecting privacy and confidentiality.*
- *We accept responsibility for the short- and long-term consequences for our own communication and expect the same of others.*

Source: National Communication Association. Reprinted by permission.

"African American culture." But lest we be guilty of stereotyping, we need to recognize that within any large culture—especially a culture based on race or nationality—there will be enormous differences. The Kansas farmer may in some ways be closer to the Chinese farmer than to the Wall Street executive. Further, as an individual born into a particular race and nationality, you don't necessarily have to adopt the attitudes, beliefs, and values that may be dominant among the people of that race and nationality.

In a similar way, gender can be considered a cultural variable—largely because cultures teach boys and girls different attitudes, beliefs, values, and ways of communicating and relating to one another. In other words, you act like a man or a woman in part because of what your culture has taught you about how men and women should act. This does not, of course, deny that biological differences also play a role in the differences between male and female behavior. In fact, research continues to uncover biological roots of behavior once thought entirely learned, such as happiness and shyness.

There are lots of reasons for the cultural emphasis you'll find in this book (and probably in all your textbooks). Most prevalent, perhaps, are the vast demographic changes taking place throughout the United States. Whereas at one time the United States was largely a country populated by Europeans, it's now a country greatly influenced by the enormous number of new citizens from South and Central America, Africa, and Asia. And the same is true on college and university campuses throughout the nation. With these changes come different communication customs and the need to understand and adapt to these new ways of looking at communication generally and public speaking specifically.

❖ **CONSIDER** the kinds of research and evidence that would work best in speeches advocating unpopular positions, positions to which the audience is strongly opposed. What kinds of evidence would you yourself demand before you'd consider changing your present beliefs about, say, religion, drugs, or politics?

The principles for communicating information and for persuasion differ from one culture to another. If you're to understand public speaking, then you need to know how its principles vary on the basis of culture. Success in public speaking—at your job and in your social life—will depend in great part on your ability to communicate effectively with persons who may have different cultural perspectives.

Now that we've considered the essential elements of public speaking, especially culture, let's turn to what is probably your major concern: fear, or what's called "communication apprehension."

Managing Your Apprehension

Apprehension in public speaking is normal. Everyone experiences some degree of fear in the relatively formal public speaking situation. After all, in public speaking you're the sole focus of attention and are usually being evaluated for your performance. Experiencing fear or anxiety isn't strange or unique.

Although you may at first view **communication apprehension** as harmful, it's not necessarily so. In fact, apprehension can work for you. Fear can energize you. It may motivate you to work a little harder—to produce a speech that will be better than it might have been. Further, the audience cannot see the apprehension that you may be experiencing. Even though you may think that the audience can hear your heart beat faster and faster, they can't. They can't see your knees tremble. They can't sense your dry throat—at least not most of the time.

You may wish to pause here and take the self-test on pages 13–14 to measure your own level of fear of public speaking.

USING TECHNOLOGY

Visit the Gallup Organization's website at http://www.gallup.com/ and look for information on common fears that people have. Where does public speaking rank?

CRITICAL LISTENING/THINKING *Link*

Listening to Yourself

Listen critically when you talk to yourself: Listen both to self-destructive statements, which you'll want to avoid, and to self-affirming statements, which you'll want to internalize.

Self-Destructive Statements. Thoughts that damage the way you feel about yourself are self-distructive: *I'm a poor speaker. I'm boring. The audience won't like me.* Recognizing that you may have internalized such beliefs is your first step in eliminating them. Your second step is to recognize that these beliefs are self-defeating and unrealistic, which you can do by analyzing why they are unrealistic. Your third step is to substitute more realistic beliefs. For example, try replacing the unrealistic belief that audiences won't like you with the more realistic belief that most listeners are much like yourself and are supportive of other speakers.

Self-Affirming Statements. Positive and supportive thoughts are self-affirming. Remind yourself of your successes, strengths, and virtues. Concentrate on your potential, not on your limitations. Use such self-affirmations as these: *I'm friendly and can communicate this in my speeches. I can learn the techniques for controlling my fear. I'm a competent person and have the potential to be an effective speaker. I'm a good team player. I don't have to repeat my past failures. I'm flexible and can adjust to different communication situations.*

Getting Critical. What other self-affirming statements can you make about yourself as a student? As a public speaker?

Test YOURSELF

How Apprehensive Are You in Public Speaking?

This questionnaire consists of six statements concerning your feelings about public speaking. Indicate the degree to which each statement applies to you by marking whether you (1) strongly agree, (2) agree, (3) are undecided, (4) disagree, or (5) strongly disagree with each statement. There are no right or wrong answers. Don't be concerned that some of the statements are similar to others. Work quickly; just record your first impression.

_____ **1.** I have no fear of giving a speech.

_____ **2.** Certain parts of my body feel very tense and rigid while giving a speech.

_____ **3.** I feel relaxed while giving a speech.

_____ **4.** My thoughts become confused and jumbled when I am giving a speech.

_____ **5.** I face the prospect of giving a speech with confidence.

_____ **6.** While giving a speech, I get so nervous that I forget facts I really know.

❖ **HOW DID YOU DO?** To obtain your public speaking apprehension score, begin with the number 18 (selected so that you won't wind up with negative numbers) and add to it the scores for items 1, 3, and 5. Then, from this total, subtract the scores from items 2, 4, and 6. A score above 18 shows some degree of apprehension. Most people score above 18, so if you scored relatively high, you're among the vast majority of people.

USING TECHNOLOGY

The popular psychology magazine *Psychology Today* maintains a wonderful website devoted to many of the topics covered in this text (http://www.psychologytoday.com/HTDocs/prod/ptoselftest/self_test.asp). Of special interest are the self-tests, which will help you learn more about yourself. Log on to this website and take one or more of these self-tests. Other websites containing self-tests include All the Tests (http://www.allthetests.com) and Queendom.com (http://www.queendom.com).

❖ **WHAT WILL YOU DO?** As you read the suggestions for reducing apprehension in the text, consider what you can do to incorporate these into your own public speaking experiences. Consider how these suggestions might be useful in reducing apprehension more generally—for example, in social situations and in small groups and meetings. An extremely thorough discussion of communication apprehension may be found in Richmond and McCroskey (1998), *Communication Apprehension*. Briefer discussions may be found at www.ablongman.com/devito; look for "general and specific apprehension," "degrees of apprehension," "positive and normal apprehension," and "culture and communication apprehension."

Source: McCroskey, J. C. (2001). *An introduction to rhetorical communication* (8th ed.). Boston: Allyn & Bacon. Reprinted by permission of the author.

There are several ways you can deal with your own public speaking apprehension: (1) Reverse the factors that cause apprehension, (2) practice performance visualization, and (3) systematically desensitize yourself.

Reversing the Factors That Cause Apprehension

If you can reverse or at least lessen the factors that cause apprehension, you'll be able to reduce your apprehension significantly. So let's look first at the factors that seem most important in creating apprehension and then at some suggestions for reversing these factors. Research has identified the following five factors as being especially important in contributing to your fear in public speaking (Beatty, 1988; Richmond & McCroskey, 1998):

◆ **Inexperience:** Having no experience in public speaking and seeing it as new and totally different from other situations you have been in

◆ **Subordinate status:** Seeing yourself as less important or lower in status than the members of your audience

◆ **Conspicuousness:** Seeing yourself as the center of attention

◆ **Lack of similarity:** Seeing yourself as very different from your audience

◆ **Prior history:** Having memories of previous times when you were apprehensive

You can reduce the impact of these factors by following a few simple suggestions.

◆ **Gain experience.** New and different situations such as public speaking are likely to make anyone anxious, so try to reduce their newness and differentness. The best way to do this is to get as much public speaking experience as you can. With experience your initial fears and anxieties will give way to feelings of control, comfort, and pleasure. Experience will show you that the feelings of accomplishment you gain from public speaking are rewarding and will outweigh any initial anxiety. Try also to familiarize yourself with the public speaking context. For example, try to rehearse in the room in which you will give your speech.

◆ **Think positively.** When you see yourself as inferior—when, for example, you feel that others are better speakers or that they know more than you do—your anxiety increases. Therefore, think positive thoughts and be especially thorough in your preparation so as to build your own confidence. At the same time, maintain realistic expectations for yourself. Fear increases when you feel that you can't meet your own expectations or the expectations of your audience (Ayres, 1986). Your second speech does not have to be better than that of the previous speaker, but it should be better than your own first one.

◆ **See public speaking as conversation.** When you're the center of attention, as you are in public speaking, you feel especially conspicuous, and this often increases anxiety. It may help, therefore, to think of public speaking as another type of conversation (some theorists call it "enlarged conversation"). Or, if you're comfortable talking in small groups, visualize your audience as an enlarged small group; it may dispel some of the anxiety you feel.

Please, no talking!

Cartoon by George Abbott as appeared in *New York Teacher*/City Edition.

◆ **Stress similarity.** When you feel similar to (rather than different from) your audience, your anxiety should lessen. Therefore, try to emphasize the similarities between yourself and your audience. This is especially important when your audience consists of people from cultures different from your own (Stephan & Stephan, 1992): In such cases you're likely to feel fewer similarities with your listeners and therefore to experience greater anxiety (Gudykunst & Nishida, 1984; Gudykunst, Yang, & Nishida, 1985). So with all audiences, but especially with multicultural groups, stress similarities such as shared attitudes, values, or beliefs. This tactic will make you feel more at one with your listeners and therefore more confident as a speaker.

◆ **Prepare and practice thoroughly.** Much of the fear you experience is a fear of failure. Adequate and even extra preparation will lessen the possibility of failure and the accompanying apprehension. Because apprehension is greatest during the beginning of the speech, try memorizing the first few sentences of your speech. If there are complicated facts or figures, be sure to write them out and plan to read them. This way you won't have to worry about forgetting them completely.

◆ **Move about and breathe deeply.** Physical activity—including movements of the whole body as well as small movements of the hands, face, and head—lessens apprehension. Using a visual aid, for example, will temporarily divert attention from you and will allow you to get rid of your excess energy as you move to display it. Also, try breathing deeply a few times before getting up to speak. You'll feel your body relax, and this will help you overcome your initial fear of walking to the front of the room.

◆ **Avoid chemicals as tension relievers.** Unless prescribed by a physician, avoid any chemical means for reducing apprehension. Tranquilizers,

marijuana, or artificial stimulants are likely to create problems rather than reduce them. And, of course, alcohol does nothing to reduce public speaking apprehension (Himle, Abelson, & Haghightgou, 1999). These chemicals can impair your ability to remember the parts of your speech, to accurately read audience feedback, and to regulate the timing of your speech.

Practicing Performance Visualization

Performance visualization is a technique designed specifically to reduce the outward signs of apprehension and also to reduce the negative thinking that often creates anxiety (Ayres & Hopf, 1992, 1993; Ayres, Hopf, & Ayres, 1994).

First, develop a positive attitude and a positive self-perception. Visualize yourself in the role of the effective public speaker. Visualize yourself walking to the front of the room—fully and totally confident, fully in control of the situation. The audience is in rapt attention and, as you finish, bursts into wild applause. Throughout this visualization, avoid all negative thoughts. As you visualize yourself as this effective speaker, take note of how you walk, look at your listeners, handle your notes, and respond to questions; also, think about how you feel about the public speaking experience.

Second, model your performance on that of an especially effective speaker. View a particularly competent public speaker on video, for example, and make a mental movie of it. As you review the actual and mental movie, shift yourself into the role of speaker; become this speaker.

Systematically Desensitizing Yourself

Systematic desensitization is a technique for dealing with a variety of fears, including those involved in public speaking (Goss, Thompson, & Olds, 1978; Richmond & McCroskey, 1998; Wolpe, 1957). The general idea is to create a hierarchy of behaviors leading up to the desired but feared behavior (say, speaking before an audience). One specific hierarchy might look like this:

5. Giving a speech in class
4. Introducing another speaker to the class
3. Speaking in a group in front of the class
2. Answering a question in class
1. Asking a question in class

The main objective of this experience is to learn to relax, beginning with relatively easy tasks and progressing to the behavior you're apprehensive about—in this case giving a speech in class. You begin at the bottom of the hierarchy and rehearse the first behavior mentally over a period of days until you can clearly visualize asking a question in class without any uncomfortable anxiety. Once you can accomplish this, move to the second level. Here you visualize a somewhat more threatening behavior; say, answering a question. Once you can do this, move to the third level, and so on until you get to the desired behavior.

In creating your hierarchy, use small steps to help you get from one step to the next more easily. Each success will make the next step easier. You might then go on to engage in the actual behaviors after you have comfortably visualized them: ask a question, answer a question, and so on.

Preparing a Public Speech: In Brief

This section answers the FAQs you're likely to be wondering about by providing a brief overview of the public speaking process. By following the 10 steps outlined in this chapter and diagrammed in Figure 1.2, you'll be able to prepare and present an effective first speech almost immediately. The remainder of the text elaborates on these steps and will help you fine-tune your public speaking skills.

Step 1: Select Your Topic and Purpose

The first step in preparing a speech is to select the topic (or subject) and the purpose you hope to achieve. Let's look first at the topic. For your classroom speeches—where the objective is to learn the skills of public speaking—there are thousands of suitable topics. Suggestions may be found everywhere and anywhere. Take a look at the "Dictionary of Topics" on the text's Companion Website; it lists hundreds of suitable topics from abortion, academic freedom, and acupuncture to women, words, youth, and zodiac.

10. Deliver your speech

9. Rehearse your speech

8. Construct your introduction, conclusion, and transitions

7. Word your speech

6. Organize your speech materials

5. Support your main points

4. Develop your thesis and main points

3. Research your topic

2. Analyze your audience

1. Select your topic and purpose

❖ **FIGURE 1.2**

The Steps in Preparing and Presenting a Public Speech

As you can see, this figure presents the 10 steps in a linear fashion. The process of constructing a public speech, however, doesn't always follow such a logical sequence. So you'll probably not progress simply from Step 1, to 2, to 3, through to 10. Instead, after selecting your topic and purpose (Step 1) you may progress to Step 2 and analyze your audience. On the basis of this analysis, however, you may wish to go back and modify your topic, your purpose, or both. Similarly, after you research the topic (Step 3), you may want more information about your audience. You may, therefore, return to Step 2.

What makes a topic "suitable"? First, the topic of a public speech should be *worthwhile*; it should address an issue that has significant implications for the audience.

A topic should also be *appropriate* both to you as the speaker and to your audience. Try not to select a topic just because it will fulfill the requirements of an assignment. Instead, select a topic about which you know something and would like to learn more.

Topics should also be *culturally sensitive*. Culture plays an extremely important role in determining what people consider appropriate or worthwhile. For example, it would be considered inappropriate for an American businessperson in Pakistan to speak about politics or in Nigeria about religion or in Mexico about illegal aliens (Axtell, 1993). Because you're a college student, you can assume, to some extent, that the topics you're interested in will also prove interesting to your classmates.

Topics must also be *limited in scope.* Probably the major problem for beginning speakers is that they attempt to cover a huge topic in five minutes: the history of Egypt, why our tax structure should be changed, or the sociology of film. Such topics are too broad and cause the speaker to try to cover too much. In these cases, all the speaker succeeds in doing is telling the audience what it already knows.

Once you have your general topic, consider your general purpose. Generally, public speeches are designed to inform, to persuade, or to serve some ceremonial or special occasion function.

The *informative speech* seeks to create understanding: to clarify, enlighten, correct misunderstandings, or demonstrate how something works.

The *persuasive speech* seeks to influence attitudes or behaviors: to strengthen or change audience attitudes or to inspire hearers to take some specific action.

The *special occasion speech*, containing elements of both information and persuasion, serves to introduce another speaker or a group of speakers, present a tribute, secure the goodwill of the listeners, or entertain the audience.

Your speech also will have a specific purpose. For example, specific informative purposes might be to inform the audience about a proposed education budget or to describe the way a television pilot is audience tested. Specific persuasive purposes might be to persuade an audience to support a proposed budget or to influence them to vote for Smith. Specific purposes for special occasion speeches might include introducing a Nobel Prize winner in nuclear physics or celebrating Veteran's Day.

Step 2: Analyze Your Audience

In public speaking your audience is central to your topic and purpose. In most cases, and especially in a public speaking class, you'll be thinking of both your audience and your topic at the same time; in fact, it's difficult to focus on one without also focusing on the other. Your success in informing or persuading an audience rests largely on the extent to which you know them and the extent to which you've adapted your speech to them. Ask yourself, Who are they? What do they already know? What would they want to know more about? What special interests do they have? What opinions, attitudes, and beliefs do they have? Where do they stand on the issues you wish to address? What needs do they have?

For example, if you're going to speak on social security and health care for the elderly or on the importance of the job interview, it's obvious that the age of your listeners will influence how you develop your speech. Similarly, men and women often view topics differently. For example, if you planned to speak on caring for a newborn baby, you'd approach an audience of men very differently from an audience of women. With an audience of women, you could probably assume a much greater knowledge of the subject and a greater degree of comfort in dealing with it. With an audience of men, you might have to cover such elementary topics as the type of powder to use, how to test the temperature of a bottle, and the way to prepare a bottle of formula.

Step 3: Research Your Topic

If the speech is to be worthwhile and if both you and the audience are to profit from it, you need to research the topic. First, read some general source—an encyclopedia article or a general article in a magazine or on the Web. You might pursue some of the references in the article or seek out a book or two in the library. For some topics, you might want to consult individuals; professors, politicians, physicians, or people with specialized information are useful sources and are now easy to reach through e-mail. Or you might begin by accessing a database, assembling a bibliography, and reading—beginning with the most general source and continuing with increasingly specific articles.

DEVELOPING STRATEGIES

Audience Analysis. John is planning to give a speech on the need for a needle exchange program in his state. But he knows nothing of the audience other than that the occasion will be a high school PTA meeting. He has no information about the audience's cultural background, gender, social attitudes, or religious beliefs. What can John do to prepare for this difficult situation?

USING TECHNOLOGY

Visit the Reference Desk (www.refdesk.com) and select one online research resource that you think would be useful to students preparing speeches for this class. What types of information does this resource contain? Why do you think this information would prove useful?

RESEARCH Link

General Research Principles

Here are a few principles to help you research your speeches more effectively and more efficiently.

Examine What You Know. Begin your search by examining what you already know. Winston Churchill followed this guideline when preparing his speeches, and it will prove useful to you as well. Write down what you know, for example, about books, articles, or websites on the topic that you're familiar with; jot down names of people who might know something about the topic. Also consider what you know from your own personal experiences and observations. In this way you can attack the problem systematically and not waste effort and time.

Begin with a General Overview. Continue your search by getting an authoritative but general overview of the topic. An encyclopedia article, book chapter, or magazine article in print or online will serve this purpose well. This general overview will help you see the topic as a whole and understand how its various parts fit together.

Consult Increasingly Specific Sources. Follow up the general overview with increasingly more detailed and specialized sources. Fortunately, many general articles contain references or links to direct this next stage of your search for more specific information.

Research Activity. If you have access, log on to Research Navigator (www.researchnavigator.com) and read the sections under "Research Process" that you still may not be sure about. Sections under this tab explain the contents of Research Navigator and tell how you can use it most efficiently and effectively. As you learn about research, consider which of the general principles seem especially useful to your own public speaking research.

Step 4: Develop Your Thesis and Main Points

In developing your **thesis** or main assertion, identify the one idea that you want your audience to remember after you've concluded your speech. This one central idea is your thesis. It's the essence of what you want your audience to get out of your speech. If your speech is informative, then your thesis is the main idea that you want your audience to understand; for example, "A newspaper company has three divisions." If your speech is persuasive, then your thesis is the central idea that you want your audience to accept or believe; for example, "We should adopt the new e-mail system."

Once you have worded your thesis, identify its component ideas—the main ideas you want to use to clarify or support your thesis. We'll call these the *main points* of the speech. You can identify these main points by asking strategic questions of your thesis. For informative speeches the most helpful questions are "What?" and "How?" Phrasing your thesis as a question beginning with "what" or "how" will help you identify the main points. For example, for the thesis "A newspaper company has three divisions", you'd ask, "What are the divisions?" The answer to this question will yield your main points. Following one mass communication theorist (Rodman, 2001), we can list these main points in the form of a brief outline like this:

Thesis: "A newspaper company has three divisions." (What are the divisions?)

I. The publishing division makes major decisions on the entire paper.

II. The editorial division produces news and features.

III. The business division sells advertising and prints the paper.

For a persuasive speech, the question you'd ask of your thesis is often "Why?" For example, if your thesis is "We should adopt the new e-mail system," then the inevitable question is "Why should we adopt the new system?" Your answers to this question will identify the major parts of the speech, which might look like this:

Thesis: "We should adopt the new e-mail system." (Why should we adopt the new e-mail system?)

I. The new system is easier to operate.

II. The new system enables you to check your spelling.

III. The new system provides more options for organizing messages.

Step 5: Support Your Main Points

Once you've identified your thesis and main points, turn your attention to supporting each point. Tell the audience what it needs to know about the newspaper divisions. Convince the audience that the new e-mail system is easier to use, has a spell-checker feature, and provides useful options for organizing e-mails.

In the informative speech your supporting materials primarily amplify—describe, illustrate, define, exemplify—the various concepts you discuss. For example, you want the causes of inflation to come alive for the audience. You want your listeners to see and feel the drug problem, the crime rate, or the economic hardships of the people you're talking about. Supporting materials accomplish this. Presenting definitions, for example, helps the audience to understand specialized terms; definitions breathe life into concepts that may otherwise be too abstract or vague. Statistics (summary figures that explain various trends) are essential for certain topics. Presentation aids—charts, maps, actual objects, slides, films, and so on—enliven normally vague concepts. Because presentation aids have become so important in public speaking, you may want to include these in each of your speeches. If you start using these with your first speeches, you'll develop considerable facility by the end of the semester. The best way to do this is to read Chapter 5's section on presentation aids (pages 106–123) immediately after you complete this chapter and to begin incorporating such aids into all your speeches.

In a persuasive speech your support is proof—material that offers evidence, argument, and motivational appeal and establishes your credibility. Proof helps you convince the audience to agree with you. Let's say, for example, that you want to persuade the audience to believe that the new e-mail system is easier to operate (your first main point, as noted above). To do this you need to give your audience good reasons for believing in its greater ease of operation. Your point might be supported this way:

❖ **CONSIDER** the mistakes speakers make when they talk about highly complex subjects and what they could do to be more effective. How might you plan to guard against at least one of these common mistakes?

I. The new e-mail system is easier to operate.

   A. It's easier to install.

   B. It's easier to configure to your personal preferences.

   C. It makes it easier to save and delete messages.

Step 6: Organize Your Speech Materials

Organize your materials to help your audience understand and retain what you say. You might, for example, select a simple topical pattern. This involves dividing your topic into its logical subdivisions or subtopics. Each subtopic becomes a main point of your speech, and each is treated about equally. You'd then organize the supporting materials under each of the appropriate points. The body of the speech, then, might look like this:

I. Main point I

   A. Supporting material for I

   B. Supporting material for I

II. Main point II

   A. Supporting material for II

   B. Supporting material for II

   C. Supporting material for II

III. Main point III

   A. Supporting material for III

   B. Supporting material for III

Step 7: Word Your Speech

Because your audience will hear your speech only once, make what you say instantly intelligible. Don't talk down to your audience; but do make your ideas, even complex ones, easy to understand at one hearing.

Use words that are simple rather than complex, concrete rather than abstract. Use personal and informal rather than impersonal and formal language. For example, use lots of pronouns (*I, me, you, our*) and contractions (*can't* rather than *cannot*; *I'll* rather than *I will*). Use simple and direct rather than complex and indirect sentences. Say "Vote in the next election" instead of "It is important that everyone vote in the next election."

Perhaps the most important advice at this point is that you should not write out your speech word for word. This will only make you sound as if you're reading to your audience. You'll lose the conversational quality that is so important in public speaking. Instead, outline your speech and speak with your audience, using the outline to remind yourself of your main ideas and the order in which you want to present them.

Title your speech. Create a title that's relatively short (so it's easy to remember)—two, three, or four words are often best. Choose a title that will attract the attention and arouse the interest of the listeners and that has a clear relationship to the major purpose of your speech.

Step 8: Construct Your Introduction, Conclusion, and Transitions

The last items to consider are the introduction, conclusion, and transitions.

Introduction

In introducing your speech, try to accomplish three goals. First, gain your listeners' attention. A provocative statistic, a little-known fact, an interesting story, or a statement explaining the topic's significance will help secure this initial attention.

Second, establish connections among yourself, the topic, and the audience. Tell audience members why you're speaking on this topic. Tell them why you're concerned with the topic and why you're competent to address them. These are questions that most audiences will automatically ask themselves. Here's one example of how this might be done.

> You may be wondering why a twenty-five-year-old woman with no background in medicine or education is talking to you about AIDS education. I'm addressing you today as a mother of a child with AIDS, and I want to talk with you about my child's experience in school—and about every child's experience in school—your own children as well as mine.

> Third, orient your audience; tell them what you're going to talk about.

> I'm going to explain the ways in which war movies have changed through the years. I'm going to discuss examples of movies depicting World War II, the Korean War, and Vietnam.

Conclusion

In concluding your speech, do at least two things. First, summarize your ideas. For example, you might restate your main points, summing up what you've told the audience.

Let's all support Grace Moore. She's our most effective negotiator. She's honest, and she knows what negotiation and our union are all about.

Second, wrap up your speech. Develop a crisp ending that makes it clear to your audience that your speech is at an end.

I hope then that when you vote on Tuesday, you'll vote for Moore. She's our only real choice.

Transitions

After you've completed the introduction and conclusion, review the entire speech to make sure that the parts flow into one another and that the movement from one part to another (say, from the introduction to the first major proposition) will be clear to the audience. Transitional words, phrases, and sentences will help you achieve this smoothness of movement.

◆ Connect your introduction's orientation to your first major proposition: *"Let's now look at the first of these three elements,* the central processing unit, in detail. The CPU is the heart of the computer. It consists of. . . ."

◆ Connect each main point to the next: *"But not only is* cigarette smoking dangerous to the smoker, *it's also* dangerous to the nonsmoker. Passive smoking is harmful to everyone. . . ."

◆ Connect your last main point to your conclusion: *"As we saw,* there were three sources of evidence against the butler. He had a motive; he had no alibi; he had the opportunity."

Step 9: Rehearse Your Speech

You've prepared your speech to deliver it to an audience, so your next step is to practice it. Rehearse your speech, from start to finish, out loud, at least four times before presenting it in class. During these rehearsals, time your speech to make sure that you stay within the specified time limits. Practice any words or phrases you have difficulty with; consult a dictionary to clarify any doubts about pronunciation. Include in your outline any notes that you want to remember during the actual speech—notes to remind you to use a presentation aid or to read a quotation.

Step 10: Deliver Your Speech

In your actual presentation, use your voice and bodily action to reinforce your message. Make it easy for your listeners to understand your speech. Any vocal or body movements that draw attention to themselves (and away from what you're saying) obviously should be avoided. Here are a few guidelines that will prove helpful.

1. When called on to speak, approach the front of the room with enthusiasm; even if, like most speakers, you feel nervous, show your desire to speak with your listeners.

2. When at the front of the room, don't begin immediately; instead, pause, engage your audience eye to eye for a few brief moments, and then begin to talk directly to the audience. Talk at a volume that people can hear easily without straining.

3. Throughout your speech, maintain eye contact with your entire audience; avoid concentrating on only a few members or looking out of the window or at the floor.

USING TECHNOLOGY

Using your favorite search engine, search for "public speeches." What kinds of speeches are available on the Web? You may want to bookmark these addresses and save them in a "Public Speeches" folder.

Summary of Concepts and Skills

This first chapter has looked at the nature of public speaking and at probably the most important obstacle to public speaking—namely, communication apprehension. The chapter also introduced, in brief, the 10 steps to preparing and delivering a public speech.

Studying Public Speaking

Public speaking is a transactional process in which *(a)* a speaker *(b)* addresses *(c)* a relatively large audience with *(d)* a relatively continuous message.

◆ Studying public speaking will help you
  ■ Increase your personal and social abilities.
  ■ Enhance related academic and professional skills in organization, research, style, and the like.
  ■ Refine your general communication competencies.
  ■ Improve your public speaking abilities—as speaker, as listener, and as critic—which results in personal benefits as well as benefits to society.

◆ The essential elements of public speaking are:
  ■ Speaker, the one who delivers the speech
  ■ Messages, the verbal and nonverbal signals
  ■ Channels, the medium through which the signals pass from speaker to listener
  ■ Noise, the interference that distorts messages
  ■ Audience, the intended receivers of the speech
  ■ Context, the physical, sociopsychological, temporal, and cultural space in which the speech is delivered
  ■ Delivery, the actual sending of the message, the presentation of the speech
  ■ Ethics, the moral dimension of communication

◆ Especially important in influencing public speaking is culture.

■ Because of demographic changes and economic interdependence, cultural differences have become more significant.
■ Increased understanding of the role of culture in public speaking will help you improve your skills in a context that is becoming increasingly intercultural.

Managing Your Apprehension

Communication apprehension is fear of speaking and is often especially high in public speaking. In managing your fear of public speaking, try to

◆ Reverse the factors that contribute to apprehension (inexperience, subordinate status, conspicuousness, dissimilarity, and prior history).

◆ Acquire relevant public speaking techniques for managing apprehension.

Preparing a Public Speech: In Brief

In preparing and presenting a public speech follow these 10 steps:

◆ Select your topic and purpose.
◆ Analyze your audience.
◆ Research your topic.
◆ Develop your thesis and main points.
◆ Support your main points.
◆ Organize your speech materials.
◆ Word your speech.
◆ Construct your introduction, conclusion, and transitions.
◆ Rehearse your speech.
◆ Deliver your speech.

Vocabulary Quiz

Introducing Public Speaking

Match the terms of public speaking with their definitions. Record the number of the definition next to the appropriate term.

_____ audience

_____ noise

_____ context

_____ public speech

_____ ethics

_____ culture

_____ apprehension

_____ channel

_____ thesis

_____ transitions

1. Anything that interferes with the listener receiving the message the speaker sends.
2. The listeners to a public speech.
3. A relatively continuous message delivered to a relatively large audience in a unique context.
4. The physical, psycho-sociological, temporal, and cultural environment in which the public speech is delivered and received.
5. The medium that carries the message signals from speaker to listener.
6. The rightness or wrongness of acts such as public speaking.
7. The collection of beliefs, attitudes, values, and ways of behaving that are shared by a group of people and passed down from generation to generation through communication.
8. Words, phrases, or sentences that connect one part of the speech to another.
9. The central theme or main idea of a speech.
10. Fear or anxiety, as in fear of public speaking.

Web Explorations

Companion Website

www.ablongman.com/devito

Two self-tests and further discussions of communication apprehension are offered online: "How Apprehensive Are You in Conversations?" (self-test), "How Shy Are You?" (self-test), "General and Specific Apprehension," "Degrees of Apprehension," "Positive and Normal Apprehension," "Culture and Communication Apprehension," and "Developing Confidence." In addition, a complete annotated speech, "Adverse Drug Effects," is presented and will help you review the steps for preparing a public speech.

Public Speaking Exercises

These exercises, presented at the end of each chapter, are designed to stimulate you to think more actively about the concepts and skills covered in the chapter and to help you practice your developing public speaking skills.

The last exercise in each chapter involves analyzing a speech. A complete speech is presented here with annotations to guide you in understanding what an excellent speech looks like. You might use the methods of these speakers in your own speeches. As a complement to these exercises, suggestions for short speeches, based on the content of the chapters, are available at www. ablongman.com/devito; see "Short Speech Technique."

1.1 Constructing a Speech

Consult the "Dictionary of Topics" on the text's website at www.ablongman.com/devito for suggestions for speech topics. Select a topic and develop an outline by following these steps:

1. Formulate a specific thesis.
2. Formulate a specific purpose suitable for an informative or persuasive speech of approximately five minutes.
3. Analyze this class as your potential audience and identify ways that you can relate this topic to their interests and needs.
4. Generate at least two main points from your thesis.
5. Support these points with examples, illustrations, definitions, and so on.

6. Construct an introduction that gains attention and orients your audience.
7. Construct a conclusion that summarizes your main ideas and brings the speech to a definite close.

Discuss these outlines in small groups or with the class as a whole. Try to secure feedback from other members on how you can improve your outline.

1.2 Analyzing a Speech of Introduction

One of the first speeches you may be called upon to make is the speech of introduction, illustrated here. It may prove useful to review this speech and its accompanying annotations to get an overview of the parts of the speech. This speech will then give you reference points for examining the steps in preparing a public speech, as presented in Figure 1.2.

The relatively brief speech of introduction illustrated here is a commonly used first assignment in public speaking classes. It is designed to give each person in the class an early and nonthreatening public speaking experience and at the same time give class members a chance to get to know each other. (A different type of speech of introduction is discussed in Chapter 11, "Speaking on Special Occasions.")

In the speech presented here, one student introduces another student to the class. The speech, although fairly complete and detailed, would take about three minutes to deliver.

[Introduction]

It's a real pleasure to introduce Joe Robinson to you. I want to tell you a little about Joe's background, his present situation, and his plans for the future.

[Transition]

Let's look first at Joe's past.

[Body, first main point (the past)]

Joe comes to us from Arizona, where he lived and worked on a small ranch with his father and grandpar-

In this introduction, the speaker accomplishes several interrelated purposes: to place the speech in a positive context, to explain the purpose of the speech and orient the audience, to tell them what the speech will cover, and to indicate that it will follow a time pattern—beginning with the past, moving to the present, and then ending with the proposed future. What other types of opening statements might be appropriate? In what other ways might you organize a speech of introduction?

This transitional statement alerts listeners that the speaker is moving from the introduction to the first major part of what is called the "body" of the speech.

The speaker here gives us information about Joe's past that makes us see him as a unique individual. We also learn something pretty significant about Joe: the fact that his

ents—mostly working with dairy cows. Working on a farm gave Joe a deep love and appreciation for animals, which he carries with him today and into his future plans.

Joe's mother died when he was three years old, so he lived with his father most of his life. When his father, an air force lieutenant, was transferred to Stewart Air Force Base here in the Hudson Valley, Joe thought it would be a great opportunity to join his father and continue his education.

Joe also wanted to stay with his father to make sure he eats right, doesn't get involved with the wrong crowd, and meets the right woman to settle down with.

[Transition]

So Joe and his father journeyed from the dairy farm of Arizona to the Hudson Valley.

[Second main point (the present)]

Right now, with the money he saved while working on the ranch and with the help of a part-time job, Joe's here with us at Hudson Valley Community College.

Like many of us, Joe is a little apprehensive about college and worries that it's going to be a difficult and very different experience, especially at 28. Although an avid reader—mysteries and biographies are his favorites—Joe hasn't really studied, taken an exam, or written a term paper since high school, some 10 years ago. So he's a bit anxious but at the same time looking forward to the changes and the challenges of college life.

And again, like many of us, Joe's a bit apprehensive about taking a public speaking course.

Joe is currently working for a local animal shelter. He was especially drawn to this particular shelter because of their no-kill policy; lots of shelters will kill the animals they can't find adopted homes for, but this one sticks by its firm no-kill policy.

[Transition]

But it's not the past or the present that Joe focuses on, it's the future.

[Third main point (the future)]

Joe is planning to complete his AB degree here at Hudson Valley Community and then move on to the State University of New Paltz, where he intends to major in communication with a focus on public relations.

His ideal job would be to work for an animal rights organization. He wants to help make people aware of the ways in which they can advance animal rights and stop so much of the cruelty to animals common throughout the world.

mother died when he was very young. The speaker continues here to answer one of the questions that audience members probably have; namely, why this somewhat older person is in this class and in this college. If this were a longer speech, what else might the speaker cover here? What else would you want to know about Joe's past?

Here the speaker shows that Joe has a sense of humor in his identifying why he wanted to stay with his father, the very same things that a father would say about a son. Can you make this more humorous?

Here's a simple transition, alerting the audience that the speaker is moving from the first main point (the past) to the second (the present). In what other ways might you state such a transition?

Here the speaker goes into the present and gives Joe a very human dimension by identifying his fears and concerns about being in college and taking this course and in his concern for animals. The speaker also explains some commonalities between Joe and the rest of the audience (for example, feeling apprehension in a public speaking class are shared by nearly everyone). Some textbooks suggest that telling an audience that a speaker has apprehension about speaking is a bad idea. What do you think of this disclosure in this context?

This transition tells listeners that the speaker has finished talking about the past and present and is now moving on to the future.

The speaker moves to the future and identifies Joe's educational plans. Having a plan is one thing that everyone has in common, and Joe's plan is something that most in the class would want to know about. The speaker also covers Joe's career goals, again, something the audience is likely to be interested in. In this the speaker also reveals important aspects of Joe's interests and belief system—his concern for animals and his dedication to building his career around this abiding interest. What kinds of information might this speech of introduction give you about the attitudes and beliefs of its intended audience?

[Transition, Internal Summary]

Joe's traveled an interesting road from a dairy farm in Arizona to the Hudson Valley, and the path to New Paltz and public relations should be just as interesting.

This transition (a kind of internal summary) tells you that the speaker has completed the three part discussion (past, present, and future) and offers a basic summary of what has been discussed.

[Conclusion]

Having talked with Joe over the last few days, I'm sure he'll do well—he has lots of ideas, is determined to succeed, is open to new experiences, and enjoys interacting with people. I'd say that gives this interesting dairy farmer from Arizona a pretty good start as a student in this class, as a student at Hudson Valley Community, and as a soon-to-be public relations specialist.

In this concluding comment the speaker appropriately expresses a positive attitude toward Joe and summarizes some of Joe's positive qualities. These qualities are then tied to the past-present-future organization of the speech. Although the speaker doesn't say "thank you"—which can get trite when 20 speakers in succession say this—it's clear that this is the end of the speech from the last sentence, which brings Joe into his future profession. How effective do you think this conclusion is? What other types of conclusions might the speaker have used in this speech?

2 Listening and Criticism

Why Read This Chapter?

It will enable you to become a more effective listener and critic of public speeches by helping you to:

❖ improve your listening effectiveness in public speaking (or in any oral communication situation) by identifying pitfalls to avoid and strategies for effectiveness that you'll want to make a part of your general listening behavior

❖ analyze public speaking effectiveness and apply the insights to your own speeches

❖ express your evaluations in ways that will help speakers you listen to improve their skills

> " It takes two to speak the truth—one to speak, and another to listen. "
>
> **—Henry David Thoreau**

When you improve your listening skills and become a more effective listener, you will gain numerous benefits. Effective listening will help you increase the amount of information you learn and will decrease the time you need to learn it. It will help you distinguish logical from illogical appeals and thus decrease your chances of getting duped. And, not surprisingly, effective listening will help you become a better public speaker. When you listen effectively in public speaking, you'll see more clearly what works and what doesn't work (and why). So effective listening will help you identify the principles of public speaking to follow, along with the pitfalls to avoid.

Listening to Speeches

Listening is often thought to be the same as hearing; it's just something that takes place when you're in hearing range of speech. Actually, listening and hearing are not the same; listening is a lot more complex than hearing.

What Is Listening?

Listening can be described as a series of five steps: receiving, understanding, remembering, evaluating, and responding. The process is represented in Figure 2.1.

Receiving
Unlike listening, hearing begins and ends with the first stage: receiving. Hearing is something that just happens when you get within earshot of some auditory

A&B Public Speaking Website

(www.ablongman.com/pubspeak)
In addition to the Companion Website introduced in Chapter 1 (p. 4), Allyn & Bacon, this book's publisher, also maintains an extensive public speaking website. As you can see from its home page, this website highlights several crucial public speaking processes: assessing and analyzing the audience and situation, researching your topic, organizing your speech, and delivering the speech.

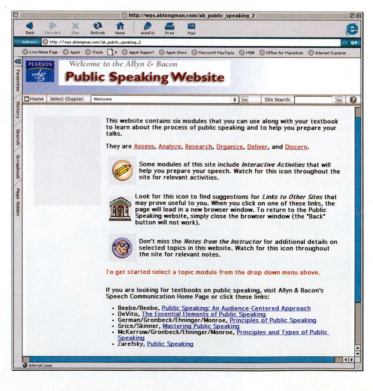

stimulus. Listening is quite different; it begins (but does not end) with receiving a speaker's messages. The messages a listener receives are both verbal and nonverbal; they consist of words as well as gestures, facial expressions, variations in volume and rate, and lots more, as we will see throughout this book.

At this stage of listening you recognize not only what is said but also what is not said. For example, you receive both the politician's summary of accomplishments in education as well as his or her omission of failed promises to improve health care programs.

Receiving messages is a highly selective process. You don't listen to all the available auditory stimuli. Rather, you selectively tune in to certain messages and tune out others. Generally, you listen most carefully to messages that you feel will prove of value to you or that you find particularly interesting. At the same time, you give less attention to messages that have less value or interest. Thus, you may listen carefully when your instructor tells you what will appear on the examination but may listen less carefully to an extended story or to routine announcements. To improve your receiving skills:

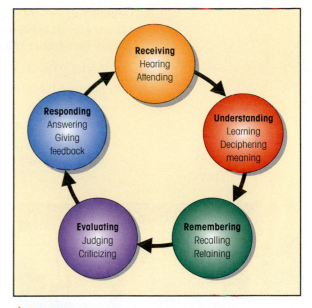

◆ **FIGURE 2.1**
The Process of Listening

This five-step model draws on a variety of models that listening researchers have developed (Alessandra, 1986; Barker, 1990; Brownell, 1987; Steil, Barker, & Watson, 1983).

◆ Look at the speaker; make your mind follow your body and focus attention on the person speaking.

◆ Focus your attention on the speaker's verbal and nonverbal messages, on what is said and on what isn't said.

◆ Avoid attending to distractions in the environment.

◆ Focus your attention on what the speaker is saying rather than on any questions or objections you may have to what the speaker is saying.

Understanding

Understanding a speaker means grasping not only the thoughts that are expressed but also the emotional tone that accompanies these thoughts; for example, the urgency or the joy or sorrow expressed in the message. To enhance understanding:

◆ Relate the new information the speaker is giving to what you already know.

◆ See the speaker's messages from the speaker's point of view; avoid judging the message until you fully understand it as the speaker intended it.

◆ Rephrase (paraphrase) the speaker's ideas into your own words as you continue to listen.

Remembering

Messages that you receive and understand need to be retained at least for some period of time. In public speaking situations you can augment your memory by taking notes or by taping the messages.

What you remember is actually not what was said, but what you think (or remember) was said. Memory for speech isn't reproductive; you don't simply reproduce in your memory what the speaker said. Rather, memory is

USING TECHNOLOGY

Visit one of the many humor sites on the Net (search for "humor," "jokes," or "anecdotes"). What techniques of the best humor writers might you try using in your own speeches to make your audience want to listen?

reconstructive; you actually reconstruct the messages you hear into a system that seems to make sense to you. This is well illustrated in the exercise "Do You Really Remember What You Hear?" at the end of this chapter. In remembering:

♦ Identify the thesis or central idea and the main points.

♦ Summarize the message in a more easily retained form, being careful not to ignore crucial details or important qualifications.

♦ Repeat names and key concepts to yourself.

♦ Identify the organizational pattern and use it (visualize it) to organize what the speaker is saying.

❖ **CONSIDER** the kinds of listening obstacles that this contractor may face as she details the work that needs to be done. In anticipation of these obstacles, what might she do to lessen their effects?

Evaluating

Evaluating consists of judging the message and the speaker's credibility, truthfulness, or usefulness in some way. At this stage your own biases and prejudices become especially influential. These will affect what you single out for evaluation and what you'll just let pass. They will influence what you judge good and what you judge bad. In some situations evaluation is more in the nature of critical analysis, a topic explored in detail later in this chapter. When evaluating:

♦ Resist evaluation until you feel you understand (at least reasonably well) the speaker's point of view.

♦ Distinguish facts from inferences (see Chapter 7), opinions, and personal interpretations that you're making as well as those made by the speaker.

♦ Identify any biases, self-interests, or prejudices that may lead the speaker to slant unfairly what he or she is presenting.

♦ Identify any biases that may lead you to remember what supports your attitudes and beliefs and to forget what contradicts them.

Responding

Responding occurs in two phases: (1) nonverbal (and occasionally verbal) responses you make while the speaker is talking and (2) responses you make after the speaker has stopped talking. Responses made while the speaker is talking should support the speaker and show that you're listening. These include what nonverbal researchers call backchanneling cues—gestures that let the speaker know that you're listening, such as nodding your head, smiling, and leaning forward (Burgoon, Buller, & Woodall, 1995).

Responses made after the speaker has stopped talking are generally more elaborate and might include questions of clarification ("I wasn't sure what you meant by reclassification"); expressions of agreement ("You're absolutely right on this, and I'll support your proposal when it comes up for a vote"); and expressions of disagreement ("I disagree that Japanese products are superior to those produced in the United States").

RESEARCH *Link*

Research Time Management

Because a great deal of your time—in this course and in numerous others—will be spent on research, you should learn to use your research time efficiently. Here are a few suggestions:

Multitask. Combine your research tasks and do them simultaneously. For example, when going to the library or logging on to the Internet, have more than one task in mind. If you know the topics of your next few speeches, or if you're writing a sociology paper on a related topic, do the research for both at the same time.

Watch Detours. When you are searching the Net, it's easy to get lured into taking long detours. These are often excellent learning experiences and are not necessarily detrimental. For purposes of time management, however, it will help if you keep your purpose clearly in mind—even to the point of writing it down—as you surf the Net or lurk among the chat groups.

Access Your Library from Home. If possible, access your college library's online catalog of books from home; it will save you time if you can go to the library with your searches already completed. If your library subscribes to full text databases that can be accessed from your home computer (ProQuest and Lexis-Nexis are popular examples), you may be able to do all your research from the comfort of your home.

Learn the Available Resources. Learn what is available, where, and in what form. Spend a few hours in the library learning where some of the most useful materials are located or how they can be accessed. Learn the computer search facilities that are available at your college library and at neighboring public or college libraries for accessing newspapers, research articles, corporate reports, magazines, or any type of media you may wish to use. Learn, too, the Internet search engines and search directories (see the Chapter 7 Research Link, p. 176) and how to use them efficiently.

Consult Your Librarian. One useful but often overlooked suggestion is to consult your librarian. Librarians are experts in the very researching issues that may be giving you trouble. They'll be able to help you access biographical material, indexes of current articles, materials in specialized collections at other libraries, and a wide variety of computerized databases.

Research Activity. Research Navigator (www.researchnavigator.com) has lots of useful information to help you become a more efficient researcher. If you have access, read the sections you find particularly interesting under the "Research Process" tab.

◆ Use a variety of backchanneling cues to support the speaker; using only one cue—for example, nodding constantly—will make it appear that you're not listening but are on automatic pilot.

◆ Support the speaker in your final responses by saying something positive.

◆ Own your own responses: State your thoughts and feelings as your own, and use I-messages. For example, say, "I think the new proposal will entail greater expense than you outlined" rather than "Everyone will object to the plan because it will cost too much."

Culture and Listening

Listening is difficult, partly because of the inevitable differences between the communication systems of speaker and listener. Because each person has had a unique set of experiences, each person's communication and meaning system is going to be different from the next person's system. When speaker and listener

"Of course I'm paying attention. I've pressed the mute button."

come from different cultures, the differences and their effects are naturally much greater. Here are just a few areas where misunderstandings can occur.

Language and Speech

Even when speaker and listener speak the same language, they speak it with different meanings and different accents. No two speakers speak exactly the same language. Every speaker speaks an idiolect—a unique variation of the language. Speakers of the same language will sometimes have different meanings for the same terms because they have had different experiences.

Speakers and listeners who have different native languages and who may have learned English as a second language will have even greater differences in meaning. Translations are never precise and never fully capture the meaning in the other language. If your meaning for *house* was learned in a culture in which everyone lived in their own house with lots of land around it, then communicating your meaning for *house* with someone whose meaning was learned in a neighborhood of high-rise tenements is going to be difficult. Although you'll each hear the same word, the meanings you'll each develop will be drastically different. In adjusting your listening—especially when in an intercultural setting—understand that the speaker's meanings may be very different from yours even though you each know and speak the same language.

Another aspect of speech is the speaker's accent. In many classrooms throughout the United States, there will be a wide range of accents, both regional and foreign. People whose native language is tonal such as Chinese (in which differences in pitch signal important meaning differences), may speak English with variations in pitch that may seem unnatural to others. Those whose native language is Japanese may have trouble distinguishing *l* from *r*, as Japanese does not make this distinction. Regional accent differences may make it difficult for people from Mississippi and Maine, for example, to understand each other; words even may have different meanings in different regions, and this may make communication more difficult than if the speakers were from the same area.

Nonverbal Differences

As you listen to other people, you also "listen" to their **nonverbal communication**. If their nonverbal messages are drastically different from what you expect on the basis of the verbal message, the nonverbals may be seen as a kind of noise or interference or they may be seen as contradictory messages.

Additionally, speakers from different cultures have different display rules, cultural rules that govern which nonverbal behaviors are appropriate and which are inappropriate in a public setting. Also, different cultures may give very different meanings to the same nonverbal gesture. For example, Americans consider direct eye contact an expression of honesty and forthrightness, but the Japanese often view this as a lack of respect. The Japanese will glance at the other person's face rarely and then only for very short periods (Axtell, 1990). Among some Latin Americans and Native Americans, direct eye contact between, say, a teacher and a student is considered inappropriate, perhaps aggressive; appropriate student behavior is to avoid eye contact with the teacher.

DEVELOPING STRATEGIES

Self-Identification. Serena is planning to give a speech in favor of gay marriage. Serena herself is heterosexual, and she wonders if she should identify her affectional orientation in the speech. If Serena were giving her speech to your class, what would you see as the advantages and disadvantages of including reference to her own affectional orientation? Would the advantages and disadvantages you identified be different if Serena were a lesbian?

Ethnocentrism

Ethnocentrism is the tendency to evaluate the values, beliefs, and behaviors of your own culture as being more positive, logical, and natural than those of other cultures. The nonethnocentric, on the other hand, would see both himself or herself and others as different but equal, with neither being inferior nor superior. Ethnocentric listening occurs when you listen to members of other cultures and consider them to be lacking in knowledge or expertise because they are from another culture, or when you acknowledge members of your own culture as knowledgeable and expert simply because they are from your own culture. Similarly, you're listening ethnocentrically when you listen to ideas about other cultures and view these as inferior simply because they differ from those of your own culture, or when you view ideas of your own culture as superior simply because they are from your own culture.

Ethnocentrism exists on a continuum. People are not either ethnocentric or not ethnocentric; most are somewhere between these polar opposites. And, of course, your degree of ethnocentrism varies depending on the group on which you focus. For example, if you're Greek American, you may have a low degree of ethnocentrism when dealing with Italian Americans (because of the similarities in the cultures of Greeks and Italians) but a high degree when dealing with Japanese Americans (because of the greater differences between the Greek and Japanese cultures). Most important for our purposes is that your degree of ethnocentrism—and we're all ethnocentric to some degree—will influence your listening effectiveness.

Recognizing the tendency toward ethnocentrism is the first step in combating any excesses. In addition, try following the suggestions for effective listening offered in this chapter, especially when you're in an intercultural public speaking situation. Also, expose yourself to culturally different experiences, but resist the temptation to evaluate these through your own cultural filters. For many this will not be an easy experience; however, in light of the tremendous advantages to be gained through increased intercultural experiences, the effort seems well worth it.

"I've seen most of Spike Lee's movies, so I know what you must be going through."

© The New Yorker Collection 1996 Robert Weber from cartoonbank.com. All Rights Reserved.

Gender and Listening

According to Deborah Tannen (1990) in her best-selling *You Just Don't Understand: Women and Men in Conversation*, women seek to build rapport and establish a closer relationship and so use listening to achieve these ends. Men, on the other hand, tend to play up their expertise, emphasize it, and use it to dominate the interaction. Women are apt to play down their expertise and are more interested in communicating supportiveness. Tannen argues that the goal of a man in conversation is to be accorded respect, so he seeks to show his knowledge and expertise. A woman, on the other hand, seeks to be liked, so she expresses agreement.

Men and women also show that they're listening in different ways. Women are more apt to give lots of listening cues such as interjecting *yeah* or *uh-huh*, nodding in agreement, and smiling. A man is more likely to listen quietly,

? DEVELOPING STRATEGIES

Cultural Sensitivity. Arthur is listening to Jack giving a speech of unbelievable cultural insensitivity. Arthur wonders if he should continue to listen attentively and thus encourage Jack to cause further damage to cultural understanding, or if he should give Jack negative feedback and perhaps wake him up.

without giving a lot of listening cues as feedback. Tannen argues, however, that men do listen less to women than women listen to men. The reason, says Tannen, is that listening places a person in an inferior position, whereas speaking places the speaker in a superior role.

As a result of these differences, men may seem to assume a more combative posture while listening, as if getting ready to argue. They also may appear to ask questions that are more argumentative or that are designed to puncture holes in your position as a way to play up their own expertise. Women are more likely to ask supportive questions and perhaps to offer more positive criticism than men. Women also use more cues in listening in a public speaking context. They let the speaker see that they're listening. Men, on the other hand, seem to use fewer listening cues in a public speaking situation.

Men and women act this way to both men and women; their customary ways of communicating don't seem to change depending on whether the speaker is male or female. There's no evidence to show that these differences represent any negative motives—any conscious aim on the part of men to prove themselves superior or of women to ingratiate themselves. Rather, these differences in listening are largely the result of the ways in which men and women have been socialized.

Guidelines for Listening More Effectively

Effective listening is extremely important, because you spend so much time listening. In fact, if you measured importance by the time you spend on an activity, listening would be your most important communication activity. Studies conducted from 1929 to 1980 show that listening is the most often used form of communication (occupying about 45 to 53 percent of your communication time), followed by speaking (about 16 to 30 percent), reading (about 16 to 17 percent), and writing (about 9 to 14 percent) (Barker, Edwards, Gaines, Gladney, & Holley, 1980; Rankin, 1929; Steil, Barker, & Watson, 1983; Werner, 1975; Wolvin & Coakley, 1996). This was true of high school and college students as well as of adults from a wide variety of fields. With the widespread use of the Internet, these studies have become dated, and today their findings are of limited value. However, anecdotal evidence (certainly not conclusive in any way) suggests that listening is probably still the most used communication activity. Just think of how you spend your day; listening probably occupies a considerable amount of time. Listening is also important in your professional life; regardless of what profession you enter, you'll always need the skills of effective listening (Allen, 1997; Salopek, 1999).

❖ **CONSIDER** the potential listening problems that this librarian may face as she explains new (and highly complex) online services. What might she have done in her preparation to deal with these anticipated problems?

Listen Actively

The first step in listening improvement is to recognize that it isn't a passive activity. You cannot listen without effort. Listening is a difficult process. In many ways it's more demanding than speaking. In speaking you control the situation; you can talk about what you like in the way you like. In listening, however, you have to follow the pace, the content, and the language of the speaker.

RESEARCH *Link*

Research Notes

The more accurate your research notes are, the less time you'll waste going back to sources to check on a date or spelling. Accurate records also will prevent you from going to sources you've already consulted but may have forgotten about. The following suggestions may prove helpful to you as you take notes during the research process.

Create Folders. If you want to collect your material on paper, loose-leaf notebooks or simple manila folders work well to keep everything relating to a speech or article in the same place. If you want to file your material electronically, create a general folder and subfolders as you need them. This will work especially well if you can scan into your folder material you find in print. By using a notebook or folder, you can retain the sources consulted, quotations, ideas, arguments, suggested references, preliminary outlines, and material you've printed or downloaded in one place.

Key Your Notes. Notes are most effective when they're keyed to specific topics. For example, let's say that your speech is to be on animal experimentation. Your notebook or major folder might

be titled *Animal Experimentation.* The notebook divisions or subfolders might then be labeled, "Basic Information" (statistics on animal experimentation, people to contact, organizations involved in this issue), "Arguments for Animal Experimentation," and "Arguments against Animal Experimentation." Taking notes as you prepare your preliminary outline will help focus your research and will remind you of those topics for which you need more information. It also will help you keep the information logically organized.

Take Complete Notes. Make sure your notes are complete (and legible). If you have to err, then err on the side of too much detail. You can always cut a quotation or select one example out of the three at a later time. As you take notes, be sure to identify the source of the material—so that you can find that reference again should you need it and so that you can reference it in your speech outline. When you use material from the Web, be sure to print out or save to folder the Web page, noting the URL and the date you accessed this site. In this way, you'll be able to cite a source even if the Web page disappears, a not unlikely possibility.

Research Activity. Construct your folder and subfolders for your next speech. Then, if you have access, consult Research Navigator (www.researchnavigator.com) and, if you haven't already done so, read the section on "Creating Effective Notes" under the "Research Process" tab.

The best preparation for **active listening** is to act like an active listener. Recall, for example, how your body almost automatically reacts to important news. Almost immediately you sit up straighter, cock your head toward the speaker, and remain relatively still and quiet. You do this almost reflexively, because this is how you listen most effectively. This isn't to say that you should be tense and uncomfortable, but only that your body should reflect your active mind. In listening actively:

◆ Use your listening time to think about what the speaker is saying, summarizing the speaker's thoughts, formulating questions, drawing connections between what the speaker says and what you already know.

◆ Work at listening. Listening is hard, so be prepared to participate actively. Avoid "the entertainment syndrome," the expectation that you'll be amused and entertained by a speaker (Floyd, 1985). Set aside distractions (newspapers, magazines, headphones) so that your listening task will have less competition.

◆ Assume there's value in what the speaker is saying. Resist assuming that what you have to say is more valuable than the speaker's remarks.

USING TECHNOLOGY

Visit the International Listening Association's website at http://www.listen.org. What resources are available to someone learning about listening?

◆ Take notes if appropriate. In some instances you'll want to take notes while the speaker is speaking. Taking notes may be helpful if you want to ask a question about a specific item of information or if you want to include a specific statement in your critical evaluation.

◆ Avoid becoming preoccupied with yourself. If you focus on yourself, you'll invariably miss much of what the speaker is saying. Similarly, avoid becoming preoccupied with external issues, with what you did last Saturday, or with your plans for the evening. The more you entertain thoughts of external matters, the less effectively you listen.

Listen for Total Meaning

The meaning of a message isn't only in the words; it's also in the speaker's nonverbal behavior.

The meanings communicated in a speech will also depend on what the speaker does not say. The speaker on contemporary social problems who omits references to homeless people or to drug abuse communicates important messages by these very omissions. For example, listeners may infer that the speaker is poorly prepared, that the speaker's research was inadequate, or that the speaker is trying to fool the audience by not mentioning these issues. As a listener, therefore, be particularly sensitive to the meanings that significant omissions may communicate. As a speaker, recognize that most inferences that audiences draw from omissions are negative and will reflect negatively on your credibility and on the total impact of your speech. In listening for total meaning:

◆ Focus on both verbal and nonverbal messages. Recognize both consistent and inconsistent "packages" of messages and take these cues as guides for drawing inferences about the meaning the speaker is trying to communicate. Ask questions when in doubt.

◆ See the forest, then the trees. Connect the specifics to the speaker's general theme rather than merely remembering isolated facts and figures.

◆ Balance your attention between the surface and the underlying meanings. Don't disregard the literal (surface) meaning of the speech in your attempt to uncover the more hidden (deeper) meanings.

◆ Resist the temptation to filter out difficult or unpleasant messages. You don't want to hear that something you believe is untrue or to be told that people you respect are doing bad things, and yet these are the very messages you need to listen to with great care. These are the messages that will lead you to examine and reexamine your implicit and unconscious assumptions. If you filter out this kind of information, you risk failing to correct misinformation. You risk losing new and important insights.

Listen with Empathy

Try to feel what the speaker feels—to empathize with the speaker. **Empathy** means feeling what others feel, seeing the world as they see it, walking in their shoes (Eisenberg & Strayer, 1987). Of course, you can never feel exactly what the speaker is feeling, but you can try to feel something of what he or she is feeling. Listen to emotions as well as to thoughts and ideas.

◆ See the speaker's point of view. Before you can understand what the speaker is saying, you have to see the message from the speaker's vantage point. Try putting yourself in the role of the speaker and looking at the topic from the speaker's perspective.

◆ Understand the speaker's thoughts and feelings. Don't consider your listening task complete until you've understood what the speaker is feeling as well as thinking.

◆ Avoid "offensive listening." Offensive listening is the tendency to listen to bits and pieces of information that will enable you to attack the speaker or to find fault with something the speaker has said.

◆ Don't distort messages because of the "friend-or-foe" factor; in other words, avoid listening for positive statements about friends and negative statements about enemies. For example, if you dislike Fred, make the added effort to listen objectively to Fred's speeches or to comments that might reflect positively on Fred.

Listen with an Open Mind

Listening with an open mind is difficult. It isn't easy to listen to arguments attacking your cherished beliefs. Listening often stops when such remarks are made. Yet in these situations it's particularly important to continue listening openly and fairly. To listen with an open mind, try these suggestions.

◆ Avoid prejudging. Delay both positive and negative evaluation until you've fully understood the intention and the content of the message being communicated.

◆ Avoid filtering out difficult, unpleasant, or undesirable messages. Avoid distorting messages through oversimplification or leveling, the tendency to eliminate details and to simplify complex messages to make them easier to remember.

◆ Recognize your own **biases**. They may interfere with accurate listening and cause you to distort message reception to fit your own prejudices, and expectations. Biases may also lead to sharpening—when an item of information takes on increased importance because it seems to confirm your stereotypes or prejudices.

◆ Avoid **assimilation**—the tendency to reconstruct messages so they reflect your own attitudes, prejudices, needs, and values. Assimilation is the tendency to hear relatively neutral messages ("Management plans to institute drastic changes in scheduling") as supporting your own attitudes and beliefs ("Management is going to screw up our schedules again").

◆ Whether in a lecture auditorium or in a small group, avoid prejudging some speeches as uninteresting or irrelevant. All speeches are, at least potentially, interesting and useful. If you prejudge them and then tune them out, you may not be proved wrong; however, you will close yourself off from potentially useful information. Most important, perhaps, is that you're not giving the other person a fair hearing.

Listen Ethically

As a listener you share not only in the success or failure of any communication but also in the moral implications of the communication exchange.

? DEVELOPING STRATEGIES

Ethical Listening. Anita is teaching a class in public speaking, and one of her students, a sincere and devout Iranian Muslim, gives a speech on "why women should be subservient to men." After the first two minutes of the speech, half the class walks out, returning 10 minutes later, after the speech is over. Anita decides to address this incident. What would you advise Anita to say?

Consequently, bear ethical issues in mind when listening as well as when speaking. Two major principles govern ethical listening:

◆ Give the speaker an honest hearing. Avoid prejudging the speaker before hearing her or him out. Try to put aside prejudices and preconceptions and to evaluate the speaker's message fairly. At the same time, try to empathize with the speaker. You don't have to agree with the speaker, but try to understand emotionally as well as intellectually what he or she means. Then accept or reject the speaker's ideas on the basis of the information offered, not on the basis of some bias or prejudice or incomplete understanding.

◆ Give the speaker honest responses and feedback. In a learning environment such as a public speaking class, listening ethically means giving honest and constructive criticism to help the speaker improve. It also means reflecting honestly on the questions speakers raise. Much as the listener has a right to expect an active speaker, the speaker has the right to expect a listener who will actively deal with, rather than just passively hear, the message of a speech.

Criticizing Speeches

In learning the art of public speaking, you can gain much insight from the criticism offered by others as well as from your own efforts to critique others' speeches. This section considers the nature of criticism in a learning environment, the influence of culture on criticism, and the standards and principles for evaluating a speech and for making criticism easier and more effective.

What Is Criticism?

Critics and criticism are essential parts of any art. The word *criticism* comes into English from the Latin *criticus*, which means "able to discern," "able to judge." Speech **criticism,** therefore, is the process of evaluating a speech, of rendering a judgment of its value. Note that there is nothing inherently negative about criticism; criticism may be negative, but it also may be positive.

Perhaps the major value of criticism in the classroom is that it helps you improve your public speaking skills. Through the constructive criticism of others, you'll learn the principles of public speaking more effectively. You'll be shown what you do well; what you could improve; and, ideally, how to improve. As a listener–critic you'll also learn the principles of public speaking through assessing the speeches of others. Just as you learn when you teach, you also learn when you criticize.

When you give criticism—as you do in a public speaking class—you're telling the speaker that you've listened carefully and that you care enough about the speech and the speaker to offer suggestions for improvement.

Of course, criticism can be difficult—for the critic (whether student or instructor) as well as for the person criticized. As a critic, you may feel embarrassed or uncomfortable about offering evaluation. After all, you may think, "Who am I to criticize another person's speech; my own speech won't be any better." Or you may be reluctant to offend, fearing that your criticism may make the speaker feel uncomfortable. Or you may view criticism as a confrontation that will do more harm than good.

But reconsider this view. By offering criticism you're helping the speaker; you're giving the speaker another perspective that should prove useful in future speeches. When you offer criticism, you're not claiming to be a better speaker; you're simply offering another point of view. It's true that by offering criticism, you're stating a position with which others may disagree. That's one of the things that will make this class and the study of public speaking exciting and challenging.

Criticism is also difficult to receive. After working on a speech for a week or two and dealing with the normal anxiety that comes with giving a speech, the last thing you want is to stand in front of the class and hear others say what you did wrong. Public speaking is ego-involving, and it's normal to take criticism personally. But if you learn how to give and how to receive criticism, it will help you improve your public speaking skills. Constructive criticism also can serve as an important support mechanism for the developing public speaker, a way of patting the speaker on the back for all the positive effort.

Culture and Criticism

There are vast cultural differences in what is considered proper when it comes to criticism. For example, criticism will be viewed very differently depending on whether members come from an **individualist culture** (which emphasizes the individual and places primary value on the individual's goals) or a **collectivist culture** (which emphasizes the group and places primary value on the group's goals).

Individual and collective tendencies are not mutually exclusive; this isn't an all-or-none cultural orientation but rather a matter of emphasis. For example, in basketball, you may follow an individualist orientation and compete with other members of your team for most baskets or most valuable player award. However, in a game you will act with a collective orientation to benefit the entire group—in this case, to enable your team to win the game. In actual practice both individual and collective tendencies will help you and your team achieve your goals. At times, however, these tendencies may conflict; for example, do you shoot for the basket and try to raise your own individual score, or do you pass the ball to another player who is better positioned to score the basket and thus benefit your team?

Those who come from cultures that are highly individualist and competitive (the United States, Germany, and Sweden are examples) may find public criticism a normal part of the learning process. Those who come from cultures that are more collectivist and therefore emphasize the group rather than the individual (Japan, Mexico, and Korea are examples) are likely to find giving and receiving public criticism uncomfortable. Thus, people from individualist cultures may readily criticize speakers and are likely to expect the same "courtesy" from listeners. "After all" such a person might reason, "if I'm going to criticize your skills to help you improve, I expect you to help me in the same way." Persons from collectivist cultures, on the other hand, may feel that it's more important to be polite and courteous than to help someone learn a skill. Cultural rules that maintain peaceful relations among the Japanese (Midooka, 1990) and norms of politeness among many Asian cultures (Fraser, 1990) may conflict with the classroom cultural norm to express honest criticism. In some cultures being kind to the person is more important than telling the truth, and so members may say things that are complimentary but untrue in a strict literal sense.

Collectivist cultures place a heavy emphasis on face-saving—on allowing people always to appear in a positive light (James, 1995). In these cultures people may prefer not to say anything negative in public. In fact they may even be reluctant to say anything positive lest any omission be construed as negative. Japanese executives, for instance, are reluctant to say no in a business meeting for fear of offending the other person. But their yes, properly interpreted in light of the context and the general discussion, may mean no. In cultures in which face-saving is especially important, communication rules such as the following tend to prevail:

◆ Don't express negative evaluation in public; instead, compliment the person.

◆ Don't prove someone wrong, especially in public; express agreement even if you know the person is wrong.

◆ Don't correct someone's errors; don't even acknowledge them.

◆ Don't ask difficult questions, lest the person not know the answer and lose face or be embarrassed; generally, avoid asking questions.

The difficulties that these differences may cause may be lessened if they're discussed openly. Some people may become comfortable with public criticism once it's explained that the cultural norms of most public speaking classrooms include public criticism just as they incorporate informative and persuasive speaking and written outlines. Others may feel more comfortable offering written criticism as a substitute for oral and public criticism. Or perhaps private consultations can be arranged.

Guidelines for Criticizing More Effectively

A useful standard to use in evaluating a classroom speech is the speech's degree of conformity to the principles of the art. Using this standard, you'll evaluate a speech positively when it follows the principles of public speaking established by the critics, theorists, and practitioners of public speaking (as described throughout this text) and evaluate it negatively if it deviates from these principles. These principles include speaking on a subject that is worthwhile, relevant, and interesting to listeners; designing a speech for a specific audience; and constructing a speech that is based on sound research. A critical checklist for analyzing public speeches that is based on these principles is presented on the inside back cover of this book.

Before reading the specific suggestions for making critical evaluations a more effective part of the total learning process and avoiding some of the potentially negative aspects of criticism, take the following self-test, which asks you to identify what's wrong with selected critical comments.

 **YOURSELF**

What's Wrong with These Critical Evaluations?

For the purposes of this exercise, assume that each of the following 10 comments represents the critic's complete criticism. What's wrong with each?

1. I loved the speech. It was great. Really great.
2. The introduction didn't gain my attention.

3. You weren't interested in your own topic. How do you expect us to be interested?
4. Nobody was able to understand you.
5. The speech was weak.
6. The speech didn't do anything for me.
7. Your position was unfair to those of us on athletic scholarships; we earned those scholarships.
8. I found four things wrong with your speech. First, . . .
9. You needed better research.
10. I liked the speech; we need more police on campus.

❖ **HOW DID YOU DO?** Before reading the following discussion, try to explain why each of these statements is ineffective. Visualize yourself as the speaker receiving such comments and ask yourself if these comments would help you in any way. If not, then they are probably not very effective critical evaluations.

❖ **WHAT WILL YOU DO?** To help you improve your criticism, try to restate the basic meaning of each of these comments but in a more constructive manner.

Stress the Positive

Egos are fragile, and public speaking is extremely personal. Speakers understand what Noel Coward meant when he said, "I love criticism just as long as it's unqualified praise." Part of your function as a critic is to strengthen the

---

CRITICAL LISTENING/THINKING Link

Listening to Criticism

Here are some suggestions for making listening to criticism a less difficult and more productive experience:

Accept the Critic's Viewpoint. Criticism reflects the listener's perception. Because of this, the critic is always right. If the critic says that he or she wasn't convinced by your evidence, it doesn't help to identify the 10 or 12 research sources that you used in your speech; this critic was simply not convinced. Instead, consider why your evidence was not convincing. Perhaps you didn't make clear how the evidence was connected to your thesis or perhaps you raced through it too quickly.

Listen Openly. Public speaking is highly ego-involving, so it's tempting to block out criticism. If you do, however, you'll lose out on useful suggestions for improvement. So listen to criticism with an open mind, and let the critics know that you're really paying attention to what they have to say. In this way you'll encourage critics to share their perceptions more freely; in the process you'll gain valuable insights into how you come across to an audience.

Separate Speech Criticism from Personal Criticism. Always recognize that when some aspect of your speech is criticized, your personality or your worth as an individual isn't being criticized or attacked.

Seek Clarification. If you don't understand the criticism, ask for clarification. For example, if you're told that your specific purpose was too broad but it's unclear to you how you might narrow it, ask the critic to explain—being careful not to appear defensive or confrontational.

Getting Critical. How would you describe the last time you received criticism? Did you follow the suggestions offered here? If not, how would the situation have changed if you had followed these suggestions?

❖ **CONSIDER** how a politician might criticize opponents or opposing points of view, yet avoid giving the audience the impression of running a negative campaign. What types of critical statements should a politician avoid?

already positive aspects of someone's public speaking performance. Positive criticism is particularly important in itself, but it's almost essential as a preface to negative comments. There are always positive characteristics about any speech, and it's more productive to concentrate on these first. Thus, instead of saying (as in the self-test), "The speech didn't do anything for me," tell the speaker what you liked first, then bring up a weak point and suggest how it might be improved.

When criticizing a person's second or third speech, it's especially helpful if you can point out specific improvements ("You really held my attention in this speech," "I felt you were much more in control of the topic today than in your first speech").

Remember, too, that communication is irreversible. Once you say something, you can't take it back. Remember this when offering criticism, especially criticism that may be negative. If in doubt, err on the side of gentleness.

Be Specific

Criticism is most effective when it's specific. General statements such as "I thought your delivery was bad," "I thought your examples were good," or, as in the self-test, "I loved the speech . . . Really great" and "The speech was weak" are poorly expressed criticisms. These statements don't specify what the speaker might do to improve delivery or to capitalize on the examples used. In commenting on delivery, refer to such specifics as eye contact, vocal volume, or whatever else is of consequence. In commenting on the examples, tell the speaker why they were good. Were they realistic? Were they especially interesting? Were they presented dramatically?

In giving negative criticism, specify and justify—to the extent that you can—positive alternatives. Here's an example.

> I thought the way you introduced your statistics was vague. I wasn't sure where the statistics came from or how recent or reliable they were. It might have been better to say something like "The U.S. Census figures for 2000 show. . . ." That way we would know that the statistics were as recent as possible and the most reliable available.

Be Objective

In criticizing a speech, transcend your own biases as best you can, unlike the self-test's example ("Your position was unfair . . .; we earned those scholar-ships"). See the speech as objectively as possible. Assume, for example, that you're strongly for a woman's right to an abortion and you encounter a speech diametrically opposed to your position. In this situation you'll need to take special care not to dismiss the speech because of your own biases. Examine the speech from the point of view of a detached critic; evaluate, for example, the va-lidity of the arguments and their suitability to the audience, the language, and the supporting materials. Conversely, take special care not to evaluate a speech positively because it presents a position with which you agree, as in "I liked the speech; we need more police on campus."

Be Constructive

Your primary goal should be to provide the speaker with insight that will prove useful in future public speaking transactions. For example, to say that "The in-troduction didn't gain my attention" doesn't tell the speaker how he or she might have gained your attention. Instead, you might say, "The example about the computer crash would have more effectively gained my attention in the in-troduction."

Another way you can be constructive is to limit your criticism. Cataloging a speaker's weak points, as in "I found four things wrong with your speech," will overwhelm, not help, the speaker. If you're the sole critic, your criticism natu-rally will need to be more extensive. If you're one of many critics, limit your crit-icism to one or perhaps two points. In all cases, your guide should be the value your comments will have for the speaker.

Focus on Behavior

Focus criticism on what the speaker said and did during the actual speech. Try to avoid the very natural tendency to read the mind of the speaker—to assume that you know why the speaker did one thing rather than another. Compare the critical comments presented in Table 2.1. Note that those in the first column, "Criticism as Attack," try to identify the reasons the speaker did as he or she did; they try to read the speaker's mind. At the same time, they blame the speaker for what happened. Those in the second column, "Criticism as Support," focus on

USING TECHNOLOGY

If you have access, explore Video Workshop to see a wide variety of examples of public speaking. Alternatively, or in addition, visit History and Politics Out Loud (http://www. hpol.org), the History Channel (http://www.historychannel.com/ speeches), or C-Span (http:// www.c-span.org/classroom/ lang/speeches.asp) and read (and in some cases hear and see) one of the speeches. What two or three things does the speaker do that you find effective?

TABLE 2.1	Criticism as Attack and as Support
Can you develop additional examples to illustrate criticism as attack and as support?	
CRITICISM AS ATTACK	**CRITICISM AS SUPPORT**
"You weren't interested in your topic."	"I would have liked to see greater variety in your delivery. It would have made me feel that you were more interested."
"You should have put more time into the speech."	"I think it would have been more effective if you had looked at your notes less."
"You didn't care about your audience."	"I would have liked it if you had looked more directly at me while speaking."

the specific behavior. Note, too, that those in the first column are likely to encourage defensiveness; you can almost hear the speaker saying, "I was so interested in the topic." Those in the second column are less likely to create defensiveness and are more likely to be appreciated as honest reflections of how the critic perceived the speech.

Own Your Criticism

In giving criticism, own your comments; take responsibility for them. The best way to express this ownership is to use "I-messages" rather than "you-messages." Instead of saying, "You needed better research," say, "I would have been more persuaded if you had used more recent research."

Avoid attributing what you found wrong to others. Instead of saying, "Nobody was able to understand you," say, "I had difficulty understanding you. It would have helped me if you had spoken more slowly." Remember that your criticism is important precisely because it's your perception of what the speaker did and what the speaker could have done more effectively. Speaking for the entire audience ("We couldn't hear you clearly" or "No one was convinced by your arguments") will not help the speaker, and it's likely to prove demoralizing.

Employing I-messages also will prevent you from using "should messages," a type of expression that almost invariably creates defensiveness and resentment. When you say "You should have done this" or "You shouldn't have done that," you assume a superior position and imply that what you're saying is correct and that what the speaker did was incorrect. On the other hand, when you own your evaluations and use I-messages, you're giving your perceptions; it's then up to the speaker to accept or reject them.

Recognize Your Ethical Obligations

Just as the speaker and listener have ethical obligations, so does the critic. Here are a few guidelines. First, the ethical critic *separates personal feelings about the speaker* from his or her evaluation of the speech. A liking for the speaker shouldn't lead you to give positive evaluations of the speech, nor should disliking the speaker lead you to give negative evaluations of the speech.

A CASE OF *Ethics*

Criticizing a Speech

You and your best friend are taking a public speaking course together, and your friend just gave a pretty terrible speech. Unfortunately, the instructor has asked you to offer a critique of it. The wrinkle here is that you've noticed that the grades your instructor gives for the speeches seem heavily influenced by what student critics say. So, in effect, your critique will largely determine your friend's grade. You'd like to give your friend a positive critique so he can earn a good grade—which he badly needs. Besides, you figure, you can always tell him the truth later and even help him to improve.

How might you give an honest critique and still be a good friend? More generally, what ethical obligations does a critic have?

Second, the ethical critic *separates personal feelings about the issues* from an evaluation of the validity of the arguments. The ethical critic recognizes the validity of an argument even if it contradicts a deeply held belief; similarly, he or she recognizes the fallaciousness of an argument even if it supports a deeply held belief.

Third, the ethical critic *is culturally sensitive,* is aware of his or her own ethnocentrism, and doesn't negatively evaluate customs and forms of speech simply because they deviate from her or his own. Similarly, the ethical critic does not positively evaluate a speech just because it supports her or his own cultural beliefs and values. The ethical critic does not discriminate against or favor speakers simply because they're of a particular sex, race, nationality, religion, age group, or affectional orientation.

Summary of Concepts and Skills

This chapter has looked at listening and criticism and offered suggestions for making your listening and your criticism more effective.

Listening to Speeches
Listening is central to public speaking.

- Listening is a five-stage process: (1) receiving the verbal and nonverbal messages, (2) understanding the speaker's thoughts and emotions, (3) remembering and retaining the messages, (4) evaluating or judging the messages, and (5) responding or reacting to the messages.
- Cultural differences in language and speech, nonverbal behavioral differences, ethnocentrism, and gender can create listening difficulties.
- Among the principles for effective listening are these:
  - Listen actively (use listening time; work hard; assume value; and, if appropriate, take notes).
  - Listen for total meaning (focus on both verbal and nonverbal messages, connect specifics to the general thesis, attend to both surface and deep meanings).
  - Listen with empathy (see speaker's point of view, understand speaker's feelings and thoughts, avoid offensive listening).
  - Listen with an open mind (avoid prejudging and filtering out difficult messages, recognize your own biases).
  - Listen ethically (give the speaker an honest hearing and honest feedback).

Criticizing Speeches
Criticism is crucial to mastering the principles of public speaking.

- Criticism is a process of judging and evaluating a work. Criticism can (1) identify strengths and weaknesses and thereby help you improve as a public speaker, (2) identify standards for evaluating all sorts of public speeches, and (3) show that the audience is listening and is concerned about the speaker's progress.
- Cultures differ in their views of criticism and in the rules they consider appropriate. For example, members of individualist cultures may find public criticism easier and more acceptable than people from collectivist cultures.
- Among the principles for effective criticism are these:
  - Stress the positive.
  - Be specific.
  - Be objective.
  - Be constructive.
  - Focus on behavior.
  - Own your criticism.
  - Recognize your ethical obligations.

Vocabulary Quiz

Listening and Criticism

Match the terms of listening and criticism with their definitions. Record the number of the definition next to the appropriate term.

_____ listening

_____ receiving, understanding, remembering, evaluating, and responding

_____ ethnocentrism

_____ assimilation

_____ empathy

_____ criticism

_____ I-messages

_____ collectivist culture

_____ conformity to the principles of the art standard

_____ remembering

1. Begins with receiving and ends with responding.

2. The tendency to evaluate the values and beliefs of one's own culture as more positive or logical than those of another culture.

3. The tendency to reconstruct messages so that they reflect your own attitudes and prejudices.

4. Feeling what another is feeling, seeing as another sees.

5. The process of evaluating a work such as a speech.

6. A reconstructive rather than a reproductive process.

7. An orientation focusing on the needs of the social group rather than the individual.

8. An approach to public speaking criticism based on the degree to which the speech followed the rules and principles of the art.

9. The stages or steps involved in listening.

10. Messages that acknowledge the speaker's responsibility for what he or she says.

Web Explorations

Companion Website

www.ablongman.com/devito

If you'd like to explore further the topic of listening and criticism, see one or more of the following in Chapter 2: "How Good a Listener Are You?" (a self-test on listening effectiveness), "How to Listen with Questions," "Obstacles to Effective Listening," and "Standards for Criticism."

Public Speaking Exercises

2.1 Do You Really Remember What You Hear?

To illustrate the reproductive nature of memory, try to memorize the following list of 12 words (Glucksberg & Danks, 1975). Don't worry about the order of the words. Only the number remembered counts. Take about 20 seconds to memorize as many words as possible. Don't read any further until you've tried to memorize the list of words.

Word List

bed	dream	comfort
rest	wake	sound
awake	night	slumber
tired	eat	snore

Now close the book and write down as many of the words from this list as you can remember.

How did you do? If you're like my students, you not only remembered a good number of the words on the list but you also "remembered" at least one word that was not on the list: *sleep*. You did not simply reproduce the list; you reconstructed it. In this case you gave the list a meaning and part of that meaning included the word *sleep*. This happens with all types of messages; the messages are reconstructed into a meaningful whole, and in the process a distorted version of what was said is often "remembered."

2.2 Understanding Your Own Listening Barriers

Most of us put on blinders when we encounter particular topics or particular spokespersons. Sometimes these blinders prevent us from listening fairly and objectively. For example, you may avoid listening to certain people or reading certain newspapers because they frequently contradict your beliefs. Sometimes these blinders color the information you take in, influencing you to take a positive view of some information (because it may support one of your deeply held beliefs) and a negative view of other information (because it may contradict such beliefs).

Read over the following speech situations and identify at least one barrier that you (or someone else) might set up for each situation.

1. Bill Cosby on educating children
2. Bill Gates on financial mistakes the government must avoid
3. A representative from General Motors urging greater restrictions on foreign imports
4. A homeless person petitioning to be allowed to sleep in the local public library
5. An Iranian couple talking about the need to return to fundamentalist Islamic values
6. A person with AIDS speaking in favor of lower drug prices

2.3 Analyzing a Poorly Constructed Informative Speech

The sample speeches presented throughout most of this book are good examples and are designed to illustrate the effective application of the principles of public speaking. Here, however, is an especially poor speech, constructed to illustrate clearly and briefly some of the major faults with informative speeches. This exercise can be returned to several times throughout the course. As the course progresses, the responses will become more complete, more insightful, and more effective.

After you have reviewed the speech and the comments on the right, phrase your criticism in the form of a relatively formal critique of one to two minutes. Assume that this is a student's first speech and that you're the public speaking instructor. What do you say?

THREE JOBS

Well, I mean, hello. Er . . . I'm new at public speaking, so I'm a little nervous. I've always been shy. So don't watch my knees shake.

Ehm, let me see my notes here. [Mumbles to self while shuffling notes: "One, two, three, four, five—oh, they're all here."] Okay, here goes.

Three jobs. That's my title, and I'm going to talk about three jobs.

This nervous reaction is understandable but is probably best not shared with the listeners. After all, you don't want the audience to be uncomfortable for you.

Going through your notes makes the audience feel that you didn't prepare adequately and may just be wasting their time.

This is the speaker's orientation. Is this sufficient? What else might the speaker have done in the introduction? The title

The Health Care Field. This is the fastest growing job in the country; one of the fastest, I guess I mean. I know that you're not interested in this topic and that you're all studying accounting. But there are a lot of new jobs in the health care field. The *Star* had an article on health care and said that health care will be needed more in the future than it is now. And now, you know, like they need a lot of health care people. In the hospital where I work—on the west side, uptown—they never have enough health aides and they always tell me to become a health aide, like you know, to enter the health care field. To become a nurse. Or maybe a dental technician. But I hate going to the dentist. Maybe I will.

I don't know what's going to happen with the president's health plan, but whatever happens, it won't change the need for health aides. I mean, people will still get sick, so it really doesn't matter what happens with health care.

The Robotics Field. This includes things like artificial intelligence. I don't really know what that is, but it's like growing real fast. They use this in making automobiles and planes and I think in computers. Japan is a leading country in this field. A lot of people in India go into this field, but I'm not sure why.

The Computer Graphics Field. This field has a lot to do with designing and making lots of different products, like CAD and CAM. This field also includes computer-aided imagery—CAI. And in movies, I think. Like *Star Wars* and *Terminator 2*. I saw *Terminator 2* four times. I didn't see *Star Wars* but I'm gonna rent the video. I don't know if you have to know a lot about computers or if you can just like be a designer and someone else will tell the computer what to do.

I got my information from a book that Carol Kleiman wrote, *The 100 Best Jobs for the 1990s and Beyond*. It was summarized in last Sunday's *News*.

My conclusion. These are three of the fastest growing fields in the U.S. and in the world I think—but not in Third World countries, I don't think. China and India and Africa. More like Europe and Germany. And the U.S.—the U.S. is the big one. I hope you enjoyed my speech. Thank you.

I wasn't as nervous as I thought I'd be. Are there any questions?

seems adequate but is not terribly exciting. After reading the speech, try to give it a more appealing title. In general, don't use your title as your opening words.

Here the speaker shows such uncertainty that we question his or her competence.

And we begin to wonder, why is the speaker talking about this to us?

A report in the Star *may be entertaining, but it doesn't constitute evidence. What does this reference do to the credibility you ascribe to the speaker?*

Everything in the speech must have a definite purpose. Asides such as this comment about not liking to go to the dentist are probably best omitted.

Here the speaker had an opportunity to connect the topic with important current political events but failed to say anything that was not obvious.

Introducing these topics like this is clear but is probably not very interesting. How might each of the three main topics have been introduced more effectively?

Notice how vague the speaker is—"includes things like," "and I think in computers," "I'm not sure why." Language like this communicates very little information to listeners and leaves them with little confidence that the speaker knows what he or she is talking about.

Again, there is little that is specific. CAD and CAM are not defined and CAI is explained as "computer-aided imagery," but unless we already knew what these were, we would still not know even after hearing the speaker. Again, the speaker inserts personal notes (for example, seeing Terminator 2 *four times) that have no meaningful connection to the topic.*

The speaker uses only one source and, to make matters worse, doesn't even go to the original source but relies on a summary in the local newspaper. Especially with a topic like this, listeners are likely to want a variety of viewpoints and additional reliable sources.

Note too that the speech lacked any statistics. This is a subject that demands facts and figures. Listeners will want to know how many jobs will be available in these fields, what these fields will look like in 5 or 10 years, how much these fields pay, and so on.

Using the word conclusion *to signal that you're concluding is not a bad idea, but work it into the text instead of using it like a heading in a book chapter.*

Again, the speaker makes us question his or her competence and preparation by the lack of uncertainty. Again, personal comments are best left out.

3 Selecting Your Topic, Purpose, and Thesis

Why Read This Chapter?

It will enable you to develop a more effective speech by helping you to:

❖ find a topic that is interesting to you and to your audience

❖ phrase a purpose statement that crystallizes what you hope to achieve in your speech and that will guide you as you prepare the speech

❖ prepare for your speech by formulating a thesis sentence: a statement of your central idea, the one thing you want your audience to understand and remember

> "There is no such thing as an uninteresting subject; there are only uninteresting people."
>
> **—Gilbert Keith Chesterton**

Now that the basic steps in public speaking preparation have been established along with the fundamentals of controlling apprehension and the basics of listening and criticizing, you can focus on selecting a topic (and narrowing it down so that you can cover it in the allotted time), selecting a purpose, and framing your central idea or thesis.

Your Topic

Perhaps the first question you have is "What do I speak about?" Of course, the answer to this question will change as your life situation changes; in the years ahead you'll most likely speak on topics that grow out of your job or your social or political activities. In the classroom, however, where your objective is to learn the skills of public speaking, there are literally thousands of subjects to talk about. And yet you'll want to keep two standards in mind as you think about your topics. First, make sure your topic deals with matters of substance; your topic should be important enough to merit the time and attention of a group of intelligent people. Second, make sure your topic is appropriate to your audience; it should be culturally sensitive. In many Arab, Asian, and African cultures, for example, discussing sex in an audience of both men and women would be considered obscene and offensive. In Scandinavian cultures, on the other hand, sex is expected to be discussed openly and without embarrassment or discomfort. Table 3.1 provides a very brief list of some taboo topics.

TABLE 3.1	Taboo Speech Topics

Each culture has its own taboo topics—subjects that should be avoided, especially by visitors from other cultures. Here are several examples that Roger Axtell, in *Do's and Taboos Around the World* (1993), recommends that visitors from the United States avoid. These examples are not exhaustive; rather, they illustrate that each culture defines differently what topics are appropriate for public discussion.

CULTURE	TABOOS
Caribbean	Race, local politics, religion
Colombia	Politics, criticism of bullfighting
Egypt	Middle Eastern politics
Iraq	Religion, Middle Eastern politics
Japan	World War II
Libya	Politics, religion
Mexico	Mexican-American War, illegal aliens
Nigeria	Religion
Pakistan	Politics
Philippines	Politics, religion, corruption, foreign aid
South Korea	Internal politics, criticism of the government, socialism or communism
Spain	Family, religion, jobs, negative comments on bullfighting

DEVELOPING STRATEGIES

Taboo Topics. Michael, a student in this public speaking class, wonders if any topic would be considered taboo for class presentation. What topics, if any, would you consider taboo and advise Michael not to address in his speeches in this class? Why?

Finding Topics

Here are four ways to find topics: surveys, news items, brainstorming, and the idea generator.

Surveys

Look at some of the national and regional polls concerning what people think is important—polls that identify the significant issues, the urgent problems. For example, one survey of 10,000 executives in the 1990s identified the 10 topics that those individuals believed would be most important for the next few years: dealing with change, customer service, global marketplace opportunities, future strategies, total quality, new technologies, productivity and performance in business, diversity, legal issues, and health and fitness (Weinstein, 1995).

Survey data are now easier than ever to get, because many of the larger poll results are available on the Internet. For example, the Gallup Organization maintains a website at http://www.gallup.com that includes national and international surveys on political, social, consumer, and other issues speakers often talk about. The Polling Report website also will prove useful; it provides a wealth of polling data on issues such as political science, business, journalism, health, and social science (www.pollingreport.com). Another source is the search directories, such as Hotbot or Yahoo!, where you can examine the major directory topics and any subdivisions of those you'd care to pursue—a process that's explained later in this chapter. Many search engines and browsers provide lists of "hot topics," which are often useful starting points. These topics are exactly the topics that people are talking about and therefore often make excellent speech topics.

Or you can conduct a survey yourself. Roam through the nonfiction section of your bookstore (online, if you prefer—for example, at Amazon, www.amazon.com, Barnes and Noble, www.bn.com, or Borders, www.borders.com) and you'll quickly develop a list of the topics book buyers consider important. A glance at your newspaper's best-seller list will give you an even quicker overview.

News Items

Other useful starting points are newspapers and newsmagazines. Here you'll find the important international and domestic issues, the financial issues, and the social issues all conveniently packaged in one place. The editorial page and the letters to the editor also are useful indicators of what people are concerned about.

Newsmagazines such as *Time* and *Newsweek* and financial magazines such as *Forbes, Money,* and *Fortune* (in print or online) will provide a wealth of suggestions. Similarly, news shows such as *20/20, 60 Minutes,* and *Meet the Press* and even the ubiquitous talk shows (and their corresponding websites) often identify the very issues that people are concerned with and on which there are conflicting points of view.

Brainstorming

Another useful method for finding a topic is **brainstorming,** a technique designed to enable you to generate lots of topics in a relatively short time (DeVito, 1996; Osborn, 1957). You begin with your "problem," which in this case is "What will I talk about?" You then record any and all ideas that occur to you. Allow your mind to free-associate. Don't censor yourself; instead, allow your ideas to flow as freely as possible. Record all your thoughts, regardless of how silly or inappropriate they may seem. Write them down or record them on tape. Try to generate as many ideas as possible. The more ideas you think of, the better your chances of finding a suitable

USING TECHNOLOGY

Visit one of the news websites (see the Research Link on page 222 for ideas), or go to the newspaper links website containing links to newspapers throughout the country and the world (http://www.newspaperlinks.com). Browse through a few papers. Identify three or four issues discussed in the news that would make appropriate speech topics for this class.

❖ **CONSIDER** the topics that television news shows select. These topics can be useful starting points for developing an informative or persuasive speech. Focusing on just this week, what topics are the media highlighting?

topic in your list. After you've generated a sizable list—it should take you no longer than five minutes—read over the list or replay the tape. Do any of the topics on your list suggest other topics? If so, write these down as well. Can you combine or extend your ideas? Which ideas seem workable? The use of this technique in small groups is explained more fully in Chapter 12, "Speaking in Small Groups."

The Idea Generator: Dictionary of Topics

The idea generator system is actually a method both for discovering topics and for limiting them. It consists of using a dictionary of general topics and a series of questions that you can ask of any subject. The first part of the idea generator, "Ideas: The Dictionary of Topics," will help you find a suitable topic. It's simply a dictionary-like listing of subjects within which each topic is broken down into several subtopics. These subtopics should begin to suggest potential subjects for your informative and persuasive speeches (Table 3.2). The second part of

---

TABLE 3.2	**Ideas: The Dictionary of Topics**

This table presents just a few general topics to illustrate how you can use existing lists as ideas for speech topics. Lists like these will stimulate you to think of subjects dealing with topics you're interested in but may not have thought of as appropriate to a public speech. Each topic is broken down into several subtopics that should stimulate you to see these as potential ideas for your informative and persuasive speeches. Just a small sampling of topics is presented here; a much more extensive "dictionary of topics" may be found at www.ablongman.com/devito.

Abortion arguments for and against; techniques of; religious dimension; legal views; differing views of

Academic freedom nature of; censorship; teachers' role in curriculum development; and government; and research; restrictions on

Acupuncture nature of; development of; current practices in; effectiveness of; dangers of

Adoption agencies for; procedures; difficulties in; illegal; concealment of biological parents; search for birth parents

Advertising techniques; expenditures; ethical; unethical; subliminal; leading agencies; history of; slogans

Age ageism; aging processes; aid to the aged; discrimination against the aged; treatment of the aged; different cultural views of aging; sex differences

Aggression aggressive behavior in animals; in humans; as innate; as learned; and territoriality

Agriculture science of; history of; in ancient societies; technology of; theories of

Air pollution travel; embolism; law; navigation; power; raids

Alcoholism nature of; Alcoholics Anonymous; Al Anon; abstinence; among the young; treatment of

Amnesty in draft evasion; in criminal law; and pardons; in Civil War; in Vietnam War; conditions of

Animals experimentation; intelligence of; aggression in; ethology; and communication

the idea generator, *"Topoi: The System of Topics,"* will help you limit your topic, a process to which we now turn.

Limiting Topics

Probably the major error beginning speakers make is to try to cover a huge topic in too short a period of time. The inevitable result is that such speakers cannot cover anything in depth; they touch on everything superficially. To be suitable for a public speech, a topic must be limited in scope; it must be narrowed down to fit the time restrictions and yet permit some depth of coverage.

Another reason to narrow your topic is that it will help you focus your collection of research materials. If your topic is too broad, you'll be forced to review a lot more research material than you're going to need. On the other hand, if you narrow your topic, you can search for research materials more efficiently. Here are three methods for narrowing and limiting your topic: topoi, tree diagrams, and search directories.

USING TECHNOLOGY

One of the best websites for suggesting topics (and appropriate purposes and theses) is LibrarySpot (www.libraryspot.com). It provides links to reference words, lists of top websites, answers to frequently asked questions, and lots more. It will be well worth a visit.

RESEARCH Link

Libraries

Libraries, the major depositories of stored information, have evolved from a concentration on print sources to their present-day focus on computerized databases. Increasingly you'll go to one virtual or online library to access other virtual libraries or databases maintained by local and national governments, cultural institutions, and various corporations and organizations. Of course, you'll also go to a brick-and-mortar library, because it houses materials that are not on the Net or that you want to access in print. Because each library functions somewhat differently, your best bet in learning about a specific library—such as your own college library—is to talk with your librarian about what the library has available, what kinds of training or tours it offers, and how materials are most easily accessed. Here are a few online libraries that you'll find especially helpful.

- For a list of library catalogs that will help you find the location of the material you need, try www.libdex.com/. By clicking on "library-type index" you'll get a list of categories of libraries; for example, *government* or *medical* or *religious*.
- The largest library in the United States is the Library of Congress, which houses millions of books, maps, multimedia, and manuscripts. Time spent at this library (begin with www.loc.gov) will

be well invested. The home page will guide you to a wealth of information.
- Maintained by the National Archives and Records Administration, the presidential libraries may be accessed at www.archives.gov/.
- The Virtual Library is a collection of links to 14 subject areas; for example, agriculture, business and economics, computing, communication and media, and education. Visit this at www.vlib.org (see the home page on p. 56).
- If you're not satisfied with your own college library, visit the libraries of some of the large state universities, such as the University of Pennsylvania (http://www.library.upenn.edu/cgi-bin/res/sr.cgi) or the University of Illinois (http://gateway.library.uiuc.edu).
- The Internet Public Library (www.ipl.org) is actually not a library; it's a collection of links to a wide variety of materials. But it will function much like the reference desk at any of the world's best libraries.
- Quick Study, the University of Minnesota's Library Research Guide (http://tutorial.lib.umn.edu), will help you learn how to find the materials you need and will answer lots of questions you probably have about research.

Research Activity. Log on to one of the libraries mentioned in this research link and identify two or three ways in which this library can be of value to the courses you're taking this semester or to your future speeches.

Virtual Library

(www.vlib.org)
Visit this virtual library and discover a world of information that will be useful in your speeches and throughout your college and professional careers.

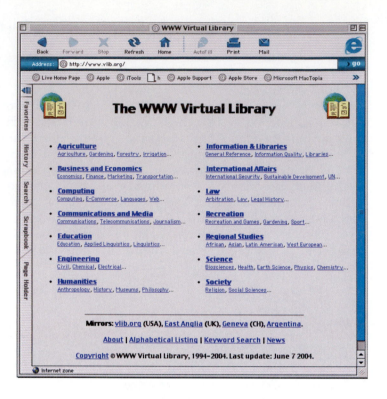

"For me, it all began one gray chilly morning in the grim maternity ward of a borderline hospital on the Upper West Side."

© The New Yorker Collection 2003 Robert Weber from cartoonbank.com. All Rights Reserved.

The Idea Generator: *Topoi,* The System of Topics

The second half of the idea generator is *"Topoi,* The System of Topics," a technique that comes from the classical rhetorics of ancient Greece and Rome but today is used more widely as a stimulus to creative thinking (DeVito, 1996). Using this method of *topoi,* you ask yourself a series of questions about your general subject. The process will help you see divisions of your general topic on which you might want to focus. In Table 3.3 the columns on the left contain seven general questions (*Who? What? Why? When? Where? How?* and *So?*) and a series of subquestions (which will vary depending on your topic). The right column illustrates how some of the questions on the left might suggest specific aspects of the general subject of "homelessness."

Tree Diagrams

Tree diagrams help you to divide your topic repeatedly into its significant parts. Starting with the general topic, you divide it into its parts. Then you take one of these parts and divide it into its parts. You continue with this dividing process until the topic seems manageable—until you believe you can reasonably cover it in some depth in the time allotted.

Figure 3.1 on page 58 illustrates a tree diagram that begins with the topic of mass communication. Take the topic of television programs as the first general topic area. Television programs, without some limitation, would take a lifetime to cover adequately. So you might divide this topic into such subtopics as

TABLE 3.3	*Topoi*, The System of Topics

These questions should enable you to use general topics to generate more specific ideas for your speeches. Try this system on any one of the topics listed in the Dictionary of Topics at www. ablongman.com/devito. You'll be amazed at how many topics you'll be able to find. Your problem will quickly change from "What can I speak on?" to "Which one of these should I speak on?" Here's an example on the topic of homelessness.

GENERAL QUESTIONS	SUBJECT-SPECIFIC QUESTIONS
Who? Who is he or she? Who is responsible? To whom was it done?	Who are the homeless? Who is the typical homeless person? Who is responsible for the increase in homelessness? Who cares for the homeless?
What? What is it? What effects does it have? What is it like? What is it different from? What are some examples?	What does it mean to be homeless? What does homelessness do to the people themselves? What does homelessness do to the society in general? What does homelessness mean to you and me?
Why? Why is there homelessness? Why does it happen? Why does it not happen?	Why are there so many homeless people? Why did this happen? Why does it happen in the larger cities more than in smaller towns? Why is it more prevalent in some countries than in others?
When? When did it happen? When will it occur? When will it end?	When did homelessness become so prevalent? When does it occur in the life of a person?
Where? Where did it come from? Where is it going? Where is it now?	Where is homelessness most prevalent? Where is there an absence of homelessness?
How? How does it work? How is it used? How do you do it? How do you operate it? How is it organized?	How does someone become homeless? How can we help the homeless? How can we prevent others from becoming homeless?
So? What does it mean? What is important about it? Why should I be concerned with this? Who cares?	Why is homelessness such an important social problem? Why must we be concerned with homelessness? How does all this affect me?

comedy, children's programs, educational programs, news, movies, reality programs, soap operas, game shows, and sports. You might then take one of these topics, say comedy, and divide it into subtopics. Perhaps you might consider it on a time basis and divide television comedy into its significant time periods: pre-1960, 1961–1989, 1990 to the present. Or you might focus on situation comedies. Here you might examine a topic such as women in situation comedies, race relations in situation comedies, or family relationships in situation comedies. The resultant topic is at least beginning to look manageable.

Search Directories

A more technologically sophisticated way of both selecting and limiting your topic is to let a search directory do some of the work for you. A search directory is a nested list of topics. You go from the general to the specific by selecting a topic, and then a subdivision of that topic, and then a subdivision of that

DEVELOPING STRATEGIES

Limiting a Topic. Jay wants to give a speech on women's rights, but she can't seem to narrow her topic down to manageable proportions. Everything she comes across seems important and cries out for inclusion. What advice would you give to Jay to help her limit and focus her general topic?

❖ **FIGURE 3.1**

A Tree Diagram for Limiting Speech Topics

How would you draw a tree diagram for limiting topics beginning with such general subjects as immigration, education, sports, transportation, or politics? An alternative method for limiting topics with the "fishbone diagram" may be found at www.ablongman.com/devito.

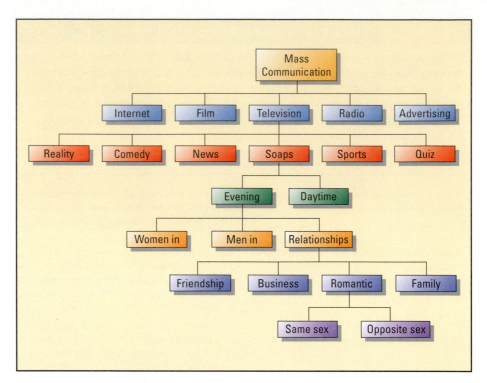

subdivision. Eventually you'll be directed to relatively specific areas and websites that will suggest topics that may be suitable for a classroom speech.

Your Purpose

The purpose of your speech is the goal you want to achieve; it identifies the effect that you want your speech to have on your audience. In constructing your speech you'll first identify your general purpose and then your specific purpose.

General Purposes

The three major purposes of public speeches are to inform, to persuade, and to serve some special occasion function. In the **informative speech** you seek to create understanding: to clarify, to enlighten, to correct misunderstandings, to demonstrate how something works. In this type of speech you'll rely most heavily on materials that amplify—examples, illustrations, definitions, testimony, visual aids, and the like.

In the **persuasive speech** you try to influence attitudes or behaviors; you seek to strengthen or change existing attitudes or get the audience to take some action. In this type of speech you'll rely heavily on materials that offer proof—on evidence, argument, and psychological appeals, for example.

In the special occasion speech, which contains elements of information and persuasion, you might, for example, introduce another speaker or a group of speakers, present a tribute, try to secure the goodwill of the listeners, toast your friends' anniversary, or "just" entertain your listeners.

CRITICAL LISTENING/THINKING *Link*

Listening to Primary and Secondary Sources

As a listener and as a researcher, be sure to distinguish between primary and secondary source material. Primary sources include, for example, an original research study reported in an academic journal, a corporation's annual report, and an eyewitness report of an accident. With primary sources there is nothing (or very little) standing between the event (say, an accident) and the reporting of it (the eyewitness testimony). Secondary sources include, for example, a summary of research appearing in a popular magazine, a television news report on a corporation's earnings, and a report by someone who talked to someone who witnessed an accident. With secondary sources someone stands between the actual event and the report; for example, a science reporter reads the scientist's monograph (primary source), then writes up a summary for the popular press (secondary source). As a listener and speaker you'll hear and use both types of source material. Yet there are important differences that you should keep in mind.

Secondary source material is less reliable than primary source material, because it is a step removed from the actual facts or events. The writer of secondary material may have forgotten important parts, may be biased and so may have slanted the reporting to reflect his or her attitudes, or may have distorted the material because he or she misunderstood the data. On the other hand, the writer may have been able to express complicated scientific data in simple language—often making it easier for a nonscientist to understand than the original report. When using or listening to secondary sources, examine the information for any particular spin the writer may be giving the material. If possible, check the primary source material itself to see if anything was left out or if the conclusions are really warranted on the basis of the primary evidence.

Getting Critical. Review one or more of the speeches contained in this text or on the Companion Website (www.ablongman.com/devito). What primary sources did the speaker use? What secondary sources did the speaker use? Which were more effective in informing and in influencing you?

Specific Purposes

Once you have chosen your general purpose, develop your specific purpose by identifying more precisely what you aim to accomplish. For example, in an informative speech, your specific purpose would identify the information you want to convey to your audience. Here are a few examples on the topic of AIDS:

General purpose: To inform.

Specific purposes: To inform my audience of the recent progress in AIDS research.

To inform my audience of our college's plans for AIDS Awareness Day.

To inform my audience of the currently used tests for HIV infection.

You may find it helpful to view your specific informative purposes in behavioral terms, identifying how you want the audience to demonstrate what they've learned from your speech. Here are a few examples:

After listening to my speech, listeners should be able to describe the procedures for systematic desensitization.

❖ **CONSIDER** the general speech purposes that you hear most often in business, educational, or political settings. How would you classify them in terms of information and persuasion?

After listening to my speech, listeners should be able to define the three major differences between communism and capitalism.

After listening to my speech, listeners should be able to demonstrate the five steps of active listening.

In a persuasive speech, your specific purpose identifies what you want your audience to believe, to think, or perhaps to do. Here are a few examples:

General purpose: To persuade.

Specific purposes: To persuade listeners to use systematic desensitization to reduce their apprehension.

To persuade listeners to believe that capitalism is superior to communism.

To persuade listeners to use active listening more often.

As you formulate your specific purposes, there are three guidelines to keep in mind: Use an infinitive phrase; limit your specific purposes; and use specific terms.

Use an Infinitive Phrase

Begin the statement of each specific purpose with the word *to* and elaborate on your general purpose, for example: *To inform my audience of the new registration procedures* or *To persuade my audience to contribute a book for the library fund raiser* or *To introduce the main speaker of the day*.

Limit Your Specific Purpose

Limit your specific purposes in two ways. First, avoid the common pitfall of trying to accomplish too much in too short a time. For example, *To persuade my audience of the prevalence of date rape in our community and that they should attend the dating seminars offered on campus* contains two specific purposes. Select one or

DEVELOPING STRATEGIES

Defining Purpose. Shawn is considering developing his 10-minute persuasive speech around one of the following purposes: to persuade his listeners (1) to vote for the pro-life candidate in the upcoming election, (2) to contribute $250 to the college's scholarship fund, or (3) to attend a religious ceremony of a religion other than the listeners' own. If the audience was your public speaking class, how would you suggest Shawn rephrase or redefine any one of these purposes?

the other. Beware of specific purposes that contain the word *and;* it's often a sign that you have more than one purpose.

Second, limit your specific purposes to what you can reasonably develop in the allotted time. Specific purposes that are too broad are useless. Note how

RESEARCH *Link*

Using and Evaluating Internet Resources

Although you'll no doubt use a variety of research sources—both print and electronic—it's a lot easier to do your research by computer. Perhaps the greatest advantage is that in computer research, you browse through a larger number of sources in less time and with greater accuracy and thoroughness than you could do with archives of printed materials. Also, you can usually do this research at your own convenience and from your own home.

In using computerized sources—on CD-ROMs and, most often, on the Web—you've already noticed that the amount of information available often makes finding specific information difficult. Two general guides will help you at the start. First, learn the databases that contain the information you want to find. A database is simply an organized collection of information contained in one place. A dictionary, an encyclopedia, an index to magazines, and a collection of abstracts from hundreds of journals are all examples of databases. Databases may be in print (for example, *Psychological Abstracts*) or computerized (for example, the communication database in Research Navigator). Because each library subscribes to a different set of databases, find out which databases are available at your college library as well as at other libraries to which you have access. Review the available databases, single out those that will be especially helpful to you, and learn as much as you can about them. For example, if you're researching a medical topic, then the *Medline* database will prove especially useful. *Medline* can be searched for free at the National Library of Medicine's website at www.nlm.nih.gov. If you're looking for sociological statistics, then the U.S. census figures will be essential; you'll want to become familiar with the Census Bureau's website at www.census.gov.

Second, learn about the search engines and directories that will help you find the information you need, and learn how to use them efficiently. Most engines and directories use similar symbols to help you search their databases; for example, the use of *and*, *or*, *not*, and + and – (see the Research Link in Chapter 7, p. 176). At the same time, however, each engine and directory makes use of its own particular search mechanisms. Learn the techniques for the engines and directories you use most often.

As you research your topic, keep in mind that anyone can "publish" on the Internet, making it essential that you subject everything you find on the Net to critical analysis, a topic also discussed in the Critical Listening/Thinking boxes on pages 62 and 107. An article on the Internet can be written by world-renowned scientists or by elementary school students; by fair and objective reporters or by people who would spin the issues to serve their own political, religious, or social purposes. It's not always easy to tell which is which. Find out what the author's qualifications are. One useful technique is to pursue the Internet links often included in these documents to the sources from which they derived—say, the original statistics or predictions or arguments. Recognize also, however, that much information on the Internet is identical to the information you regularly read in print. Encyclopedias, newspapers and newsmagazines, and professional journals that appear on the Internet are identical to the print copies, so there's no need to draw distinctions between print and Internet information when dealing with sites such as these.

Research Activity. Read one of the many guides to evaluating Internet sources. Using your favorite search engine search for "evaluating" + Internet + research or sources; visit www.slu.edu/departments/english/research, http:// nuevaschool.org/~debbie/library/research/research.html, http://www.uwec.edu/library/Guides/tenc.html, or http://lib.nmsu.edu/instruction/evalcrit.html; or if you have access, log on to Research Navigator (www.researchnavigator.com) and read the section on "Finding and Evaluating Sources" under the "Research Process" tab. On the basis of these insights, construct a list of three, four, or five questions you might ask in evaluating an Internet resource.

broad and overly general are such purposes as *To inform my audience about clothing design* or *To persuade my audience to improve their health.*

Note how much more reasonable the following restatements are for a relatively short speech: *To inform my audience of the importance of color in clothing design* and *To persuade my audience to exercise three times a week.*

Use Specific Terms

Phrase your specific purposes with specific terms. The more precise your specific purposes, the more effectively they will guide you in the remaining steps of preparing your speech. Instead of the overly general *To persuade my audience to do something about AIDS,* consider the more specific *To persuade my audience to contribute food to homebound persons with AIDS.*

Your Thesis

Your thesis is your central idea; it's the theme, the essence of your speech. It's your point of view and what you want the audience to absorb from your speech. The thesis of Lincoln's Second Inaugural Address was that Northerners

---

○○ CRITICAL LISTENING/THINKING *Link*

Listening to Research Findings for Reliability

Reliability in research findings or conclusions means that these are sources you can count on, sources that are trustworthy and dependable. In estimating how reliable a speaker's conclusions are, ask yourself if the conclusions have been arrived at logically rather than, say, emotionally. Does the author offer clear evidence and sound arguments to support conclusions—rather than, say, anecdotes or testimonials?

Another way to estimate reliability in published works is to look at the publisher. Major textbook and trade book publishers go to enormous effort to ensure the accuracy of what appears in print or on their websites, so the information they provide is generally reliable. Some publishers, however, are arms of special interest groups with specific corporate, religious, political, or social agendas. If this is the case with one of the sources you have selected, try to balance this publisher's perspective with information that represents other views of the issue.

If an article appears in a journal sponsored by a major organization such as the American Psychological Association or the National Communication Association, you can be pretty sure that experts in the field have carefully reviewed the article before publication. Again, if an article appears in a well-respected major newspaper like the *New York Times,* the *Washington Post,* or the *Wall Street Journal,* or in any of the major newsmagazines or news networks (or online on their websites), you can be pretty sure that the information is reliable.

Do realize that these claims of accuracy are generalizations and that errors do occur. Both academic journals and newspapers have printed fraudulent articles. In September 2003 the *New York Times*, one of the world's great newspapers, experienced a significant credibility gap for printing as fact articles that turned out to be no more than fiction. So inaccuracies do creep into even the most respected sources.

Getting Critical. How reliable do you find the information in your college textbooks? In the *National Enquirer*? In the stories covered by television newsmagazine shows such as *20/20* or *60 Minutes*?

and Southerners should work together for the entire nation's welfare; the thesis of the *Rocky* movies was that the underdog can win; the thesis of Dr. Martin Luther King Jr.'s "I Have a Dream" speech was that true equality is a right of African Americans and all people.

In an informative speech your thesis states what you want your audience to learn. For example, a suitable thesis for an informative speech on jealousy might be "There are two main theories of jealousy." Notice that here, as in all informative speeches, the thesis is relatively neutral and objective.

In a persuasive speech your thesis states what you want your audience to believe or accept; it summarizes the claim you're making or the position you're taking. For example, let's say that you're planning to present a speech against using animals for experimentation. Your thesis statement might be something like this: "Animal experimentation should be banned." Here are a few additional examples of persuasive speech theses:

◆ We should all contribute to AIDS research.

◆ Everyone should get tested for HIV infection.

◆ Condoms should be distributed free of charge.

This is what you want your audience to believe as a result of your speech. Notice that in persuasive speeches the thesis statement puts forth a point of view, an opinion. The thesis is arguable and debatable.

Be sure to limit the thesis statement to one central idea. A statement such as "Animal experimentation should be banned, and companies engaging in it should be prosecuted" contains not one but two basic ideas.

In preparing your speech, state your thesis as a simple declarative sentence. This will help you focus your thinking, your collection of materials, and your organizational pattern. You may, however, state your thesis in various different ways when you present it to your audience. You may state it to your audience as

A CASE OF *Ethics*

Evaluating Theses

You're a public speaking instructor, and your students are getting ready to deliver their first round of speeches. You've asked them to submit their thesis statements to you so that you can make sure they're on the right track and can offer whatever help may be needed. Among the theses you receive are the following:

1. The Neo-Nazi movement deserves our support.
2. You can cheat on your income tax with two great strategies.
3. Growing marijuana can be fun and profitable.
4. The Holocaust has been exaggerated.
5. Employers should have the right to discriminate on the basis of religion, sex, affectional orientation, race, or nationality.

Would it be ethical to allow these speeches to be delivered in class? On the other hand, would it be ethical to censor the points of view of your students? More generally, what ethical obligations does an instructor have in regulating (or not regulating) issues spoken on in a college classroom?

you phrased it for yourself—for example, "Animal experimentation must be banned" or "I want to tell you in this brief speech why animal experimentation must be stopped." Or you may decide to state your thesis as a question—for example, "Why should we ban animal experimentation?" or "Are there valid reasons for banning animal experimentation?"

The different beliefs that different cultures have about religion, politics, education, family, sex, justice, and just about any topic you can think of will influence how an audience responds to you and your speech. Because of this you need to take these cultural beliefs into consideration as you prepare your speech. To explore your own facility in examining such cultural beliefs, you may wish to take the accompanying self-test, "How Are Cultural Beliefs and Theses Related?"

Test YOURSELF

How Are Cultural Beliefs and Theses Related?

Assume that you're giving a speech to your public speaking class. Evaluate each of the cultural beliefs listed below in terms of how effective each would be if you used it as a thesis in your speech. Use the following scale:

A = The audience would favorably accept this thesis and would welcome a speaker with this point of view.
B = The audience would listen fairly openly to the speaker.
C = Some members would listen openly and others wouldn't.
D = The audience would not listen very openly to the speaker.
E = The audience would definitely reject this thesis and would not welcome a speaker with this point of view.

_____ **1.** The welfare of the family must come first, even before your own welfare.

_____ **2.** Sex outside of marriage is morally wrong.

_____ **3.** Winning is all-important; it's not how you play the game, it's whether or not you win that matters.

_____ **4.** The strong are responsible for caring for the weak, the rich for the poor.

_____ **5.** Work is a positive good; people should work hard because it's the right thing to do.

_____ **6.** Money is good; the quest for financial success is a perfectly respectable (even noble) one.

_____ **7.** Getting to heaven should be life's major goal.

_____ **8.** Gay and lesbian relationships are equal in all ways to heterosexual relationships.

_____ **9.** Immigration to the United States should be significantly reduced.

_____ **10.** In a marriage a wife should submit graciously to her husband's leadership.

❖ **HOW DID YOU DO?** This test was designed to help you think about the possible influence of cultural beliefs and values on a sampling of theses that speakers might develop speeches from or use as basic assumptions. These beliefs will influence the way your audience looks at your speech and especially at the thesis you've developed. For example, if your audience believes that sex outside of marriage is morally wrong and sinful, then a speech advocating safe sex for teenagers (other than abstinence) will encounter a very different attitude than would a talk advocating abstinence. It's essential for you to understand the beliefs and values of your audience so you can effectively adapt your speech to them.

❖ **WHAT WILL YOU DO?** Because of the influence that an audience's cultural beliefs will have on the way they listen to and react to your speech, listen carefully to the beliefs and values of your audience as they're expressed in classroom comments and questions. Ask questions to discover how your audience feels about the theses you may be planning to address. Use audience analysis forms when appropriate (see Chapter 4, pages 75–77).

USING TECHNOLOGY

Log on to UNESCO's website on cultural issues (http://www. unesco.org/culture/news/ html_eng/index_en.shtml). What can you learn about your own culture that you didn't know before? What can you learn about cultures you know little about?

RESEARCH Link

General Reference Works

Begin researching your topic with general reference works, one of the best of which is the standard encyclopedia. Any good encyclopedia will give you a general overview of your subject and suggestions for additional reading. The most comprehensive and the most prestigious is the *Encyclopaedia Britannica*, available in print (32 volumes), on CD-ROM, and online. A variety of other encyclopedias also are available on CD-ROM or online, among them, *Compton's Multimedia Encyclopedia, Grolier's, Collier's,* and *Encarta*. CD-ROM and online encyclopedias have great advantages; for example, they allow you to locate articles, maps, diagrams, and even definitions of difficult terms more easily and efficiently than hard-copy volumes. Video illustrations and audio capabilities enable you to see the volcano exploding and the heart pumping blood and to hear the pronunciation of foreign terms and the music of particular instruments. Hypertext capabilities enable you to get additional information on any term or phrase that is highlighted in the video display. Simply select the highlighted phrase and you'll get this other article on screen. Most of the CD-ROM encyclopedias have accompanying websites that provide periodic updates of the articles and additional materials, thus ensuring both recency and completeness. A useful place to start is with www.internetoracle.com/encyclop.htm, which provides hot links to a wide variety of online encyclopedias, both general and specific.

Should you want information on the world's languages, household income, presidential elections, the countries of the world, national defense, sports, noted personalities, economics and employment, the environment, awards and prizes, science and technology, health and medicine, maps, world travel information, or postal rates, an almanac will prove extremely useful. Numerous inexpensive almanacs, published annually, are among the most up-to-date sources of information on many topics. The most popular are *The World Almanac and Book of Facts* (also available on CD-ROM), *The Universal Almanac,* and *The Canadian Almanac and Directory*. The *Information Please Almanac*'s website provides access to a wide variety of almanacs (www.infoplease.com/almanacs.html). Another useful source is the Internet Public Library's list of almanac resources at www.ipl.org/ref/RR/static/ref05.00.00.html.

Research Activity. Log on to one of the websites mentioned here; explore one research source you think might be especially useful to members of your class; and, in a two-minute speech, explain the source's value to the class.

Use Your Thesis to Generate Main Ideas

Within each thesis there is an essential question that allows you to explore and subdivide the thesis. Your objective is to find this question and use it to help you discover the major propositions that will support this thesis. For example, let's take a hypothetical proposed bill—call it the Hart Bill—and let's say your thesis is "The Hart Bill provides needed services for senior citizens." When the thesis is stated in this form, the obvious question suggested is "What are the needed services?" The answer to this question suggests the main parts of your speech; let's say, health, food, shelter, and recreational services. These four areas then become the four main points of your speech.

Some public speaking instructors and trainers advise speakers to include their main points in the statement of the thesis. If you did this, your thesis for the above speech would be "The Hart Bill provides needed health, food, shelter, and recreational services for senior citizens." You may find it helpful to use the briefer thesis statement for some speech topics and purposes and the more expanded thesis statement for others.

Regardless of whether you use the brief or the expanded thesis, an outline of the main ideas would look like this:

Purpose:	To inform.
Specific purpose:	To inform my audience of the provisions of the Hart Bill.
Thesis:	The Hart Bill provides needed services for senior citizens. *Or:* The Hart Bill provides needed health, food, shelter, and recreational services for senior citizens.

  I. The Hart Bill provides needed health services.

 II. The Hart Bill provides needed food services.

III. The Hart Bill provides needed shelter services.

IV. The Hart Bill provides needed recreational services.

❖ **CONSIDER** the theses of the last few college lectures you heard and how these theses were presented (directly, indirectly, early, late). What system of thesis presentation do you prefer? Why?

The remainder of the speech would then be filled in with supporting materials. Under part I, for example, you might identify several health services and explain how the Hart Bill would provide them. This first main point of your speech might, in outline, look something like this:

I. The Hart Bill provides needed health services.

   A. Neighborhood clinics will be established.

   B. Medical hotlines will be established.

In the completed speech, this first main point and its two subordinate statements might be spoken like this:

> The Hart Bill provides senior citizens with the health services they need so badly. Let me give you some examples of these necessary health services. One of the most important services will be the establishment of neighborhood health clinics. These clinics will help senior citizens get needed health advice and medical care right in their own neighborhoods.
>
> A second important health service will be the health hotlines. These phone numbers will be for the exclusive use of senior citizens. These hotlines will connect seniors with trained medical personnel who will be able to give advice and send emergency medical services to seniors as needed.

Use Your Thesis to Organize

The thesis will provide you with useful guidelines in selecting your organizational pattern. For example, let's suppose your thesis is "We can improve our own college education." Your answer to the inherent question "What can we do?" will suggest a possible organizational pattern. If, for example, you identify the remedies in the order in which they should be taken, then a time-order pattern will be appropriate. If you itemize a number of possible solutions, all of which are of about equal importance, then a topical pattern will be appropriate. These and other patterns are explained in detail in Chapter 6, "Organizing Your Speech."

Use Your Thesis Strategically

Because the thesis sentence will focus the audience's attention on your central idea and reveal your position on the issue you're addressing, you'll want to consider the persuasive implications of stating your thesis. You have several options. For example:

- State your thesis early in the speech.
- State your thesis late in the speech.
- State your thesis explicitly and directly.
- Don't state your thesis; allow the audience to infer it.

Here are a few guidelines that will help you make a strategically effective decision about how and when to present your thesis.

- In an informative speech, state your thesis early, clearly, and directly: "Immigration patterns are predicted to change drastically over the next 50 years"; "Carpal tunnel syndrome can be corrected with surgery"; or "A PDA can organize your life."

? DEVELOPING STRATEGIES

Statement of Thesis. Tony and Claire want to give their speeches on opposite sides of Megan's Law—the law requiring that community residents be notified if a convicted sex offender is living in the neighborhood. Tony is against the law and Claire is for it. If Tony and Claire were giving their speeches to your class, what would you advise each of them to do concerning his or her thesis statement?

◆ In a persuasive speech addressed to a neutral or positive audience, state your thesis explicitly and early in your speech: "Immigration laws should be changed"; "Avoid carpal tunnel syndrome with rest and exercise"; or "Get a PDA today."

◆ In a persuasive speech whose audience is hostile to your position, give your evidence and arguments first and gradually move the audience into a more positive frame of mind before stating your thesis.

◆ When you are speaking to a relatively uneducated or uninformed audience, it is probably best to state your thesis explicitly. If the thesis is not explicit, the listeners may fail to grasp what your thesis is and therefore may be less likely to change their attitudes or behaviors.

◆ Recognize, too, that there are cultural differences in the way a thesis should be stated. In some Asian cultures, for example, making a point too directly or asking directly for audience compliance may be considered rude or insulting.

Summary of Concepts and Skills

In this chapter we considered the speech topic and ways to find and limit it, the speech purposes and how to phrase them, and speech theses and how to use them to best effect.

Your Topic

Suitable speech topics are topics that are worthwhile; appropriate to the speaker, audience, and occasion; and culture sensitive.

◆ Topics may be found through:
  - Surveys
  - News items
  - Brainstorming
  - Dictionary of topics
◆ Speech topics may be limited by:
  - *Topoi*, the system of topics
  - Tree diagrams
  - Search directories

Your Purpose

Speech purposes are both general (for example, to inform or persuade) and specific (for example, to inform audience of the new health plan options) and should be:

◆ Phrased as an infinitive phrase
◆ Limited to one main point and to what can reasonably be accomplished
◆ Phrased with precise terms

Your Thesis

Speech theses should be phrased as complete declarative sentences, should be clear and specific, and should be limited to one central idea or focus. Theses may be used to:

◆ Generate main ideas
◆ Suggest organizational patterns
◆ Focus audience attention

Vocabulary Quiz

Topics, Purposes, and Theses

Match the terms for topics, purposes, and theses with their definitions. Record the number of the definition next to the appropriate term.

_____ taboos
_____ tree diagrams
_____ brainstorming
_____ specific purpose
_____ topic
_____ culture-sensitive
_____ general purpose
_____ thesis
_____ topoi
_____ search directories

1. The general subject matter of a speech.
2. Cultural prohibitions against certain messages.
3. A technique for generating lots of ideas.
4. A set of questions that you can apply to a wide variety of issues.
5. One method for limiting a topic.
6. A useful method for finding and limiting topics.
7. The main idea of a speech.
8. An infinitive phrase that identifies a speaker's general goal.
9. A phrase that identifies what a speaker wants the audience to do or think.
10. One of the qualities of an appropriate speech topic.

Web Explorations

Companion Website
www.ablongman.com/devito
In Chapter 3 you'll find an extensive list of potential public speaking topics in "The Dictionary of Topics" and another way of limiting topics in the "Fishbone Diagram." In addition, an exercise providing insight into "Generating Main Points from Thesis Statements" is provided.

Public Speaking Exercises

3.1 Brainstorming for Topics

With a small group of students or with the class as a whole sitting in a circle, brainstorm for suitable speech topics. Be sure to appoint someone to write down all the contributions or use a recorder.

After this brainstorming session, consider:

1. Did any members give negative criticism (even nonverbally)?
2. Did any members hesitate to contribute really wild ideas? Why?
3. Was it necessary to restimulate the group members at any point? Did this help?

4. Did some useful speech topics emerge in the brainstorming session?

3.2 Limiting Topics

Here are a few overly general topics. Using one of the methods discussed in this chapter (or any other method you're familiar with), limit each topic to a subject that would be reasonable for a 5- to 10-minute speech.

1. Dangerous sports
2. Race relationships
3. Parole
4. Censorship on the Internet
5. Ecological problems
6. Problems faced by college students
7. Morality
8. Health and fitness
9. Ethical issues in politics
10. Urban violence

3.3 Using Cultural Beliefs as Assumptions in Public Speaking

Evaluate each of the cultural beliefs listed below in terms of how effective each would be if used as a basic assumption by a speaker addressing your public speaking class. Use the following scale: A = the audience would accept this assumption and welcome a speaker with this point of view; B = some members would listen

openly and others wouldn't; or C = the audience would reject this assumption and would not welcome a speaker with this point of view. On the basis of this analysis, what might you do and what should you not do in your next speech?

_____ 1. A return to religious values is the best hope for the world.

_____ 2. Embryonic stem cell research should be encouraged.

_____ 3. The invasion of Iraq was morally unjustified.

_____ 4. Winning is all important; it's not how you play the game, it's whether or not you win that matters.

_____ 5. Keeping the United States militarily superior is the best way to preserve world peace.

3.4 Analyzing a Poorly Constructed Persuasive Speech

This speech was written to illustrate some really broad as well as some rather subtle errors that a beginning speaker might make in constructing a persuasive speech. First, read the entire speech without reading any of the questions in the right-hand column. Then, after you've read the entire speech, reread each paragraph and respond to the critical thinking questions. What other questions might prove productive to ask?

XXX HAS GOT TO GO

You probably didn't read the papers this weekend, but there's a XXX movie, I mean video, store that moved in on Broad and Fifth Streets. My parents, who are retired teachers, are protesting it, and so am I. My parents are organizing a protest for the next weekend.

There must be hundreds of XXX video stores in the country and they all need to be closed down. I have a lot of reasons.

First, my parents think it should be closed down. My parents are retired teachers and have organized protests over the proposed new homeless shelter and to prevent the city from making that park on Elm Street. So they know what they're doing.

The XXX video place is un-Christian. No good Christian people would ever go there. Our minister is against it and is joining in the protest.

These stores bring crime into the neighborhood. I have proof of that. Morristown's crime increased after the

What do you think of the title of the speech? Visualizing yourself as a listener, how would the opening comment make you feel? Does the speaker gain your attention? What thesis do you think the speaker will support? Does mentioning "my parents" help or hurt the speaker's credibility?

What is the speaker's thesis? What impression are you beginning to get of the speaker?

How do the speaker's parents sound to you? Do they sound like credible leaders with a consistent cause? Professional protesters (with perhaps a negative agenda)? What evidence is offered to support the assertion that we should believe the speaker's parents? Is this adequate? What would you need to know about people before believing them?

What does this statement assume about the audience? How would this statement be responded to by your public speaking class? What are some reasons why the speaker might not have explained how XXX video stores are un-Christian?

What do you think of the reasoning used here? Are there other factors that could have influenced Morristown's crime

XXX video store opened. And in Martinsville, where they got rid of the video store, crime did not increase. If we allow the video store in our own town, then we're going to be like Morristown and our crime is going to increase.

These stores make lots of garbage. The plastic wrappings from the videos will add to our already overextended and overutilized landfill. And a lot of them are going to wind up as litter on the streets.

The XXX Video House stays open seven days a week, 24 hours a day. People will be forced to work at all hours and on Sunday, and that's not fair. And the store will increase the noise level at night, with cars pulling up and all.

The XXX Video House—that's it's name, by the way—doesn't carry regular videos that most people want. So why do we want them?

The XXX Video House got a lease from an owner who doesn't even live in the community, someone by the name of, well, it's an organization called XYX Management. And their address is Carlson Place in Jeffersonville. So they don't even live here.

A neighboring store owner says he thinks the store is in violation of several fire laws. He says they have no sprinkler system and no metal doors to prevent the spread of a fire. So he thinks they should be closed down, too.

Last week on *Oprah* three women were on and they were in the XXX movie business, and they were all on drugs, and had been in jail, and they said it all started when they went into the porno business. One woman wanted to be a teacher, another wanted to be a nurse, and the other wanted to be a beautician. If there weren't any XXX video stores then there wouldn't be a porn business; and, you know, pornography is part of organized crime and so if you stop pornography you take a bite out of crime.

One of the reasons I think it should be closed is that the legitimate video stores—the ones that have only a small selection of XXX movies somewhere in the back—will lose business. And if they continue to lose business, they'll leave the neighborhood and we'll have no video stores.

That's a lot of reasons against XXX movie houses. I have a quote here: Reason is "a portion of the divine spirit set in a human body." Seneca.

In conclusion and to wrap it up and close my speech, I want to repeat and say again that the XXX video stores should all be closed down. They corrupt minors. And they're offensive to men and women and especially women. I hope you'll all protest with the Marshalls—my mother and father—and there'll be lots of others there too. My minister, I think, is coming too.

increase? Is there any evidence that getting rid of the video store resulted in the stable crime rate in Martinsville? What assumption about the audience does the speaker make in using Martinsville and Morristown as analogies?

Do you agree with this argument about the garbage? Is this argument in any way unique to the video store? Is it likely that people will open the wrappers and drop them on the street?

What validity do you give to each of these arguments? Given the 24-hour policy, how might you construct an argument against the video store? Are there advantages of a neighborhood store's 24-hour policy that the audience may be thinking of, thus countering the speaker's argument? If there are, how should the speaker deal with them?

On hearing this, would you be likely to extend this argument and start asking yourself "Do we now close up all stores that most people don't want?"

Is there a connection between who the owner is and whether the video store should or shouldn't be closed? Could the speaker have effectively used this information in support of the thesis to close the video store?

What credibility do you ascribe to the "neighboring store owner"? Do you begin to wonder if the speaker would simply agree to have the store brought up to the fire code laws?

What is the cause and what is the effect that the speaker is asserting? How likely is it that the proposed cause actually produced the effect? Might there have been causes other than the pornography that might have led these women into drugs? What credibility do you give to people you see on talk shows? Does it vary with the specific talk show? Do you accept the argument that there would be no pornography business without video stores? What would have to be proved to you before you accepted this connection? How do you respond to the expression "Take a bite out of crime"?

Is the speaker implying that this is the real reason against XXX video stores? Do you start wondering if the speaker is against XXX video stores—as seemed in the last argument—or just against stores that sell these exclusively? What effect does this impression have on your evaluation of the speaker's credibility and the speaker's thesis?

How do you feel about the number of "reasons"? Would you have preferred fewer reasons more fully developed or more reasons? What purpose does this quotation serve?

In light of this conclusion might the speaker have introduced the speech differently? What does the speaker's thesis seem to be now? What do you think of the argument that XXX video stores are offensive? What effect does this argument have, being stated here in the conclusion? Do you think you'd go to the protest? Why or why not?

4 Analyzing and Adapting to Your Audience

Why Read This Chapter?

It will enable you to tailor your speech to your specific audience by helping you to:

- ❖ discover something about who your audience is—the demographics or sociology of your listeners (age, culture, gender, religion, for example) and their psychology (willingness to listen, attitudes toward your thesis, for example)
- ❖ adapt your speech to these specific listeners
- ❖ adapt to your audience during the actual speech

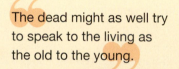

> The dead might as well try to speak to the living as the old to the young.
>
> **—Willa Cather**

You can inform or persuade an audience only if you know who they are, what they know, and what they believe. Once you have this information, you can begin to tailor your speech to these specific listeners. In this chapter we look at the nature of today's audiences, ways to analyze the sociology and psychology of the audience, and some suggestions for adapting to the audience during the actual speech.

Audiences and Audience Analysis

The public speaking audience is best defined as a group of people with the common purpose of listening and responding to a speech. It can be of almost any size—five people listening to a street orator, 20 students in a classroom, thousands at a stadium listening to a political or religious speaker. **Audience analysis** is the process of discovering useful information about these listeners so as to tailor a speech to them.

The Audience: Two Basic Characteristics

Among all the qualities that might be said to characterize today's audiences, two stand out: uniqueness (no audience is like any other audience) and diversity (audiences are never truly homogeneous). Let's look at each of these briefly.

All Audiences Are Unique

Each public speaking audience you address is unique. Audiences are unique because people are different and unique as individuals; but even when you address the same persons repeatedly (as you will in this course and in various business and other situations), the individuals are not necessarily the same as they were the last time you addressed them. For example, audiences on September 10 and on September 12, 2001, may have been composed of the same people, but probably very few audience members were the same in attitudes and beliefs on those two different dates. Not only world events but also personal experiences change us all—even if in less dramatic ways—to some extent and in some way.

All Audiences Are Diverse

As important as uniqueness is the contemporary audience's diversity—in age, race, gender, religion, affectional orientation, nationality, economic situation, relationship status, occupation, political affiliation, attitudes, values, and beliefs, and in hundreds of other ways. If you're in a typical college classroom in the United States, your classroom audience represents a diverse group of people. Further, each subgroup within this diverse group is itself diverse. People of the same age will differ in race, gender, religion, and so on. And those of the same religion will differ from one another in age, nationality, politics, and so on. As you prepare to learn about your audience, keep this notion of diversity in mind. It will help you focus on your audience as a mix of unique individuals rather than a blend.

In addition to being sensitive to cultural differences, develop sensitivity to those in your audience who may have one or more disabilities. Scan your audience for any listeners who may have difficulty in hearing or seeing you. Don't identify them or in any way call attention to them, but keep their needs in mind as you present your speech. Here are just a few suggestions for such a situation; these hints would be helpful with any audience but which are especially significant when your listeners have sight or hearing disabilities.

1. If there are blind or partially sighted people in the audience, explain your visual aids in a bit more detail. For example, instead of saying, "As you can see from the graph, we're in good shape," consider saying, "As you can see from this graph, which shows a 40 percent increase in sales, we're in good shape." If you're using handouts, be especially sure to explain fully what their purpose is, and make it a point to reiterate the information on them. If you're writing on the chalkboard, say aloud what you're writing.

2. If you notice persons with hearing deficits, be sure to maintain an adequate volume (loudness) and to speak distinctly. Be especially careful not to drop your voice at the ends of sentences. If you see your audience leaning forward or struggling to hear you, increase your volume.

3. Use normal vocabulary, and don't avoid topics that you would speak on to (for example) an audience of all sighted people. Don't avoid terms such as *see, hear, look, listen*, or even *blind* or *deaf*. Don't avoid illustrating your speech with an example from a television show or a song.

4. Try to eliminate as much noise as you can. For example, audible noise might include the sounds of voices in nearby hallways or other classrooms; visual "noise" might take the form of sun washing out the colors on your slides. Sometimes something as simple as closing the door or pulling the shades is all that's necessary to make your speech more understandable.

5. In talking about people with disabilities, use language that emphasizes the person rather than the disability. Thus, it's preferable to refer to "persons with disabilities" rather than "disabled persons." If your speech topic requires you to discuss people with a specific disability, be sure you have done adequate research on the terms preferred by that population. For example, many people born with *achondroplastic dwarfism* prefer to be referred to as "little people." In general, people with disabilities are able in most respects; in only some situations does the specific disability come into play.

And, of course, persons with disabilities have responsibilities too. So, if you have hearing problems, take a seat close to the front of the room. If you hear better in one ear than the other, be sure to position yourself on the proper side of the room. If you have vision problems, be sure to bring your glasses and to sit as close to the front as is comfortable.

Learning about Your Audience

You can seek out audience information in four general ways: observation, data collection, interviewing, and inference (Sprague & Stuart, 1996). Let's explore each.

Observe

Think about your audience based on the way they present themselves physically. What can you infer about their economic status from their clothing and jewelry, for example? Might their clothing reveal any conservative or liberal

Gallup Poll

(www.gallup.com)
Visit the Gallup Organization website (or any other polling website you'd like) and search for information on college students that might prove of value in your speech. How might this information prove of value to you as you prepare your next several speeches?

leanings? Might clothing provide clues to attitudes on economics or politics? What do they do in their free time? Where do they live? What do they talk about? Are different cultures represented? Do your observations give you any clue as to what audience members' interests or concerns might be? Be careful that this analysis doesn't turn into stereotyping based on appearance; rather, use visual cues to give you hints as to the nature of the audience.

Collect Data Systematically

A useful way to secure information about your audience is to use a questionnaire. Let's say you've taken a course in website design and are thinking about giving an informative speech on ways to design effective Web pages. One thing you'll need to know is how much your audience already knows about Web design. A questionnaire asking them about their experience with Web design can help you judge the level at which to approach the topic, the information that you can assume the audience already has, the terms you need to define, and so on. You might also want to find out how much experience the audience members have had with web pages, either as users or as designers.

To help you answer these and other relevant questions, you might compose a questionnaire. If your class is set up as a listserv, or if members can communicate through some Web group (like BlackBoard or WebCT), these questionnaires will be extremely easy to distribute: You can do it with one e-mail

USING TECHNOLOGY

Visit a major polling organization's website, where you'll find a wide variety of information on all sorts of attitudes and opinions on economics, business, politics, lifestyles, buying habits, and more (search for "opinion poll" or, if you have access, visit Research Navigator at www.researchnavigator for lots of suggestions). The Cornell Institute for Social and Economic Research maintains a useful website with hot links to a wide variety of polls and surveys at www.ciser.cornell.edu/info/polls.shtml. One of the most extensive polling websites is the Gallup Organization's at www.gallup.com; see its home page above. Can you find a poll that would help you in preparing your next speech?

questionnaire sent to the listserv (see the Research Link on p. 105). Other members of the class can then respond to the questionnaire, and you can tabulate the results and use the information you discover as you prepare your speech. Do caution other members of the listserv that they should send back questionnaires directly and only to you. If classmates return questionnaires to the listserv, then everyone in the class will get everyone else's responses; in a class of 25 students, each person would receive 625 responses. If your class is not established as a listserv, you can still distribute printed questionnaires before class begins or as students are leaving.

Audience questionnaires are even more useful as background for persuasive speeches. Let's say you plan to give a speech in favor of allowing single people to adopt children. To develop an effective speech, you need to know your audience's attitudes toward single parent adoption. Are they in favor of this idea? Opposed to it? Do they have reservations? If so, what are they? Are they undecided? To answer such questions, you might use a questionnaire such as that presented in Figure 4.1.

Interview Members of Your Audience

In a classroom situation you can easily take the time to interview members of your audience in order to find out more about them. But if you're to speak to an audience you'll not meet prior to your speech, you might interview those who know

---

◖◗ RESEARCH *Link*

Experts

A frequently useful source of information is the expert: anyone with specialized knowledge, anyone who has information about something that others don't have. Usually experts are people who are extremely knowledgeable about a particular topic—images of world-renowned scientists come quickly to mind. But the term *expert* also can refer to a teenager who witnessed an accident, experienced homelessness, or won the national spelling bee.

The faculty of your college or university is one of the best, if rarely used, sources of expert information for almost any speech topic. Regardless of what your topic is, a faculty member of some department likely knows a great deal about the topic. At the very least, faculty members will be able to direct you to appropriate sources. Experts in the community can serve similar functions. Local politicians, religious leaders, doctors, lawyers, museum directors, and the like often are suitable sources of information.

Beyond your college or university lies a world of experts—religious and business leaders, politicians, educators at other colleges and research institutes, medical personnel, researchers in almost any field imaginable. Ask yourself if your speech and your audience could profit from the insights of experts. If your answer is yes—and few topics could not so profit—then consider the steps suggested in Chapter 9 (p. 225) for interviewing such experts—either in person, by telephone, or, as is becoming increasingly popular, over the Internet, especially in e-mail or chat groups.

Of course, if 500 public speaking students all descend on the faculty or on the community, chaos can easily result. So going to these experts is often discouraged as a class assignment. But it's often a useful practice for speeches you'll give later in life.

Research Activity. Make a list of the experts that you might ideally interview for your next speech. Why would each be useful, and how would you use the information this expert provided?

Audience Questionnaire for a Persuasive Speech

What are the disadvantages to stating your position on the issue in your questionnaire? Can you identify any possible advantages?

AUDIENCE QUESTIONNAIRE

I'm planning to give my persuasive speech on adoption. I'd like to know your attitudes on a few issues relating to this topic. I'd appreciate it if you'd complete this questionnaire and return it to jdevito@hunter.cuny.edu.

1. How do you feel about single people's adopting children?

_____ strongly in favor of it
_____ in favor of it
_____ neutral
_____ opposed to it
_____ strongly opposed to it

2. Is your attitude the same for interracial adoption? For gays and lesbians who adopt? Please explain.

3. What are your main reasons for your current attitudes?

4. What underlying values and beliefs do you think contribute to your current attitudes?

Thanks,
Joe

the audience members better than you do. For example, you might talk with the person who invited you to speak and inquire about the audience's culture, age, gender, knowledge and educational levels, religious background, and so forth.

Use "Intelligent Inference and Empathy"

Use your knowledge of human behavior and human motivation and try to adopt the perspective of the audience. Intelligent inference and empathy will help you estimate your listeners' **attitudes, beliefs,** and **values,** and even their thoughts and their emotions on your topic (Sprague & Stuart, 1996). For example, let's say you're addressing your class on the need to eliminate (or expand) affirmative action. What might you infer about your audience—are they likely to be in favor of affirmative action or opposed to it? Can they be easily classified in terms of their liberal or conservative leanings? How informed are they likely to be about the topic and about the advantages and disadvantages of affirmative action? What feelings might they have about affirmative action?

DEVELOPING STRATEGIES

Audience Attitudes. Jack is planning to give a persuasive speech to your class urging listeners to support the National Rifle Association in its efforts to fight gun control. He wonders, first, what attitudes the members of the class have on this topic, and second, how he can adjust his speech on the basis of these (predicted) attitudes. How would you advise Jack?

Analyzing Audience Sociology

Let's look at six major sociological or demographic variables: (1) cultural factors, (2) age, (3) gender, (4) affectional orientation, (5) educational and intellectual levels, and (6) religion and religiousness.

Cultural Factors

Nationality, race, and cultural identity are crucial in audience analysis. Largely because of different training and experiences, various cultural groups will have different interests, values, and goals. Further, cultural factors also will influence each of the remaining factors; for example, attitudes toward age and gender will differ greatly from one culture to another (Harris & Johnson, 2000).

The use of cultural information about your audience to help you select the right motivational appeals may be effective only in certain situations. For example, researchers have found that appeals to self-interest have greater influence on audiences from individualist cultures than on audiences from collectivist cultures. And appeals to other-interests are relatively more influential on audiences of collectivist cultures than on people from individualist cultures (Han & Shavitt, 1994; Dillard & Marshall, 2003). Thus, using an audience's cultural information to select appeals works best when you speak to audiences that are almost exclusively from one cultural orientation and when all or almost all members of that audience subscribe to the specific values you are addressing (Dillard & Marshall, 2003).

You can use cultural information to avoid offending members of the audience, however. Consider some general questions you might ask yourself:

1. Are the attitudes and beliefs held by different cultures relevant to your topic and purpose? Find out what these are. For example, the degree to which listeners are loyal to family members, feel responsibility for the aged, and believe in the value of education will vary from one culture to another. Build your appeals around your audience's attitudes and beliefs.

2. Will the varied cultures differ in their goals or in ideas about how to change their lives? For example, groups that have experienced recent oppression may be more concerned with immediate goals and immediate means of affecting change in their lives. Many want revolutionary rather than evolutionary change. They may have little patience with the more conservative posture of the majority that tells them to be content with small gains. You see this division even within groups in which some people want to take it slow and some want more dramatic change; you see it in disputes within the African American community, the Hispanic community, and the gay and lesbian community. And of course you see this in other countries throughout the world; in China, for example, there are those who want democracy now and those who are content to let changes come more slowly. Among the Israelis, as among the Palestinians, there are those who want revolutionary and those who want evolutionary changes.

3. Are the differences within cultures relevant to your topic and purpose? Speakers who fail to demonstrate an understanding of cultural differences will be distrusted. For example, speakers, especially those who are seen to be outsiders, who imply that all African Americans are athletic and all lesbians

USING TECHNOLOGY

Visit http://www.odci.gov/cia/publications/ for the *World Factbook*, a source that contains information on more than 250 countries. Or take a look at InfoNation, published by the United Nations, which contains information on all UN member nations (www.un.org/). Can you locate any information here that might be of use in one of your future speeches?

are masculine will quickly lose credibility. Many African Americans are poor athletes, and many lesbians are extremely feminine. Avoid any implication that you're stereotyping audience members (or the groups to which they belong). It's sure to work against achieving your purpose.

Continue for a moment your focus on culture, and examine your own public speaking openness to those who are culturally different by taking the accompanying self-test, "How Open Are You Interculturally?"

Test YOURSELF

How Open Are You Interculturally?

Select an adjective denoting a specific culture (national, racial, or religious) different from your own, and substitute this culture for the phrase *culturally different* in each statement below. Indicate how likely you are to do what the statement suggests, using the following scale: Very likely = 5, likely = 4, neither likely nor unlikely = 3, unlikely = 2, and very unlikely = 1.

_____ **1.** Listen openly and fairly to a speech by a *culturally different* person.

_____ **2.** Critique a speech by a *culturally different person* with the same degree of objectivity and supportiveness that you'd give to someone who was culturally similar to you.

_____ **3.** Evaluate evidence in a speech by a *culturally different* person with exactly the same standards that you'd use in evaluating evidence presented by someone culturally similar to you.

_____ **4.** Attribute the same degree of credibility to the *culturally different* person that you'd attribute to those who were culturally similar to you.

_____ **5.** Participate in a work team with a *culturally different* person with the same degree of willingness and enthusiasm that you'd have working with someone culturally similar to you.

❖ **HOW DID YOU DO?** This test was designed to raise questions rather than to provide answers about your degree of openness in public speaking. High scores for any question or group of questions indicate considerable intercultural openness; low scores indicate a lack of intercultural openness.

❖ **WHAT WILL YOU DO?** Use these numbers for purposes of thinking critically about your intercultural openness rather than to indicate any absolute level of openness or closed-mindedness. Did you select the "culturally different" group on the basis of how positive or negative your attitudes were? What group would you be most open to interacting with? Least open?

Age

Different age groups have different attitudes and beliefs largely because they have had different experiences in different contexts. Take these differences into consideration in preparing your speeches.

❖ **CONSIDER,** if you were a comedian like Jim Carrey pictured here, speaking to students at your college and joking about various topics. What two or three topics would you avoid joking about? What two or three topics would you assume would be safe?

In examining the following questions, recognize that culture will greatly influence attitudes toward age. Among some Native Americans and Chinese, for example, there is great respect for the aged, and the elders are frequently asked for advice and guidance by the young. Among some groups in the United States—though certainly not all or even necessarily a majority—the aged are often ignored and devalued. Programs for the aged, scholarships for students, or parental and child responsibilities are likely to be regarded very differently by members of these different cultures.

1. **Do the age groups in your audience differ in the goals, interests, and day-to-day concerns that may be related to your topic and purpose?** Graduating from college, achieving corporate success, raising a family, and saving for retirement are concerns that differ greatly from one age group to another. Learn your audience's goals. Know what they think about and worry about. Connect your points and supporting materials to these goals and concerns. Show the audience how they can more effectively achieve their goals, and you'll have a favorable outcome.

2. **Do the groups differ in their ability to absorb and process information?** With a young audience, it may be best to keep up a steady, even swift pace. If possible, use visuals. Make sure their attention doesn't wander. With older persons, you may wish to maintain a more moderate pace.

3. **Do the groups differ in their respect for tradition and the past?** Is one age group (traditionally the young) more likely to view innovation and change positively? Might appeals to tradition be more appropriate for an older audience? Might appeals to discovery, exploration, newness, and change find a more receptive hearing among the young?

Gender

Gender is one of the most difficult audience variables to analyze. The rapid social changes taking place today make it difficult to pin down the effects of gender. At one time researchers focused primarily on biological sex differences. Now, however, many researchers are focusing on psychological sex roles. When we focus on a psychological sex role, we consider a person feminine if that person has internalized those traits (attitudes and behaviors) that society considers feminine and rejected those traits society considers masculine. We consider a person masculine if that person has internalized those traits society considers masculine and rejected those traits society considers feminine. Thus, a biological woman may display masculine sex-role traits and behaviors, and a biological man may display feminine sex-role traits and behaviors (Pearson, West, & Turner, 1995).

Because of society's training, biological males generally internalize masculine traits and biological females generally internalize feminine traits. So there's probably great overlap between biological sex roles and psychological sex roles, even though they're not equivalent.

CRITICAL LISTENING/THINKING *Link*

Listening to Gender Differences

Imagine that you're listening to a variety of speakers who evidence the following behaviors. Which ones do you imagine as men and which do you imagine as women? Can you group the behaviors into two categories: "communication behaviors characteristic of men" and "communication behaviors characteristic of women"? Are some behaviors equally characteristic of both men and women?

1. This speaker is emotional rather than logical.
2. This speaker is vague rather than precise.
3. This speaker jumps from one idea to another.
4. This speaker is more social and personal than businesslike.
5. This speaker lacks force and power.

Although popular stereotypes imply that these behaviors are all more characteristic of women, careful research on gender differences (for example, Kramarae, 1981; Coates & Cameron, 1989; Burgoon & Bacue, 2003; Pearson, West, & Turner, 1995; Arliss, 1991) finds none of the behaviors more characteristic of one gender than another.

Getting Critical. Given these popular stereotypes (which you may or may not hold personally), what advice would you give male public speakers? Female public speakers?

Although it's not possible to make generalizations about all men or all women, you may be able to make some assumptions about the men and women in your *specific audience.* Here are some questions to guide your analysis of this very difficult audience characteristic.

1. Do men and women differ in the values they consider important and that are related to your topic and purpose? Traditionally, men have been found to place greater importance on theoretical, economic, and political values. Traditionally, women have been found to place greater importance on aesthetic, social, and religious values. Of course, you're unlikely ever to find yourself speaking to an audience of all "traditional" men and "traditional" women. Rather, your audience is likely to be composed of men and women whose values overlap. Be careful not to assume that the women in your audience are religious simply because they're women and that the men, because they're men, are not; or that the men are interested in sports and the stock market but that the women are not.

2. Will your topic be seen differently by men and by women? Although both men and women may find the topic important, they may nevertheless view it from different perspectives. For example, men and women don't view such topics as abortion, date rape, performance anxiety, anorexia, equal pay for equal work, or exercise in the same way. So if you're giving a speech on date rape on campus, you need to make a special effort to relate the topic and your purpose to the attitudes, knowledge, and feelings that the men and the women in your audience bring with them.

3. Will men or women respond differently to the language and style of your speech? Research shows that men and women differ in language usage a lot less than the stereotypes might have us believe. And yet research does support at least two differences: Women are more polite than men in their speech and are more indirect, especially when stating something that is unpleasant or negative (Holmes 1995; Pearson, West, & Turner, 1995). Depending on your specific audience, you may want to make the inference—based on this research—that women have less favorable reactions to slang or to expressions you might label vulgar. Your best bet, of course, is to avoid slang or any expression that may be interpreted as vulgar and to avoid this especially when your audience is mixed. You also may want to infer that women will prefer a more indirect form of criticism or argument, a less confrontational style of speaking, than will men.

Affectional Orientation

Within just the last decade or so, the issue of affectional orientation has received enormous media attention—especially when you compare it to the way the subject was viewed 40 or 50 years ago. The *New York Times*, for example, now regularly features same-sex unions along with those of opposite-sex couples in their Sunday Styles section, and gay and lesbian celebrities and fictional characters are common in the media. Despite these changes, because of the social climate, much of the gay and lesbian experience remains unreported and unknown. Yet you can be reasonably sure that in all your public speaking experiences, you will never address an audience that is totally heterosexual.

If it's difficult to generalize about culture or gender, it's even more difficult to generalize about affectional orientation. Again, however, you may find a few general questions helpful.

1. Will the affectional orientation of the audience members influence the way they see your topic? If your topic is politics, the military's current policies on gay men and lesbians, taxes, marriage, or any of a host of other topics, the answer is probably yes. Polls and frequent news items consistently report on attitudes among gay men and lesbians that differ from those of heterosexuals in significant ways. But don't assume that heterosexuals and homosexuals necessarily see things differently on every topic. There are differences but there are also many similarities.

2. Will the attitudes and behaviors of the audience conform to popular stereotypes of gay men, lesbians, and heterosexual men and women? Here the answer is a clear no. The differences within any large group are always great. So be very careful when you assume sameness among members of any large group. You're going to find that heterosexual women vary greatly in their attitudes toward most issues, just as do gay men, for example. Portrayals of the heterosexual male as boorish or the gay male as compulsively neat are likely to destroy your credibility with most educated audiences.

3. Should the affectional orientation of audience members influence your language and style? Although clearly the answer is that it should not, you might want to be on the lookout for stereotypical portrayals in your examples or for using language that is not as inclusive as it might be. As you consider this issue, try to assume the perspective of the audience member who is most unlike you and to ask yourself if your examples or language might prove offensive.

Educational and Intellectual Levels

An educated person may not be very intelligent; conversely, an intelligent person may not be well educated. In most cases, however, education and intelligence do seem to go together. Further, they seem to influence the reception of a speech in similar ways. So we'll consider these factors together, using the shorthand "educated" to refer to both qualities.

In looking at the education and intelligence of your audience, consider asking questions such as the following:

1. Is the educational level of audience members related to their level of social or political activism? Generally, educated people are more responsive to the needs of others. They more actively engage in causes of a social and political nature. Appeals to humanitarianism and broad social motives should work well with an educated audience. When speaking to less-educated groups, concentrate on the value your speech has to their immediate needs and to the satisfaction of their immediate goals.

2. Will the interests and concerns of audience members differ on the basis of their educational level? Generally, educated people are more concerned with issues outside their immediate field of operation. They're concerned with international affairs, economic issues, and the broader philosophical and sociological issues confronting the nation and the world. Educated groups recognize that these issues affect them in many ways. Often uneducated people don't see the connection. Therefore, when speaking to a less-educated audience, draw connections explicitly to relate such topics to their more immediate concerns.

3. Will educational levels influence how critical the audience will be of your evidence and argument? More educated audiences will probably be less swayed by appeals to emotion and to authority (see Chapter 10). They'll be more skeptical of generalizations (as you should be of my generalizations in this chapter). They'll question the validity of statistics and frequently will demand better substantiation of your propositions. Therefore, pay special attention to the logic of your evidence and arguments in addressing an educated audience.

Religion and Religiousness

Today there's great diversity among the religious backgrounds of audiences. And the attitudes of religions vary widely on numerous issues: abortion, same-sex marriage, women's rights, and divorce (Bates & Fratkin, 1999). Attitudes also vary within religions; almost invariably there are conservative, liberal, and middle-of-the-road groups within each (Henslin, 2000). In some Christian communities, for example, gay men and lesbians may be ordained ministers and same-sex marriages may be performed. In other Christian communities the attitudes are vastly different. Generalizations here, as with gender, are changing rapidly.

1. Will religious audience members see your topic or purpose from the point of view of religion? Religion permeates all topics and all issues. On a most obvious level, we know that views on such issues as birth control, abortion, and divorce are closely connected to religion. Similarly, attitudes about premarital sex, marriage, child rearing, money, cohabitation, responsibilities toward parents, and thousands of other issues are clearly influenced by religion. Religion also is important, however, in areas where its connection isn't so obvious. For example, religion influences people's ideas concerning such topics as obedience to authority; responsibility to government; and the usefulness of such qualities as honesty, guilt, and happiness.

2. Does your topic or purpose attack the religious beliefs of any segment of your audience? Even people who claim total alienation from the

USING TECHNOLOGY

Visit the Information Please religion website page (http://www.infoplease.com/ipa/A0779433.html), which lists hot links to comprehensive websites for a variety of different religions. What can you learn from these websites that will help you analyze and adapt to your audience?

religion in which they were raised may still have strong emotional (though perhaps unconscious) ties to that religion. These ties may continue to influence such individuals' attitudes and beliefs. When dealing with any religious beliefs (and particularly when disagreeing with them), recognize that you're likely to meet stiff opposition. Proceed slowly and inductively. Present your evidence and argument before expressing your disagreement.

3. Do the religious beliefs of your audience differ in any significant ways from the official teachings of their religion? Don't assume that the rank-and-file members of a faith necessarily accept religious leaders' opinions or pronouncements. Official statements by religious leaders often take more conservative positions than those of laypeople.

Other Audience Factors

No list of audience characteristics can possibly be complete, and the list presented here is no exception. You'll need another category—"other factors"—to identify any additional characteristics that might be significant to your particular audience. For example:

◆ **Are the audience's occupation and income relevant to your speech?** Is your audience's level of job security and occupational pride related to your topic, purpose, or examples? Will people from different economic levels have different preferences for immediate or long-range goals? Will different groups have different demands on their time that will influence their ability to comply with suggestions to, say, participate in social or political causes?

◆ **Is the audience's relational status relevant?** Will the relational status of your audience members influence the way they view your topic or purpose? Will singles be interested in hearing about the problems of selecting preschools? Will those already in long-term relationships be interested in the depression many people who are not in close relationships experience during the holidays?

❖ **CONSIDER** whether, as a juror in a trial, you'd be influenced by the sex of the lawyers. Would you favor your own sex, the opposite sex, or would you respond to them regardless of sex?

◆ **Are the special interests of the audience relevant?** Do the special interests of your audience members relate to your topic or purpose? What special interests do the audience members have? What occupies their leisure time? How can you integrate these interests into your examples and illustrations or use them as you select quotations?

◆ **Are the audience's political beliefs relevant?** Will audience members' political affiliations influence how they view your topic or purpose? Are they politically liberal? Conservative? Might this influence how you develop your speech?

◆ **Are organizational relationships relevant?** Might audience members' affiliations give you cues as to their other beliefs and values? Might you use references to these organizations in your speech, perhaps as examples or illustrations?

Context Characteristics

In addition to analyzing specific listeners, think about the specific context in which you'll speak. Here are a few questions you might ask as you prepare your speech:

◆ **How many listeners will you address?** Generally, the larger the audience, the more formal the speech presentation should be. With a small audience, you may be more casual and informal. In a large audience you'll have a wider variety of religions, a greater range of occupations and income levels, and so on. All the variables noted earlier will be intensified in a large audience. Therefore, you'll need supporting materials that will appeal to all members.

◆ **Where will you speak?** The physical environment—indoors or outdoors, room or auditorium, sitting or standing audience—will obviously influence your speech presentation. Also, consider the equipment that is available. Is there a chalkboard, flip chart, or transparency projector? Is there a slide projector and screen? Is there a computer with the projector for showing computer slides? Are chalk and markers available? As Chapter 5 will emphasize, it's vital that you check on the compatibility of the equipment in the room with the equipment on which you prepared your materials. If at all possible, rehearse in the room you'll be speaking in with the same equipment that you'll have when you deliver your speech.

◆ **Why are you speaking?** What's the occasion? When you give a speech as a class assignment, for example, you'll probably be operating under a number of restrictions—time limitations, the type of general purpose you can use, the types of supporting materials, and various other matters. When you are invited to speak because of who you are, you'll have greater freedom to talk about what interests you—which, by virtue of the fact that you were invited, will also interest the audience.

◆ **When will you speak?** If your speech is to be given in an early morning class, say around 8 A.M., then take into consideration that some of your listeners will still be half asleep. Express your appreciation for their attendance; compliment their attention. If necessary, wake them up with your voice, gestures, attention-gaining materials, visual aids, and the like. If your speech is in the evening, when most of your listeners are anxious to get home, recognize this fact as well.

RESEARCH *Link*

Specialized Reference Works

In addition to general encyclopedias (discussed in Chapter 3, p. 65), there are also many specialized encyclopedias. Those devoted to religion include the *New Catholic Encyclopedia* (15 volumes), which contains articles on such topics as philosophy, science, and art as these have been influenced by and have influenced the Catholic Church; *Encyclopaedia Judaica* (16 volumes plus yearbooks), which emphasizes Jewish life and includes biographies and detailed coverage of the Jewish contribution to world culture; and *Encyclopedia of Islam* and *Encyclopaedia of Buddhism,* which cover the development, beliefs, institutions, and personalities of Islam and Buddhism, respectively. Supplement these with appropriate websites devoted to specific religions, for example, http://www.utm.edu/martinarea/fbc/bfm.html (Southern Baptist Convention), http://www.catholic.org/ index.html (Catholicism), http://www.hindunet.org (Hinduism), http://www.utexas.edu/students/amso (Islam), and http://jewishnet.net (Judaism).

For the physical, applied, and natural sciences, there's the 20-volume *McGraw-Hill Encyclopedia of Science and Technology*. This is complemented by annual supplements. *Our Living World of Nature* is a 14-volume popular encyclopedia that deals with natural history from an ecological point of view (the online version is by subscription). *The International Encyclopedia of the Social Sciences* concentrates on the theory and methods of the social sciences in 17 well-researched volumes. Other widely used specialized encyclopedias include the *Encyclopedia of Bioethics* (4 volumes), the *Encyclopedia of Religion* (16 volumes), and the *Encyclopedia of Philosophy* (4 volumes). Also check *The Internet Encyclopedia of Philosophy* at www.utm.edu/research/iep.

Research Activity. Locate a specialized encyclopedia—print or online—that you think will prove of value to students in your public speaking course. In a two-minute speech explain how it is accessed, what it is (what areas it covers), and why this might be of value to others in the class.

Analyzing Audience Psychology

It is helpful to analyze audience psychology along such dimensions as willing-to-unwilling, favorable-to-unfavorable, and knowledgeable-to-unknowledgeable.

How Willing Is Your Audience?

Audiences gather with varying degrees of willingness to hear a speaker. Some are anxious to hear the speaker and may even have paid a substantial admission price. The "lecture circuit," for example, is a most lucrative aspect of public life. But whereas some audiences are willing to pay to hear a speaker, others don't seem to care one way or the other. Other audiences need to be persuaded to listen (or at least to sit in the audience). Still other audiences gather because they have to. For example, negotiations on a union contract may require members to attend meetings where officers give speeches.

Your immediate concern, of course, is with the willingness of your fellow students to listen to your speeches. How willing are they? Do they come to class because they have to, or do they come because they're interested in what you'll say? If they're a willing group, then you have few problems. If they're an unwilling group, all is not lost; you just have to work a little harder in adapting your speech. Here are a few suggestions to help change your listeners from unwilling to willing.

◆ **Get their interest and attention as early in your speech as possible.** Then maintain this attention throughout your speech by using little-known facts, humor, quotations, startling statistics, examples, narratives, audiovisual aids, and the like. For example, Judith Maxwell (1987), then chair of the Economic Council of Canada, used humor to gain the interest and attention of her audience. She then quickly connected this humor to the topic of her talk:

> Yogi Berra said something once that's relevant to a discussion of economic forecasting. "If you don't know where you're going, you could wind up somewhere else." Whether we are business economists or economists in the public sector, what society expects from us is advice on how to "know where we are going."

◆ **Reward the audience for their attendance and attention.** Do this in advance of your main arguments. Let the audience know you're aware they're making a sacrifice in coming to hear you speak. Tell them you appreciate it. One student, giving a speech close to midterm time, said simply:

> I know how easy it is to cut classes during midterm time to finish the unread chapters and do everything else you have to do. So I especially appreciate your being here this morning. What I have to say, however, will interest you and will be of direct benefit to all of you.

◆ **Relate your topic and supporting materials directly to your audience's needs and wants.** Show the audience how they can save time, make more money, solve their problems, or become more popular. If you fail to do this, then your audience has good reason for not listening.

How Favorable Is Your Audience?

Audiences vary in the degree to which they're favorable or unfavorable toward your thesis or point of view. And even within the same audience, of course, you're likely to have some who agree with you and others who disagree and perhaps still others who are undecided. If you hope to change an audience's attitudes, beliefs, or behaviors, you must understand their present position. The unfavorably disposed audience is especially difficult to confront and so needs special handling. Here are a few suggestions for dealing with this type of audience.

◆ **Clear up any possible misapprehensions that may be causing the disagreement.** Often disagreement is caused by a lack of understanding. If you feel this is the case, then your first task is to clear this up. For example, if the audience is hostile to the new team approach you are advocating because they wrongly think it will result in a reduction in their autonomy, then explain to them very directly, saying something like:

> I realize that many people oppose this new team approach because they feel it will reduce their own autonomy and control. Well, it won't; as a matter of fact, with this approach, each person will actually gain greater control, greater power, greater autonomy.

◆ **Build on commonalities; emphasize not the differences between you and your listeners but the similarities.** Stress what you and the audience share as people, as interested citizens, as fellow students. Theorist and critic Kenneth Burke (1950) argued that we achieve persuasion through

? DEVELOPING STRATEGIES

Unwilling Audience. Joe is scheduled to give a speech on careers in computer technology to a group of high school students who have been forced to attend this Saturday career day. The audience definitely qualifies as unwilling. What advice can you give Joe to help him deal with this type of audience?

CASTING A WIDE NET

ELECT   ELECT

MANKOFF

"Fellow-earthlings . . ."

identification with the audience. Identification involves emphasizing similarities between speaker and audience. When audience members see common ground between themselves and you, they become more favorable to both you and your speech.

◆ Here, for example, Alan Nelson (1986) identified with the city of his audience in the introduction to a talk on the sanctuary movement:

> Returning to the Golden Gate, my home area, reminds me of another harbor and a beautiful statue . . . the Statue of Liberty, which has stood for 100 years in New York Harbor, is being rededicated this year and represents the heritage of America.

◆ **Organize your speech inductively.** Try to build your speech from areas of agreement, through areas of slight disagreement, up to the major differences between the audience's attitudes and your own position. Let's say, for example, that you represent management and you wish to persuade employees to accept a particular wage offer. You might begin with such areas of agreement as the mutual desire for improved working conditions or for long-term economic growth. Once areas of agreement are established, it's easier to bring up differences such as, perhaps, the need to delay salary increases until next year. In any disagreement or argument, there are still areas of agreement; emphasize these before considering areas of disagreement.

◆ **Strive for small gains.** Don't try to convince a pro-life group to contribute money for the new abortion clinic or a pro-choice group to vote against liberalizing abortion laws in a five-minute speech. Be content to get your listeners to see some validity in your position and to listen fairly. About-face changes take a long time to achieve. To attempt too much persuasion or too much change can result only in failure or resentment.

◆ **Acknowledge the differences explicitly.** If it's clear to the audience that they and you are at opposite ends of the issue, it may be helpful to acknowledge this very directly. Show the audience that you understand and respect their position but that you'd like them to consider a different way of looking at things. Say something like:

> I know you don't all agree that elementary school teachers should have to take tests every several years to maintain their licenses. Some teachers are going to lose their licenses, and that isn't pleasant. And we all feel sorry that this will happen. What isn't widely known, however, is that the vast majority of teachers will actually benefit from this proposal. And I'd like an opportunity to sketch out the benefits that many of us will enjoy as a result of this new testing procedure.

How Knowledgeable Is Your Audience?

Listeners differ greatly in the knowledge they have. Some listeners will be quite knowledgeable about your topic, others will be almost totally ignorant. Mixed audiences are the most difficult ones.

? DEVELOPING STRATEGIES

Unfavorable Audience. Nancy is scheduled to give a speech to the school board arguing that the school board president should be dismissed for incompetence. Although she has a convincing case, she faces two problems: (1) The school board wants to keep things the way they are, because the president allows them to do what they want; and (2) the president is extremely well liked by the entire community. What advice would you give Nancy?

If you're unaware of the audience's knowledge level, you won't know what to assume and what to explain. You won't know how much information will overload the channels or how much will bore the audience to sleep. Perhaps you want to show that their previous knowledge is now inadequate. Perhaps you want to demonstrate a new slant to old issues. Or perhaps you want to show that what you have to say will not repeat but instead will build on the already extensive knowledge of the audience. However you accomplish this, you need to make the audience see that what you have to say is new. Make them realize that you won't simply repeat what they already know.

Treat audiences that lack knowledge of the topic very carefully. Never confuse a lack of knowledge with a lack of ability to understand.

◆ **Don't talk down to your audience.** This is perhaps the greatest communication error that teachers make. Having taught a subject for years, they face, semester after semester, students who have no knowledge of the topic. As a result, many teachers tend to talk down to the students and, in the process, lose their audience.

◆ **Don't confuse a lack of knowledge with a lack of intelligence.** An audience may have no knowledge of your topic but be quite capable of following a clearly presented, logically developed argument. Try especially hard to use concrete examples, audiovisual aids, and simple language. Fill in background details as required. Avoid jargon and specialized terms that may not be clear to someone new to the subject. In sum, never overestimate your audience's knowledge, but never underestimate their intelligence.

◆ **Let your listeners know that you're aware of their knowledge and expertise.** Try to do this as early in the speech as possible. Emphasize that what you have to say will not be redundant. Tell them that you'll be presenting recent developments or new approaches. In short, let them know that they'll not be wasting their time listening to your speech.

◆ **Emphasize your credibility, especially your competence in this general subject area** (see Chapter 10). Let your listeners know that you have earned the right to speak. Let them know that what you have to say is based on a firm grasp of the material.

Here, for example, Richard Colino (1986) established his credibility early in a speech on satellite technology:

> I'm pleased to be here today to discuss the impact of the Information Age on national policies—a subject which merits more analysis and debate than it gets. I'm the Director General and Chief Executive of the International Telecommunications Satellite Organization, better known as INTELSAT. However, my commentary on a series of issues and themes today represents my personal, rather than official INTELSAT, views.

Analysis and Adaptation during the Speech

In addition to analyzing your audience and making adaptations in your speech *before* delivering the speech, devote attention to analysis and adaptation *during* the speech. This during-the-speech analysis is especially important when you

❖ **CONSIDER** the ways college instructors adapted to classes you've attended. For example, have you seen instructors respond to puzzled looks, elaborate on an example that didn't seem to work as planned, or pick up the pace when there's more to cover than time allows? What one suggestion would you offer to help the typical college instructor to better adapt his or her lectures to the classroom audience?

DEVELOPING STRATEGIES

Audience Inactivity. Temple is giving a speech on the problem of teenage drug abuse and notices that several entire back rows of the audience have totally tuned him out; they're reading, chatting, working on their laptops. What might Temple do to encourage these audience members to listen?

know little of your audience or find yourself facing an audience very different from the one you expected. Here are a few suggestions.

Focus on Listeners as Message Senders

As you're speaking, look at your audience. Remember that just as you're sending messages to your listeners, they're also sending messages to you. Pay attention to these messages; on the basis of what they tell you, make the necessary adjustments.

Remember that members of different cultures operate with different "display rules," cultural rules that state what types of expressions are appropriate to reveal—and what expressions are inappropriate to reveal and should be kept hidden. Some display rules call for open and free expression of feelings and responses; these listeners will be easy to read. Other display rules call for little expression, and these listeners will be difficult to read.

You can make a wide variety of adjustments to each type of audience response. For example, if your audience shows signs of boredom, increase your volume, move closer to them, or tell them that what you're going to say will be of value to them. If your audience shows signs of disagreement or hostility, stress a similarity you have with them. If your audience looks puzzled or confused, pause a moment and rephrase your ideas, provide necessary definitions, or insert an internal summary. If your audience seems impatient, say, for example, "my last argument . . ." instead of your originally planned "my third argument. . . ."

Ask "What If" Questions

The more preparation you put into your speech, the better prepared you'll be to make on-the-spot adjustments and adaptations. For example, let's say you have been told that you're to explain the opportunities available to the nontraditional student at your college. You've been told that your audience will consist mainly of working women in their 30s and 40s who are just beginning college. As you prepare your speech with this audience in mind, ask yourself "what if" questions. For example:

◆ What if the audience has a large number of men?

◆ What if the audience consists of women much older than 40?

◆ What if the audience members also come with their spouses or their children?

Keeping such questions in mind will force you to consider alternatives as you prepare your speech. This way, you'll have extra options readily available if you face an audience that is not what you're used to or is different from what you expected.

A CASE OF *Ethics*

Respecting Audience Interests

You've just been hired by an advertising agency to design a campaign to promote a cereal that's extremely high in sugar and saturated fat—both of which you know are not healthy. The job, however, is a particularly good one, and should you succeed on this account, your future in advertising would be assured. Yet you wonder if you can ethically give persuasive force to selling this product, which is not in the best interests of your "audience," the consumer.

What would you do in this situation? More generally, what ethical guidelines should a speaker follow in balancing self- and audience interests?

Address Audience Responses Directly

Another way of dealing with audience responses is to confront them directly. To people who disagree with you, for example, you might say:

> Regardless of your present position, hear me out and see if this new way of doing things will not simplify your accounting procedures.

Or, to those who seem puzzled, you might say:

> This plan may seem confusing, but bear with me; it will become clear in a moment.

Or, to those who seem impatient, you might respond:

> I know this has been a long day, but give me just a few more minutes and you'll be able to save hours recording your accounts.

By responding to your listeners' reactions and feedback, you acknowledge their needs. You let them know that you hear them, that you're with them, and that you're responding to their very real concerns.

DEVELOPING STRATEGIES

Negative Feedback. While giving his speech Kevin notices from the expressions on the faces of his audience that they are totally against his thesis and are ready to tune him out. What would be the best thing Kevin could do to induce the audience to continue listening and to give him a fair hearing?

Summary of Concepts and Skills

This chapter has looked at the audience and particularly at how you can analyze your listeners and adapt your speeches to them.

Audiences and Audience Analysis

In seeking information about your audience, consider the values of observation, collecting data systematically (for example, with audience questionnaires), interviewing members, and using intelligent inference and empathy.

Analyzing Audience Sociology

In analyzing the sociology of your audience, consider especially the following characteristics:

- ◆ Cultural factors
- ◆ Age
- ◆ Gender (biological sex role and psychological sex role)
- ◆ Affectional orientation
- ◆ Educational and intellectual levels
- ◆ Religion and religiousness

In addition, look into your audience's occupation and income status, relational status, special interests, and political attitudes and beliefs, and consider context characteristics.

Analyzing Audience Psychology

In analyzing audience psychology consider their willingness, degree of favor, and their knowledge level.

- ◆ In adapting to an unwilling audience,
  - ■ Secure their attention as early as possible.
  - ■ Reward the audience for their attendance and attention.
  - ■ Relate your topic and supporting materials to the audience's needs and interests.

- ◆ In adapting to an unfavorable audience,
  - ■ Clear up any possible misunderstandings.
  - ■ Build on the similarities you have with the audience.
  - ■ Build your speech from areas of agreement up to the major differences.
  - ■ Strive for small gains.
- ◆ In adapting to an unknowledgeable audience,
  - ■ Avoid talking down to your listeners (or to any audience).
  - ■ Avoid confusing a lack of knowledge with a lack of intelligence.
- ◆ In adapting to a knowledgeable audience,
  - ■ Let your listeners know that you're aware of their expertise.
  - ■ Establish your credibility.

Analysis and Adaptation during the Speech

Not only during the preparation of a speech but also during its actual presentation,

- ◆ Focus on audience members as message senders, not merely message receivers.
- ◆ Ask "what if" questions as you prepare your speech.
- ◆ Address audience responses directly.

Vocabulary Quiz

Audience Analysis and Adaptation

Match the terms of audience analysis and adaptation with their definitions. Record the number of the definition next to the appropriate term.

_____ value

_____ "what if" questions

_____ audience questionnaire

_____ attitude

_____ psychological analysis

_____ belief

_____ context factors

_____ display rules

_____ sociological analysis

_____ audience

1. A group of people gathered to hear a public speech.
2. The conviction a person has about the truth or falsity of something.
3. The worth a person perceives an object, person, or idea to have.
4. Cultural rules regulating what is considered appropriate or inappropriate emotional expression.
5. Analysis of the demographic characteristics of an audience.
6. Factors such as the audience size, the physical environment, the occasion, and the time of a speech.
7. An audience's predisposition to respond for or against a speaker's thesis.
8. Analysis of the attitudes, beliefs, and values of the audience.
9. A useful aid in analyzing and adapting to an audience.
10. A means for discovering what listeners know or think about a topic or thesis.

Web Explorations

Companion Website
www.ablongman.com/devito

Additional insight into the public speaking audience and how you can better adapt your speeches to specific audiences are provided in a variety of discussions and exercises and in a self-test: "Audience Attitudes, Beliefs, and Values," "How Active Is Your Audience?," "How Homogeneous Is Your Audience?," "Predicting Listeners' Attitudes," "Analyzing an Unknown Audience," and "How Well Do You Know Your Audience?" An excellent speech on sexual harassment by Meleena Erikson, "See Jane, See Jane's Dilemma," is presented with annotations and questions for analysis.

Public Speaking Exercises

4.1 Analyzing Your Public Speaking Class

Using a 10-point scale, with 1 being "extremely unfavorable," 5 being "relatively neutral," and 10 being "extremely favorable," consider how favorable or unfavorable the attitudes of members of your class would be toward each of the following theses: (1) Individual states should be allowed to fly the Confederate flag if they wish. (2) Parents who prevent their children from receiving the latest scientific cures because of a belief in faith healing should be prosecuted. (3) Same-sex marriage should be legalized. (4) Medicinal marijuana should be readily available. (5) Random drug testing should be allowed in colleges.

After you've indicated your scores, discuss these potential public speaking theses with the class as a whole and consider how you'd adapt a speech advocating any one of these theses to both a favorable and an unfavorable audience.

4.2 Analyzing an Unknown Audience

This experience should familiarize you with some of the essential steps in analyzing an audience on the basis of relatively little evidence and in predicting their attitudes on the basis of that analysis. The class should be broken up into small groups of five or six members. Each group will be given a different magazine; their task is to analyze the audience (i.e., the readers or subscribers) of that particular magazine in terms of the characteristics discussed in this chapter. The only information the groups will have about their audience is that they're avid and typical readers of the given magazine. Pay particular attention to the types of articles published in the magazine, the advertisements, the photographs or illustrations, the editorial statements, the price of the magazine, and so on. Magazines that differ widely from one another are most appropriate for this experience.

After the audiences have been analyzed, try to identify at least three favorable and three unfavorable attitudes that each audience probably holds on contemporary issues. On what basis do you make these predictions? If you had to address this audience and advocate a position with which it disagreed, what adaptations would you make? What strategies would you use to prepare and present this persuasive speech?

Each group should share with the rest of the class the results of their efforts, taking special care to point out not only their conclusions but also the evidence and reasoning they used in arriving at the conclusions.

4.3 Predicting Listeners' Attitudes

Analyze the audience in each of the five situations presented below in terms of their willingness, favorableness, and knowledge. On the basis of this analysis, what one suggestion would you give the speaker to help her or him better adapt the speech to this audience?

1. Film students listening to Woody Allen talk about how to break into films.

2. High school athletes listening to a college athletic director speaking against sports scholarships.

3. Pregnant women listening to an advertising executive speak on how advertisers try to protect consumers.

4. Office managers listening to an organizational communication consultant speaking on ways to increase employee morale and productivity.

5. Chicago high school seniors listening to a college recruiter speak on the advantages of a small rural college.

4.4 Analyzing a Speech

Here is an informative speech on "Plasti-Bone," a new procedure to handle bone injuries and diseases. This speech was given by Nicole Martin, University of Texas at Austin.

JUST PRESS PRINT

The year is 2413, and once again Earth is being threatened by an evil force. This time the fate of mankind rests in the hands of Bruce Willis and the "Fifth Element." Unfortunately, the Fifth Element—Earth's savior—played with thespian excellence by Milla Jovavich, is attacked on her way to Earth, and all that is left of her is a single piece of bone. However, scientists of her time, using her remains, are able to literally print her back to life using a tissue reformulator. The Earth is saved, Bruce and Milla fall in love, and all is good in the universe again. Flashback to today, where *Business Week* of June 23, 2003, explains that doctors have invented a new method for replacing bone tissue destroyed by injury or disease, and our reality begins to look curiously like a science-fiction movie. The website for the Center for Orthopedics and Sports Medicine, last updated April 3, 2003, estimates that there are nearly half a million bone graft surgeries performed each year, and the bone printer, or "Plasti-Bone," is set to revolutionize the way doctors and patients handle physical injuries and bone diseases—simply by printing out new bone material.

So, to better understand the implications of a technique that the *Ventura County Star* of July 21, 2003, expects will reap $80 billion in sales by the year 2010, let's, first, examine what Plasti-Bone is; second, identify how the process works and its benefits; and, finally, explore the limitations and future prospects of the technology that the *Dallas Medical Journal* of August 2003 calls "another beneficial blurring of the line between computing and care."

In 1998 the U.S. Navy began funding an investigation into solutions to amputation for wounded naval troops. It took five years, but in 2003 Advanced Ceramics Research of Tucson, Arizona, answered the call with Plasti-Bone, an artificial substance that can be used to fix or replace broken or damaged bones. For this next sequence, revisit your inner child and think of a really large and expensive Play-Doh Fun Factory where the outgoing material is inserted into the body rather than eaten by a five-year-old. According to *Navy News Week* of June 16, 2003, the idea is to gain a precise 3-D image

In this opener the speaker connects a popular movie with the rather complicated process that is the subject of the speech. How effectively would this opener gain the attention of members of your class?

If you were giving this speech to your class, what audience factors would be significant? How important would such factors as the following be: culture, age, gender, affectional orientation, educational and intellectual levels, or religion and religiousness?

Here the speaker provides a detailed orientation. The speech, we learn here, will be in three parts: (1) the nature of Plasti-Bone, (2) the way the process works and its benefits, and (3) the limitations and future of the technology. Is this about the right level of detail for an orientation if this audience were your class? If not, what would you do differently?

Here the speaker begins the first main point, focusing on what Plasti-Bone is. As you can tell, the process is fairly complex; but the speaker helps the uninformed listener understand Plasti-Bone with a clever analogy to Play-Doh. It's a good example of how you can explain the unknown by relating it to something known.

Now that you know something about the speech topic, how would you evaluate your class on such psychological dimen-

of a bone before injury by using either a CAT scan or a magnetic resonance imaging system. For example, if the right forearm is broken, doctors use a mirror image of the left forearm to figure out how the implant should be shaped. With our Play-Doh machine, the various shape molds are included in the box. But the image for Plasti-Bone is created through "rapid prototyping"—basically, a 3-D printer. The machine prints a plastic or ceramic material—called a graft or template—into the shape specified by the 3-D image data sent by the computer. The *Plain Dealer* of July 3, 2003, reveals that rapid prototyping machines squeeze out complex shapes, extruding a thin thread from a nozzle that weaves back and forth under computer control; layers of the resulting mesh stack to make a model, or part, which is then used as a scaffold into which human bone can regenerate. Admittedly, a little more complicated than our Play-Doh Fun Factory—but immensely more fascinating as well.

Now what makes Plasti-Bone so unique is the material. The *Times-Picayune* of August 19, 2003, explains that the base material for the scaffold is a polymer called polybutalyne terephthalate, or PBT, a chemical cousin to the plastic used for milk jugs. The only difference is that PBT is coated with calcium phosphate, which attaches to bone cells, allowing the structure to be absorbed by the body. Within a matter of months inside the body, the PBT-based Plasti-Bone begins to function, amazingly, just like a real bone.

Now, the Fifth Element's medical miracle was a lot of special effects—but how the Plasti-Bone process works and its medical benefits are almost as divine. At the moment, reconstructing crushed or severely damaged bones is a painstaking process, states the *New Scientist* of June 20, 2003. To bridge gaps, surgeons use scaffolds made of biocompatible materials and bone grafts taken from elsewhere in the body, with strength provided by steel pins. Unfortunately, explains the *Deseret Morning News* of Salt Lake City on July 21, 2003, these metallic inserts can't be absorbed by the body and must eventually be replaced. In fact, the 2004 *Navy Opportunity Forum* explains that with current implant materials, loss of strength occurs before substantial bone growth has taken place, and 20 percent failure is the norm. Plasti-Bone, however, works in quite a different way. The *News Illustrated* of August 17, 2003, describes the surgical implantation process: The damaged bone pieces are surgically removed and the sterilized computer-generated graft is implanted; the graft is glued into place with a ceramic paste that is harmless to the body yet strong enough to eliminate the need for support pins; then a cast is placed over the limb to keep it immobile. The result is a bone implant that surrounding natural bone slowly will grow into over the next four to six months. Not bad for a bone that, according to the previously

sions as willingness to listen, degree of favorableness to the topic, and knowledge? What two or three major adjustments to the speech as presented here would you make on the basis of your audience analysis?

Here the speaker continues with the explanation of Plasti-Bone by explaining what it consists of.

Here the speaker begins the second main point and explains the benefits and advantages of the Plasti-Bone process. The speaker succeeds in explaining the benefits of this process by neatly comparing it to the process that is currently widely used.

cited *New Scientist*, will take only an hour and a half to create.

But the speed of the Plasti-Bone process isn't all that's remarkable: The Scripps Howard News Service of July 21, 2003, states that the porous nature of the Plasti-Bone material allows blood flow through the healing area, while the material is tough enough to resist the corrosiveness of human blood. Eventually, the implant is "bioresorbed" and replaced with a completely natural bone. As University of Arizona orthopedics professor John Szivek states in the *Arizona Daily Star* of July 17, 2003, "Once it's dissolved, it's gone, and the body doesn't have to deal with it and the surgeon doesn't have to go back in to take it out." And, amazingly, Ranji Vaidyanathan, principle investigator at Advanced Ceramics Research, confirms in a personal interview on March 16, 2004, that the technology will cost patients an amount significantly less than current procedures, which range between $5,000 and $6,000.

In order to save the world, Bruce Willis and the Supreme Being had to overcome a devious villain and a big ball of evil matter. Though not as threatening, Plasti-Bone's future has its own share of obstacles—but its ending promises to be equally supreme. Unfortunately, Plasti-Bone's arrival on the market could take a little time. *Biotech Week* of July 9, 2003, explains that only tissue cultures and animals have been used to test the new material. But as Vaidyanathan states in the previously cited *Dallas Medical Journal*, in tests rats with Plasti-Bone have been up and running just a few weeks after implantation. The product currently is awaiting approval of safety from the U.S. Food and Drug Administration to begin human testing, and as a result, the product will probably not be seen on the market for a few years.

After approval, though, Plasti-Bone's potential makes it a possible fifth element in its own right. In addition to the half a million bone graft surgeries each year, the Dr. Joseph F. Smith Medical Library website, last accessed and updated on March 12, 2004, reveals that 65,000 amputations are performed annually in the United States, with a long rehabilitation process, and that the average infection rate is 15 percent. According to the *Engineer* of May 30, 2003, Plasti-Bone holds the promise to improve recovery time and minimize infections rates for patients. Consider American climber Aron Ralston, who—according to *People Yearbook* magazine of 2004—and just about every major magazine and newspaper in May of last year—amputated his own arm after a thousand-pound boulder fell on him during an expedition in Colorado. Even though the probability of being crushed by a huge boulder is low, had Plasti-Bone been available, Ralston might have had the opportunity to "grow" his natural arm back without resorting to the

The speaker continues here with another advantage of Plasti-Bone, namely that it's porous and resistant to corrosion and that ultimately it is replaced with natural bone.

Notice this brief qualification of the credentials of the person whose testimony is used here.

The speaker here begins the third main point of the speech—the limitations and problems associated with the process.

If you were giving this speech to your class, what kinds of audience responses might you expect? What might you do to deal effectively with these responses?

Throughout this speech you'll find a number of references to websites effectively woven into the fabric of the speech. You don't have to give the URLs of websites you cite in your speeches, but you probably should have them ready just in case someone asks a question or would like to access the site.

current prosthetic arm that he now uses. And in a press release from the Office of Naval Research on June 12, 2003, this medical innovation offers significant benefits to bones damaged by cancer. According to the American Cancer Society's publication *Cancer Facts and Figures 2004*, about 2,500 cases of cancer in the bones will be diagnosed this year, with about 1,300 deaths from these cancers expected. With Plasti-Bone, patients will be able to remove the cancerous bones—saving their bodies and their lives.

Thanks to Bruce Willis, Earth was once again saved from doom and destruction, and very soon damaged bones and limbs will offer the same thanks to Plasti-Bone. By examining what Plasti-Bone is, how it works and its benefits, and the limitations and future prospects of the process, while it is clear we are still a ways away from having cruise ships that take us to the depths of the universe or flying automobiles, the success of Plasti-Bone could soon have scientists of today actually living the life of the movies—and all they have to do is press "print."

Here the speaker returns to the introductory example of Bruce Willis and signals that the conclusion is coming. The speaker summarizes the speech by reiterating the three main points that were covered and ends by again referring back to the movie talked about in the introduction.

5 Using Supporting Materials and Presentation Aids

Why Read This Chapter?

It will contribute to your public speaking success by helping you to:

❖ select supporting materials (such as examples and statistics) to make your speech come alive in the minds of the audience—to maintain their interest and attention, clarify complex ideas, and influence their attitudes and beliefs

❖ develop interesting and appropriate presentation aids, including PowerPoint presentations, to further inform and persuade—aids that contribute to your achieving your speech purpose

> "He or she is greatest who contributes the greatest original practical example."
>
> —Walt Whitman

This chapter will begin by examining the various types of supporting materials and explaining how to use them most effectively: examples, narratives, testimony, and statistics. Next we will turn to presentation aids and their effective use.

As you begin to collect your speech materials, keep in mind the complex issue of plagiarism. Because of the importance of this topic, a special box explaining the nature of plagiarism and, especially, ways to avoid it is presented on pages 100–101.

USING TECHNOLOGY

To supplement the discussion of plagiarism presented here, if you have access, visit Research Navigator (www.researchnavigator. com) and read the section on "Understanding and Avoiding Plagiarism" available under the "Research Process" tab.

Supporting Materials

Supporting materials are a vital part of an effective public speech; they add concreteness, help maintain interest and attention, and provide vital information and persuasive appeal. In this section we cover examples, narration, testimony, and statistics. In the next section we consider a special kind of support, the presentation aid. For additional forms of support, see Table 5.1 on page 109.

Examples

Examples are specific instances that are explained in varying degrees of detail. A relatively brief specific instance is referred to as an example; a longer and more detailed example is referred to as an illustration; and an example told in story-like form is referred to as a narative, as discussed in the next section. In using examples, keep in mind that their function is to make your ideas vivid and easily understood; examples are not ends in themselves. Make them only as long as necessary to ensure that your purpose is achieved.

Use examples when you want to make an abstract idea concrete. Specific examples can make the audience see what you mean when you talk about such abstract concepts as "persecution," "denial of freedom," "love," or "friendship." Your examples also encourage listeners to see *your* mental pictures of these concepts rather than seeing their own. In a speech on free speech and song lyrics, Sam Brownback (1998, p. 454), a U.S. senator from Kansas, uses some pretty powerful examples to make his point:

> Women are objectified, often in the most obscene and degrading ways. Songs such as Prodigy's single "Smack My Bitch Up" or "Don't Trust a Bitch" by the group "Mo Thugs" encourage animosity and even violence towards women. The alternative group Nine Inch Nails enjoyed both critical and commercial success with their song "Big Man with a Gun" which describes forcing a woman into oral sex and shooting her in the head at pointblank range.
>
> Shock-rock bands such as "Marilyn Manson" or "Cannibal Corpse" go ever further, with lyrics describing violence, rape, and torture. Consider just a few song titles by the group "Cannibal Corpse," "Orgasm by Torture," or "Stripped, Raped and Strangled." As their titles indicate, the lyrics to these songs celebrate hideous crimes against women.

Use relevant examples. Make sure your example is directly relevant to the proposition you want it to support, and make its relationship with your assertion explicit. Remember that although this relationship is clear to you (because you've constructed the speech), the audience is going to hear your speech only

PLAGIARISM

What is plagiarism?

The word *plagiarism* refers to the process of passing off the work (ideas, words, illustrations) of others as your own. Understand that plagiarism is not the act of using another's ideas—we all do that. It is using another's ideas without acknowledging that they are the ideas of this other person; it is passing off the ideas as if they were yours.

Plagiarism exists on a continuum, ranging from representing as your own an entire term paper or speech written by someone else to using a quotation or research finding without citing the author. Plagiarism also can include getting help from a friend without acknowledging this assistance.

In some cultures—especially collectivist cultures (cultures that emphasize the group and mutual cooperation, such as Korea, Japan, and China)—teamwork is strongly encouraged. Students are encouraged to help other students with their work. In the United States and in many other individualist cultures (cultures that emphasize individuality and competitiveness), teamwork without acknowledgment is considered plagiarism.

In U.S. colleges and universities, plagiarism is a serious violation of the rules of academic honesty and can bring serious penalties, sometimes even expulsion. And it's interesting to note that instructors are mobilizing and are educating themselves in techniques for detecting plagiarism. Further, as with all crimes, ignorance of the law is not an acceptable defense against charges of plagiarism. This last point is especially important, because many people plagiarize through a lack of information as to what does and what does not constitute plagiarism.

Why is plagiarism unacceptable?

Here are just a few reasons why plagiarism is wrong.

- *Plagiarism is a violation of another's intellectual property rights. Much as it would be unfair to take another person's watch without permission, it's unfair to take another person's ideas without acknowledging that you did it.*
- *You're in college to develop your own ideas and your own ways of expressing them; plagiarism defeats this fundamental purpose.*
- *Evaluations (everything from grades in school to promotions in the workplace) assume that what you present as your work is in fact your work.*

How can a person avoid plagiarism?

A few guidelines will help you avoid plagiarism.

Let's start with the easy part. You do not have to, and should not, cite sources for common knowledge—information that is readily available in numerous sources and is not likely to be disputed. For example, the population of Thailand, the amendments to the U.S. Constitution, the actions of the United Nations, or the way the heart pumps blood all are widely available knowledge, and you would not cite the almanac or the political science text from which you got this information. On the other hand, if you were talking about the attitudes of people from Thailand or the reasons the constitutional amendments were adopted, then you would need to cite your sources, because this information is not common knowledge and may well be disputed.

For information that is not common knowledge, you need to acknowledge your source. Three simple rules will help you avoid even the suggestion of plagiarism:

1. *Acknowledge the source of any ideas you present that are not your own.* If you learned of an idea in your history course, then cite the history instructor or the textbook. If you read an idea in an article, then cite the article.

2. *Acknowledge the words of another.* It's obvious what to do when you're quoting another person exactly; then of course, you need to cite the person you're quoting. You also should cite the person even when you paraphrase his or her words, because you are still using the other person's ideas. When paraphrases need to be credited may not always be clear, so some of the plagiarism websites established by different universities include exercises and extended examples; see, for example, Indiana University's site at www.indiana.edu/~uts/wts/plagiarism.html or Purdue University's at http://owl.english.purdue.edu/handouts/print/reseach/r-plagiar.html. The same is true when you use the organizational structure of another person; just say, for example, "I'm following the line of reasoning proposed by James McCroskey in his discussion of apprehension."

3. *Acknowledge help from others.* If your roommate gave you examples or ideas or helped you style your speech, acknowledge the help. For example, notice how some of the award-winning speeches that are reprinted as models in this book give credit to the speakers' speech coaches.

once. Show the audience exactly how your example relates to the assertion or concept you're explaining. Here for example, New York's Mayor Rudolph Giuliani, in his address to the United Nations after the World Trade Center attack of September 11, 2001, gave relevant examples to support his proposition that we are a land of immigrants and must continue to be so (http://www.washingtonpost.com/wp-srv/nation/specials/attached/transcripts/giulianitext_100101.html):

> New York City was built by immigrants and it will remain the greatest city in the world so long as we continue to renew ourselves with and benefit from the energizing spirit from new people coming here to create a better future for themselves and their families. Come to Flushing, Queens, where immigrants from many lands have created a vibrant, vital commercial and residential community. Their children challenge and astonish us in our public school classrooms every day. Similarly, you can see growing and dynamic immigrant communities in every borough of our city: Russians in Brighton Beach, West Indians in Crown Heights, Dominicans in Washington Heights, the new wave of Irish in the Bronx, and Koreans in Willow Brook on Staten Island.

Distinguish between real and hypothetical examples. Don't try to foist a hypothetical example on the audience as a real one. If they recognize it, they'll resent your attempt to fool them. Use phraseology such as the following to let the audience know when you're using a hypothetical example:

◆ We could imagine a situation such as . . .

◆ I think an ideal friend would be someone who . . .

◆ A hypothetical example of this type of friendship would be like . . .

If the example is real, let the audience know this as well. Help the audience to see what you want them to see with such statements as "A situation such as this occurred recently; it involved . . ." or "I have a friend who . . ." or simply "An actual example of this was reported when . . . ."

Narration

Narratives, or stories, are often useful as supporting materials in a speech. Narration gives the audience what it wants: a good story. It helps you maintain attention, because listeners automatically seem to perk up when a story is told. If your narrative is a personal story, then it's likely that it will increase your credibility and show you as a real person. Listeners like to know about speakers, and the personal narrative meets this desire. Notice how you remember the little stories that celebrities tell during television interviews.

The main value of narration is that it allows you to bring an abstract concept down to specifics. For example, to illustrate the dangers of greed, you might retell the fable of the man and woman who killed the goose that laid the golden egg: Thinking that they'd get all the gold at once, they lost the very thing that could have made them rich. To illustrate determination, you might tell the story of any of numerous great people who rose to prominence against the odds.

Freeality.com

(www.freeality.com)
Visit freeality.com and browse through some of the available resources. Record those that might be of special value when you are collecting supporting materials for your speeches as well as for your other courses.

Narratives may be of different types, and each type serves a somewhat different purpose. Following Clella Jaffe (2001) we distinguish three general types of narrative: explanatory, exemplary, and persuasive.

1. **Explanatory narratives** explain the way things are. The biblical book of Genesis, for example, explains the development of the world.
2. **Exemplary narratives** provide examples of excellence to follow or admire. The stories of the lives of saints and martyrs are exemplary narratives, as are the Horatio Alger type of success stories. Similarly, many motivational speakers, such as Richard Simmons and Marianne Williamson, often include exemplary narratives in their speeches and will tell their own story of being out of shape or unenlightened.
3. **Persuasive narratives** try to strengthen or change beliefs and attitudes. When Sally Struthers tells us of the plight of the starving children, she's using a persuasive narrative. The parables in religious writings are persuasive narratives that urge readers to lead life in a particular way.

Keep narratives short and few in number. In most cases, one or possibly two narratives are sufficient in a short five- to seven-minute speech. Be sure you don't get carried away and elaborate more than necessary, especially if the narrative is personal.

Maintain a reasonable chronological order. Events happen in time and are best recounted in a time sequence. Avoid shifting back and forth through time. Start at the beginning and end at the end.

Make explicit the connection between your story and the point you're making. Be sure that the audience will see the connection between the story and the purpose of your speech. If they don't, you risk not only losing the effectiveness of the story but also losing your listeners' attention as they try to figure out why you told that story.

Testimony

The term *testimony* refers to the opinions of experts or to the accounts of witnesses. Testimony helps to amplify your speech by adding a note of authority to your arguments.

Testimony may, therefore, be used in either of two ways. First, you may be concerned the opinions, beliefs, predictions, or values of some authority or expert. For example, you might want to state an economist's predictions concerning inflation and depression, or you might want to support your analysis by citing an art critic's evaluation of a painting or art movement. Second, you may want to use the testimony of an eyewitness to some event or situation. For example, you might cite the testimony of someone who saw an accident, of a person who spent two years in a maximum-security prison, or of a person who had a particular operation.

Stress the competence of the person. Whether the person is an expert or a witness, make sure the audience sees this person as competent. To cite the predictions of a world-famous economist of whom your audience has never heard will mean little, so first explain the person's

"The proposal sounds good. Of course, I still have to run it by my people over at the Psychic Friends Network."

❖ **CONSIDER** the one person (living or dead, available for an interview or unavailable) you would most like to interview for your next speech. What questions would you ask? What impact do you think this type of testimony would have on your audience?

competence. To prepare the audience to accept what this person says, you might introduce the testimony by saying, for example:

> This prediction comes from the world's leading economist, who has successfully predicted all major finacial trends over the past 20 years.

Stress the unbiased nature of the testimony. If the audience perceives the testimony to be biased—whether or not it really is—it will have little effect. You want to check out the biases of a witness so that you may present accurate information. But you also want to make the audience see that the testimony is in fact unbiased. You might say something like this:

> Researchers and testers at *Consumer Reports,* none of whom have any vested interest in the products examined, found wide differences in car safety. Let's look at some of these findings. In the October 2001 issue, for example, . . .

Stress the recency of the testimony. When you say, for example, "General Bailey, who was interviewed last week in the *Washington Post,* noted that the United States has twice the military power of any other world power," you show your audience that your information is recent and up-to-date.

Suggestions for orally citing the sources of testimony or any other evidence are given in the Research Links in Chapter 8.

Statistics

Let's say you want to show that the salaries for home health aides should be raised, that defendants' level of wealth influences their likelihood of criminal conviction,

---

☐
☐
☐ A CASE OF *Ethics*
☐
☐
☐ **Misleading Your Audience**
☐
☐ In a speech on false arrests, you develop a hypothetical story about a college
☐ student who gets arrested and is held unlawfully in custody for several days.
☐ As you rehearse this story, you realize it would be a lot more convincing if
☐ the audience were allowed to think that the story was true and that the per-
☐ son was you. Actually, you wouldn't be *saying* that it was you or that it wasn't
☐ you; you'd just be allowing the audience to form their own conclusions.
☐
☐ *Would it be ethical to allow your audience to believe that this incident*
☐ *actually happened to you? If not, what might you do to present this*
☐ *persuasive illustration ethically? More generally, what ethical guides should*
☐ *a speaker follow in using hypothetical examples?*

RESEARCH *Link*

E-Mail and Listservs

E-mail may prove useful in public speaking in several ways. For example, you can write to specific people who may be experts in the topic you're researching. Internet services are now making it quite easy to locate a person's e-mail address. Try, for example, the Netscape people page—which you can access from Netscape's home page or by going to http://guide.netscape.com/guide/people.html—or Yahoo's directory (http://www.yahoo.com/search/people/) and their links to numerous other directories such as Yahoo's white pages (http://www.yahoo.com/Reference/White-Pages/). Another useful people search tool is http://www.procd.com/hl/direct.htm. Also, try the sites that specialize in e-mail addresses such as Four11 (http://www.four11.com), WhoWhere? (http://www.whowhere.com), and Switchboard (www.switchboard.com). Four11 also provides a directory of regular telephone numbers as well as special directories for government personnel and for celebrities.

Of course, e-mail (and instant messaging) also can let you communicate with your instructor, with other students, or with those who share your topic interests, who often can help you secure needed information and helpful feedback.

You also can join a mailing list or listserv that focuses on the topic you're researching and learn from the collective insights of all members. In joining a listserv remember to lurk before contributing; get a feel for the group and for the types of messages they send. Read the FAQs to avoid asking questions that have already been answered.

Some classes are set up with listservs, chat rooms, or message boards so that you can communicate with everyone else through e-mail. For example, such a group would enable you to distribute an audience analysis questionnaire to see what your audience knew about your topic or what their attitudes were about a variety of issues. The sample questionnaires discussed in Chapter 4 would be excellent to distribute via e-mail and would enable you to find out what you need to know about your audience to adjust your speech to them. Or you could set up a critique group with a few others from your class to provide mutual feedback on speeches or outlines, or even to offer moral support. Such a group also would be helpful for people who wanted to ask questions or to try out an idea before presenting it in the actual speech.

Research Activity. Using your favorite search engines, search for any newsletters or discussion groups that deal with your speech topic or with any of your other academic pursuits this semester. What can you find that's of interest?

or that significant numbers of people get their news from the Internet. To support these types of propositions, you might use *statistics*—summary figures that help you communicate the important characteristic of a complex set of numbers. For most speeches and most audiences, simple statistics work best; for example, measures of central tendency, correlation, and percentages. Let's consider each of these types of simple statistics as they might be used in public speaking.

Measures of central tendency describe the general pattern in a group of numbers. Two useful measures are the *mean* (the arithmetic average of a set of numbers) and the *median* (the middle score; 50 percent of the cases fall above and 50 percent fall below it). When you use a mean or a median, make it clear why this figure is important. For example, if you wanted to show that home health aides should be paid higher salaries, you might compare the mean salaries of home health aides to the means for other health care workers or for workers who have similar education and responsibilities. Once this difference was clear to your audience, you could relate it to your thesis and demonstrate that this salary difference, this gap between the two means, was significant and needed to be redressed.

USING TECHNOLOGY

Excellent aids for using and interpreting statistics may be found at http://nilesonline.com/stats/. This site will assist you in understanding and evaluating research results and in using statistics in your own speeches.

Measures of correlation describe how closely two or more things are related. For example, there's a high positive correlation between smoking and lung cancer; smokers have a much greater incidence of lung cancer than non-smokers. Correlations also can be negative. For example, there's a negative correlation between the amount of money you have and the likelihood that you'll be convicted of a crime. As your money increases, the likelihood of criminal conviction decreases. When using correlations make clear to your audience why the relationship between, say, money and criminal conviction is important and how this correlation relates to the proposition you want to support.

Percentages allow you to express a score as a portion of 100. That is, saying that 78 percent of people favor coffee over tea means that 78 out of every 100 people favor coffee over tea. Percentages are useful if you want to show, for example, the amount of a proposed tuition increase, the growth of cable television over the past 10 years, or various divorce rates in different parts of the world. In some cases you might want to compare percentages. For example, you might compare the percentage tuition increase at your school to the national average increase or to the increase for schools similar to yours. To illustrate the growth of the Internet as a news medium, you might note that in 1995 only 4 percent of Americans got their news from the Internet but that by 2002 that percentage had grown to 40 percent.

In using statistics, consider these few suggestions:

◆ Make sure the statistics are clear to your audience—remember, your listeners will hear these figures only once. Round off figures so they're easy to comprehend and retain. Instead of saying, "The median income of workers in this city is $49,347," consider saying "around $50,000" or "just under $50,000."

◆ Make the significance of the statistics explicit. For example, if you state that the average home health aide makes less than $30,000 a year, you need to relate that figure to the salaries of other workers and to your proposition that home health aide salaries need to be increased. Don't just rattle off statistics; use them to support a specific proposition.

◆ Reinforce your oral presentation of statistics with some type of presentation aid—perhaps a graph or a chart. Numbers are difficult to grasp and remember if they're presented without visual reinforcement. When possible, let your audience see *and* hear the numbers; they'll be better able to see their relevance and remember them.

◆ Use statistics in moderation. Most listeners' capacity for numerical data presented in a speech is limited, so use statistics sparingly.

Presentation Aids

As you plan your speech, consider using some kind of presentation aid—a visual or auditory means for clarifying ideas. Ask yourself how you can visually present what you want your audience to remember. For example, if you want your audience to see the growing impact of the sales tax, consider showing them a chart of rising sales tax over the last 10 years. If you want them to see that Brand A is superior to Brand X, consider showing them a comparison chart identifying the su-

CRITICAL LISTENING/THINKING *Link*

Listening to Research Findings for Currency, Fairness, and Sufficiency

When you hear research reported by a speaker, or when you collect research yourself, listen to it critically for currency, fairness, and sufficiency.

Currency. Generally, the more recent the material, the more useful it will be. With some topics—for example, unemployment statistics, developments in AIDS research, or tuition costs—the currency of the information is crucial to its usefulness. To ensure currency check important figures in a recent almanac (for example, the *Information Please Almanac* is available online in full text at www.infoplease.com); in a newspaper (most major newspapers have free online access, generally following the format www.nameofpaper.com, or access the *New York Times* through Research Navigator at www.ablongman.com), or at a frequently updated Internet source such as Federal Statistics at www.fedstats.gov.

Fairness. Does the author of the material present the information objectively, or is there a bias favoring one position? Reviewing a range of research in the area will help you see how other experts view the issue. It will also enable you to see if this author's view of the situation takes into consideration all sides of the issue and if these sides are represented fairly and accurately.

Sufficiency. Is the collected information sufficient to prove the case? The opinion of one dietitian is insufficient to support the usefulness of a particular diet; statistics on tuition increases at five private colleges are insufficient to illustrate national trends in tuition costs.

Getting Critical. Read one of the speeches in this text or on the text's Companion Website (www.ablongman.com/devito). How current, fair, and sufficient do you feel the research information is? In what ways might the information have been made more current, less biased, and/or more sufficient?

periority of Brand A. Presentation aids are not added frills—they are integral parts of your speech. They will help you gain your listeners' attention and maintain their interest; they can add clarity, reinforce your message, and contribute to your credibility and confidence (Sojourner & Wogalter, 1998).

◆ **Presentation aids help you gain attention and maintain interest.** Americans today have grown up on multimedia entertainment. We are used to it and we enjoy it. It's not surprising, then, that we as members of an audience appreciate it when a speaker makes use of visuals or audio aids. We perk up when the speaker says, "I want you to look at this chart showing the employment picture for the next five years" or "Listen to the vocal range in this voice." Presentation aids provide variety in what we see and hear, something audiences will appreciate and respond to favorably.

◆ **Presentation aids add clarity.** Let's say you want to illustrate the growth of the cable television industry in the United States over the last 20 years. You could say, for example, "In 1977 there were 12 million subscribers, in 1982 there were 29 million subscribers, in 1987 there were . . . ." But this gets boring pretty fast. Further, the numbers you want the audience to appreciate are difficult to retain in memory,

"It sort of makes you stop and think, doesn't it."

© The New Yorker Collection 2003 Sam Gross from cartoonbank.com. All Rights Reserved.

so by the time you get to the current figures, they've already forgotten the previous figures. As a result, the very growth that you want your audience to see is likely to get lost. It would be much easier to communicate this kind of information in a bar graph.

◆ **Presentation aids reinforce your message.** Presentation aids help ensure that your listeners understand and remember what you've said. Visual aids help you present the same information in two different ways: verbally, as audience members hear you explain the aid, and visually, as they see the chart, map, or model. The same is true with audio aids. For example, you might discuss the range of vocal variety and at the same time provide recorded samples. This kind of one-two punch helps the audience understand your ideas more clearly and remember them more accurately.

◆ **Presentation aids contribute to credibility and confidence.** If you use appropriate and professional-looking presentation aids—and shortly we'll see how you can do this—your listeners are likely to see you as a hightly credible speaker, as someone who cares enough about both them and the topic to do this "extra" work. When listeners view you as credible and have confidence in you, they're more likely to listen carefully and to believe what you have to say.

◆ **Presentation aids help reduce apprehension.** When you have to concentrate on coordinating your speech with your presentation aids, you're less likely to focus on yourself—and self-focus often increases apprehension. In addition, the movement involved in using presentation aids relaxes many speakers, and with greater relaxation comes greater confidence.

Types of Presentation Aids

Among the presentation aids you have available are the object itself, models of the object, graphs, word charts, maps, people, photographs and illustrations.

The Object Itself

As a general rule (to which there are many exceptions), the best presentation aid is the object itself. Bring it to your speech if you can. Notice that infomercials sell their products not only by talking about them but by showing them to potential buyers. You see what George Foreman's Lean Mean Grilling Machine looks like and how it works. You see the jewelry, the clothing, the new mop from a wide variety of angles and in varied settings.

Models

Models—replicas of the actual object—are useful for a variety of purposes. For example, if you wanted to explain complex structures such as the human hearing or vocal mechanism, the brain, or the structure of DNA, a model would prove useful. Models help to clarify relative size, position, and how each part interacts with each other part.

Graphs

Graph are useful for showing differences over time, clarifying how a whole is divided into parts, and comparing different amounts or sizes. Figure 5.1 on page 110 shows a variety of graphs that can be drawn freehand or generated with the graphics capabilities of any word-processing or presentation software. Keep

TABLE 5.1	Additional Forms of Support
FORM OF SUPPORT	**SUGGESTIONS FOR USING**
Quotations add spice and wit as well as authority to your speeches.	Quotations work best when they are short, easily comprehensible to the audience, and related directly to the point you're trying to make.
Definitions clarify and explain the meaning of specific terms and are especially helpful when you are introducing complex terminology or when you wish to provide a particular perspective on a subject.	Use definitions only when they are needed; don't define terms the audience already understands. And make sure the definitions add clarity and that they themselves don't need definition.
Comparisons and contrasts help to clarify two ideas, events, or concepts.	Focus on the most crucial similarities and differences. Avoid itemizing comparisons and contrasts; they often create confusion when they are drawn in too much detail. If necessary, supplement your oral discussion with a visual aid such as a chart or a slide that identifies the most crucial information.
Simple statement of fact or of a series of facts often helps to illustrate or support a statement or position.	Make sure that the fact or series of facts is clearly linked to the proposition it supports. When using a series of facts, state the facts' connection with the proposition when introducing the facts and again after you complete the list of facts.
Repetition (repeating your idea in the same words at strategic places throughout your speech) and *restatement* (repeating your idea in different words) are helpful in adding clarity and emphasis to your ideas and will help you compensate for the inevitable lapses in audience attention.	Avoid unnecessary repetition and restatement; be careful that you don't bore the audience by repeating what they already understand.

USING TECHNOLOGY

First, select a quotation that you can use in your next speech from the offerings at (http://www.bartleby.com, http://www.yahoo.com/Reference/Quotations/, or http://us.imdb.com/. Second, search for information on the author of the quotation (see some of the biography sites mentioned in the Research Link on p. 250). Third, integrate the quotation and some relevant information about the author into your speech.

your graphs as simple as possible. In a pie chart, for example, don't have more than five segments. Similarly, in a bar graph limit the number of items to five or fewer. As in the graphs shown in Figure 5.1, be sure you add the legend, the labels, and the numerical values you wish to emphasize.

Word Charts

Word Charts (which also can contain numbers and even graphics) are useful for identifying the key points in one of your propositions or in your entire speech—in the order in which you cover them, of course. Slide 5 in Figure 5.2 on page 117 is a good example of a simple word chart that identifies the major topics discussed in the speech. Or you could use a word chart to identify the steps in a process—for example, the steps in programming a VCR, in dealing with sexual harassment, or in downloading the latest version of Netscape. Another use of charts is to show information you want your audience to write down. Emergency phone numbers, addresses, or titles of recommended books and websites are examples of the type of information that listeners will welcome in written form.

DEVELOPING STRATEGIES

Graphs. Gabrielle has asked your advice on the kinds of graphs that would be most effective in illustrating each of the following propositions: (1) School violence is increasing; (2) inflation is under control; (3) the divorce rate is increasing. What suggestions can you offer Gabrielle?

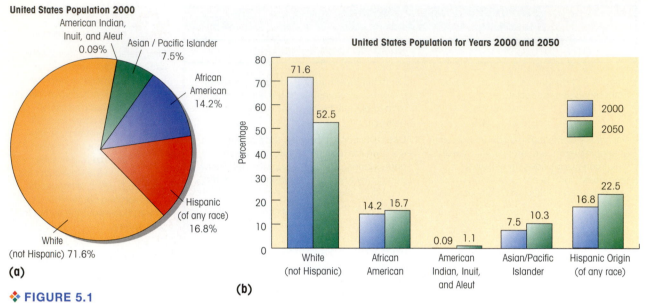

United States Population 2000

(a)

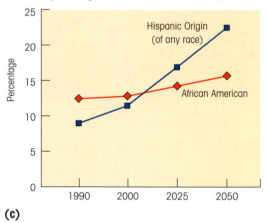

(b)

(c)

❖ **FIGURE 5.1**

Assorted Graphs

A pie chart (a) shows the cultural diversity in the population of the United States as recorded by the 2000 census. The pie chart is particularly helpful for showing relative proportions. However, the pie chart is useful only when the total equals 100 percent. A bar graph (b) illustrates the population figures for 2000 (the same figures that appear in the pie chart) and projected figures for the year 2050. This graph enables you to see at a glance the changes in population that are predicted in the five groups over the next 50 years. A line graph (c) illustrates the percentages of African Americans and Hispanics for four different periods: the actual percentages as recorded in 1990 and 2000 and the projected percentages for the years 2025 and 2050. This graph not only enables you to see the changes over the years but also enables you to compare the relative changes of the two groups. Additional groups could have been added but the graph would become increasingly difficult to read. The figures for all graphs are taken from the Census Bureau website (www.census.gov).

Maps

If you want to illustrate the locations of geographic features such as cities, lakes, rivers, or mountain ranges, maps will obviously prove useful as presentation aids. But maps also can be used for illustrating population densities, immigration patterns, world literacy rates, varied economic conditions, the spread of diseases, and hundreds of other issues you may wish to examine in your speeches. A wide variety of maps may be downloaded from the Internet and then shown as slides or transparencies. Chances are you'll find a map on the Internet for exactly the purpose you need.

People

If you want to demonstrate the muscles of the body, different voice patterns, skin complexions, or hairstyles, consider using people as your aids. Aside from the obvious assistance they provide in demonstrating their muscles or voice

USING TECHNOLOGY

Visit a website devoted to maps. Two exceptional ones are the Library of Congress map collections (http://memory.LOC.gov/ammem/gmdhtml/gmdhtml.html) or the University of Texas map collection (www.lib.utexas.edu/libs/pcl/map_collection/map_collection.html). How might you use maps in your future speeches?

qualities, people help to secure and maintain the attention and interest of the audience.

Photographs and Illustrations

Types of trees, styles of art, kinds of exercise machines, or the horrors of war—all can be made more meaningful with photographs and illustrations. The best way to use these images is to convert them to slides. If you're using a computer presentation program (explained below) and you have a scanner, you can import your photos into your presentation with relative ease. Or you can have them converted to slides. Once they're converted to slides, you'll be able to project them in a format large enough for everyone to see clearly. You'll also be able to point to specific parts of the photo as you explain the devastation of war or the fine art of combining colors and textures. You can also convert the images to transparencies to use with a transparency projector, although you'll lose some of the detail that you would have in slides. Another way to use photographs and illustrations is to have them enlarged to a size large enough for the entire audience to see. Try to mount these on cardboard so they'll be easier to handle. Most copy shops provide this service—though the cost may be considerable, especially if you have several photos to convert and you need them in color. Nevertheless, this is an option that may prove useful in some situations. Passing pictures around the room is generally a bad idea. Listeners will wait for the pictures to circulate to them, will wonder what the pictures contain, and will miss a great deal of your speech in the interim.

❖ **CONSIDER** how you might integrate any of the numerous kinds of maps into your next speech. How might maps have been used in speeches you've heard so far in this class?

The Media of Presentation Aids

Once you've decided on the type of presentation aid you'll use, you need to decide on the medium you'll use to present it. Acquire skill in using both low-tech (the chalkboard or flip chart) and high-tech (the computerized slide show) resources. In this way you'll be able to select your presentation aids from the wide array available, choosing on the basis of the message you want to communicate and the audience to whom you'll be speaking.

Chalkboards

The easiest aid to use, though not necessarily the most effective, is the chalkboard. The chalkboard may be used effectively to record key terms or important definitions or even to outline the general structure of your speech. Don't use it when you can present the same information with a preplanned chart or model. It takes too long to write out anything substantial. If you do write on the board, be careful not to turn your back to the audience, even briefly. In just a few moments, you can easily lose the attention of your audience.

Chartboards

Chartboards are useful when you have one or two relatively simple graphs or charts that you want to display during your speech. If you want to display them for several minutes, be sure you have a way of holding them up. For example, bring

CRITICAL LISTENING/THINKING *Link*

Listening to Galileo and the Ghosts

"Galileo and the Ghosts" is a technique for seeing a topic or problem through the eyes of a particular group of people (von Oech, 1990; Higgins, 1994; DeVito, 1996). In "ghost-thinking" (analogous to ghostwriting), you select a team of four to eight "people"—for example, historical figures like Galileo or Aristotle, fictional figures like Wonder Woman or James Bond, or persons from other cultures or of a different gender or affectional orientation. Selecting people who are very different from you and from one another will increase the chances that different perspectives will be raised.

You pose a question or problem and then ask yourself how each of these ghostthinkers would answer your question or solve your problem, allowing yourself to listen to what each has to say. Of course, you're really listening to yourself—but to yourself acting in the role of another person. The technique forces you to step outside of your normal role and to consider the perspective of someone totally different from you.

Getting Critical. Select a ghostthinking team and ask for suggestions for speech topics or for supporting materials for your next speech.

masking tape if you intend to secure them to the chalkboard, or enlist the aid of an audience member to hold them up. Black lettering on a white board generally works best; it provides the best contrast and is the easiest for people to read.

Flip Charts

Flip charts, large pads of paper (usually about 24 × 24 inches) mounted on a stand or easel, can be used to record a variety of information that you reveal by flipping the pages as you deliver your speech. For example, if you were to discuss the various departments in an organization, you might have the key points relating to each department on a separate page of your flip chart. As you discussed the advertising department, you'd show the chart relevant to the advertising department. When you moved on to discuss the personnel department, you'd flip to the chart dealing with personnel.

Slides and Transparencies

Slides and transparencies are helpful in showing a series of visuals that may be of very different types; for example, photographs, illustrations, charts, or tables. The slides can easily be created with many of the popular computer programs (see "Computer-Assisted Presentations," p. 116). To produce actual 35mm slides, you'll need considerable lead time, so be sure to build this into your preparation time. If you don't have access to slide projectors or if you don't have the lead time needed to construct the slides, consider the somewhat less sophisticated transparencies. You can create your visual in any of the word processing or spreadsheet programs you normally use, then use a laser printer or copier to produce the transparencies.

Audio and Videotapes, CDs, and DVDs

Consider the value of using music or recorded speech to support your ideas—and also to add a note of variety that will set your speeches apart from most other speakers' presentations. A speech on advertising jingles, music styles, or dialects would be greatly helped, for example, by having actual samples for the audience to hear on CDs or tapes. Similarly, videotapes can serve a variety of purposes in public speaking. Basically, you have two options with videotapes. First, you can tape a scene from a film or television show with your VCR and show it at the appropriate time in your speech. Thus, for example, you might videotape examples of sexism in television sitcoms, violence on television talk shows, or types of families depicted in feature films and show these excerpts during your speech. Second, you can create your own video with a simple camcorder. Videos are best used in small doses; in many instances just 20- or 30-second excerpts will prove sufficient to illustrate your point. Avoid using long excerpts that will divert attention from your message; just use enough video to help your listeners understand the point you're making, not to rehash the plot of the entire movie.

Handouts

Handouts, printed materials that you distribute to the audience, are especially helpful in explaining complex material and also in providing listeners with a permanent record of some aspect of your speech. Handouts are also useful for presenting complex information that you want your audience to refer to throughout the speech. Handouts encourage listeners to take notes—especially if you leave enough white space or even provide a specific place for notes—which keeps them actively involved in your presentation. A variety of handouts can be easily prepared with many of the computer presentation packages that we'll consider in the last section of this chapter. Of course, if you distribute your handouts during your speech, you run the risk of your listeners reading the handout and not concentrating on your speech. On the other hand, if they're getting the information you want to communicate—even if it's primarily from the handout—that isn't too bad. You can encourage listeners to listen to you when you want them to and to look at the handout when you want them to by simply telling them "Look at the graph on the top of page 2 of the handout; it summarizes recent census figures on immigration" or "We'll get back to the handout in a minute; now, however, I want to direct your attention to this next slide" (or "to the second argument"). If you distribute your handouts at the end of the speech, they won't interfere with your presentation but may never get read. After all, listeners might reason, they heard the speech, so why bother going through the handout as well? To counteract this very natural tendency, you might include additional material on your handout and mention this to your audience when you distribute it.

Once you have the idea you want to present in an aid and you know the medium you want to use, direct your attention to preparing and using the aid so it best serves your purpose.

Preparing Presentation Aids

In preparing presentation aids make sure that they add clarity to your speech, that they're appealing to the listeners, and that they're culturally sensitive.

Clarity is the most important consideration. To achieve clarity, follow a few simple suggestions:

1. Use colors that will make your message instantly clear; light colors on dark backgrounds or dark colors on light backgrounds provide the best contrast

and seem to work best for most purposes. Be careful of using yellow, which is often difficult to see, especially if there's glare from the sun.

2. Use direct phrases (not complete sentences); use bullets to highlight your points or your support (see Figure 5.2, pp. 117–118). Just as you phrase your propositions in parallel style, phrase your bullets in parallel style; in many cases this involves using the same part of speech (for example, all nouns or all infinitive phrases). And make sure that any connection between a graphic and its meaning is immediately clear. If it isn't, explain it.

3. Use the aid to highlight a few essential points; don't clutter it with too much information. Four bullets on a slide or chart, for example, are as much information as you should include.

4. Use typefaces that can easily be read from all parts of the room.

5. Give the aid a title—a general heading for the slide, chart, or transparency—to further guide your listeners' attention and focus.

Presentation aids should be appealing to your audience. At the same time, although presentation aids should be attractive enough to engage the attention of the audience, they should not be so attractive that they're distracting. The almost nude body draped across a car may be effective in selling underwear, but would probably detract if your objective is to explain the profit-and-loss statement of General Motors.

Presentation aids should be culturally sensitive. Be sure, too, that they can easily be interpreted by people from other cultures. Just as what you say will be interpreted within a cultural framework, so too will the symbols and colors you use in your aid. For example, when speaking to international audiences, you need to use universal symbols or explain those that are not universal. Be careful, that icons don't reveal an ethnocentric bias (see the following self-test). For example, using the American dollar sign to symbolize "wealth" might be quite logical in your public speaking class but might be interpreted as ethnocentric if used with an audience of international visitors.

Test YOURSELF

Can You Distinguish Universal from Culture-Specific Icons?

Here are 10 icons and the meaning intended to be conveyed. Write U if you think the symbol is universal throughout all cultures and CS if you think the symbol is culture specific. What reasons do you have for each of your choices?

_____ **1.** ♀ ♂ , female/male

_____ **2.** 🎓 , college/college graduation

_____ **3.** 🌎 , the world

_____ **4.** 💡 , good idea/creativity

_____ **5.** ♿ , wheelchair access

_____ **6.** , good luck

_____ **7.** , fire

_____ **8.** , atom/atomic/radioactive

_____ **9.** , no smoking

_____ **10.** , music

❖ **HOW DID YOU DO?** Icons 1, 5, 7, 8, 9, and 10 would be considered universal; the others are specific to different cultures. Icon 3 is universal in depicting the world, although the positioning of the globe (with North America at the center, for example) would be considered culture-specific.

❖ **WHAT WILL YOU DO?** Before selecting icons or any visual representations, ask yourself how your audience will interpret them. This will be especially important if you're from a culture very different from the majority of your audience. As always, when in doubt, find out; ask questions.

Using Presentation Aids

Your presentation aids will be more effective if you follow a few simple guidelines.

◆ _Know your aids intimately._ Be sure you know in what order your aids are to be presented and how you plan to introduce them. Know exactly what goes where and when. Do all your rehearsal with your presentation aids so that you'll be able to introduce and use them smoothly and effectively.

◆ _Test the presentation aids before giving your speech._ Be certain that aids can be seen easily from all parts of the room. Don't underestimate, for example, how large lettering must be to be seen by those in the back of the room.

◆ _Rehearse your speech with the presentation aids incorporated into the presentation._ Practice your actual movements with the aids you'll use. If you're going to use a chart, how will you use it? Will it stand by itself? Will you ask another student to hold it for you?

◆ _Integrate presentation aids into your speech seamlessly._ Just as a verbal example should flow naturally into the text and seem an integral part of the speech, so should the presentation aid. It should appear not as an afterthought but as an essential part of the speech.

◆ _Avoid talking to your aid._ Talk to your audience at all times. Know your aids so well that you can point to what you want without breaking eye contact with your audience.

◆ _Use your aid only when it's relevant._ Show each aid when you want the audience to concentrate on it and then remove it. If you don't remove it, the audience's attention may remain focused on the visual when you want them to focus on what you'll be saying next.

Computer-Assisted Presentations

There are a variety of presentation software packages available; PowerPoint, Corel Presentations, and Lotus Freelance are among the most popular and are very similar in what they do and how they do it. Figure 5.2 on pages 117–118 illustrates what a set of slides might look like; the slides are built around the speech outline discussed in Chapter 6 (pp. 156–159) and were constructed in PowerPoint. As you review this figure, try to visualize how you'd use a slide show to present your next speech.

Computer-assisted presentations possess all of the advantages of aids already noted (for example, maintaining interest and attention, adding clarity, and reinforcing your message). In addition, however, they have advantages all their own, so many in fact that you'll want to seriously consider using this technology in your speeches. They give your speech a professional, up-to-date look, and in the process add to your credibility. They show you're prepared and care about your topic and audience.

Ways of Using Presentation Software

Presentation software enables you to produce a variety of aids. For example, you can construct your slides on your computer and then have 35mm slides developed from disk. To do this you'd have to have a slide printer or send them out (you can do this via modem) to a lab specializing in converting electronic files into 35mm slides. You may have access to a slide printer at your school, so do check first. Similarly, your local office supply store or photocopy shop may have exactly the services you need.

Or you can create your slides and then show them on your computer screen. If you're speaking to a very small group, it may be possible to have your listeners gather around your computer as you speak. With larger audiences, however, you'll need a computer projector or LCD projection panel. Assuming you have a properly equipped computer in the classroom, you can copy your entire presentation to a floppy, Zip, or CD-ROM disk and bring it with you the day of the speech.

Computer presentation software also enables you to print out a variety of materials: slides, slides with speaker's notes, slides with room for listener notes, and outlines of your speech. You can print out your complete set of slides to distribute to your listeners. Or you can print out a select portion of the slides, or even slides that you didn't have time to cover in your speech but which you'd like your audience to look at later. The most popular options are to print out two, three, or up to six slides per page. The two-slide option provides for easy readability and would be especially useful for slides of tables or graphs that you want to present to your listeners in an easy-to-read size. The three-slide option is probably the most widely used; it prints the three slides down the left side of the page with space for listeners to write notes on the right. This option is useful if you want to interact with your audience and you want them to take notes as you're speaking. Naturally, you'd distribute this handout before you begin your speech, during your introduction, or perhaps at that point when you want your listeners to begin taking notes. A sample three-slide printout with space for notes is provided in Figure 5.3 on page 119. If you want to provide listeners with a complete set of slides, then the six-slide option may be the most appropriate. You can, of course, also print out any selection of slides you wish—perhaps only those slides that contain graphs, or perhaps only those slides that summarize your talk.

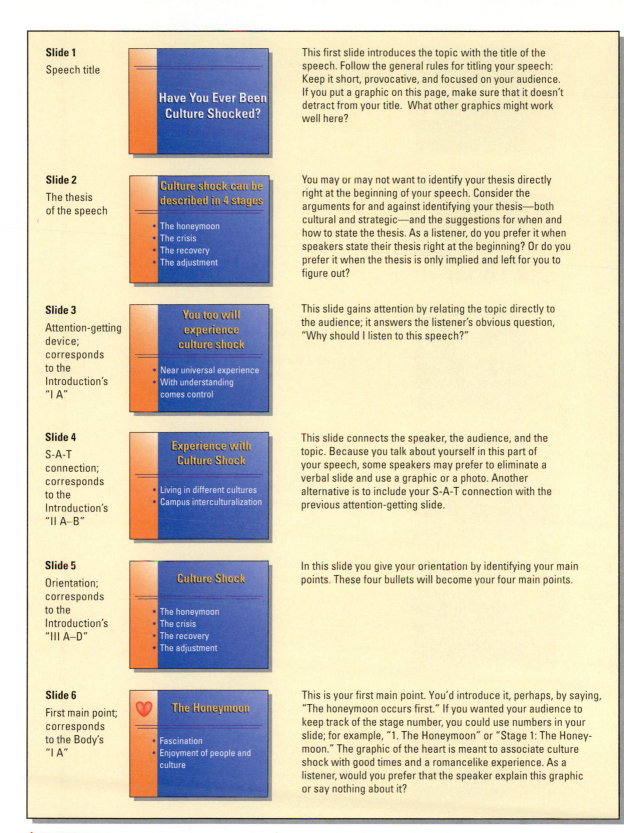

Slide 1

Speech title

Have You Ever Been Culture Shocked?

This first slide introduces the topic with the title of the speech. Follow the general rules for titling your speech: Keep it short, provocative, and focused on your audience. If you put a graphic on this page, make sure that it doesn't detract from your title. What other graphics might work well here?

Slide 2

The thesis of the speech

Culture shock can be described in 4 stages
- The honeymoon
- The crisis
- The recovery
- The adjustment

You may or may not want to identify your thesis directly right at the beginning of your speech. Consider the arguments for and against identifying your thesis—both cultural and strategic—and the suggestions for when and how to state the thesis. As a listener, do you prefer it when speakers state their thesis right at the beginning? Or do you prefer it when the thesis is only implied and left for you to figure out?

Slide 3

Attention-getting device; corresponds to the Introduction's "I A"

You too will experience culture shock
- Near universal experience
- With understanding comes control

This slide gains attention by relating the topic directly to the audience; it answers the listener's obvious question, "Why should I listen to this speech?"

Slide 4

S-A-T connection; corresponds to the Introduction's "II A–B"

Experience with Culture Shock
- Living in different cultures
- Campus interculturalization

This slide connects the speaker, the audience, and the topic. Because you talk about yourself in this part of your speech, some speakers may prefer to eliminate a verbal slide and use a graphic or a photo. Another alternative is to include your S-A-T connection with the previous attention-getting slide.

Slide 5

Orientation; corresponds to the Introduction's "III A–D"

Culture Shock
- The honeymoon
- The crisis
- The recovery
- The adjustment

In this slide you give your orientation by identifying your main points. These four bullets will become your four main points.

Slide 6

First main point; corresponds to the Body's "I A"

The Honeymoon
- Fascination
- Enjoyment of people and culture

This is your first main point. You'd introduce it, perhaps, by saying, "The honeymoon occurs first." If you wanted your audience to keep track of the stage number, you could use numbers in your slide; for example, "1. The Honeymoon" or "Stage 1: The Honeymoon." The graphic of the heart is meant to associate culture shock with good times and a romancelike experience. As a listener, would you prefer that the speaker explain this graphic or say nothing about it?

❖ **FIGURE 5.2**
A Slide Show

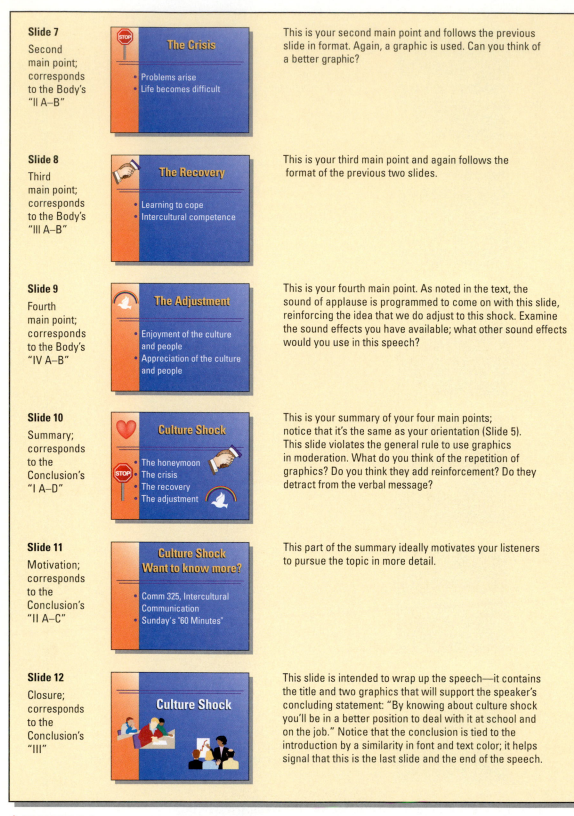

Slide 7

Second main point; corresponds to the Body's "II A–B"

This is your second main point and follows the previous slide in format. Again, a graphic is used. Can you think of a better graphic?

Slide 8

Third main point; corresponds to the Body's "III A–B"

This is your third main point and again follows the format of the previous two slides.

Slide 9

Fourth main point; corresponds to the Body's "IV A–B"

This is your fourth main point. As noted in the text, the sound of applause is programmed to come on with this slide, reinforcing the idea that we do adjust to this shock. Examine the sound effects you have available; what other sound effects would you use in this speech?

Slide 10

Summary; corresponds to the Conclusion's "I A–D"

This is your summary of your four main points; notice that it's the same as your orientation (Slide 5). This slide violates the general rule to use graphics in moderation. What do you think of the repetition of graphics? Do you think they add reinforcement? Do they detract from the verbal message?

Slide 11

Motivation; corresponds to the Conclusion's "II A–C"

This part of the summary ideally motivates your listeners to pursue the topic in more detail.

Slide 12

Closure; corresponds to the Conclusion's "III"

This slide is intended to wrap up the speech—it contains the title and two graphics that will support the speaker's concluding statement: "By knowing about culture shock you'll be in a better position to deal with it at school and on the job." Notice that the conclusion is tied to the introduction by a similarity in font and text color; it helps signal that this is the last slide and the end of the speech.

❖ **FIGURE 5.2**
A Slide Show (*continued*)

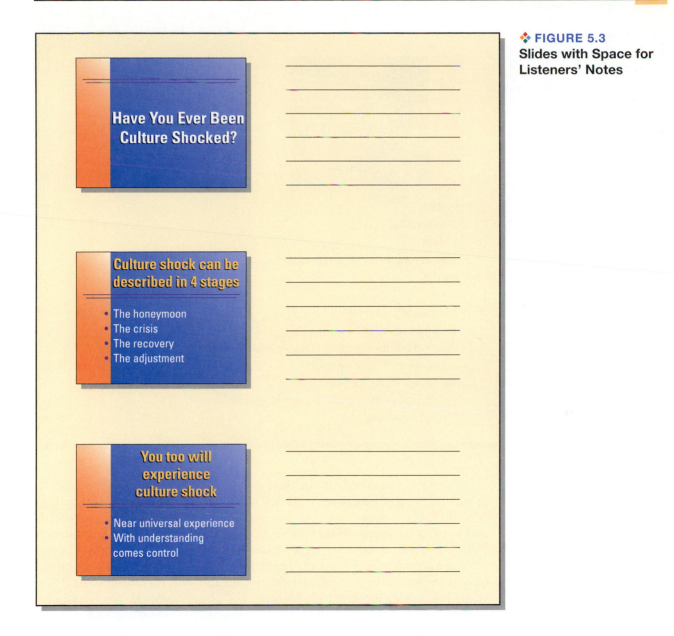

❖ FIGURE 5.3
**Slides with Space for
Listeners' Notes**

Another useful option is to print out your slides with your speaker's notes. That way you'll have your slides and any notes you may find useful—examples you want to use, statistics that would be difficult to memorize, quotations that you want to read to your audience, delivery notes, or anything that you care to record. The audience will see the slides but not your speaker's notes. It's generally best to record these notes in outline form, with key words rather than complete sentences. This will prevent you from falling into the trap of reading your speech. A sample printout showing a slide plus speaker's notes is provided in Figure 5.4 on page 120.

Another useful printout is the speech outline. Two outline options are generally available: the collapsed outline and the full outline. The collapsed outline contains only the slide titles and is useful if you want to give your audience a general outline of your talk. If you want your listeners to fill in the outline with

❖ **FIGURE 5.4**
Slide and Speaker's Notes

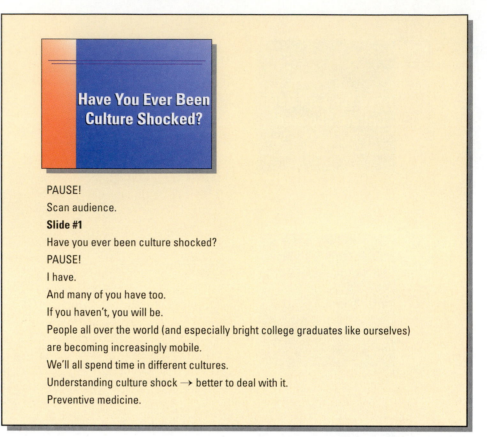

the information you'll talk about, then you can distribute this collapsed outline at the beginning of your speech. The full outline option (slide titles plus bullets) is useful for providing listeners with a relatively complete record of your speech and also can be helpful if you cover a lot of technical information that listeners will have to refer to later. You might hand out a full outline, for example, if you were giving a speech on company health care or pension plans and you wanted to provide your listeners with detailed information on each option, or if you wanted to provide listeners with addresses and phone numbers. You would normally distribute a full outline not at the beginning but after your speech, because such a complete outline could lead your audience to read and not to listen.

You also can create overhead transparencies from your computer slides. You can make these on many printers and most copiers simply by just substituting transparency paper for regular paper.

Suggestions for Designing Slides

Your slides will be more effective and easier to produce if you follow these few simple suggestions.

Use the templates provided by your software. Allow the design wizards to help you choose colors and typefaces. These are created by professional designers who are experts at blending colors, fonts, and designs into clear and appealing renderings.

Use consistent typeface, size, and color. Give each item in your outline that has the same level head (for example, all your main ponts) the same typeface, size, and color throughout your presentation. This will help your listeners follow the organization of your speech. If you're using one of the predesigned templates, this will be done for you. Notice that this principle is followed for the most part in the slides in Figure 5.2—but that it's broken in one case, to connect the introduction and the conclusion, which are in a color and typeface different from the rest of the slides. Another way you might break this rule would be to design your internal summaries a bit differently from the regular slides to signal their unique function. This would prove especially effective in a long speech with frequent internal summaries.

Be brief. Your objective in designing these slides is to provide the audience with key words and ideas that will reinforce what you're saying in your speech; you don't want your audience to spend their time reading rather than listening. Generally, put one complete thought on a slide, and don't try to put too many words on one slide.

Use colors for contrast. Remember that many people have difficulty distinguishing red from green; so if you want to distinguish ideas, it is probably best to avoid this color pairing. Similarly, if you're going to print out your slides in shades of gray, make sure the tones you choose provide clear contrasts. Also, be careful that you don't choose colors that recall holidays that have nothing to do with your speech—for example, red and green for Christmas or orange and black for Halloween. Remember, too, the cultural attitudes toward different colors; for example, among some Asian cultures, writing a person's name in red means that the person has died.

Use only the visuals that you really need. Presentation software packages make inserting visuals so easy that they sometimes encourage us to include too many visuals. Most presentation packages provide a variety of graphic pictures, animated graphics, photos, and videos that are useful for a wide variety of speeches. With the help of a scanner, you can add your own visuals. Use visuals when you have room on the slide and when the visual is directly related to your speech thesis and purpose. In deciding whether or not to include a visual, ask yourself if the inclusion of this graph or photo will advance the purpose of your speech. If it does, use it; if it doesn't, don't. In using video, remember that this takes up enormous amounts of disk space. If you're using floppy disks, a several-second video can take up a full third or even half of your disk; if you're using Zip disks or CDs, you'll have enough room for just about any speech you'd make.

Use transitions. As verbal transitions help you move from one part of your speech to another, presentational transitions help you move from one slide to the next with the desired effect—blinds folding from left or right or top or bottom or a quick fade. Don't try to use too many different transitions in the same talk; it will detract attention from what you're saying. Generally, it's best to use the same type of transition for all your slides in a single presentation. You might vary this a bit by, say, having the last slide introduced by a somewhat different transition, but any more variation is likely to work against the listeners focusing on your message. In choosing transitions select one that is consistent with your speech purpose; don't use a perky black-and-yellow checkerboard transition in a speech on child abuse, for example.

Use sound effects. A wide variety of sound effects come with most presentation packages, ranging from individual sounds—foghorn, drumroll, or doorbell—to excerpts from musical compositions. Consider using sound effects in your speech, perhaps especially with your transitions. But, as with graphics, go

? DEVELOPING STRATEGIES

Slide Show Speech. Bree is planning a slide show, but she worries that using slides for each topic she discusses might be too much repetition. And yet she wants to gain some experience in using this technique, as it's widely used in the field she hopes to enter. What advice would you give Bree to help her make sure that her slides complement rather than repeat what she says?

USING TECHNOLOGY

Take one of the many available PowerPoint tutorials available online. A tutorial may be on your own computer or may be available somewhere on your campus. If not, visit one of the excellent tutorials from different colleges that are available to everyone; for example, visit Florida Gulf Coast University at www.fgcu.edu/support/office2000/ppt/, the University of Rhode Island at http://einstein.cs.uri.edu/tutorials/csc101/powerpoint/ppt.html, or Indiana–Purdue University at http://www.science.iupui.edu/SAC98/pp.htm. If you need more advanced training, try the University of Northern Iowa's advanced tutorial at http://www.uni.edu/plschool/index/profdev/briley/Advppt.html. What can you add to the information presented here?

easy; overdoing it is sure to make your speech seem carelessly put together. In the slides in Figure 5.2, I programmed "applause" (one of the readily available sound effects) to come on as Slide 9—the adjustment—comes on. As you read through the slides in Figure 5.2, you may find additional places where sound could be used effectively.

Use build effects. Help focus your listeners' attention with "build effects," the ways in which your bulleted items come onto the screen. For example, you can have each bulleted phrase fly from the top of the screen into its position; with the next mouse click, the second bullet flies into position. Or you can have your bullets slide in from right to left or from left to right. And so on.

Use charts and tables when appropriate. Charts and tables are useful, as noted above, when you want to communicate complex information that would take too much text for one slide to explain. You have a tremendous variety of chart and graph types (for example, pie, bar, and cumulative charts) and tables to choose from. If you're using presentation software that's part of a suite, then you'll find it especially easy to import files from your word processor or spread sheet. Also, consider the advantages of chart animation. Just as you can display bullets as you discuss each one, you can display the chart in parts so as to focus the audience's attention on exactly the part of the chart you want. You can achieve somewhat the same effect with transparencies by covering up the chart and gradually revealing the parts you want the audience to focus on.

Anticipate questions. If there's a question-and-answer period following your speech, consider preparing a few extra slides for your responses to questions

you anticipate being asked. Then, when someone asks you a predicted question, you can say: "I anticipated that someone might ask that question; it raises an important issue. The data are presented in this chart." You can then show the slide and explain it more fully. This is surely going the extra mile, but it can help make your speech a real standout.

Use the spell-check. You don't want professional-looking slides with misspellings; it can ruin your credibility and seriously damage the impact of your speech.

Anticipate technical problems. If you're planning to use a slide show, for example, consider what you'd do if the slide projector didn't arrive on time or the electricity didn't work. A useful backup procedure is to have transparencies and handouts ready just in case something goes wrong.

❖ **CONSIDER** the common errors that slide-show speakers make. What two or three principles would you urge slide-show speakers to follow?

Rehearsing with Presentation Programs

Presentation packages are especially helpful for rehearsing your speech and timing it precisely. As you rehearse, the computer program records the time you spend on each slide and will display that time under each slide; it will also record the presentation's total time. You can see these times at the bottom of each slide in a variety of views, but they won't appear in the printed handout, such as appears in Figure 5.3. You can use these times to program each slide so you can set it to run automatically. Or you can use the times to see if you're devoting the amount of time to each of your ideas that you want to. If you find in your rehearsal that your speech is too long, these times can help you see which parts may be taking up too much time and perhaps could be shortened.

Presentation software allows you to rehearse individually selected slides as many times as you want. But make sure that you go through the speech from beginning to end toward the end of your rehearsal period. Rehearse with this system as long as improvements result; when you find that rehearsal no longer serves any useful purpose, then stop.

Another type of rehearsal is to check out the equipment available in the room you'll speak in and its compatibility with the presentation software you're using. If possible, rehearse with the very equipment you'll have available on the day you're speaking. In this way you can adjust to or remedy any incompatibilities or idiosyncrasies that are identified. Further, you'll discover how long it takes to warm up the slide projector or to load PowerPoint, so you won't have to use up your speaking time for these preparations.

The Actual Presentation

During your actual presentation you can control your slides with your mouse, advancing to the next one or going back to a previously shown slide. If you set the package to run automatically, programming each slide to be shown for its own particular amount of time, you won't be tied to the mouse—assuming you don't have a remote mouse. You can, of course, override the automatic programming by simply clicking your mouse either to advance or to go back to a slide that perhaps went by too quickly.

As with any presentation aid, make sure that you focus on the audience; don't allow the computer or the slides to get in the way of your immediate contact with the audience.

Consider using the pen—actually your mouse—to write on and highlight certain words or figures in the slides. But it's not very easy to write with a mouse, so don't plan on writing very much. Underlining or circling key terms and figures is probably the best use for the pen.

Summary of Concepts and Skills

In this chapter we focused on supporting materials, especially examples, narration, testimony, and statistics, and we considered presentation aids at some length.

Supporting Materials

Examples are specific instances explained in varying degrees of detail and are most effective when:

◆ They are used to explain a concept rather than as ends in themselves.

◆ The relationship between the concept and the example is explicit.

◆ The distinction between a real and a hypothetical example is clear.

Narratives, stories that illustrate an assertion, can be explanatory, exemplary, or persuasive; they can be presented in first or third person and are most effective when they are:

◆ Relatively short

◆ Presented in chronological order

◆ Clearly connected to the speech purpose

◆ Presented in climax order

Testimony is the opinion of an expert or witness that is often used to lend authority or otherwise amplify assertions. Testimony is especially effective when:

- The competence of the authority is stressed.
- The unbiased nature of the testimony is stressed.
- The recency of the observation or opinion is stressed.

Statistics are figures that summarize the important characteristics of an otherwise complex set of numbers and are especially effective when they are:

- Clear
- Meaningful to the audience
- Connected to the proposition they support
- Visually and verbally reinforced
- Used in moderation

Presentation Aids

Common types of presentation aids are: the actual object, models, graphs, word charts, maps, people, and pictures and illustrations. Among the available media for presentation aids are the chalkboard, chartboards, flip charts, slide and transparency projections, audio and videotapes, and handouts.

In using presentation aids:

- Know your aids intimately.

- Test your aids before using them.
- Don't talk to your presentation aid.
- Use the aid when it's relevant.

Computer-assisted presentations offer a variety of advantages.

- Presentation software can provide great choice and flexibility; facilitate rehearsal and timing; facilitate the printing of handouts; and enable you to construct computer slide presentations, 35mm slides, handouts, and transparencies.

- In designing slides, consider using the templates provided. Aim for consistency in typeface, size, and color; seek brevity; and consider using color contrasts to emphasize your ideas. Use only the visuals you need; use transitions, sound effects, and build effects; employ charts and tables effectively consider preparing additional slides for anticipated questions; use the spell-check.

- Rehearse your speech with your presentation software, time your speech carefully, and make sure that you have all the needed equipment.

- During the actual presentation, make sure that your audience has enough but not too much time to spend on each slide, that your slides don't dominate the speech and obscure your speaker–audience contact, and that you use the pen when appropriate.

Vocabulary Quiz

Supporting Materials and Presentation Aids

Match the terms dealing with supporting materials with their definitions. Record the number of the definition next to the appropriate term.

_____ presentation software
_____ models
_____ flip chart
_____ illustration
_____ pie chart
_____ bullets
_____ narration
_____ testimony
_____ statistics
_____ restatement

1. A longer and more detailed example.
2. A story that allows the speaker to create a specific illustration of a general or abstract concept.
3. The opinions of experts or eyewitnesses.
4. Summary figures.
5. Large pad of paper, usually mounted on a stand.
6. Replicas of actual objects.
7. Short phrases that highlight the essential concepts in a speech.
8. Computer programs that enable speakers to present their ideas visually (and often with sound).
9. Repetition of an idea in different words.
10. Visual aid that enables the speaker to illustrate how some whole is divided into parts and the relative sizes of the various parts.

Web Explorations

Companion Website
www.ablongman.com/devito
Additional insight into presentation aids is provided in several items in the Companion Website's Chapter 5.

"Some Typefaces" (table) will help you select appropriate fonts for your PowerPoint slides. In addition, see "Color and Culture" (table) and the exercises "Analyzing Presentation Aids" and "Coloring Meanings."

Public Speaking Exercises

5.1 Amplifying Statements

Select one the following overly broad statements and amplify it, using at least three different methods of amplification. Because the purpose of this exercise is to provide greater insight into amplification forms and methods, you may, for this exercise, invent facts, figures, illustrations, examples, and the like.

1. Significant social contributions have been made by persons over 65.
2. The writer of this article is an authority.
3. Attitudes toward women in the workplace have changed over the last 20 years.
4. The college sounds ideal.
5. September 11, 2001, was a world-changing, life-changing event.
6. The athlete enjoyed a lavish lifestyle.

5.2 Critically Evaluating Testimony

If you were presenting testimony from one of the following "experts," how would you establish the person's qualifications so that your audience would accept what he or she said?

1. Nutritionist on the importance of a proper diet
2. Real estate agent advising to buy real estate now
3. Nurse on the nature of eating disorders
4. Pet store owner on how to feed your pet
5. Teacher on how to write a book

5.3 Analyzing Presentation Aids

Select a print advertisement and analyze the visuals. For purposes of this exercise, consider the text of the ad as the spoken speech and the visuals in the ad as the presentation aids for the speech.

1. What types of aids were used?
2. What functions did the presentation aids serve?
3. Were the aids clear?
4. Were they relevant?
5. Were the aids appealing?
6. Were the aids culturally sensitive?

5.4 Analyzing a Speech

In the following speech Matthew Sanchez presents a powerful argument against diplomatic immunity. Read the speech and respond to the questions in the margins.

DIPLOMATIC IMMUNITY UNJUSTIFIED

Matthew Sanchez

Imagine an evening outing: you and your two children decide to have a fun night out. You look up to your

Did the title grab your attention? Do you think it was effective for the speaker to reveal his purpose and thesis in the title?

rearview mirror to see a car slam into the back of your car—WHAM—killing your children. You survive the crash and so does the individual who rear-ended you. You are told by the police that the driver was drunk the night of the accident, but that no crimes applied to him. Murder, vehicular homicide, and driving under the influence of alcohol are just meaningless statements to this person.

According to the *USA Today* of June 4, 1996, "There are more than 18,000 of these individuals, not including their family members, who are immune to all law in the U.S." And the one thing that they have in common is that they are foreign diplomats.

What was once thought to be a great international resolution is quickly becoming a great international dilemma. Despite repeated derogatory reports about diplomatic immunity, UN policy officials fail to reform diplomatic international law.

Today, I would like to speak to all of you about why diplomatic immunity's current application is not justified.

First, we will examine the purpose of diplomatic immunity. Second, I will explain the problem that diplomatic immunity has created. And third, I will offer an amendment to diplomatic immunity.

First, we will examine the purpose of diplomatic immunity. According to the *U.S. Department of State Dispatch* on June 28, 1996, "Diplomatic immunity is defined as a principle of international foreign law in which certain foreign government officials are not subject to local courts and/or other authorities." Simply put, you do not have to obey the law if you are a foreign diplomat. This concept is derived from the premise that upon entering into another country, you may be unaware of their laws and societal norms. But the question arises, is it possible to be a foreign diplomat and at the same time be unaware of laws in other nations?

The Economist of October 13, 1996, gives us the answer to this question: "In 1961 the Vienna Convention of Consular Practices established most modern diplomatic relations, including the concept of diplomatic immunity. Today there are more than 160 nations including the U.S. who are members of these treaties. These treaties grant foreign diplomats and their families complete immunity to all aspects of Foreign Law in hopes of protecting them from unfair prosecution at the hands of a foreign court."

Now that we have examined the purpose of diplomatic immunity, let us look at the problems that diplomatic immunity has created. *Time* magazine of November 2, 1996, states that foreign diplomats living in New York City often refuse to pay their debts. This leaves little recourse for U.S. creditors since it is impossible to sue a foreign mission. *New York Magazine*

Did the speaker establish the relevance of the topic? If you were in the audience, would you be concerned about this topic?

How effective was the speaker's orientation?

Did the speaker establish an S–A–T (speaker–audience–topic) connection? How would you have done it?

Notice the transition from the first point (the purpose of diplomatic immunity) to the second point (the problems of diplomatic immunity). In what other ways might you have phrased this transition?

of the same month goes on to say that "Total estimated foreign diplomatic debt is between 5.3 and 7 million dollars." Take a moment, please, and imagine the adverse ramifications that a deficit of 7 million dollars would have on your city's budget. Where in the world is your city going to get that kind of money? Unfortunately the first place that local government goes to for money is our taxpayer dollars. Instead of building better parks, schools, and highways, our taxes will be spent on foreign diplomat debt. On January 17, 1997, ABC interviewed New York Mayor Rudolph Giuliani as to what he thought about diplomatic immunity and he had quite a bit to say. He poured out that the Russian Federation alone owes over 15,000 unpaid traffic violations to the city of New York. Furthermore, when one of his officers accosted a man about parking in front of a fire hydrant, the man responded by punching out the officer. After subduing the culprit and taking him to jail the police found out three things about him. First, that he was drunk, second that he was a diplomat, and third that because of diplomatic immunity nothing could be done to this criminal and he had to be released back out onto the streets of New York. In a current dispute, Friday April 18, 1997, carloads of diplomats from the Russian Embassy blocked in a moving van on a public street in Washington, D.C., that was transporting Russian artifacts from one museum to another. The diplomats parked one car in front of the van and one car in back of the van and did not move for days.

These are reasons enough that diplomatic immunity must be amended. But they are nothing compared to what CBS News states on January 17, 1997. In 1981 a British police woman was out patrolling her nightly route, when she was shot in the head by a Libyan sniper. This assassin also happened to be a member of the Libyan Embassy and was therefore immune to prosecution. Furthermore, Jud Aspen in the book *Diplomatic Crime* writes [that] after getting into an argument with a bartender, a Brazilian official then decided to leave, only to come back with a 45 caliber handgun and kill the bartender. He then fled the U.S. and because of diplomatic immunity's sanctions, nothing could be done to this cold-blooded murderer.

In yet another example, the son of the attaché from Ghana came to the U.S. in 1986 and raped his first victim. Since then he has caught onto his freedom from law in other nations and has raped over 16 other women in the New York area alone. New York Detective Pat Christenson said that after he released the handcuffs, the diplomat laughed in his face, laughed in the rape victim's face and then left the office. The victim asked the detective why her rapist was let go and he responded, "Ma'am, I am sorry; there is nothing I can do. He is the son of a diplomat."

Specific examples are essential to a speech topic like this. How would you have handled the examples? Would you have used fewer examples but developed them in more detail? Or, would you have used more examples but developed them in less detail?

On January 15, 1997, UPI stated "Second ranked Georgian Diplomat Gregory Makardze was allegedly under the influence of alcohol and when driving in a downtown Washington area, his car collided with a set of parked cars, killing 16-year-old Jovianna Waltrick." Joseph A. Thomasino, student of International Law at Johns Hopkins University, told me that unless Georgian President Eduard Shevardnadze decides to waive diplomatic immunity, we cannot sue this diplomat. Fortunately, Shevardnadze did waive diplomatic immunity in this case. However, Washington, D.C., *News Online* updated April 15, 1997, stated that Makardze pleaded not guilty. But realize relying on another country's goodwill to waive diplomatic immunity is not the solution, because the problem of diplomatic immunity still exists.

As citizens of the USA we should be appalled that a person foreign to our country can walk into our own backyard and get away with murder. But, we should also be embarrassed that on January 4, 1997, CNN stated that one of our own diplomats was in Russia in 1986 and while driving under the influence of alcohol killed a woman and her three children while they were peacefully walking alongside of the road.

As Julius Caesar once wrote, "The inviolability of diplomats is acknowledged by most civilized people, but there must be a limit. How do you protect, for example, people guilty of cold-blooded murder?"

I have defined the problems resulting from diplomatic immunity; now let us look at the solution. Moderate Exemption Directive Reform is the solution to diplomatic immunity, wherein foreign diplomats and their families remain immune to all aspects of foreign law, except for two: theft and the violation of safety of others. These two concepts are universal in nature. That means all 160 nations in the UN label them as crimes. So there is no confusion on the part of the diplomat for not knowing any better since his own country prosecutes these crimes. Mortimer J. Adler in the book *Six Great Ideas* states, "Justice is fairness; it is giving to each what he is due."

Diplomatic immunity is not just; it is not fair because it does not punish criminals. Moderate Exemption Directive Reform is just because it does punish criminals. It gives them what they are due. Therefore, your tax dollars are safe, because people not paying what they owe is a form of theft. And rapists like the son of the attaché from Ghana shall be put behind bars because when they violate the safety of another human being it is considered a crime.

So, let us recap. The original intent of diplomatic immunity was to protect diplomats from unfair prosecution in a foreign court. We have discovered that diplomatic immunity has long since gone out of control and that something must be done. The solution is to have

Notice how you pay especially close attention to the anecdotes. And notice, too, how much easier they are to follow than other parts of the speech. For example, you could probably repeat the anecdote about the moving van or about the rapist without any difficulty. But you'd probably have a hard time repeating the first major proposition of the speech. Which of these examples was the most compelling? Why?

How effective is this transition? Would it have been more effective to summarize both major propositions and then introduce the solution? In what other ways might you have phrased this transition?

How effective were the several quotations the speaker used? How did they contribute to the overall effectiveness of the speech?

Does the speaker succeed in convincing you that Moderate Exemption Directive Reform is an effective solution?

How effective is the speaker in summarizing the major points of the speech?

moderate exemption amend the way that diplomatic immunity is currently administered.

In closing, diplomatic immunity has proven itself to be retrogressive to a foreign diplomat's mission and abusive to a hosting country and its citizens. Nolan Kirkpatrick, in the book *Living Issues in Ethics,* states, "Moral choices reside upon an understanding of Justice." Making diplomats accountable for their actions will, in turn, enable them to become better decision makers. But for now, your brother's murder, your close friend's sexual assault, and worst of all, those children whom you love so much that lost their lives to a drunk driver one night could all end up victims to the international criminal otherwise known as the foreign diplomat.

Sanchez, M. (1997). Diplomatic immunity unjustified. In L. G. Schnoor (Ed.), *Winning orations of the Interstate Oratorical Association* (pp. 19–21). Mankato, MN: Interstate Oratorical Association.

How would you evaluate the speaker's use of research materials? How effectively did the speaker integrate the materials into the oral presentation?

How effective is the speaker's closing? How would you have closed the speech?

6 Organizing Your Speech

Why Read This Chapter?

It will enable you to organize your speech by helping you to:

❖ put your ideas in proper relation to one another so that your audience can more easily follow, understand, and remember what you say

❖ see the speech as a whole so you can decide if the parts of the speech are appropriately developed and connected to each other with clear transitions

❖ select an organizing pattern that best fits your topic, purpose, thesis, and audience

❖ develop outlines of your speech that will help you rehearse and deliver your speech

> If you're going to play the game properly, you'd better know every rule.
>
> —Barbara Jordan

Organizing your speech will yield several significant benefits. One such benefit is that the organizing process will help guide your speech preparation; once you can see the speech as a whole (even in a preliminary and unfinished form), you'll be able to see what needs further developing and what needs paring down. Organizing your speech will also help you achieve your purpose: Whether your aim is to inform or to persuade, your audience will be better able to follow your thinking if you present it in an organized pattern. They'll also find an organized speech easier to remember. Lastly, when you present a clearly organized speech, you enhance your own credibility; your audience is more likely to see you as a competent person and as someone who is truly concerned with achieving your purpose.

In this chapter we first look at organizing the body of the speech, in which you set forth your main ideas. Once you've accomplished this, you can move on to develop your introduction, your conclusion, and the transitions that hold the pieces of the speech together. As you are developing these parts of the speech, you'll also be preparing outlines of your speech.

The Body of the Speech

Begin organizing your speech by selecting and wording your main points. Let's look first at how you can select and word your main points and then at how you can logically arrange them.

Select and Word Your Main Points

Chapter 3's discussion of the thesis showed how you can develop your main points or propositions by asking strategic questions. To see how this works in detail, imagine that you're giving a speech to a group of high school students on the values of a college education. Your thesis is: "A college education is valuable." You then ask, "Why is it valuable?" From this question you generate your main points. Your first step may be to brainstorm this question and generate as many answers as possible without evaluating them. You may come up with answers such as the following:

1. It helps you get a good job.
2. It increases your earning potential.
3. It gives you greater job mobility.
4. It helps you secure more creative work.
5. It helps you to appreciate the arts more fully.
6. It helps you to understand an extremely complex world.
7. It helps you understand different cultures.
8. It allows you to avoid taking a regular job for a few years.
9. It helps you meet lots of people and make new friends.
10. It helps you increase your personal effectiveness.

There are, of course, other possibilities, but for purposes of illustration, these 10 possible main points will suffice. But not all 10 are equally valuable or relevant to your audience, so you should look over the list to see how to make it shorter and more meaningful. Try these suggestions:

1. Eliminate those points that seem least important to your thesis. On this basis you might want to eliminate number 8, as this seems least consistent with your intended emphasis on the positive values of college.

2. Combine those points that have a common focus. Notice, for example, that the first four points all center on the values of college in terms of jobs. You might, therefore, consider grouping these four items into one proposition:

A college education helps you get a good job.

This point might become a main point, which you could develop by defining what you mean by a "good job." This main point or proposition and its elaboration might look like this:

I. A college education helps you get a good job.

   A. College graduates earn higher salaries.

   B. College graduates enter more creative jobs.

   C. College graduates have greater job mobility.

Note that A, B, and C are all aspects or subdivisions of a "good job."

3. Select those points that are most relevant or interesting to your audience. On this basis you might eliminate numbers 5 and 7, on the assumption that the audience will not see learning about the arts or different cultures as exciting or valuable at the present time. You also might decide that high school students would be more interested in increasing personal effectiveness, so you might select number 10 for inclusion as a second main point:

A college education increases your personal effectiveness.

Earlier you developed the subordinate points in your first proposition (the A, B, and C of I above) by defining more clearly what you meant by a "good job." Follow the same process here by defining what you mean by "personal effectiveness." It might look something like this:

II. A college education helps increase your personal effectiveness.

   A. A college education helps you improve your ability to communicate.

   B. A college education helps you acquire the skills for learning how to think.

   C. A college education helps you acquire coping skills.

Follow this same general procedure to develop the subheadings under A, B, and C. For example, point A might be divided into two major subheads:

   A. A college education helps improve your ability to communicate.

      1. College improves your writing skills.

      2. College improves your speech skills.

Develop points B and C in essentially the same way, defining more clearly (in B) what you mean by "learning how to think" and (in C) what you mean by "coping skills."

4. Use two, three, or four main points. For your class speeches, which will generally range from 5 to 15 minutes, use two, three, or four main points. Too many main points will result in a speech that's confusing, contains too much information, and proves difficult to remember.

5. **Word each of your main points in the same (parallel) style.** Statements phrased in parallel style share the same grammatical structure and many of the same words. Julius Caesar's famous "I came, I saw, I conquered" is a good example of parallel style: Each statement is structured the same way, using the pronoun *I* plus a verb in the past tense. Phrase points labeled with roman numerals in parallel style. Likewise, phrase points labeled with capital letters and subordinate to the same roman numeral (for example, A, B, and C under point I or A, B, and C under point II) in a similar style. Parallel styling will help the audience follow and remember your speech. Notice in the following that the first outline is more difficult to understand than the second, which is phrased in parallel style.

Not This	This
The mass media serve four functions.	The mass media serve four functions.
I. The media entertain.	I. The media entertain.
II. The media function to inform their audiences.	II. The media inform.
III. Creating ties of union is a major media function.	III. The media create ties of union.
IV. The conferral of status is a function of all media.	IV. The media confer status.

6. **Develop your main points so they're separate and discrete.** Don't allow your main points to overlap each other. Each section labeled with a roman numeral should be a separate entity.

Not This	This
I. Color and style are important in clothing selection.	I. Color is important in clothing selection.
	II. Style is important in clothing selection.

Organize Your Main Points

Once you've identified the main points you wish to include in your speech, organize them into a clearly identified organizational pattern. For online assistance with organizing your speech see the accompanying website (www.ablongman.com/pubspeak). Here we consider some of the more useful patterns.

Topical Pattern

When your topic conveniently divides itself into subdivisions, each of which is clear and approximately equal in importance, the topical pattern is useful. A speech on important cities of the world might be organized into a topical pattern, as might speeches on problems facing the college graduate, great works of literature, the world's major religions, and the like. For example, the topical pattern would be an obvious choice for organizing a speech on the powers of the government. The topic itself divides into three parts: legislative, executive, and judicial. Similarly, a talk on the major stock exchanges might follow a topical pattern; a sample outline might look like this:

"It's confusing when everybody has a pointer."

The Stock Exchanges

I. The New York Stock Exchange focuses on the largest companies.

II. The Nasdaq focuses largely on technology companies.

III. The American Stock Exchange focuses on the smaller companies.

Here is another example: a speech on ways to help people who have disabilities, in which each subtopic is treated about equally. The speaker is seeking to persuade the audience to devote some of their leisure time to helping people with disabilities, using the thesis "Leisure time can be well used to help people." Asking a strategic question of this thesis—"How can leisure time be spent helping people with disabilities?" or "What can we do to help people with disabilities?"—lets the speaker easily identify the main points:

Helping Others

I. Read for the blind.

   A. Read to a blind student.

   B. Make a recording of a textbook for blind students.

II. Run errands for students confined to wheelchairs.

III. Type for students who can't use their hands.

Temporal Pattern

With the temporal (time) pattern, your speech is organized chronologically into two, three, or four major parts—beginning with the past and working up to the present or the future, or beginning with the present or the future and working back to the past. The temporal (sometimes called "chronological") pattern is especially appropriate for informative speeches in which you wish to describe events or processes that occur over time. It's also useful when you wish to tell a story, demonstrate how something works, or explain how to do something. Most historical topics lend themselves to organization by time. The events leading up to the Civil War, the steps toward a college education, or the history of writing would all be appropriate for temporal patterning. A speech on television scheduling might be organized in a temporal pattern, covering each of the four television periods in a time sequence beginning with the morning and ending with the evening—a pattern everyone would find easy to follow.

Television Scheduling

I. Morning television gets people ready for their day.

II. Daytime television keeps the homebound viewer company.

III. Prime-time television appeals to everyone.

IV. Late-night television appeals to adults.

Spatial Pattern

Organizing your main points on the basis of space is useful when you wish to describe objects or places—progressing from top to bottom, from left to right, from inside to outside, or from east to west, for example. The structure of a place, an object, or even an animal is easily placed into a spatial pattern. You might describe the layout of a hospital, school, or skyscraper, or perhaps even the skeletal structure of a dinosaur, with a spatial pattern of organization. Here's an example of an outline describing the structure of the traditional textbook using a spatial pattern:

The Textbook

I. The front matter contains the preface and the table of contents.

II. The text proper contains the chapters.

III. The back matter contains the glossary, bibliography, and index.

Problem–Solution Pattern

The problem–solution pattern is especially useful in persuasive speeches, in which you want to convince the audience that a problem exists and that your solution would solve or lessen the problem. Let's say that you want to persuade your audience that jury awards for damages should be limited. A problem–solution pattern might be appropriate here. In the first part of your speech, you'd identify the problem(s) created by these large awards; in the second part you'd present the solution. A sample outline for such a speech might look something like this:

Jury Awards

I. Jury awards for damages are out of control. [the general problem]

    A. These awards increase insurance rates. [a specific problem]

    B. These awards increase medical costs. [a second specific problem]

    C. These awards place unfair burdens on business. [a third specific problem]

II. Jury awards need to be limited. [the general solution]

    A. Greater evidence should be required before a case can be brought to trial. [a specific solution]

    B. Part of the award should be turned over to the state. [a second specific solution]

    C. Realistic estimates of financial damage must be used. [a third specific solution]

Here's another example to clarify the problem–solution organizational pattern. In this speech the speaker seeks to persuade the audience that cigarette advertising should be banned from all media. The thesis is that "Cigarette advertising should be abolished." Asking the strategic question "Why should it be abolished?" suggests the main points:

Smoking

I. Cigarette smoking is a national problem.

    A. Cigarette smoking causes lung cancer.

    B. Cigarette smoking pollutes the air.

    C. Cigarette smoking raises the cost of health care.

II. Cigarette smoking would be lessened if advertisements were prohibited.

III. Fewer people would start to smoke.

IV. Smokers would smoke less.

In delivering such a speech, a speaker might begin like this:

> I think we all realize that cigarette smoking is a national problem that affects each and every one of us. No one escapes the problems caused by cigarette smoking—not the smoker and not the nonsmoker. Cigarette smoking causes lung cancer. Cigarette smoking pollutes the air. And cigarette smoking raises the cost of health care for everyone.

RESEARCH Link

Newsgroups and Chat Groups

Newsgroups are discussion forums for the exchange of ideas on a wide variety of topics. There are thousands of newsgroups on the Internet; you can post your messages, read the messages of others, and respond to the messages you read. Newsgroups are much like listservs, in that they bring together a group of people interested in communicating about a common topic. Some newsgroups also include messages from news services such as the Associated Press or Reuters.

Newsgroups are useful to the public speaker for a variety of reasons. The most obvious reason is that newsgroups are sources of information; they contain news items, letters, and papers on just about any topic you can think of. You can also save the news items you're particularly interested in to your own file. An especially useful search engine for discussion groups is Google (http://groups.google.com/; see the home page on p. 137), although you can use any search engine to search for groups in which you might be interested (see the Research Link in Chapter 7). Google will search the available newsgroups for the topics you request. You simply submit key words that best describe your research topic, and the program will search its database of newsgroups and provide you with a list of article titles and authors along with each article's date and relevance score. You then click on any of the titles that seem most closely related to what you're looking for.

Newsgroups offer lots of advantages to the researching public speaker. Newsgroups that get news feeds are especially useful, because the information is so current and is likely to be more detailed than you'll find in newspapers—which have to cut copy to fit space limitations. You're also likely to find a greater diversity of viewpoints than you'll encounter in, say, most newspapers or newsmagazines. Another advantage is that through newsgroups you can ask questions and get the opinions of others for your next speech. Newsgroups also provide an easily available and generally receptive audience to whom you can communicate your thoughts and feelings.

Chat groups such as you'll find on the commercial Internet service providers (ISPs) enable you to communicate with others in real time; this is called *synchronous conversation* as opposed to *asynchronous conversation,* in which there's a delay between message sending and message receiving. Real-time communication obviously has its advantages: You can ask questions, respond to feedback, and otherwise adjust your message to the specific receivers. One great disadvantage, however, is that you may not find anyone you want to talk with when you log on. Unlike e-mail, real-time chat doesn't let you leave a message. Chat groups, like listservs and newsgroups, are subject specific; and because there are so many of them (they number in the thousands), you're likely to find at least one group dealing with any topic you're researching.

Research Activity. What newsgroups and chat groups can you locate that might prove of value to you in your future speeches or in your other academic pursuits?

Let's look first at the most publicized of all smoking problems: lung cancer. There can be no doubt—the scientific evidence is overwhelming—that cigarette smoking is a direct cause of lung cancer. Research conducted by the American Cancer Institute and by research institutes throughout the world all come to the same conclusion: cigarette smoking causes lung cancer. Consider some of the specific evidence. A recent study—reported in the January, 2004, issue of the . . . .

Cause–Effect Pattern

The cause–effect pattern is useful in speeches in which you want to show your audience the causal connection existing between two events or elements. Your speech divides into two major sections—causes and effects. For example, a speech on the reasons for highway accidents or birth defects might lend itself to a cause–effect pattern. Here you might first consider, say, the causes of highway

Google

(www.google.com)
Explore the many capabilities of Google. In addition to discussion groups, what else can you find through Google that might be of value to a public speaker?

accidents or birth defects and then some of the effects; for example, the number of deaths, the number of accidents, and so on.

In some cases you might want to place the effects first and then discuss the causes. Let's say you want to demonstrate the causes for the increase in AIDS in your state. You might use an effect–cause pattern that might look something like this:

AIDS

I. AIDS is increasing. [general effect]

   A. AIDS is increasing among teenagers. [a specific effect]

   B. AIDS is increasing among IV drug users. [a second specific effect]

   C. AIDS is increasing among women. [a third specific effect]

II. Three factors contribute to this increase. [general causal statement]

   A. Teenagers are ignorant about how the HIV virus is transmitted. [a specific cause]

   B. IV drug users exchange tainted needles. [a second specific cause]

   C. Men and women are not practicing safe sex. [a third specific cause]

The Motivated Sequence

The **motivated sequence** is another pattern for organizing a speech in such a way that your audience responds positively to your purpose (McKerrow, Gronbeck, Ehninger, & Monroe, 2000). This approach was developed by communication professor Alan H. Monroe in the 1930s, originally as a way to organize sales presentations. Now it's widely used in all sorts of oral and written communications. In fact, you'll probably find that you can analyze almost any persuasive message—from political speeches to television advertisements to Internet ribbon ads—in terms of the motivated sequence. The motivated sequence is especially appropriate for speeches designed to move listeners to action (to persuade the audience to do something). But you'll find it useful for informative speeches as well.

The organizational patterns we have considered so far divide speeches into three parts—introduction, body, and conclusion. The motivated sequence works a little differently; it organizes the speech into five parts or steps:

Step 1. Attention: Gain your listeners' attention.

Step 2. Need: Demonstrate that there's a problem, that your listeners have a need.

Step 3. Satisfaction: Show how your listeners can resolve their problem or satisfy their need.

Step 4. Visualization: Show your listeners what the situation would be like with this problem eliminated, with this need satisfied.

Step 5. Action: Tell your listeners what they must do to resolve their problem, to satisfy their need.

While walking down the street one day, a young boy with a shoe-shine box called out to a Wall Street-type executive:

Hey, man. You look great. But your shoes are a mess. You don't want to walk into a meeting with mud on your shoes, do you? I can fix that for you. You'll look a lot better for that meeting if you have shined shoes. Sit right here and I'll polish them up.

In this brief "advertisement" the young boy executed all five steps of the motivated sequence:

Hey, man. You look great. [Step 1. Attention: Caught the attention of a passerby with a simple compliment.]

But your shoes are a mess. You don't want to walk into a meeting with mud on your shoes, do you? [Step 2. Need: Demonstrated that the man had a problem and a need for change existed.]

I can fix that for you. [Step 3. Satisfaction: Told the man that the problem can be corrected.]

You'll look a lot better for that meeting if you have shined shoes. [Step 4. Visualization: Showed how things would be better if the problem was resolved.]

Sit right here and I'll polish them up. [Step 5. Action: Told the man what he had to do to resolve the problem and satisfy the need.]

Let's look at each of these steps in more detail and see how you might use each of them in actual speeches.

DEVELOPING STRATEGIES

Gaining Attention. Sherry wants to give a speech opposing a proposed youth center, arguing that the way to fight youth crime is by mandating harsher sentences for all youth crimes. She wants to gain the audience's attention and connect it to her topic. How might she do this?

Step 1: Gain Attention. In this step you gain the audience's undivided attention and get them to focus on you and your message. If you execute this step effectively, your audience should be anxious and ready to hear what you have to say. I'll explain and illustrate these devices later in this chapter in discussing the introduction (pp. 145–148).

Regardless of what attention device you use, demonstrate your enthusiasm. Enthusiasm is highly contagious: If you show that you're enthusiastic, your attitude is likely to infect the audience, and they too will become involved and energized. Deliver your opening remarks with appropriate gestures, and vary bodily movement. Similarly, vary your voice so that it demonstrates your own involvement in the subject of your speech.

In phrasing your introductory remarks, involve the audience directly. Use *you* if appropriate, and use connecting pronouns—*us* and *we*—that show that you and your listeners are involved in this together.

For example, in a speech in which you try to persuade your listeners to vote in favor of establishing a community youth center, you might gain attention by using a provocative question: *If you could reduce juvenile crime by some 20 percent by just flipping a lever, would you do it?* Or you might make reference to specific audience members: *I know that several of you here have been the victims of juvenile vandalism. Thom, your drug store was broken into last month by three teenagers who said they did it because they were bored. And Loraine, your video rental shop's windows were broken by teenagers who, in a drunken spree, decided to have a rock fight. And . . . .*

Step 2: Establish the Need. In the second part of the motivated sequence, you demonstrate that there's a problem, that something is wrong, that a need exists. Your listeners should feel that they have something to learn (if you are making an informative speech) or that they have to change their attitudes or do something (if it's a persuasive speech). Here are some examples, first for informative speeches and second for persuasive speeches.

State the problem or need. If you're giving an informative speech, the problem or need might be lack of information. For example, in an informative speech on how to gain access to your credit history, you might establish the need for information by saying, "You need access to your credit history because it's the best way to prevent yourself from being a victim of fraud," or, "Millions of people become victims of credit fraud because they don't have access to their own credit history," or, "You're more likely to become a victim of fraud if you don't regularly check your credit history."

If you're giving a persuasive speech, you might focus on your listeners' need to change their attitudes or their behaviors. For example, in a speech aiming to persuade your listeners to participate actively in the political process, you might establish the need by saying something like this: "You need to participate actively in the politics of your city if you want elected officials to address your needs and the needs of people like you." Or, in a speech on the need to establish a community youth center as a way of reducing juvenile crime, you might say, "Juvenile crime has been increasing dramatically in our community over the last several years. We need to do something about it."

Show why this is really a problem. Make sure your audience understands that this problem affects them directly—that it is not simply some abstract problem that will not touch them personally. You also might support the existence of need with illustrations, statistics, testimony, and other forms of support we already explored in Chapter 5. Too, you might show your listeners how this need affects those values that motivate their behavior, such as their financial status, their career goals, and their individual happiness (motivators that we'll examine in more detail in Chapter 10). In the speech on the youth center, you might say, "Federal crime statistics show that juvenile crime is likely to increase over the next several years, and it will happen in our community if we don't take a stand and do something about it *now*," or "Next year, your store, Jack, or yours, Shauna, may be broken into."

? DEVELOPING STRATEGIES

Establishing the Need. How might Sherry demonstrate the need to establish harsher sentences? How might she show that youth crime is a real problem for her specific audience?

Step 3: Satisfy the Need. In this step you present the "answer" or the "solution" that would eliminate the problem or satisfy the need that you demonstrated in Step 2. On the basis of this satisfaction step, your listeners should now believe that what you're informing them about or persuading them to do will effectively satisfy the need. So show here how the problem can be solved and why your solution will work.

Show your listeners that your plan will satisfy the need or solve the problem. Here you might say quite simply, "The best way to reduce credit card fraud is to check your credit history regularly," or, "Like our neighboring towns, we need to create a youth center for high school students to reduce juvenile crime and vandalism."

Show why your solution will work. You want your audience to understand that what you're asking them to believe or do will actually lead to resolving the problem or satisfying the need you identified in Step 2. So you might say something like: "Youth crime has been dramatically reduced in all of our neighboring towns since they established youth centers. The same will happen here."

This step is also a good place to answer any objections you anticipate from your listeners. For example, if you anticipate that audience members will object to the youth center for fear it would increase their taxes, you might answer this now. For example, you might say, "A major portion of the financing will be secured from New York State grants, and local merchants have already agreed to contribute whatever additional financing is needed. So this youth center will impose absolutely no financial burden on anyone."

Notice that in an informative speech you could have stopped after the satisfaction step, because you would have accomplished your goal of informing the audience about the youth centers and how they can effectively reduce juvenile crime. In a persuasive speech, on the other hand, you must continue at least as far as Step 4, visualization (if your purpose is limited to strengthening or changing attitudes or beliefs) or go on to Step 5, action (if your purpose is to get your listeners to do something).

Step 4: Visualize the Need Satisfied. In this step of the motivated sequence, you take the audience beyond the present time and place and enable them to imagine, to visualize, the situation as it would be if the problem were eliminated, if the need were satisfied as you suggested in Step 3. Through this visualization you aim to intensify your listeners' feelings or beliefs. You can achieve this visualization with any one or combination of these basic strategies.

Demonstrate the benefits that your listeners will receive if your ideas are put into operation. You might, for example, point to the decrease in crime that accompanies the establishment of youth centers, or to the social and vocational skills that the students will learn there. Or you could visualize the need satisfied by returning to your introductory examples and say something like: "Wouldn't it have been great if Thom's drugstore was never broken into and that the time, energy, and expense that Thom had to go through could have been spent taking a well-deserved vacation? And Loraine, wouldn't it have been nice if your windows had never been broken? And . . . ."

Demonstrate the negative effects that will occur if your plan is not put into operation. Here you might argue, for example, that without such a youth center, juvenile crime will increase or students will fail to learn safe sex practices normally

CRITICAL LISTENING/THINKING *Link*

Listening to Analogies

Analogies are comparisons and may be of two types: figurative and literal. **Figurative analogies** compare items from different classes—for example, the flexibility afforded by a car with the freedom of a bird, a college degree with a passport to success, playing baseball with running a corporation. Figurative analogies are useful for illustrating possible similarities; they provide vivid examples that are easily remembered. But they do not constitute evidence of the truth or falsity of an assertion. Speakers who present figurative analogies as proof may be doing so because there is no real evidence.

Literal analogies compare items from the same class, such as two cars or two cities. For example, in a literal analogy you might argue (1) that the towns of Marlboro and Accord are similar—both are small cities, both have similar numbers of youth, both are in New York State, and so on; and (2) that therefore the effects Marlboro experienced with their youth

center will be the same in Accord. In listening to literal analogies, pose two questions:

- *Are the cases compared alike in essential respects?* Or do the two cases differ from each other in ways that the speaker doesn't mention but that might influence the comparison? For example, do the two towns differ in their populations' predominant religion, in average income, in available youth facilities, or in types and/or rates of youth crime?
- *Do the differences make a difference?* Obviously, not all differences are significant. A difference in religion may not be significant, but a difference in types of youth crimes may prove significant and may weaken the comparison. For example, youth centers may be helpful in reducing the number of offenses when they're relatively minor but may make no difference when the offenses are more serious.

Getting Critical. What kinds of analogies might you develop to support such assertions as (1) colleges must establish hate speech guidelines or (2) Internet communication should be free of censorship?

taught at these youth centers that are not currently taught at home or in the schools.

Demonstrate the combined positive and negative effects. You might combine both the demonstration of the positive effects that will result if your plan is put into operation and the negative effects that will result if your plan is denied. You might then say something like this: "Without a youth center teen crime is likely to increase, as the statistics from similar towns that I'll show will illustrate. But with such a center juvenile crime is likely to decrease, and I'll also show you very recent and very dramatic statistics from towns just like ours that had the foresight to establish such centers."

DEVELOPING STRATEGIES

Visualizing the Need Satisfied. How might Sherry visualize what it will be like with harsher sentences for all youth crimes?

Step 5: Ask for Action. In this final step you tell the audience what they should do to ensure that the need (as demonstrated in Step 2) is satisfied (as described in Step 3). Here you want to move the audience in a particular direction; for example, to vote in favor of additional research funding for AIDS or against cigarette advertising, to attend the next student government meeting, or to contribute free time to for the blind. In completing this step consider two basic strategies.

Tell the audience exactly what they must do. Frequently, speakers use emotional appeals here (see Chapter 10). Or you might give your listeners guidelines for future action, saying something like this: "Proposition 14, establishing

DEVELOPING STRATEGIES

Asking for Action. Sherry wants to ask her audience to support harsher sentences for all youth crimes in a straw poll to be conducted next week. How might she phrase her action step?

a youth center in the old post office building, is coming up for a vote next week. Vote *yes*, and urge your family members, your friends, and your work colleagues to also vote *yes*. It will make our town a better place for us all."

Remind your listeners of the connections you've established throughout your speech. Throughout your motivated sequence speech, you've established a series of important connections and relationships. Make sure your listeners remember them and see how the action you ask for here is related. Make sure they see that the action you ask for here will satisfy the need and enable them to live in a world (in a community, in our example of the youth center) that is a lot better than it would be otherwise.

Stress specific advantages. Stress the specific advantages of these behaviors to your specific audience. In other words, don't ask your audience to engage in behaviors solely for abstract reasons. Give them concrete, specific reasons why they will benefit from the actions you want them to engage in. Instead of telling your listeners that they should devote time to reading to blind students because it's the right thing to do, show them how much they will enjoy the experience and how much they will personally benefit from it.

Because your organizational pattern serves primarily to help your listeners follow your speech, you might want to tell your listeners (in your introduction or as a transition between the introduction and the body of your speech) what pattern you'll be following. Here are just a few examples:

- In explaining the goals of television scheduling, we'll start with morning TV and go through the day to late-night TV.
- I'll first explain the problems with jury awards and then propose three workable solutions.
- First we'll look at the increase in AIDS, and then we'll look at three of the causes.

❖ **CONSIDER** the speeches of politicians, especially those urging citizens to vote for them. Read a recently delivered political speech in your newspaper, on the Internet, or in the periodical *Vital Speeches of the Day.* How did the speaker gain attention, establish need, satisfy the need, visualize the need satisfied, and urge action?

Additional Organizational Patterns

The six patterns just considered are the most common and the most useful for organizing most public speeches. But there are other patterns that might be appropriate for different topics.

◆ The *structure–function pattern* is useful in informative speeches in which you want to discuss how something is constructed (its structural aspects) and what it does (its functional aspects). This pattern might be useful, for example, in a speech explaining what a business organization is and what it does, identifying the parts of a university and how they operate, or describing the sensory systems of the body and their various functions. This pattern also might be useful in a discussion of the nature of a living organism: its anatomy (that is, its structures) and its physiology (that is, its functions).

◆ Arranging your material in a *comparison-and-contrast pattern* is useful in informative speeches in which you want to analyze two different theories, proposals, departments, or products in terms of their similarities and differences. In this type of speech you would be concerned not only with explaining each theory or proposal but also with clarifying how they're similar and how they're different.

◆ The *pro-and-con pattern*, sometimes called the *advantages–disadvantages pattern*, is useful in informative speeches in which you want to explain objectively the advantages (the pros) and the disadvantages (the cons) of a plan, method, or product. Or you can use this pattern in a persuasive speech in which you want to show the superiority of one plan or position over another.

◆ The *claim-and-proof pattern* is especially useful in a persuasive speech in which you want to prove the truth or usefulness of a particular proposition. It's the pattern that you see frequently in trials, where the claim made by the prosecution is that the defendant is guilty and the proof is the varied evidence designed to show that the defendant had a motive, opportunity, and no alibi. In this pattern your speech would consist of two major parts. In the first part you'd explain your claim (tuition must not be raised, library hours must be expanded, courses in AIDS education must be instituted). In the second part you'd offer your evidence or proof; for example, evidence to show why tuition must not be raised.

◆ The *multiple-definition pattern* is useful for informative speeches in which you want to explain the nature of a concept. (What is a born-again Christian? What is a scholar? What is multiculturalism?) In this pattern each major heading would consist of a different type of definition or way of looking at the concept.

◆ The *Who? What? Why? Where? When? pattern* is used by journalists and is useful when you wish to report or explain an event; for example, a robbery, political coup, war, or trial. Here the major parts of your speech would deal with the answers to several or all of these five questions.

Cultural Considerations in Organization

Cultural considerations are as important in organization as they are in all other aspects of public speaking. One factor that's especially important is whether the culture is a high-context or a low-context one (Hall & Hall, 1987). **High-context cultures** (Japanese, Arabic, Latin American, Thai, Korean, Apache, and

Mexican are examples) are those in which much of the information in communication is in the context or in the person rather than in the actual spoken message. Both speaker and listener already know the information from, say, previous interactions, assumptions each makes about the other, or shared experiences. **Low-context cultures** (German, Swedish, Norwegian, and American are examples) are those in which most information is explicitly stated in the verbal message. In formal communications, the information would be in written form as well, as it is with contracts, prenuptial agreements, or apartment leases.

To appreciate the distinction between high and low context, consider giving directions to the recycling center. Someone who knows the neighborhood (a high-context situation) probably knows the local landmarks. So you can give directions such as "next to the laundromat on Main Street" or "the corner of Albany and Elm." With a newcomer (a low-context situation), you can't assume that you have a common body of shared information; you have to use directions that even a stranger would understand—for example, "make a left at the next stop sign" or "go two blocks and then turn right."

Extending this distinction to speech organization, we can see that high-context cultures will probably prefer an organization in which the supporting materials are offered and the audience is allowed to infer the general principle or proposition themselves. Low-context culture members, on the other hand, will likely prefer an organization in which the proposition is clearly and directly stated and the supporting materials are clearly linked to the proposition.

Persons from the United States speaking in Japan, to take one well-researched example, need to be careful lest they make their point too obvious or too direct and thus inadvertently insult their audience. Speakers in Japan are expected to lead their listeners to the conclusion through example, illustration, and various other indirect means (Lustig & Koester, 1999). Persons from Japan speaking in the United States need to be careful lest their indirectness be perceived as unnecessarily vague, underhanded, or suggestive of an attempt to withhold information.

To give an example, you might organize a speech on the need for random drug testing in the workplace somewhat differently depending on whether you were addressing a high-context or a low-context audience.

High-Context Audience	**Low-Context Audience**
• Implicitness and indirectness are preferred	• Explicitness and directness are preferred
• The main point is implicitly identified only after the evidence is presented	• The main point is clearly stated at the outset, even before the evidence is presented
Drugs in the workplace cause accidents. Drugs in the workplace contribute to the national drug problem. Drugs in the workplace increase costs for employers and consumers. These are some factors we need to think about as we consider the proposal to establish random workplace drug testing.	*Random drug testing in the workplace is a must. It will reduce accidents. It will reduce the national drug problem. It will reduce costs. Let's examine each of these reasons why random drug testing in the workplace should become standard.*

DEVELOPING STRATEGIES

Gender Expectations. Michelle is running for president of the local chapter of a construction workers' union. Michelle is one of only five women in this entire local of more than 1,000 members, and she is the only woman running for this office. Michelle wonders if she should mention the issue of gender in her speech announcing her intention to run. What would you advise Michelle to do?

Introductions, Conclusions, and Transitions

Now that you have the body of your speech organized, devote your attention to the introduction, conclusion, and transitions that will hold the parts of your speech together.

Introductions

Together with your general appearance and your nonverbal messages, your introduction gives your listeners their first impression of you and your speech. And, as you know, first impressions are very resistant to change. Because of this the introduction is an especially important part of the speech. It sets the tone for the rest of the speech; it tells your listeners what kind of a speech they'll hear.

Begin collecting suitable material for your introduction as you prepare the entire speech, but wait until all the other parts are completed before you put the pieces together. In this way you'll be better able to determine which elements should be included and which should be eliminated.

Your introduction should serve three functions: gain attention, establish a speaker–audience–topic connection, and orient the audience as to what is to follow. Let's look at how you can accomplish each of these functions.

Gain Attention

Your introduction should gain the attention of your audience and focus it on your speech topic. (And, of course, it should help you maintain that attention throughout your speech.) You can secure attention in numerous ways; here are just a few.

Ask a Question. Questions are effective because they're a change from the more common declarative statements, and listeners automatically pay attention to change. Rhetorical questions—questions to which you don't expect an answer—are especially helpful in focusing the audience's attention on your subject: "Do you want to live a happy life?" "Do you want to succeed in college?" "Do you want to meet the love of your life?" "Have you ever suffered from loneliness?" Also useful are polling-type questions, questions that ask the audience for a show of hands: "How many of you have suffered through a boring lecture?" "How many of you intend to continue school after graduating from college?"

Refer to Recent Happenings. Referring to a previous speech, a recent event, or a prominent person currently making news helps gain attention, because the audience is familiar with this and will pay attention to see how you're going to connect it to your speech topic.

Use an Illustration or Dramatic Story. Much as we are drawn to soap operas, so we are drawn to illustrations and stories about people. A good example can be found in the introduction to the speech for analysis in this chapter (p. 167). Here's another example (Schnoor, 1994, p. 73):

USING TECHNOLOGY

Visit Northwestern's Douglass website, or any other of the many websites devoted to public speeches (see Using Technology, p. 45), and read over some of the speeches. What kinds of introductions and conclusions are most popular? What can you learn from these professionally prepared introductions and conclusions that you might use for your own public speeches?

An eight-year-old boy became just another victim when his mother turned unintentionally away from him for just a few seconds unaware that there was a real danger present in her home. This was enough time for her child to be burned on over half of his body. Because of the injuries he received, he was hospitalized for 16 days before he died.

Use a Quotation. Quotations are useful because the audience is likely to pay attention to the brief and clever remarks of someone they have heard of or read about. Make sure that the quotation is directly relevant to your topic; if you have to explain its relevance, it probably isn't worth using.

Cite a Little-Known Fact or Statistic. These help pique an audience's attention. Headlines on unemployment statistics, crime in the schools, and political corruption sell newspapers because they gain attention. In a speech on the need for more severe punishments for hate speech, the speaker might cite a specific hate speech incident that the audience hadn't heard of yet or the statistic that violence inspired by hate speech tripled over the last six months.

Use Humor. Humor is useful because it relaxes the audience and establishes a quick connection between speaker and listeners. In using humor make sure it's relevant to your topic, brief, tasteful, seemingly spontaneous, and appropriate to you as a speaker and to the audience. A good example occurs in actor Tim Robbins's introduction to a speech he delivered to the National Press Club on April 15, 2003 (http:www.commondreams.org/cgi-bin/print.cgi?file=views03/0416-01.htm, accessed 2/6/04):

> Thank you. And thanks for the invitation. I had originally been asked here to talk about the war and our current political situation, but I have instead chosen to hijack this opportunity and talk about baseball and show business. (Laughter.) Just kidding. Sort of.

Establish a Speaker–Audience–Topic Relationship

In addition to gaining attention, use your introduction to establish a connection among yourself as the speaker, the audience members, and your topic. Try to answer your listeners' inevitable question of why they should listen to you speak on this topic. You can establish an effective speaker–audience–topic (or S–A–T) relationship in any of numerous ways.

Establish Your Credibility. The introduction is a particularly important time to establish your competence, character, and charisma (see Chapter 10). Here, for example, the speaker establishes his credibility and in doing so establishes a connection among himself, the audience, and the topic (Jacobs, 1997, p. 461):

> I will discuss both the challenges and the opportunities of diversity. As an African American, as a person who has spent most of his adult years working to inject minorities into the mainstream of American life, and as someone who has been fortunate to join the senior management of a great global corporation, I believe that no organization can achieve its full potential unless it is capable of benefiting from diversity.

Refer to Others Present. Not only will this help you to gain attention, it will also help you to establish an effective speaker–audience–topic relationship.

In this example Harvey Mackay (1991) refers not only to the audience but also to their present thoughts and feelings:

> I'm flattered to be here today, but not so flattered that I'm going to let it go to my head. Yes, I was delighted to be asked to be your commencement speaker. But I also know the truth: By the time you're my age, 99 out of 100 will have completely forgotten who spoke at your graduation.
>
> And, I can accept that. Because I can't remember the name of my commencement speaker either. What I do remember from graduation day is the way I felt: excited, scared, and challenged. I was wondering what the world was like out there, and how I would manage to make an impact.

Express Your Pleasure or Interest in Speaking. Yukio Matsuyama (1992) effectively establishes a speaker–audience–topic relationship by humorously expressing his pleasure in addressing the audience:

> I feel very happy to be invited here today. It is always a great pleasure for me to talk about Japan with those Americans who have a sincere interest in Japanese affairs and who don't find us inscrutable, but only intractable.

Compliment the Audience. Pay the audience an honest and sincere compliment, and they'll not only give you their attention, they'll feel a part of your speech. In some cultures—Japan and Korea are good examples—the speaker is expected to compliment the audience. It's one of the essential parts of the introduction. Visitors from the United States are often advised when speaking in a foreign country to compliment the country itself, its beauty, its culture. One caution, however: If the compliment is done to an extreme or appears insincere, it is probably best omitted. In this example musician Billy Joel compliments his audience, the graduating class of the Berklee College of Music, directly and honestly (http://www.berklee.edu/commencement/past/bjoel.html, accessed February 6, 2004):

> I am truly pleased that the road has twisted and turned its way up the East Coast to Boston. The Berklee College of Music represents the finest contemporary music school there is, and I am honored to be here with you this morning to celebrate.

Express Similarities with the Audience. By stressing your own similarity with members of the audience, you create a bond with them and become an "insider" instead of an "outsider." Here Janice Payan (1990) uses this technique most effectively:

> Thank you. I felt as if you were introducing someone else because my mind was racing back 10 years, when I was sitting out there in the audience at the Adelante Mujer conference. Anonymous. Comfortable. Trying hard to relate to our "successful" speaker, but mostly feeling like Janice Payan, working mother, glad for a chance to sit down.
>
> I'll let you in on a little secret. I still am Janice Payan, working mother. The only difference is that I have a longer job title, and that I've made a few discoveries these past 10 years that I'm eager to share with you.
>
> The first is that keynote speakers at conferences like this are not some sort of alien creatures. Nor were they born under a lucky star. They are ordinary Hispanic women who have stumbled onto an extraordinary discovery.

Orient the Audience

The introduction should orient the audience in some way as to what is to follow in the body of the speech. Preview for the audience what you're going to say. The orientation may be covered in a variety of ways.

DEVELOPING STRATEGIES

S–A–T Connection. Jack, a former software engineer, is giving an informative speech on the way metasearch engines work. If the audience were your public speaking class, how might he establish a speaker–audience–topic connection?

❖ **CONSIDER** whether your own experiences support or contradict the notion that Asian culture is a "culture of courtesy," whereas North American and Western European culture is a "culture of realism" (Culick, 1962). What might this distinction mean for your own speeches?

Give a General Idea of Your Subject. For example, you might say, very simply, "Tonight I'm going to discuss atomic waste" or "I want to talk with you about the problems our society has created for the aged."

Give a Detailed Preview. In this example Microsoft founder Bill Gates gives a detailed preview of the main points of his speech at the United Nations Media Leaders Summit on January 15, 2004 (http://www.gatesfoundation.org/ MediaCenter/Speeches/BillgSpeeches/BGSpeechMedia-04, accessed February 6, 2004):

> I hope to do three things today: explain why I believe the media's role in increasing visibility for HIV/AIDS is so important, why I'm optimistic about the opportunities ahead, and what I believe is needed to stop this epidemic.

Identify Your Goal. Here Harold Carr (1987) identifies the thesis he hopes to establish:

> I'll argue today—and certainly will be happy to debate with you during the question session—that communications during a "crisis"—however you define that term—shouldn't be all that different from communications during routine times.

Conclusions

Your conclusion is especially important because it's often the part of the speech that the audience remembers most clearly. Let your conclusion serve three major functions: to summarize, motivate, and provide closure.

Summarize
You may summarize your speech in a variety of ways.

Restate Your Thesis or Purpose. In the restatement type of summary, you recap the essential thrust of your speech, repeating your thesis or perhaps the goals you hoped to achieve. Here is how Carrie Willis (Schnoor, 2000, p. 15), a student from Tallahassee Community College, restated the importance of her thesis on "drowsy driving" and also summarized the main points of her speech:

> While this problem is as old as cars, it's not disappearing. And it won't disappear until you choose to do something about it. Today, we have gained a better understanding of the problem of falling asleep at the wheel, and why it continues to exist, while finally suggesting several initiatives to help end this epidemic. Six innocent college students were killed, all because someone didn't take the precautionary steps to avoid the tragedy. So, next time you're on the road and you find yourself dozing off, pull over and take a nap, because those 30 minutes could save your life.

Here's another example, from a speech by President Jimmy Carter to the people of Cuba (http://www.americanrhetoric.com/speeches/jimmycartercubaspeech.htm, accessed February 6, 2004):

> After 43 years of animosity, we hope that someday soon, you can reach across the great divide that separates our two countries and say, "We are ready to join the community of democracies," and I hope that Americans will soon open our arms to you and say, "We welcome you as our friends."

Restate the Importance of the Topic. Another method for concluding is to tell the audience again why your topic or thesis is so important. In this excerpt Commissioner of Internal Revenue Margaret Milner Richardson (1995, p. 203) concludes her speech by restating the importance of her topic:

> Thank you for taking this journey with me into the future. By sharing with you our vision of the future, I hope you will not only understand where we have been as an agency but where we will be in the future. You are an indispensable part of that future. I look forward to working with you to bring tax administration into the twenty-first century.

Restate Your Main Points. In this type of summary you restate your thesis and the main points you used to support it. In his conclusion Carl Wayne Hensley (1994, p. 319) restates his main points as questions:

> Now, do you see why I assert that mediation provides a sensible approach for settling divorce-related issues? Do you see why I believe that mediation has to become a way of life in America when the divorce rate is so overwhelming? Do you understand that mediation helps the couple manage conflict, helps the couple engage in a win–win exchange, and helps the couple stabilize individually? Do you see more clearly that mediation does provide a sensible approach for settling divorce-related issues?

Motivate

A second function of the conclusion—most appropriate in persuasive speeches—is to motivate your audience to do what you want them to do. In your conclusion you have the opportunity to give the audience one final push in the direction you wish them to take. Whether it's to buy stock, vote a particular way, or change an attitude, you can use the conclusion for a final motivation, a final appeal. Here are three excellent ways to motivate.

? DEVELOPING STRATEGIES

Running Overtime. David's speeches invariably run overtime. What would you advise David to do—aside from planning for the allotted time restrictions—if he gets a 30-second stop signal? Should he go directly to his conclusion? Should he apologize for going overtime and ask permission to continue? Should he just continue his speech?

Ask for a Specific Response. Specify what you want the audience to do after listening to your speech. Clarence Darrow (Peterson, 1965), in his summation speech in defense of Henry Sweet, an African American man charged with murder, directed his conclusion at motivating the jury to vote not guilty in a case that drew national and worldwide attention because of the racial issues involved. A vote of not guilty was in fact quickly returned by a jury of 12 white men.

> Gentlemen, what do you think of our duty in this case? I have watched day after day these black, tense faces that have crowded this court. These black faces that now are looking to you 12 whites, feeling that the hopes and fears of a race are in your keeping. This case is about to end, gentlemen. To them, it is life. Not one of their color sits on this jury. Their fate is in the hands of 12 whites. Their eyes are fixed on you, their hearts go out to you, and their hopes hang on your verdict. This is all. I ask you, on behalf of this defendant, on behalf of these helpless ones who turn to you, and more than that—on behalf of this great state, and this great city, which must face this problem and face it fairly— I ask you, in the name of progress and of the human race, to return a verdict of not guilty in this case!

Reiterate Speaker–Audience Agreement. In a speech designed to strengthen attitudes, it may prove of value to repeat what you and the audience believe. Here, for example, UN Secretary General Boutros Boutros-Ghali (1994, p. 130), concluded his speech on transnational crime by reminding the audience of the areas of agreement:

> It is because we support these values and recognize the need to unite against transnational crime that we have come together today. I therefore see this meeting as an opportunity for us to re-state our commitment to the triumph of the rule of law over the law of the jungle. But I also see it as an expression of our faith in international cooperation to achieve the lofty ideals of the Charter of the United Nations.

Provide Directions for Future Action. Another type of motivational conclusion is to spell out the action you wish the audience to take. Here's an example by David Archambault (1992), president of the American Indian College Fund, in a speech to the Rotary Club:

> Let us make this anniversary a time of healing and a time of renewal, a time to wipe away the tears. Let us—both Indian and non-Indian—put our minds together and see what life we can make for our children. Let us leave behind more hope than we found.

Provide Closure

The third function of your conclusion is to provide closure. Often your summary will accomplish this, but in some instances it will prove insufficient. End your speech with a conclusion that is crisp and definite. Make the audience know that you have definitely and clearly ended. Some kind of wrap-up, some sort of final statement, is helpful in providing this feeling of closure. Here are three ways you can achieve closure.

Refer to Subsequent Events. You can achieve closure by looking ahead to events that will take place either that day or soon afterwards. Notice how effectively U.S. Secretary of State Madeleine K. Albright (1998) uses this method in a speech on NATO:

Our task is to make clear what our alliance will do and what our partnership will mean in a Europe truly whole and free, and in a world that looks to us for principles and purposeful leadership for peace, for prosperity, and for freedom. In this spirit, I look forward to our discussion today and to our work together in the months and years to come.

Refer Back to the Introduction. It's sometimes useful to connect your conclusion with your introduction. Here, for example, Jill Reiss (Schnoor, 1994, p. 3), a student from George Mason University, after noting the hard work that Thomas Edison put into his inventions, concludes her speech by referring to Edison again:

> Today we've examined what ecofoam peanuts are, how they compare to other alternatives, and their problems as well as their promises as an environmentally conscious product. American Excelsior, like Thomas Edison, has been willing to invest the perspiration necessary to bring its inspirations to work.

Here's another example from one of the most famous of all farewell speeches, baseball great Lou Gehrig's farewell to baseball. In his introduction Gehrig, who was at the time dying of what has come to be called Lou Gehrig's disease, said: "Fans, for the past two weeks you have been reading about the bad break I got. Yet today I consider myself the luckiest man on the face of the earth." In the conclusion he refers back to this introductory statement, very simply:

> So, I close in saying that I might have been given a bad break, but I've got an awful lot to live for.

Thank the Audience. Speakers frequently conclude their speeches by thanking the audience for their attention or for their invitation to the speaker to address them. Here, for example, John Dalton (1994, p. 298) expresses his appreciation to the audience:

> I am very grateful to you for the opportunity to share my concerns with you, and I hope that you will give me the benefit of your own knowledge and expertise as I continue to address these matters. If at the end of my tenure as Secretary of the Navy I am remembered for having encouraged the men and women of the Navy and Marine Corps to value and adhere to personal integrity and sacrificial service to others I will be *deeply satisfied* indeed.
> Thank you very much, and God bless you.

Some Common Faults of Introductions and Conclusions

The introduction and conclusion are crucial to the success of your speech. So be especially careful to avoid the most common faults.

Don't Apologize (Generally). In much of the United States and western Europe, an apology is seen as an excuse for a lack of competence or effectiveness. To apologize in your speech is therefore to encourage your listeners to look for faults and to alert them that your speech could have and should have been better. So the general advice to avoid apologizing is reasonable in these cultures. However, in many other cultures—Japanese, Chinese, and Korean are good examples—the speaker is expected to begin with an apology. It's a way of complimenting the audience and placing them in a superior position. The speaker who doesn't apologize or act humbly may be seen as an arrogant individual who feels superior to the audience.

? DEVELOPING STRATEGIES

Gaining Attention. Nina has a great joke to tell. The joke is only tangentially related to her speech topic, but it's so great that it will immediately get the audience actively involved in the speech; this, she thinks, outweighs the fact that it isn't related to the speech. Nina asks your advice. What do you suggest?

❖ **CONSIDER** the advice on introducing and concluding a speech you'd give the advertising designer pictured here as he rehearses his proposal to present to clients. What pitfalls would you suggest he be especially careful to avoid?

Don't Rely on Gimmicks. Avoid gimmicks that gain attention but are irrelevant to the nature of the speech or inconsistent with your treatment of the topic. Thus, for example, slamming a book on the desk or telling a joke that bears no relation to the rest of your speech may accomplish the very limited goal of gaining attention, but it will not advance your purpose. Also, some listeners may resent them, feeling that you fooled them into paying attention.

Don't Preface Your Introduction. Don't preface your speech with such common but ineffective statements as "I'm really nervous, but here goes," "Before I begin my talk, I want to say . . . ," or "I hope I can remember everything I want to say."

Don't Introduce New Material in Your Conclusion. You may, of course, give new expression to ideas covered in the body of the speech, but don't introduce new material in your conclusion. Instead, use your conclusion to reinforce what you've already said in your discussion and to summarize your essential points.

Transitions

Remember that your audience will hear your speech just once. They must understand it as you speak it, or your message will be lost. Transitions help listeners understand your speech more effectively and efficiently.

Transitions are words, phrases, or sentences that connect the various parts of your speech. They provide the audience with guideposts that help them follow the development of your thoughts and arguments. You can enhance your transitions by pausing for just a brief moment before and/or after your transition. This will help the audience see that you've completed one part of your speech and are leading into the next part. You might also take a step forward or to the side before or after your transition. This will also help to reinforce the movement from one part of your speech to another. Use transitions in at least the following places:

◆ between the introduction and the body of the speech
◆ between the body and the conclusion
◆ between the main points in the body of the speech

In addition, consider using transitions:

To announce the start of a major proposition or piece of evidence:
First, . . .
A second argument . . .
A closely related problem . . .
If you want further evidence, look at . . .
Next, consider . . .

My next point . . .

An even more compelling argument . . .

To signal that you're drawing a conclusion from previously given evidence and argument:

Thus, . . .

Therefore, . . .

So, as you can see . . .

It follows, then, that . . .

To alert the audience to the introduction of a qualification or exception:

But, . . .

However, also consider . . .

To remind listeners of what has just been said and that it's connected with another issue that will now be considered:

In contrast to . . . , consider also . . .

Not only . . . , but also . . .

In addition to . . . , we also need to look at . . .

Not only should we . . . , but we should also . . .

To signal the part of your speech you're approaching:

By way of introduction . . .

In conclusion . . .

Now, let's discuss why we are here today . . .

So, what's the solution? What should we do?

To summarize: A special type of transition is the internal summary, a statement that reviews what you've already discussed. It's a statement that usually recaps some major subdivision of your speech. Incorporate internal summaries into your speech—perhaps working them into the transitions connecting your main points. Notice how the internal summary presented below reminds listeners of what they've just heard *and previews what they'll hear next:*

"Wentworth, could I take another look at that reorganization plan?"

> Inadequate recreational facilities, poor schooling, and a lack of adequate role models seem to be the major problems facing our youngsters. Each of these, however, can be remedied and even eliminated. Here's what we can do.

Outlining the Speech

The **outline** is a blueprint for your speech; it lays out the elements of the speech and their relationship to one another. With this blueprint in front of you, you can see at a glance all the elements of organization considered here—the

**USING
TECHNOLOGY**

Explore the outlining capabilities
of your word processor. You
might have to go back to your
manual for this, as—despite its
usefulness—this isn't a feature
that many people use. How
might such an application be of
assistance to you in developing
your speech outline?

introduction and conclusion, the transitions, the main points and their relationship to the thesis and purpose, and the adequacy of the supporting materials. Like a blueprint for a building, the outline enables you to spot weaknesses that might otherwise go undetected.

Begin outlining at the time you begin constructing your speech. Don't wait until you've collected all your material, but begin outlining as you're collecting material, organizing it, and styling it. In this way you'll take the best advantage of one of the major functions of an outline—to tell you where change is needed.

Constructing the Outline

After you've completed your research and have mapped out an organizational plan for your speech, put this plan (this blueprint) on paper. That is, construct what is called a "preparation outline" of your speech, using the following guidelines.

Preface the Outline with Identifying Data

Before you begin the outline proper, identify the general and specific purposes as well as your thesis. You also may want to include a working title—a title that you may change as you continue to polish and perfect your speech. This prefatory material should look something like this:

What Do Media Do?

General purpose: To inform.

Specific purpose: To inform my audience of four functions of the media.

Thesis: The media serve four functions.

These identifying notes are not part of your speech proper. They're not, for example, mentioned in your oral presentation. Rather, they're guides to the preparation of the speech and the outline. They're like road signs to keep you going in the right direction and to signal when you've gone off course.

Outline the Introduction, Body, and Conclusion as Separate Units

The introduction, body, and conclusion of the speech, although intimately connected, should be labeled separately and should be kept distinct in your outline. Like the identifying data above, these labels are not spoken to the audience but are further guides to your preparation.

By keeping the introduction, body, and conclusion as separate units, you'll be able to see at a glance if they do, in fact, serve the functions you want them to serve. You'll be able to see where there are problems and where repair is necessary. At the same time, make sure that you examine and see the speech as a whole—in which the introduction leads to the body and the conclusion summarizes your main points and brings your speech to a close.

Insert Transitions

Insert [using square brackets] transitions between the introduction and the body, between the body and the conclusion, among the main points of the body, and wherever else you think they might be useful.

Append a List of References

Some instructors require that you append a list of references to the written preparation outlines of your speeches. If this is requested, then do so at the end of the outline or on a separate page. Some instructors require that only sources cited in the speech be included in the list of references, whereas others require that the full list of sources consulted be provided (those mentioned in the speech as well as those not mentioned).

Whatever the specific requirements in your course, remember that source citations will prove most effective with your audience if you carefully integrate them into the speech. It will count for little if you consult the latest works by the greatest authorities but never mention this to your audience. So, when appropriate, weave into your speech the source material you've consulted. In your outline, refer to the source material by author's name, date, and page in parentheses; then provide the complete citation in your list of references.

In your actual speech it might prove more effective to include the source with your statement. It might be phrased something like this:

> According to John Naisbitt, author of the nationwide best seller *Megatrends*, the bellwether states are California, Florida, Washington, Colorado, and Connecticut.

Use a Consistent Set of Symbols
The following is the standard, accepted sequence of symbols for outlining.

```
I.
    A.
        1.
            a.
                (1)
                    (a)
```

Begin the introduction, the body, and the conclusion with roman numeral I. Treat each of the three major parts as a complete unit.

Not This	This
Introduction	Introduction
I.	I.
II.	II.
Body	Body
III.	I.
IV.	II.
V.	III.
Conclusion	Conclusion
VI.	I.
VII.	II.

Use Complete Declarative Sentences
Phrase your ideas in the outline in complete declarative sentences rather than as questions or as phrases. This will further assist you in examining the essential relationships. It's much easier, for example, to see if one item of information supports another if both are phrased in the declarative mode. If one is a question and one is a statement, this will be more difficult.

A CASE OF *Ethics*

Getting Help from Others

You have a speech due next week, and you're having trouble constructing your outline. But your friend, who is great at developing outlines, offers to help you write it. You could really use the help; also, in the process you figure you'll learn something about outlining. And besides, you'll fill in the outline, write it up, and deliver the speech.

Would it be ethical to accept this help? If not, how might you ethically avail yourself of your friend's help? More generally, what ethical guidelines should a speaker follow in getting help from other people?

Sample Outlines

Now that the principles of outlining are clear, here are some specific examples to illustrate how those principles are used in specific outlines. Presented here are two full-sentence preparation outlines, with annotations to guide you through the essential steps in outlining a speech; a skeletal outline that will provide a kind of template for a speech outline; and a delivery outline that will illustrate the type of outline you might use in delivering your speech.

A Preparation Outline with Annotations (Temporal Organization)

Here's a relatively detailed outline similar to outlines you may prepare in constructing your speeches. The side notes will clarify both the content and the format of a full-sentence outline.

Have You Ever Been Culture Shocked?

General purpose: To inform.

Specific purpose: To inform my audience of the four phases of culture shock.

Thesis: Culture shock can be described in four stages.

INTRODUCTION

I. Many of you have experienced or will experience culture shock.

A. Many people experience culture shock, that reaction to being in a culture very different from what you were used to.

B. By understanding culture shock, you'll be in a better position to deal with it if and when it comes.

II. I've lived in four different cultures myself.

A. I've always been interested in the way in which people adapt to different cultures.

Generally the title, thesis, and general and specific purposes of the speech are prefaced to the outline. When the outline is an assignment that is to be handed in, additional information may be requested.

Note the general format for the outline; note that the headings are clearly labeled and that the indenting helps you to see clearly the relationship that one item bears to another. For example, in Introduction II, the outline format helps you to see that A, B, C, and D are explanations (amplification and support) for II.

Note that the introduction, body, and conclusion are clearly labeled and separated visually.

The speaker assumes that the audience knows the general nature of culture shock and so does not go into detail as to its definition. But just in case some audience members don't know, and to refresh the memory of others, the speaker includes a brief definition.

B. With our own campus becoming more culturally diverse every semester, the process of culture shock becomes important for us all.

III. Culture shock occurs in four stages (Oberg, 1960).

A. The Honeymoon occurs first.

B. The Crisis occurs second.

C. The Recovery occurs third.

D. The Adjustment occurs fourth.

Here the speaker attempts to connect the speaker, audience, and topic by stressing intercultural experiences and an abiding interest in the topic. Also, the speaker makes the topic important to the listeners by referring to their everyday surroundings.

Note that references are integrated throughout the outline just as they would be in a term paper. In the actual speech, the speaker might say: "Anthropologist Kalervo Oberg, who coined the term 'culture shock,' said it occurs in four stages."

The introduction serves the three functions noted: it gains attention (by involving the audience and by stressing the importance of the topic to the audience's desire to gain self-understanding); it connects the speaker, audience, and topic in a way that establishes the credibility of the speaker; and it orients the audience as to what is to follow. This particular orientation identifies both the number of stages and their names. If this speech were a much longer and more complex one, the orientation might also have included brief definitions of each stage.

[Let's follow the order in which these four stages occur and begin with the first stage, the honeymoon.]

BODY

I. The Honeymoon occurs first.

A. The honeymoon is the period of fascination with the new people and culture.

B. You enjoy the people and the culture.

1. You love the people.
   a. For example, the people in Zaire spend their time very differently from the way New Yorkers do.
   b. For example, my first 18 years living on a farm was very different from life in a college dorm.

2. You love the culture.
   a. The great number of different religions in India fascinated me.
   b. Eating was an especially great experience.

This transition cues the audience into a four-part presentation. Also, the numbers repeated throughout the outline will further aid the audience in keeping track of where you are in the speech. Most important, it tells the audience that the speech will follow a temporal thought pattern.

Notice the parallel structure throughout the outline. For example, note that I, II, III, and IV in the body are all phrased in exactly the same way. Although this may seem unnecessarily redundant, it will help your audience follow your speech more closely and will also help you in logically structuring your thoughts.

Notice that there are lots of examples throughout this speech. These examples are identified only briefly in the outline and would naturally be elaborated on in the speech.

[But, like many relationships, life isn't all honeymoon; soon there comes a crisis.]

II. The Crisis occurs second.

A. The crisis is the period when you begin to experience problems.

1. One-third of American workers abroad fail because of culture shock (Samovar & Porter, 1991, p. 232).

2. The personal difficulties are also great.

B. Life becomes difficult in the new culture.

1. Communication is difficult.

2. It's easy to offend people without realizing it.

Notice too the internal organization of each major point. Each main assertion in the body contains a definition of the stage (IA, IIA, IIIA, and IVA) and examples (IB, IIB, IIIB, and IVB) to illustrate the stage.

Because this is a specific fact, some style manuals require that the page number should be included.

[As you gain control over the crises, you begin to recover.]

III. The Recovery occurs third.

    A. The recovery is the period when you learn how to cope.

    B. You begin to learn intercultural competence (Lustig & Koester, 1999).

        1. You learn how to communicate.

            a. Being able to go to the market and make my wants known was a great day for me.

            b. I was able to ask for a date.

        2. You learn the rules of the culture.

            a. The different religious ceremonies each have their own rules.

            b. Eating is a ritual experience in lots of places throughout Africa.

Note that each statement in the outline is a complete sentence. You can easily convert this outline into a phrase or key-word outline for use in delivery. The full sentences, however, will help you see more clearly relationships among items.

[Your recovery leads naturally into the next and final stage, the adjustment.]

IV. The Adjustment occurs fourth.

    A. The adjustment is the period when you come to enjoy the new culture.

    B. You come to appreciate the people and the culture.

The transitions are inserted between all major parts of the speech. Although they may seem too numerous in this abbreviated outline, they'll be appreciated by your audience because the transitions will help them follow your speech.

[Let me summarize the stages you go through in experiencing culture shock.]

CONCLUSION

I. Culture shock can be described in four stages.

    A. The honeymoon is first.

    B. The crisis is second.

    C. The recovery is third.

    D. The adjustment is fourth.

Notice that points I, II, III, and IV of the body correspond to I A, B, C, and D of the conclusion. Notice how the similar wording adds clarity.

II. Culture shock is a fascinating process; you may want to explore it more fully.

    A. Communication 325: Culture and Communication.

    B. Sunday's *60 Minutes*.

    C. Two great books.

This step, in which the speaker motivates the listeners to continue learning about culture shock, is optional in informative speeches.

III. By knowing the four stages, you can better understand the culture shock you may now be experiencing on the job, at school, or in your private life.

This step provides closure; it makes it clear that the speech is finished. It also serves to encourage reflection on the part of the audience as to their own culture shock.

References

Lustig, M. W., & Koester, J. (1999). *Intercultural competence: Interpersonal communication across cultures* (3rd ed.). Boston: Allyn & Bacon.

Oberg, K. (1960). Culture shock: Adjustment to new cultural environments. *Practical Anthropology* 7: 177–182.

Samovar, L. A., & Porter, R. E. (1991). *Communication between cultures*. Belmont, CA: Wadsworth.

This reference list includes just those sources that appear in the completed speech.

A Preparation Outline with Annotations (Motivated Sequence Organization)

This outline illustrates how you might construct an outline and a speech using the motivated sequence. To model the five steps in the motivated sequence, we'll return to the example given earlier in the chapter—the establishment of a youth center as a means of combating juvenile crime. In a longer speech, if you wanted to persuade an audience to establish a youth center, you might want to select two or three general arguments rather than limiting yourself to the one argument about reducing juvenile crime.

The Youth Center

General purpose: To persuade.

Specific purpose: To persuade my listeners to vote in favor of Proposition 14 establishing a community youth center.

Thesis: A youth center will reduce juvenile crime.

I. If you could reduce juvenile crime by some 20 percent by just flipping a lever, would you do it?

    A. Thom's drug store was broken into by teenagers.

    B. Loraine's video store windows were broken by teenagers.

II. Juvenile crime is on the rise.

    A. The overall number of crimes has increased.

    B. In 1995 there were 32 juvenile crimes.

        1. In 1998 there were 47 such crimes.

        2. In 2000 there were 63 such crimes.

    C. The number of serious crimes also has increased.

        1. In 1995 there were 30 misdemeanors and 2 felonies.

        2. In 2000 there were 35 misdemeanors and 28 felonies.

III. A youth center will help reduce juvenile crime.

I. Attention step

The speaker asks a question to gain attention and follows it with specific examples of juvenile crime that audience members have experienced. The question and the specific examples focus on one single issue: the need to reduce juvenile crime. If the speech were a broader and longer one that included other reasons for the youth center, then it would have been appropriate to preview them here as well.

II. Need step

The speaker states the need directly and clearly and shows that a problem exists. The speaker then demonstrates that the rise in crime is significant both in absolute numbers and in the severity of the crimes. To increase the listeners' ability to understand these figures, it would help if these figures were written on a chalkboard, on a prepared chart, or on PowerPoint slides. In a longer speech, other needs might also be identified in this step; for example, the need to offer teenagers a place where they can learn useful vocational and social skills.

III. Satisfaction step

A. Three of our neighboring towns reduced juvenile crime after establishing a youth center.

   1. In Marlboro there was a 20 percent decline in overall juvenile crime.
   2. In both Highland and Ellenville the number of serious crimes declined 25 percent.

B. The youth center will not increase our tax burden.

   1. New York State grants will pay for most of the expenses.
   2. Local merchants have agreed to pay any remaining expenses.

IV. Juvenile crime will decrease as a result of the youth center.

A. If we follow the example of our neighbors, our juvenile crime rates are likely to decrease by 20 to 25 percent.

B. Thom's store would not have been broken into.

C. Loraine's windows would not have been broken.

V. Vote *yes* on Proposition 14.

A. In next week's election, you'll be asked to vote on Proposition 14, establishing a youth center.

B. Vote *yes* if you want to help reduce juvenile crime.

C. Urge your family members, your friends, and your work colleagues also to vote *yes*.

In this step, the speaker shows the listeners that the proposal to establish a youth center has great benefits and no significant drawbacks.

The speaker argues that the youth center will satisfy the need to reduce juvenile crime by showing statistics from neighboring towns. The speaker also answers the objection and removes any doubts about increased taxes. If the speaker had reason to believe that listeners might have other possible objections, those objections, too, should be answered in this step.

IV. Visualization step

Here the speaker visualizes what the town would be like if the youth center were established, using both the statistics developed earlier and the personal examples introduced at the beginning of the speech.

V. Action step

In this step the speaker asks listeners to take specific actions—to vote in favor of the youth center and to urge others to do the same. The speaker also reiterates the main theme of the speech; namely, that the youth center will help reduce juvenile crime.

Skeletal Outline

Here's a skeletal outline—a kind of template for structuring a speech. This particular outline would be appropriate for a speech using a topical organization pattern. Note that in this skeletal outline there are three main points (I, II, and III in the body). These correspond to the II A, B, and C in the introduction (where you'd orient the audience) and to the I A, B, and C in the conclusion (where you'd summarize your main points). The transitions are signaled by square brackets. As you review this outline, the faintly printed watermarks will remind you of the functions of each outline item.

USING TECHNOLOGY

Examine the templates created for the wide variety of organizational patterns presented on the Companion Website for this chapter (www.ablongman. com/devito). How can you adapt one of these templates for your next speech? What are the advantages and disadvantages of using a template in preparing a public speech?

Skeletal Outline

General purpose: your general aim (to inform, to persuade, to entertain)

Specific purpose: what you hope to achieve from this speech

Thesis: your main assertion; the core of your speech

INTRODUCTION

I. gain attention _____

II. establish speaker–audience–topic connection _____

III. orient audience _____

    A. first main point; same as I in body _____

    B. second main point; same as II in body _____

    C. third main point; same as III in body _____

[Transition: connect the introduction to the body _____]

BODY

I. first main point _____

    A. support for I (the first main point) _____

    B. further support for I _____

[Transition: connect the first major point to the second _____]

II. second main point _____

    A. support for II (the second main point) _____

    B. further support for II _____

[Transition: connect the second main point to the third _____]

III. third main point _____

    A. support for III _____

    B. further support for III _____

[Transition: connect the third main point (or all main points) to the conclusion _____]

CONCLUSION

I. summary _____

    A. first main point; same as I in body _____

    B. second main point; same as II in body _____

    C. third main point; same as III in body _____

II. motivation _____

III. closure _____

References

1. _____

2. _____

3. _____

DEVELOPING STRATEGIES

Outlining Template. Tony is giving a speech on the three major advantages and the three major disadvantages of taking vitamin supplements. Can you construct a template that would help Tony outline his speech?

A Delivery Outline

Now that you've constructed a preparation outline, you need to construct a **delivery outline**, an outline that will assist you in delivering the speech. Resist the temptation to use your preparation outline to deliver the speech. If you use your preparation outline, you'll tend to read from the outline, instead of presenting an extemporaneous speech in which you attend to and respond to audience feedback.

Instead, construct a brief delivery outline that will assist rather than hinder your delivery of the speech. Here is a sample delivery outline constructed from the preparation outline on culture shock, presented on pages 156–159. The annotations will clarify the unique features of this type of outline.

Note first that the outline is brief enough so that you'll be able to use it effectively without losing eye contact with the audience.

Notice that the outline uses abbreviations (for example, CS for *culture shock*) and phrases rather than complete sentences. This helps to keep the outline brief but also helps you to scan your message more quickly.

At the same time, however, it's detailed enough to include all essential parts of your speech, including transitions. Be careful that you don't omit essential parts even if you're convinced that you couldn't possibly forget them. Normal apprehension may cause you to do exactly that.

This outline contains delivery notes specifically tailored to your own needs; for example, pause suggestions and guides to using visual aids.

The outline is clearly divided into an introduction, body, and conclusion and uses the same numbering system as the preparation outline.

Rehearse with this delivery outline, not with your full-sentence outline. This suggestion is simply a specific application of the general rule: Make rehearsals as close to the real thing as possible.

Delivery Outline

PAUSE!
LOOK OVER THE AUDIENCE!

INTRODUCTION

I. Many experience CS
   A. CS: the reaction to being in a culture very different from your own.
   B. By understanding CS, you'll be better able to deal with it.
   PAUSE/SCAN AUDIENCE

II. I've experienced CS

III. CS occurs in 4 stages (WRITE ON BOARD)
   A. Honeymoon
   B. Crisis
   C. Recovery
   D. Adjustment

[Let's examine these stages of CS.]
   PAUSE/STEP FORWARD

BODY

I. Honeymoon
   A. fascination w/ people and culture
   B. enjoyment of people and culture
      1. people: Zaire, farm
      2. culture: religions of India, food

[But, life isn't all honeymoon—the crisis]

II. Crisis
   A. problems arise
      1. 1/3 Am. workers fail abroad
      2. personal difficulties
   B. life becomes difficult
      1. communication
      2. offend others

[As you gain control over the crises, you learn how to cope.]
   PAUSE

III. Recovery
    A. period of learning to cope
    B. you learn intercultural competence
        1. communication becomes easier
        2. you learn the culture's rules

[As you recover, you adjust.]

IV. Adjustment
    A. learn to enjoy (again) the new culture
    B. appreciate people and culture

[These then are the four stages; let me summarize.]
    PAUSE

CONCLUSION

I. CS occurs in 4 stages: honeymoon, crisis, recovery, & adjustment

II. Learn More
    A. Comm 325
    B. 60 minutes
    C. books

III. By knowing the 4 stages, you can better understand the culture shock you may now be experiencing on the job, at school, or in your private life.
    PAUSE
    ANY QUESTIONS?

A Brief Note on Organization and Flexibility

Be careful that you don't allow your organization to destroy the flexibility that you need in delivering your speech—to prevent you from adjusting and adapting your speech to the ever-changing situation. To heighten your awareness of the need for flexibility, take the following self-test (developed from an idea by Martin & Rubin, 1994, 1995).

Test YOURSELF

How Flexible Are You as a Public Speaker?

Visualize yourself in each of the following situations. Reflect for one minute on each situation, identifying as many different appropriate ways of handling the situation that you can think of in this one minute. Jot down brief abbreviations for each of the possibilities you think of. Record the number of ways you might appropriately handle each situation in the spaces provided.

_____ **1.** You're preparing a speech on abortion and planning to use some posters on both sides of the issue. Unfortunately, the person who was going to lend you the posters went on vacation, and you now have no way of getting them. These were going to be great visual aids. What might you do?

_____ **2.** Right in the middle of your speech on violence on television, a listener in the back row yells out in a perfect Austrian accent, "Hasta la vista, baby!" The entire class busts out laughing. What might you do?

_____ **3.** While you are giving your speech, one of the audience members not only falls asleep but starts snoring so loudly that everyone begins to concentrate on the snoring rather than on what you're saying. What might you do?

_____ **4.** In your speech on e-mail programs, you had planned to show the class three different programs. The first two went along without any mishaps. When you tried to show the third one, you got an error message that you didn't understand. What might you do?

_____ **5.** One of your speech assignments requires that as part of your supporting material, you interview someone with special knowledge of your speech topic. You've developed a really great speech on the dangers of taking too many vitamins, and your interviewee is going to be a nurse who suffered from excess vitamins and has just written a book on the topic. Unfortunately, the nurse is called out of town for several weeks and won't be available for the interview. What might you do?

❖ **HOW DID YOU DO?** The number of ways of handling each situation is a measure of your flexibility. The more ways you can think of, the more flexible you are.

❖ **WHAT WILL YOU DO?** If possible, share your responses with others in small groups or with the class as a whole. You should find that any group is a lot more flexible than any one person; that is, the group as a whole will come up with more possibilities than would any one individual. Can you think of other situations in which flexibility would come in handy?

Summary of Concepts and Skills

This chapter has covered ways to organize the body of the speech; prepare the introduction, conclusion, and transitions; and outline the speech.

The Body of the Speech

In organizing the body of the speech:

◆ Select your main points.
- Select the point that are most important to your thesis.
- Combine those that have a common focus.
- Select those that are most relevant to your audience.
- Use few main points (two, three, or four work best).
- Phrase your main points in parallel style.
- Separate your main points avoiding any overlap.

◆ Organize your main points.
- In a **temporal** pattern your main ideas are arranged in a time sequence.
- In a **spatial** pattern your main ideas are arranged in a space pattern—for example, left to right.
- In a **topical** pattern your main ideas (equal in value and importance) are itemized.
- In a **problem–solution** pattern your main ideas are divided into problems and solutions.
- In a **cause–effect** pattern your main ideas are arranged into causes and effects.
- In a **motivated sequence** pattern your main ideas are arranged into five steps: attention, need, satisfaction, visualization, and action.
- Additional patterns include: **structure–function, comparison-and-contrast, pro-and-con (advan-**

tages and disadvantages), **claim-and-proof, multiple-definition,** and *Who? What? Why? Where? When?*

- In selecting an organizational pattern, take into consideration the cultural composition of your audience, especially the extent to which they are from low-context or high-context cultures.

Introductions, Conclusions, and Transitions

Construct your introduction, conclusion, and transitions.

- ◆ Construct your introduction so that it:
  - Gains attention.
  - Establishes a connection among speaker, audience, and topic.
  - Orients the audience.
- ◆ Construct your conclusion so that it:
  - Summarizes your speech or some aspect of it.
  - Motivates your audience.
  - Provides crisp closure.
- ◆ Avoid the common problems of introductions and conclusions:
  - Don't apologize.
  - Don't rely on gimmicks.
  - Don't preface your introduction.
  - Don't introduce new material in your conclusion.
- ◆ Use transitions to connect the parts of your speech and give your listeners guides to help them follow your speech. Use transitions:
  - Between the introduction and the body.
  - Among the main points.
  - Between the body and the conclusion.

Outlining the Speech

- ◆ Outlines may vary from complete sentence outlines to those with just key words and phrases. In constructing your outline:
  - Preface the outline with identifying data.
  - Outline the introduction, body, and conclusion as separate units.
  - Insert transitions in square brackets.
  - Append a list of references (if required).
  - Use a consistent set of symbols.
  - Use complete declarative sentences (for your preparation outline).

Vocabulary Quiz

Organizing the Speech

Match these terms about organization with their definitions. Record the number of the definition next to the term.

_____ high-context cultures

_____ low-context cultures

_____ temporal pattern

_____ topical pattern

_____ motivated sequence

_____ transitions

_____ attention

_____ orientation

_____ closure

_____ skeletal outline

1. Organization of a speech into five steps: attention, need, satisfaction of need, visualization, and action.

2. Cultures in which much of the information in communication is in the context or in the person rather than explicitly stated in the message.

3. That part of the speech that tells the audience what the speaker will cover throughout the speech.

4. A template for structuring speeches.

5. Organization in terms of time divisions—for example, past, present, and future.

6. Organization of a speech in terms of its major parts or divisions; for example, explaining modern art in terms of its major schools (impressionism, cubism, and so on).

7. Usually the first part of a speech introduction.

8. Usually the last part of a speech conclusion.

9. Culture in which information is explicitly stated in the message; it is not assumed that both speaker and listener already have the relevant information.

10. Words, phrases, or sentences that connect the various part of your speech.

Web Explorations

Companion Website
www.ablongman.com/devito

Additional help in organizing your speech is provided in the Companion Website's Chapter 6. In "Adding and Arranging Supporting Materials" you'll find suggestions for arranging you may not have considered. Additional help in outlining is provided in "Functions of Outlines," "Using Visual Aspects to Reflect Your Organizational Pattern," and "Using One Discrete Idea per Sym-

bol." Practice in outlining is provided in a scrambled outline you're asked to unscramble: "Organizing a Scrambled Outline." Thirteen skeletal outlines similar to the model presented in this chapter but designed for different types of speeches are provided in "Skeletal Outlines." A self-test on "Flexibility in Communication" will enable you to extend your thinking about flexibility in public speaking to all areas and forms of communication.

Public Speaking Exercises

6.1 Generating Main Points

One of the skills in organizing a speech is to ask a strategic question of your thesis and from the answer to generate your main points. Below we present 10 thesis statements suitable for a variety of informative or persuasive speeches. For each thesis statement, ask a question and generate two, three, or four main points that would be suitable for an informative or persuasive speech.

Here's an example to get you started:

Thesis statement: Mandatory retirement should (should not) be abolished.

Question: Why should mandatory retirement be abolished?

 I. Mandatory retirement leads us to lose many of the most productive workers.
 II. Mandatory retirement contributes to psychological problems of those forced to retire.
III. Mandatory retirement costs corporations economic hardship because they have to train new people.

1. Buy American.
2. Tax property assets owned by religious organizations.
3. Require adoption agencies to reveal the names of birth parents to all adopted children when they reach 18 years of age.
4. Permit condom distribution in all junior and senior high schools.
5. Permit gay men and lesbians to adopt children.
6. Ban all sales of furs from wild animals.
7. Make the death penalty mandatory for those convicted of selling drugs to minors.
8. Require all students at this college to take courses on women's issues.
9. Legalize soft drugs.
10. Grant full equality to gay men and lesbians in the military.

6.2 Constructing Introductions and Conclusions

Prepare an introduction and a conclusion for a speech on one of the theses listed. Be prepared to explain the methods you used to accomplish each of these aims.

1. College isn't for everyone.
2. Maximum sentences should be imposed even for first offenders of the drug laws.
3. Each of us should donate our organs to medicine after our death.
4. Laws restricting Sunday shopping should be abolished.

5. Suicide and its assistance by others should be legalized.

6. Gambling should be legalized in all states.

7. College athletics should be abolished.

8. Same-sex marriages should be legalized.

9. Divorce should be granted immediately when there's mutual agreement.

10. Privatization of elementary and high schools should be encouraged.

6.3 Analyzing a Speech

THE COST OF JUSTICE

Adam Childers

You know, there are just some things in life that you have to fight for—like your right to crunchy-style peanut butter. And that is why, when inmate Kenneth Parker, of Nevada State Prison, was given creamy instead of crunchy peanut butter by his prison canteen two years ago, he filed a civil rights lawsuit. In this lawsuit, he demanded $5,500 dollars for the mental and emotional pain that he suffered, without the PB of his choice. Two years later, after countless hours spent by the Attorney General's office, and over $10,000 spent in taxpayer's money, this case was dismissed. As nutty as this story may sound, sadly, it is fast becoming the norm. That is because according to *Trial* magazine of May 1995, the number of inmate civil lawsuits nationwide has risen to 35,000 per year—which is roughly 30 percent of all civil lawsuits filed in the United States annually. This trend should alarm all of us, for two reasons. First, millions of dollars of our tax money are being spent needlessly on these lawsuits every year. But, even more importantly, these lawsuits are putting a financial strain on an already overburdened penal system—helping to create a situation in which our prisoners are being released early.

Does the speaker effectively capture your attention early in the introduction? How does he do this?

Does the speaker establish a speaker–audience–topic connection? Does the speaker effectively explain his interest and concern for this topic and how it is related to the audience?

Do you agree with the speaker's decision to state his thesis early in the speech? With what type of audience do you think it might have been wiser to delay the statement of the thesis until the evidence and argument had been presented?

Today we will examine this growing problem of frivolous inmate civil lawsuits. By first, uncovering their origins; secondly, understanding the problems associated with them; we will, finally, discover a few viable solutions to this current crisis.

Initially, we must understand where these lawsuits are coming from. To do so, we must take a look at Section 1983, Title 42, of the United States Code. The March 1995 edition of *Federal Probation* reports that this statute was established shortly after the Civil War, and it grants the right to citizens to sue local and state government officials when policies and practices fall below Constitutional standards. During the 1960s, the Supreme Court extended the power of this act, to give the right to prisoners to challenge their confinement—on the grounds that it violated their Constitutional rights. Over the years, these cases have proven to be instrumental in forcing improvement in prison medical care, legal access, and inmate treatment. The problem

Does the speaker effectively orient the audience? Do you have a very clear idea of how the speech will be developed? What are the speaker's three main points? How might these be stated in a preparation outline?

Does the speaker commit any of the faults common in introductions, such as apologizing or relying on gimmicks?

though, as the March 21, 1995, *New York Times* can attest, is that along with these landmark cases have come a bounty of frivolous and costly complaints. New York State Attorney General Oliver Koppel stated in a January 1996 press release that these cases consume over 20 percent of his department's resources—and he concluded by saying, "There has to be a way for prisoners to complain, but this it not it." In Mr. Koppel's home state of New York, there are 28,000 inmate lawsuits backlogged, waiting to be heard. As astounding as their figure is, it is eclipsed by the states of California, Texas, Missouri, and Florida. We can only expect these numbers to rise as these lawsuits are so easy to file. Most prisoners can cite poverty and avoid the $120 dollar filing fee. In addition, prisons are required to provide inmates with legal access and even postage to mail off their complaints. And this does not even take into account what the August 7, 1995, *National Law Journal* calls "loneliness lawsuits." This is the trend of prisoners who have nothing else better to do, filing lawsuits—to while away their time. Case in point, inmate Jerry Young of Connecticut who has congested our federal court system with a record 98 civil lawsuits in the past 12 years alone.

With an understanding of the origins and the severity of inmate civil litigation in hand, we can now turn, and understand how these lawsuits are adversely affecting our prison population and society at large.

Time magazine, of February 7, 1995, points out that our prison population has doubled in recent decades—reaching 925,000 prisoners in 1995. These prisoners do not come cheaply either. The October 17, 1995, edition of *Fortune* notes that each and every one of these prisoners costs an estimated $36,500 to house per year. With conditions such as these, obviously every dime counts. Which makes it even more unfortunate that as this same article pointed out, last year alone over $181,000,000 was spent on inmate civil lawsuits.

But even more worrisome than this are the detrimental effects that these lawsuits are having on the societal level. The January 1995 *ABA Journal* points out that the average American prisoner spends only 41 percent of his appointed time in jail, and that since 1991, 43,000 convicts have been rearrested after an early release that was due to financial troubles. Financial troubles that according to the August 30, 1995, *Washington Post*, are due in large part to these frivolous inmate lawsuits. Money wasted on these suits cannot solve our prison's problems outright, but they can help shore up a penal system that has run amok. Whether it be money spent on: Roy Clenidnen's one million dollar suit for the right to ice cream in his New York prison, or Reginald Troy's battle for veal and oysters in his Texas prison, or even Keith Polloidian's pending suit in the state of Florida,

How does the speaker make the transition to the second main point?

What organizational pattern is the speaker following? Might other organizational patterns work as well?

over the razor wire that encircles his prison, which he insists could severely lacerate him if he chose to escape. All of this money is sorely needed to ensure that our prisoners are rehabilitated, and that law-abiding citizens are kept safe.

The problems associated with inmate civil lawsuits are quite evident, but, fortunately, so too are the solutions. There are steps that we may take to alleviate this problem on a state, federal, and finally, an individual level.

First, state prisons deal with the bulk of inmate lawsuits (97 percent to be precise). The May 2, 1995, *Fortune* notes that the best step for these institutions is to require a one- to five-dollar filing fee of the prisoner's wages. The Federal District of New York recently began this practice, and has enjoyed a 35 percent decrease in cases filed.

The federal government can help lend a hand as well, with the Civil Rights of Institutionalized Persons Act, also known as CRIPA. CRIPA enables the United States Attorney General and the federal courts to certify state administrative grievance mechanisms—such as a screening process that would hear all cases, checking them for validity before they advance to the trial stage. CRIPA authorizes state and federal courts to mandate the exhaustion of these sort of grievance mechanisms before inmate cases reach the court docket. In a January 1995 United States Department of Justice report entitled, "Challenging the Conditions of our Prisons and Jails," researchers concluded that the leadership of the Districts of the United States Courts of Appeals must encourage state correctional agencies to submit new grievance mechanisms to help ensure that CRIPA is implemented.

That means that the only question left now is, What can we do to help? And, the answer is—get involved. In a telephone interview, conducted on January 23, 1996, Assistant Attorney General of Florida, Joe Bizarro, explained to me that it is only with the efforts of citizens' groups that are dedicated to tort reform that we can expect any sort of significant change. Such a group is CALA—Citizens Against Lawsuit Abuse. Based out of Houston, Texas, this is a nationwide grass-roots organization that is resolved to fight for legal reform. One of their major goals is curbing frivolous inmate lawsuits. The means that they use to achieve this end, sometimes, can be as simple as a bumper sticker sent out to all those who contact their organization. But, they can also be as complex as the many lobby groups they have formed around the nation, that are currently urging both state legislatures as well as the federal government, to change existing laws that allow these frivolous inmate lawsuits to occur. In order that you may be able to contact this organization, at the conclusion of this speech, I will distribute a card with the address and

What additional transitions can you locate in this speech? Are they effective?

Does the speaker use any internal summaries?

How effectively does the speaker summarize his main points?

Does the speaker motivate his audience to do something about the problem?

phone number of CALA—which will enable all of you to make a choice, a choice to get involved.

Today, we have examined the growing problem of frivolous inmate civil lawsuits by examining their origins and implications, and by, finally, highlighting some concrete solutions to their existence.

How does the speaker close the speech? Is this effective?

The story of Kenneth Parker and his fetish for crunchy-style peanut butter is a funny one. But, for every story like his, there is another like the one documented in the February 17, 1995, *New York Times.* This story tells of a 15-year-old Ohio girl who was caught running away from home, and sent to jail for the night. There, she was raped by a prison guard. She subsequently filed a civil rights lawsuit against the prison, but, her case was back-logged by numerous, frivolous inmate lawsuits. By the time that her case was heard—over one year later—over one hundred more children had spent time in that same jail cell. It lies in our hands to ensure that travesties of justice like this one do not take place in the future. Not only for the safety of our prisoners, but, for our own as well.

Does the speaker commit any of the faults common in conclusions, such as introducing new material or apologizing?

Can you create a brief key-word delivery outline for this speech?

Childers, A. (1996). The cost of justice. In L. G. Schnoor (Ed.), *Winning orations of the Interstate Oratorical Association* (pp. 78–80). Mankato, MN: Interstate Oratorical Association.

7 Wording Your Speech

Why Read This Chapter?

It will enable you to word your speech for greatest effectiveness by helping you to:

❖ select words that will communicate your thoughts clearly, vividly, appropriately, and in a personal style to better inform and persuade your audience

❖ phrase your sentences so that they are clear and memorable, and so that your audience will be able to easily follow your speech

> " When I read great literature, great drama, speeches, or sermons, I feel that the human mind has not achieved anything greater than the ability to share feelings and thoughts through language. "
>
> **—James Earl Jones**

Your success as a public speaker depends heavily on the way you express your ideas: on the words you select and the way you phrase your sentences. This chapter will focus on this crucial process of wording your speech, first explaining how language works and then suggesting ways to word and phrase your ideas for maximum impact and effectiveness.

How Language Works

Your use of language will greatly influence your ability to inform and persuade an audience. Five qualities of language are especially important: directness, abstraction, objectivity, orality, and accuracy.

Language Varies in Directness

Consider the following sentences:

> 1A. We should all vote for Halliwell in the next election.
>
> 1B. Vote for Halliwell in the next election.
>
> 2A. It should be apparent that we should abandon the present system.
>
> 2B. Abandon the present system.
>
> 3A. Many people would like to go to Xanadu.
>
> 3B. How many of you want to go to Xanadu?

The B-sentences are clearly more direct than the A-sentences. Note, for example, that the B-sentences address the audience directly. The A-sentences are more distant, more indirect. Indirect sentences address only an abstract, unidentified mass of people. The sentences might as well address just anyone. When you use direct sentences, you address your specific and clearly defined listeners.

Direct language, in sum, is explicit and forthright. To achieve directness, use active rather than passive sentences; say, "The professor invented the serum" rather than "The serum was invented by the professor." Use personal pronouns and personal references. Refer to your audience as "you" rather than "the audience" or "my listeners."

The preference for directness will vary considerably with the culture of the speaker and the audience. Many Asian and Latin American cultures, for example, stress the values of indirectness, largely because indirectness enables a person to avoid appearing criticized or contradicted and thereby losing face. In most of the United States, however, you're taught that directness is the preferred style. "Be up-front" and "tell it like it is" are commonly heard communication guidelines. Many Asian Americans and Latin Americans may, in fact, experience a conflict between the recommendation of style manuals to be direct and the cultural recommendation to be indirect.

Language Varies in Abstraction

Consider the following list of terms:

- ◆ entertainment
- ◆ film

- American film
- recent American film
- *Harry Potter and the Sorcerer's Stone*

At the top is the general or abstract term *entertainment*. Note that *entertainment* includes all the other items on the list plus various other items—television, novels, drama, comics, and so on. *Film* is more specific and concrete. It includes all of the items below it as well as various other items, such as Indian film or Russian film. The term excludes, however, all entertainment that is not film. *American film* is again more specific than *film* and excludes all films that are not American. *Recent American film* further limits *American film* to a time period. *Harry Potter and the Sorcerer's Stone* specifies concretely the one item to which reference is made.

Choose words from a wide range of **abstractions.** At times a general term may suit your needs best; at other times a more concrete, specific term may serve better. Generally, the specific term is the better choice.

The more general term—in this case, *entertainment*—conjures up numerous different images. One person in the audience may focus on television, another on music, another on comic books, and still another on radio. To some, *film* may bring to mind the early silent films. To others, it brings to mind postwar Italian films. To still others, it recalls Disney's animated cartoons. So as you get more specific and less abstract, you more effectively guide the images that come to your listeners' minds. Specific rather than abstract language will aid you in both your informative and persuasive goals.

Language Varies in Objectivity

The best way to explain how language varies in objectivity is to introduce two new terms: **denotation** and **connotation.** The *denotative meaning* of a term is its objective meaning. This is the meaning that you'd find in a dictionary. This meaning points to specific references. Thus, the denotation of the word *book* is, for example, the actual book, a collection of pages bound together between two covers. The denotative meaning of *dog* is a four-legged canine; the denotative meaning of *kiss* is, according to the *Random House Dictionary*, "to touch or press with the lips slightly pursed in token of greeting, affection, reverence, etc."

Connotative meaning, however, is different. The connotative meaning is your affective, or emotional, meaning for the term. The word *book* may signify boredom or excitement. It may recall the novel you have to read or perhaps this textbook that you're reading right now. Connotatively, *dog* may mean friendliness, warmth, and affection. *Kiss* may, connotatively, mean warmth, good feeling, and happiness.

Seldom do listeners misunderstand the denotative meaning of a term. When you use a term with which the audience isn't familiar, you define it and thus make sure that the term is understood. Differences in connotative meanings, however, pose difficulties. For example, you may, use the term *neighbor*, intending to communicate security and friendliness. To some of your listeners, however, the term may connote unwanted intrusions, sneakiness, and nosiness. Notice that both you and your listeners would surely agree that denotatively *neighbor* means a person who lives near another person. What you and they disagree on—and what then leads to misunderstanding—is the connotation of the term.

Cultural differences add to the complexity and difficulty of accurately communicating meaning. The meaning of the word *dog* will obviously mean one

USING TECHNOLOGY

If you're having any trouble with grammar, visit the online grammar guides of Johns Hopkins University (http://www.welch.jhu.edu/publish/guides/html), California State University (www.calstatela.edu/library/styleman.html), or Colorado State (http://writing.colostate.edu/references).

thing to a person from the United States, where *dog* signifies a "beloved pet," and quite another thing to a person from a culture where *dog* signifies "eating delicacy." *Beef* to a person from Kansas or Texas (where cattle provide much of the state's wealth) will mean something very different than *beef* does to a person from India (where the cow is a sacred animal).

As a speaker, consider the audience's evaluation of key terms before using them in your speech. When you're part of the audience, as in a public speaking class, you probably have a good idea of the meanings members have for various terms. When you address an audience very different from yourself, however, this prior investigation becomes crucial.

Language Varies in Orality

Orality refers to the degree to which a communication style resembles that of informal conversation as opposed to the more formal style of writing. You don't speak as you write. The words and sentences you use differ. The major reason for this difference is that you compose speech instantly. You select your words and construct your sentences as you think of your ideas. There's very little time in between the thought and the utterance. When you write, however, you compose your thoughts after considerable reflection. Even then you probably often rewrite and edit as you go along. Because of this, written language has a more formal tone. Spoken language is more informal, more colloquial.

Generally, spoken language, or **oral style**, uses shorter, simpler, and more familiar words than does written language. Also, there's more qualification in speech than in writing. For example, when speaking you probably make greater use of such expressions as *although, however, perhaps,* and the like. When writing, you probably edit these out.

Spoken language has a greater number of self-reference terms (terms that refer to the speaker herself or himself): *I, me, our, us,* and *you.* Spoken language also has a greater number of "allness" terms such as *all, none, every, always, never.* When you write, you're probably more careful to edit out such allness terms, realizing that such terms are usually not very descriptive of reality.

Spoken language has more pseudo-quantifying terms (for example, *many, much, very, lots*) and terms that include the speaker as part of the observation (for example, "it seems to me that . . ." or "as I see it . . ."). Further, speech contains more verbs and adverbs; writing contains more nouns and adjectives.

Oral style and written language *should* differ. The main reason why spoken and written language should differ is that the listener hears a speech only once; therefore, speech must be *instantly intelligible.* The reader, on the other hand, can reread an essay or look up an unfamiliar word. The reader can spend as much time as he or she wishes with the written page. The listener, however, must move at the pace set by the speaker. The reader may reread a sentence or paragraph if there's a temporary attention lapse; the listener doesn't have this option.

Language Varies in Accuracy

Language can reflect reality faithfully or unfaithfully. It can describe reality (as science tells us it exists) with great accuracy or with serious distortion. For example, we can use language to describe the many degrees that exist in, say, wealth, or we can describe wealth inaccurately in terms of two values, rich and poor. We can discuss these ways in which the accuracy of language may vary in

? DEVELOPING STRATEGIES

Correcting Errors. In her speech Alexx says that in a poll more than 70 percent of the students favored banning alcohol on her university's campus. Toward the end of the speech, she realizes that she mixed up the figures; only 30 percent favored banning alcohol on campus. During the question-and-answer period no one asks about the figures. Should Alexx say anything? Would your answer differ depending on whether Alexx herself favored or opposed banning alcohol from campus?

terms of the five thinking errors central to the area of language study known as General Semantics (DeVito, 1974; Hayakawa & Hayakawa, 1990; Korzybski, 1933), now so much a part of critical thinking instruction (Johnson, 1991). These five errors are polarization, fact–inference confusion, allness, static evaluation, and indiscrimination.

Polarization

The term **polarization** refers to the tendency to look at the world in terms of opposites and to describe it in terms of extremes—good or bad, positive or negative, healthy or sick, intelligent or stupid, rich or poor, and so on. It's often referred to as the "fallacy of either/or." So destructive is either/or thinking that the American Psychiatric Association identifies it as one of the major behavior characteristics of "borderline personality disorder"—a psychological disorder that lies between neurosis and psychosis and is characterized by unstable interpersonal relationships and confusion about identity.

Most people, events, and objects, of course, exist somewhere between the extremes of good and bad, health and sickness, intelligence and stupidity, wealth and poverty. Yet among all of us there's a strong tendency to view only the extremes and to categorize people, objects, and events in terms of these polar opposites.

Problems arise when polarization is used in inappropriate situations; for example, "The politician is either for us or against us." Note that these two options don't include all possibilities. The politician may be for us in some things and against us in other things, or may be neutral. Beware of speakers who imply and believe that two extreme classes include all possible classes—for example, that an individual must be pro–rebel forces or anti–rebel forces, with no other alternatives.

Fact–Inference Confusion

You can make statements about the world you observe, and you can make statements about what you have not observed. In form or structure these statements are similar and can't be distinguished by any grammatical analysis. For example,

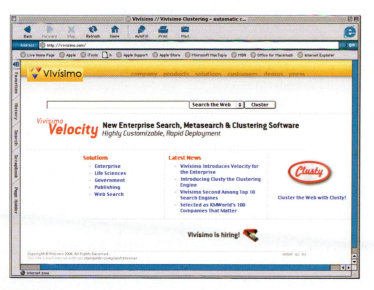

Vivisimo

(www.vivisimo.com)
Vivisimo is one of the best meta–search engines available. It presents you with results in topic clusters so you can more easily select those that seem most likely to be what you want. Try searching your next speech with Vivisimo.

you can say, "This proposal contains 17 pages" as well as "This proposal contains the seeds of its own self-destruction." Both sentences look similar in form, yet they're very different types of statements. You can observe the 17 pages, but how do you observe "the seeds of its own self-destruction"? Obviously, this isn't a descriptive but an inferential statement, a statement you make on the basis not only of what you observe, but on what you conclude.

In evaluating research, in presenting your information and arguments, and in listening to the speeches of others, beware of **fact–inference confusion;** be sure to distinguish between what is factual from what is inferential. Of course, there's nothing wrong with making inferences; the problem arises when you assume that an inference is a fact and treat it and behave as if it were a fact.

Allness

Because the world is infinitely complex, we can never know all or say all about anything—at least we can't logically say all about anything. Beware of speakers who fall into the error of **allness**—who present information as if it's all that

---

RESEARCH *Link*

Searching the Web

In most cases, searching the Web efficiently requires the use of search engines and subject directories, plus some knowledge of how these tools operate.

A **search engine** is a program that searches a database or index of Internet sites for the specific words you submit. These search engines are easily accessed through your Internet browser, and both Netscape and Internet Explorer have search functions as a part of their own home pages; they also provide convenient links to the most popular search engines and directories.

A **directory** is a list of subjects or categories of Web links. You select the category you're most interested in, then a subcategory of that, then a subcategory of that until you reach your specific topic. A directory doesn't cover everything; rather, the documents that it groups under its various categories are selected by the directory's staff members from those they deem to be especially worthwhile. Many search engines also provide directories, so you can use the method you prefer.

Some search engines are meta–search engines; these search the databases of a variety of search engines at the same time. These programs are especially useful if you want a broad search and you have the time to sift through lots of websites. Some

of the more popular include Ask Jeeves at www.ask. com, Google at www.google.com, Dog Pile at www.dogpile.com, and Vivisimo at www.vivisimo. com (see the home page shown on p. 175). Other useful search engines (some of which also contain directories) include Yahoo! (www.yahoo.com), AltaVista (www.altavista.com), and Go (http://www. go.com).

In using search engines (and in searching many CD-ROM databases), you'll often find it helpful to limit your search with "operators"—words and symbols that define relationships among the terms for which you're searching. Perhaps the most common are AND (or +), OR, and NOT (or −). Searching for *drugs AND violence* will limit your search to only those documents that contain both words—in any order. Searching for *drugs OR violence* will expand your search to all documents containing either word. And searching for *violence AND schools NOT elementary* will yield documents containing both *violence* and *schools* except those that contain the word *elementary*. Each search engine uses a somewhat different system for limiting searches, so you'll have to learn the specific system used by your favorite search engines.

Research Activity. Select one website you think would be helpful to members of this class and, in a two-minute speech, explain why they'll find the site useful.

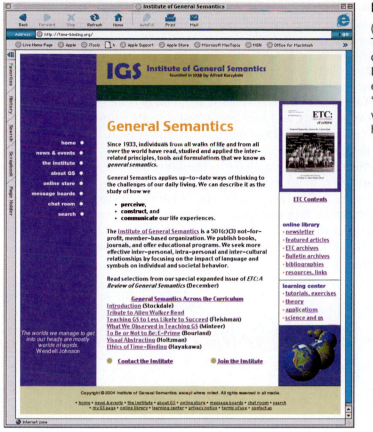

Institute of General Semantics

(http://www.time-binding.org/)
This is one of the websites maintained by organizations concerned with language. The Institute of General Semantics site is devoted especially to the area of language covered in this "Language Varies in Accuracy" section. Visit this website and see if there's anything there that will help you use language more effectively.

there is or as if it's all you need to know to make up your mind, as in *There's only one way to save social security. Never let financial considerations get in the way of romance. Always be polite.*

Disraeli's observation, "to be conscious that you are ignorant is a great step toward knowledge," is an excellent example of a nonallness attitude. If, as a critical listener, you recognize that there's more to learn, more to see, and more to hear, you'll treat what the speaker says as part of the total picture, not the whole, or the final word.

Static Evaluation

Often when you form an abstraction of something or someone—when you formulate a verbal statement about an event or person—that statement remains static and unchanging. But, the object or person to whom it refers has changed. Everything is in a constant state of change.

To avoid the error of **static evaluation,** respond to the statements of speakers as if they contained a tag that identified the time frame to which they refer. Visualize each such statement as containing a date. Look at that date and ask yourself if the statement is still true today. Thus, when a speaker says that 10 percent of the population now lives at or below the poverty level, ask yourself about the date to which that statement applies. When were the statistics compiled? Does the poverty level determined at that time adequately reflect current conditions?

Indiscrimination

Nature seems to abhor sameness at least as much as vacuums. Nowhere in the universe can you find two things that are identical. Everything is unique. Language, however, provides you with common nouns (such as *teacher*, *student*, *friend*, *enemy*, *war*, *politician*, and *liberal*) that lead you to focus on similarities. Such nouns lead you to group all teachers together, all students together, all politicians together. These words divert attention away from the uniqueness of each individual, each object, and each event. **Indiscrimination,** then, is a thinking error that occurs when you focus on classes of individuals, objects, or events rather than on the unique individual, object, or event.

Of course, there's nothing wrong with classifying. No one would argue that classifying is unhealthy or immoral. On the contrary, it's an extremely useful method of dealing with any complex matter. Classifying helps us to deal with complexity. It puts order into our thinking. The problem arises from applying some evaluative label to that class, and then using that label as an "adequate" map for each individual in the group. Put differently, indiscrimination is a denial of uniqueness.

CRITICAL LISTENING/THINKING *Link*

Listening to Fallacies: Language

In listening to and critically evaluating speeches, look carefully for *language fallacies*—ways of using language to subvert instead of clarify truth and accuracy. Earlier in this chapter we considered five thinking errors that can become barriers to language accuracy: polarization, fact–inference confusion, allness, static evaluation, and indiscrimination. Here are a few additional language fallacies—this time, words that mislead listeners or hamper their ability to understand.

- **Weasel words** are words whose meanings are slippery and difficult to pin down (Pei, 1956; Hayakawa & Hayakawa, 1990). For example, a commercial claiming that medicine M works "better than Brand X" doesn't specify how much better or in what respect Medicine M performs better. It's quite possible that it performs better in one respect but less effectively according to nine other measures. Other weasel words are "help," "virtually," "as much as," "like" (as in "it will make you feel like new"), and "more economical." Ask yourself, *Exactly what is being claimed?* For example, "What does 'may reduce cholesterol' mean? What exactly is being asserted?"

- **Euphemisms** make the negative and unpleasant appear positive and appealing, as when an executive calls the firing of 200 workers "downsizing" or "reallocation of resources." Justin Timberlake's reference to the highly publicized act with Janet Jackson during the 2004 Super Bowl as a "wardrobe malfunction" is another good example. Often euphemisms take the form of inflated language designed to make the mundane seem extraordinary, the common seem exotic ("the vacation of a lifetime," "unsurpassed vistas"). Don't let words get in the way of accurate firsthand perception.

- **Jargon,** the specialized language of a professional class (for example, the lingo of the computer hacker), becomes doublespeak when used with people who aren't members of the group and who don't know this specialized language. Don't be intimidated by jargon; ask questions when you don't understand.

- **Gobbledygook** is overly complex language that overwhelms the listener instead of communicating meaning. Ask for simplification when appropriate.

Getting Critical. Review some of the commercial websites for clothing, books, music, or any such product you're interested in. Can you find examples of misleading language?

Beware, therefore, of speakers who group large numbers of unique individuals under the same label. Beware of speakers who tell you that "Democrats are . . . ," that "Catholics believe . . . ," that "Mexicans will . . . ." Ask yourself, which Democrats, how many Catholics, which Mexicans, and so on.

Now that the general principles of language and style are understood, let's turn to some specific suggestions for improving your speech style, your words, and your sentences.

"Go ask your search engine."

 # Choosing Words

Choose carefully the words you use in your public speeches. Choose words to achieve clarity, vividness, appropriateness, and a personal style.

Clarity

Clarity in speaking style should be your primary goal. Here are some guidelines to help you make your speech clear.

Be Economical

Don't waste words. Two of the most important ways to achieve economy are to avoid redundancies and to avoid meaningless words. Notice the redundancies in the following expressions:

at 9 A.M. *in the morning*

we *first* began the discussion

the full *and complete* report

I *myself personally*

blue *in color*

*over*exaggerate

you, *members of the audience*

clearly unambiguous

approximately 10 inches *or so*

cash *money*

By withholding the italicized terms you eliminate unnecessary words. You thus move closer to a more economical and clearer style.

Use Specific Terms and Numbers

Picture these items:

◆ bracelet

◆ gold bracelet

◆ **CONSIDER** the power that economy of expression gives poetry such as that of Maya Angelou, pictured here. How might the same principles of language economy be applied to persuasive speeches? For example, why are short expressions more persuasive (usually) than long ones?

- gold bracelet with a diamond clasp
- braided gold bracelet with a diamond clasp

Notice that as we get more and more specific, we get a clearer and more detailed picture. Be specific. Don't say *dog* when you want your listeners to picture a St. Bernard. Don't say *car* when you want them to picture a limousine. Don't say *television program* when you want them to think of *20/20*.

The same is true of numbers. Don't say "earned a good salary" if you mean "earned $90,000 a year." Don't say "taxes will go up" when you mean "taxes will increase 22 percent." Don't say "the defense budget was enormous" when you mean "the defense budget was $100 billion."

Use Guide Phrases

Listening to a public speech is difficult work. Assist your listeners by using guide phrases to help them see that you're moving from one idea to another. Use phrases such as "now that we have seen how . . . , let us consider how . . ." and "my next argument . . . ." Terms such as *first, second, and also, although,* and *however* will help your audience follow your line of thinking.

Guide phrases are especially useful when your listeners aren't native speakers of the language you're speaking. And, of course, guide phrases will also prove valuable if you're speaking in a language that you have not fully mastered. The guide phrases will help compensate for the lack of language and speech similarity between speaker and audience.

Use Short, Familiar Terms

Generally, favor the short word over the long one. Favor the familiar word over the unfamiliar word. Favor the more commonly used term over the rarely used term. Say *harmless* rather than *innocuous, clarify* rather than *elucidate, use* rather than *utilize, find out* rather than *ascertain.*

Use Repetition and Restatement

Repetition and restatement will help listeners follow what you're saying and will make your speech clearer and more easily understood. These are not the same as redundancy, which involves using unnecessary words that don't communicate any information. *Repetition* means repeating something in exactly the same way, usually at different points in your speech. This will help your listeners better remember the idea and remind them of how it's connected with what you're now saying. *Restatement* means rephrasing an idea or statement in different words. This is especially helpful when the idea is new or even moderately complex. Expressing the same idea in two different ways helps clarify the concept.

Another type of restatement is the internal summary. Internal summaries—periodic summary statements or reviews of subsections of your speech—help listeners appreciate the speech as a progression of ideas and show them how one idea leads to another. Be careful not to overuse these techniques, however; you don't want to bore the audience by repeating material that doesn't need to be repeated.

Avoid Clichés

Clichés are phrases that have lost their novelty and part of their meaning through overuse. Avoid all clichés, which call attention to themselves because of their overuse. A few examples: "Tell it like it is," "free as a bird," "in the pink," "no sooner said than done," "tried and true," "for all intents and purposes," "it goes without saying," "few and far between," "no news is good news," and "mind over matter."

Distinguish between Commonly Confused Words

Many words, because they sound alike or are used in similar situations, are commonly confused. Try the accompanying self-test; it covers 10 of the most frequently confused words.

Test YOURSELF

Can You Distinguish Commonly Confused Words?

Underline the word in parentheses that you would use in each sentence.

_____ **1.** She (accepted, excepted) the award and thanked everyone (accept, except) the producer.

_____ **2.** The teacher (affected, effected) his students greatly and will now (affect, effect) a complete curriculum overhaul.

_____ **3.** Are you deciding (between, among) red and green or (between, among) red, green, and blue?

_____ **4.** I (can, may) scale the mountain but I (can, may) not reveal its hidden path.

_____ **5.** The table was (cheap, inexpensive) but has great style; the chairs cost a fortune but look (cheap, inexpensive).

_____ **6.** The professor (discovered, invented) uncharted lands and (discovered, invented) computer programs.

_____ **7.** He was (explicit, implicit) in his detailed description of the crime but made only (explicit, implicit) observations concerning the perpetrator.

_____ **8.** She was evasive and only (implied, inferred) that she'd seek a divorce. You can easily (imply, infer) her reasons.

_____ **9.** The wedding was (tasteful, tasty) and the food most (tasteful, tasty).

_____ **10.** The student seemed (disinterested, uninterested) in the test; in assigning grades the teacher was always (disinterested, uninterested).

❖ **HOW DID YOU DO?** Here are the principles that govern correct usage. (1) Use *accept* to mean "to receive" and *except* to mean "with the exclusion of." (2) Use *to affect* to mean "to have an effect or to influence," and *to effect* to mean "to produce a result." (3) Use *between* when referring to two items and *among* when referring to more than two items. (4) Use *can* to refer to ability and *may* to refer to permission. (5) Use *cheap* to refer to something that is inferior and *inexpensive* to describe something that costs little. (6) Use *discover* to refer to the act of finding something out or to learn something previously unknown, and use *invent* to refer to the act of originating something new. (7) Use *explicit* to mean "specific" and *implicit* to describe something that's indicated but not openly stated. (8) Use *to imply* to mean "to state indirectly" and *to infer* "to mean to draw a conclusion." (9) Use *tasteful* to refer to good taste and *tasty* to refer to something that tastes good. (10) Use *uninterested* to refer to a lack of interest, and use *disinterested* to mean "objective or unbiased."

❖ **WHAT WILL YOU DO?** Your use of language can greatly impact your persuasiveness. A word used incorrectly can lessen your credibility and general persuasiveness. Review your English handbook and identify other commonly confused words. Get into the habit of referring to a good dictionary whenever you have doubts about which word is preferred.

Carefully Assess Idioms

Idioms are expressions that are unique to a specific language. Perhaps the most interesting thing about idioms is that you can't deduce the meaning of an idiom from the individual words. You know the meaning of an idiom the way you know the meaning of a word. So, for example, you cannot gather the meaning of "kick the bucket" or "doesn't have a leg to stand on" from analyzing the individual words. Once you learn that "kick the bucket" means "die," the connection seems logical enough; but it's not a connection that you would have thought of merely by looking at the words. Similarly, once you learn that "he doesn't have a leg to stand on" means "he doesn't have a reasonable argument" or "he doesn't have an adequate defense," you can appreciate the idea behind the idiom—that is, that a position lacking reasonable arguments will collapse much as would a table (or a person) without legs.

The positive side of idioms is that they give your speech a casual and informal style; they make your speech sound like a speech and not like a written essay. The negative side of idioms is that they create problems for listeners who are not native speakers of your language. Many will simply not understand the meaning of your idioms. This problem is important, both because audiences are becoming increasingly intercultural and because the number of idioms we use is extremely high. If you're not convinced of this, read through any of the speeches in this text, especially in an intercultural group, and underline all idioms. You will no doubt find that you underline a great deal more than most people would have suspected.

USING TECHNOLOGY

Whether or not you speak English as a second language, visit a website devoted to ESL (for example, http://www.manythings.org/ or http://a4esl.org/). What can you learn from such websites that could supplement this chapter's discussions?

Vividness

Select words to make your ideas vivid and come alive in the minds of your listeners (Frey & Eagly, 1993; Meade, 2000).

Use Active Verbs

Favor verbs that communicate activity rather than passivity. The verb *to be,* in all its forms—*is, are, was, were, will be*—is relatively inactive. Try using verbs of action instead. Rather than saying, "The teacher was in the middle of the crowd," say, "The teacher stood in the middle of the crowd." Instead of saying, "The report was on the president's desk for three days," try, "The report sat (or slept) on the president's desk for three days." Instead of saying, "Management will be here tomorrow," consider, "Management will descend on us tomorrow," or, "Management jets in tomorrow."

Use Strong Verbs

The verb is the strongest part of your sentence. Instead of saying "He walked through the forest," consider such terms as *wandered, prowled, rambled,* or *roamed.* Consider whether one of these might not better suit your intended meaning. Consult a thesaurus for any verb you suspect might be weak. A good guide to identifying weak verbs is to look at your use of adverbs. If you use lots of adverbs, you may be using them to strengthen weak verbs. Consider cutting out the adverbs and substituting stronger verbs. Instead of *walked quickly* consider *ran, sped,* or *flew;* instead of *spoke softly* consider *whispered* or *murmured.*

Use Figures of Speech

Figures of speech are stylistic devices that have been a part of rhetoric since ancient times. Figures of speech help achieve vividness, in addition to making your speech more memorable and giving it a polished, well-crafted look. Here are some such devices that you may wish to incorporate into your next speech.

- **Alliteration** is the repetition of the same initial sound in two or more words as in "fifty famous flavors" or "the cool, calculating leader."

- **Hyperbole** is the use of extreme exaggeration, as in "He cried like a faucet" or "I'm so hungry I could eat a whale."

- **Irony** is the use of a word or sentence whose literal meaning is the opposite of that which is intended; for example, a teacher handing back failing examinations might say, "So pleased to see how many of you studied so hard."

- **Metaphor** is an implied comparison between two unlike things, as in "She's a lion when she wakes up" or "He's a real bulldozer."

- **Synecdoche** is using a part of an object to stand for the whole object, as in "all hands were on deck," in which *hands* stands for "sailors" or "crew members," or "green thumb" for "expert gardener."

- **Metonymy** is the substitution of a name for a title with which it's closely associated as in "City Hall issued the following news release," in which *City Hall* stands for "the mayor" or "the city council."

- **Antithesis** is the presentation of contrary ideas in parallel form, as in "My loves are many, my enemies are few" or in Charles Dickens's opening to *A Tale of Two Cities*: "It was the best of times, it was the worst of times."

❖ **CONSIDER** the fact that political speech—although extremely important to the welfare of the community and the country—is often quite boring. What stylistic suggestions would you offer a political candidate who was giving a campaign speech to your public speaking class?

◆ **Simile,** like metaphor, compares two unlike objects but uses the words *like* or *as;* for example, "The manager is as gentle as a lamb."

◆ **Personification** is the attribution of human characteristics to inanimate objects—"This room cries out for activity" or "My car is tired."

◆ **Rhetorical questions** are questions that are used to make a statement or to produce a desired effect rather than secure an answer—"Do you want to be popular?" "Do you want to get well?"

Use Imagery

Appeal to the senses, especially visual, auditory, and tactile senses. Make us see, hear, and feel what you're talking about.

Visual Imagery. In describing people or objects, create images your listeners can see. When appropriate, describe such visual qualities as height, weight, color, size, shape, length, and contour. Let your audience see the sweat pouring down the faces of the coal miners; let them see the short, overweight executive in a pinstriped suit smoking a cigar. Here Stephanie Kaplan (Reynolds & Schnoor, 1991), a student from the University of Wisconsin, uses visual imagery to describe the AIDS Quilt:

> The Names Project is quite simply a quilt. It's larger than 10 football fields, and composed of over 9,000 unique 3-feet-by-6-feet panels each bearing a name of an individual who has died of AIDS. The panels have been made in homes across the country by the friends, lovers, and families of AIDS victims.

Auditory Imagery. Appeal to our sense of hearing by using terms that describe sounds. Let your listeners hear the car screeching, the wind whistling, the bells chiming, the angry professor roaring.

Tactile Imagery. Use terms referring to temperature, texture, and touch to create tactile imagery. Let your listeners feel the cool water running over their bodies and the punch of the fighter; let them feel the smooth skin of the newborn baby.

Appropriateness

Use language that is appropriate to you as the speaker. Also, use language that is appropriate to your audience, the occasion, and the speech topic. Here are some general guidelines to help you achieve this quality.

Speak on the Appropriate Level of Formality

The most effective public speaking style is (usually but not always) less formal than the written essay but more formal than conversation. One way to achieve an informal style—if this seems the appropriate style on the basis of your audience analysis—is to use contractions. Say *don't* instead of *do not, I'll* instead of *I shall,* and *wouldn't* instead of *would not.* Contractions give a public speech the sound and rhythm of conversation, a quality that most listeners react to favorably.

Use personal pronouns rather than impersonal expressions. Say "I found" instead of "it became evident," or "I will present three arguments" instead of "there are three main arguments."

DEVELOPING STRATEGIES

Language Differences. Horatio, an anthropology professor, is to give an address on the topic of violence in schools twice in one day: first to the junior class at the local high school and later that day to the Education Department of his college. If Horatio is to be successful, how—if at all— should his language differ in these two situations?

Do remember, as noted elsewhere, that the expected and desirable level of formality will vary greatly from one culture to another.

Avoid Unfamiliar Terms

Avoid using terms the audience doesn't know. Avoid foreign and technical terms unless you're certain the audience is familiar with them. Similarly, avoid jargon (the technical vocabulary of a specialized field) unless you're sure the meanings are clear to your listeners. Some acronyms (NATO, UN, NOW, and CORE) are probably familiar to most audiences; most, however, are not. When you wish to use any of these types of expressions, fully explain their meaning to the audience.

Avoid Slang

Avoid **slang** or other expressions that risk offending audience members, embarrassing them, or making them feel you have little respect for them. Although your listeners may themselves use such expressions, they often resent their use by public speakers. So avoid any words or examples that may be considered "off-color."

Avoid Racist, Sexist, Ageist, and Heterosexist Terms

Avoid referring to culturally different groups with terms that carry negative connotations; be careful not to portray groups in stereotypical and negative ways.

Avoid racist language or any expressions that can be considered disparaging to members of a particular ethnic group. Using unintentionally **racist language**—qualifying someone with a racial identifier that is neither relevant nor necessary—is perhaps the most frequent mistake speakers make. For example, referring to a "Chicano professor" or an "African American mathematician" can imply that you're pointing to the rareness of Hispanics' being professors or of African Americans' being mathematicians.

Use nonsexist language. **Sexist language** is language that's derogatory to one gender (usually women). To avoid it, use gender-neutral terminology. Use "human" instead of "man" to include both sexes; use "she and he" instead of "he"; use "police officer" instead of "policeman" and "firefighter" instead of "fireman." Avoid sex-role stereotyping; for example, avoid making the hypothetical elementary school teacher female and the college professor male. Avoid referring to doctors as male and nurses as female. Avoid noting the gender of a professional with terms such as "lady lawyer" or "male nurse." When you're referring to a specific lawyer or nurse, the person's gender will become clear when you use the appropriate pronoun.

Avoid ageist expressions or language that discriminates against people because of age. Avoid popular but insulting terms referring to older people—**ageist language** such as "old-timer," "little old lady," or "over the hill." As with racism, ageism also can creep in when you qualify or describe the abilities of an older person. For example, when you refer to a "quick-witted 75-year-old" or a "responsible teenager," you're indicating that those qualities are unusual in people in those age groups. You're saying that

❖ **CONSIDER** the reasons that sexist, racist, heterosexist, or ageist language creates problems for the speaker. What problems does the speaker avoid by being more inclusive and more sensitive?

USING TECHNOLOGY

If you have any doubts as to the preferred gender-neutral term to use in your speech, visit Rensselaer Polytechnic Institute's Writing Center (http://www.rpi.edu/dept/uc/writecenter/web/genderfair.html).

quick-wittedness and being 75 years old do not normally go together and that the fact that they do in this case merits special mention. You imply the same abnormality for the linking of "responsible" and "teenager." The problem with this is that using ageist expressions is simply wrong. There are many 80-year-olds who are extremely quick-witted and many 30-year-olds who aren't.

Avoid heterosexist language, language that disparages gay men and lesbians. As with racist language, **heterosexist language** can take the form of derogatory terms for lesbians and gay men as well as more subtle kinds of language usage. As with racist and sexist language, when you qualify a professional identifier—as in "gay athlete" or "lesbian doctor," you're in effect stating that athletes or doctors are not normally gay or lesbian. Also, you're making the affectional orientation more important than it probably should be in the context of, as in the examples, sports or medicine.

Once brought to awareness, most people recognize the moral legitimacy of using language that is inclusive and refraining from using racist, ageist, or heterosexist words or phrases. There are also rhetorical reasons for avoiding such language:

◆ It's likely to offend a significant part of your audience.

◆ It's likely to draw attention to itself and away from what you're saying.

◆ It's likely to reflect negatively on your own credibility.

Avoid Ethnic Expressions (Generally)

Ethnic expressions are words and phrases that are peculiar to a particular ethnic group. At times these expressions are known only by members of the ethnic group; at other times they are known more widely but still recognized as ethnic expressions.

When you are speaking to a multicultural audience, it's generally best to avoid ethnic expressions unless they're integral to your speech and you explain them. Such expressions often seem exclusionist—that is, they highlight the connection between the speaker and the members of that particular ethnic group and the lack of connection between the speaker and all others who are not members of that ethnic group. And, of course, ethnic expressions should never be used if you're not a member of the ethnic group.

If, on the other hand, you're speaking to an audience from one ethnic group and you're also a member of that group, then such expressions are fine. Politicians who run in districts in which they and the voters are of the same national origin or language community will frequently use ethnic terms or even phrases in the native language of the audience. In these cases ethnic expressions may well prove effective; they are part of the common language of speaker and audience and will help to stress your similarities with the audience.

Use Preferred Cultural Identifiers

Perhaps the best way to avoid sexism, racism, ageism, and heterosexism is to examine the cultural identifiers to use (and not to use) in talking about members of different cultures. As always, when in doubt, find out. The preferences and many of the specific examples identified here are drawn largely from the findings of the Task Force on Bias-Free Language of the Association of American University Presses (Schwartz, 1995). Although not everyone necessarily agrees with these recommendations; they're presented here—in the words of the Task Force—"to encourage sensitivity to usages that may be imprecise, misleading, and needlessly offensive" (Schwartz, 1995, p. ix). They're not presented so that

A CASE OF *Ethics*

Qualifying Evidence

You're giving a speech on homelessness, and you want your listeners to contribute to the new halfway house that your community is building. In your research you discover (1) that the most recent statistics on the number of homeless people in your community are about 20 years old, and (2) that although many community leaders are in favor of building this halfway house, a sizable number object. So you wonder: (1) Do you have to give the date the statistics were collected? (2) Can you say simply that community leaders favor the halfway house, without going into the fact that some don't favor it?

What would you do? More generally, what ethical obligations does a speaker have for qualifying the evidence given in a speech?

you can "catch" someone being "politically incorrect" or label someone "culturally insensitive."

Generally, the term *girl* should be used only to refer to very young females and is equivalent to *boy*. Neither term should be used for people older than, say, 13 or 14. *Girl* is never used to refer to a grown woman, nor is *boy* used to refer to persons in blue-collar positions, as it once was. *Lady* is negatively evaluated by many because it connotes the stereotype of the prim and proper woman. *Woman* or *young woman* is preferred. *Older person* is preferred to *elder, elderly, senior,* or *senior citizen* (which technically refers to someone older than 65).

Generally, *gay* is the preferred term to refer to a man who has an affectional preference for other men and *lesbian* is the preferred term for a woman who has an affectional preference for other women. (*Lesbian* means "homosexual woman," so the phrase "lesbian woman" is redundant.) *Homosexual* refers to both gay men and lesbians but more often to a sexual orientation to members of one's own sex. *Gay* and *lesbian* refer to a lifestyle and not just to sexual orientation. *Gay* as a noun, although widely used, may prove offensive in some contexts, for example, "We have two gays on the team." Although used within the gay community in an effort to remove the negative stigma through frequent usage, the term *queer*—as in "queer power"or "queer Studies"—is often resented when used by outsiders. Because most scientific thinking holds that sexuality is not a matter of choice, the term *sexual orientation* is preferred to *sexual preference* or *sexual status* (which are also vague) (Rogers, 2001; Wright, 1999).

Generally, most African Americans prefer *African American* to *black* (Hecht, Collier, & Ribeau, 1993), though *black* is often used with *white* and is used in a variety of other contexts (for example, Department of Black and Puerto Rican Studies, the *Journal of Black History,* and Black History Month). The American Psychological Association recommends that both terms be capitalized, but the *Chicago Manual of Style* (the manual used by most newspapers and publishing houses) recommends using lowercase. The terms *negro* and *colored,* although used in the names of some organizations (for example, the United Negro College Fund and the National Association for the Advancement of Colored People), are not used outside of these contexts.

White is generally used to refer to those whose roots are in European cultures and usually does not include Hispanics. Analogous to *African American* is the term *European American*. Few "European Americans," however, would want to be called that; most would prefer their national origins emphasized, as in, for example, *German American* or *Greek American*. This preference may well change as Europe moves into a more cohesive and united entity. *People of color*—a literary-sounding term that may be appropriate in public speaking, but is awkward in most conversations—is preferred to *nonwhite*, which implies that whiteness is the norm and nonwhiteness is a deviation from that norm. The same is true of the term *non-Christian*.

Generally, *Hispanic* is used to refer to anyone who identifies himself or herself as belonging to a Spanish-speaking culture. *Latina* (female) and *Latino* (male) refer to people with roots in Latin American countries such as the Dominican Republic, Nicaragua, or Guatemala. *Hispanic American* refers to U.S. residents whose ancestry is culturally Spanish and includes people of Mexican, Caribbean, and Central and South American origins. But in emphasizing a Spanish heritage, the term is really inadequate, because large numbers in the Caribbean and in South America have French or Portuguese roots. *Chicana* (female) and *Chicano* (male) refer to those with roots in Mexico, though it often connotes a nationalist attitude (Jandt, 2000) and is considered offensive by many Mexican Americans. *Mexican American* is preferred.

Inuk (the plural is *Inuit*) was officially adopted at the Inuit Circumpolar Conference to refer to the indigenous peoples of Alaska, northern Canada, Greenland, and eastern Siberia. This term is preferred to *Eskimo* (a term the U.S. Census Bureau uses), which was applied to the indigenous peoples of Alaska by Europeans and derives from a term that means "raw meat eaters" (Maggio, 1997).

Indian technically should refer only to someone from India; it is incorrectly used when applied to citizens of other Asian countries or to the indigenous peoples of North America. *American Indian* or *Native American* is preferred, even though many Native Americans refer to themselves as "Indians" and "Indian people." The term *native American* (with a lowercase *n*) is most often used to refer to persons born in the United States. Although the term technically could refer to anyone born in North or South America, people outside the United States generally prefer more specific designations such as *Argentinean, Cuban,* or *Canadian*. The term *native* refers to a person born in a particular place and is distinguished from *stranger* or *foreigner*; it's not used to mean "someone having a less developed culture."

Muslim is the preferred form (rather than the older *Moslem*) to refer to a person who adheres to the religious teachings of Islam. *Quran* (rather than *Koran*) is the preferred term for the scriptures of Islam. The terms *Mohammedan* or *Mohammedanism* are not considered appropriate; they imply worship of Muhammad, the prophet, "considered by Muslims to be a blasphemy against the absolute oneness of God" (Maggio, 1997, p. 277).

Although there's no universal agreement, generally *Jewish people* is preferred to *Jews*; and *Jewess* (a Jewish female) is considered derogatory. *Jew* should be used only as a noun and is never correctly used as a verb or an adjective (Maggio, 1997).

When history was being written with a European perspective, Europe was taken as the focal point and the rest of the world was defined in terms of its

DEVELOPING STRATEGIES

Offensive Language. Eric wants to illustrate the negative effects of racist language by using these derogatory terms throughout his speech—to further drive home the point of the pain they can cause. If Eric were addressing your class, what advice would you give him?

location from Europe. Thus, Asia became "the east" or "the Orient" and Asians became *Orientals*—a term that is today considered inappropriate or "Eurocentric." Thus, people from Asia are *Asians,* just as people from Africa are *Africans* and people from Europe are *Europeans.*

In talking about people with disabilities, be especially careful to avoid terms that limit the person or define the person in terms of his or her impairment or disability. For example, avoid saying "the disabled person" or the "deaf person," and instead consider saying "the person with a disability"—or, better and more specifically, "the person with limited hearing." In addition, as with older people and different ethnic groups, scrupulously avoid any of the offensive derogatory terms that refer to various disabilities.

Personal Style

Audiences favor speakers who speak in a personal rather than an impersonal style, who speak with them rather than at them.

Use Personal Pronouns

Say *I* and *me* and *he* and *she* and *you*. Avoid such impersonal expressions as *one* (as in "One is led to believe . . .") or "this speaker," or "listeners." These expressions distance the audience and create barriers rather than bridges. Use personal pronouns in addressing the audience: Say *you* rather than *students*; say *you'll enjoy reading* . . . instead of *everyone will enjoy reading.*

Use Questions

Ask the audience questions to involve them. In a small audience, you might even briefly entertain responses. In larger audiences, you might ask the question, pause to allow the audience time to consider their responses, and then move on. When you direct questions to your listeners, they feel a part of the public speaking transaction.

Create Immediacy

Immediacy is a connectedness, a relatedness with one's listeners. Immediacy is the opposite of disconnected and separated. Here are some suggestions for creating immediacy through language:

- ◆ Use personal examples.
- ◆ Use terms that include both you and the audience; for example, *we* and *our.*
- ◆ Use specific names of audience members when appropriate.
- ◆ Express concern for the audience members.
- ◆ Reinforce or compliment the audience.
- ◆ Refer directly to commonalities between you and the audience, for example, "We are all children of immigrants" or "We all want to see our team in the playoffs."
- ◆ Refer to shared experiences and goals; for example, "We all want, we all need a more responsive PTA."
- ◆ Recognize audience feedback and refer to it in your speech. Say, for example, "I can see from your expressions that we're all anxious to get to our immediate problem."

USING TECHNOLOGY

Books about words abound on the Internet and will prove helpful in your choice of words. Visit the Internet Public Library (http://www.ipl.org/ref) or the Reference Desk (www.refdesk.com) and search for dictionaries, thesauruses, and related wordbooks. Or see http://www.yourdictionary.com/, http://dictionary.cambridge.org/, or Merriam-Webster Collegiate Dictionary at http://www.m-w.com/dictionary.htm. OneLook at http://www.onelook.com/ enables you to search lots of dictionaries in a variety of languages. To get an idea of the differences among dictionaries, look up a few words, such as "rhetoric," "persuasion," or "style," in a few of these volumes.

Phrasing Sentences

Give the same careful consideration that you give to words to your sentences as well. Here are some guidelines to help you make your sentences clear and persuasive.

Use Short Sentences

Short sentences are more forceful and economical. They are easier to comprehend and they are easier to remember. Listeners don't have the time or the inclination to unravel long and complex sentences. Help them to listen more efficiently by using short rather than long sentences.

Use Direct Sentences

Direct sentences are easier to understand. They are also more forceful. Instead of saying, "I want to tell you of the three main reasons why we should not adopt Program A," say "We should not adopt Program A. I'm going to focus on three main reasons."

Use Active Sentences

Active sentences are easier to understand. They also make your speech seem livelier and more vivid. Instead of saying "The lower court's decision was reversed by the Supreme Court," say "The Supreme Court reversed the lower court's decision." Instead of saying "The proposal was favored by management," say "Management favored the proposal."

Use Positive Sentences

Positive sentences are easier to comprehend and remember. Notice how sentences **a** and **c** are easier to understand than sentences **b** and **d**.

- **a.** The committee rejected the proposal.
- **b.** The committee did not accept the proposal.
- **c.** This committee works outside the normal company hierarchy.
- **d.** This committee does not work within the normal company hierarchy.

Vary the Types of Sentences

The advice to use short, direct, active, and positive sentences is valid most of the time. Yet too many sentences of the same type or length will make your speech sound boring. Use variety while following (generally) the preceding advice. Here are a few special types of sentences that should prove useful, especially for adding variety, vividness, and forcefulness to your speech.

Parallel Sentences. Phrase your ideas in parallel (similar, matching) style for ease of comprehension and memory. Note the parallelism in **a** and **c** and its absence in **b** and **d**.

- **a.** The professor prepared the lecture, graded the examination, and read the notices.
- **b.** The professor prepared the lecture, the examination was graded, and she read the notices.

c. Love needs two people to flourish. Jealousy needs but one.

d. Love needs two people. Just one can create jealousy.

Antithetical Sentences. Antithetical sentences juxtapose contrasting ideas in parallel fashion. In his inaugural speech, President John F. Kennedy phrased one of his most often quoted lines in antithetical structure:

> Ask not what your country can do for you; ask what you can do for your country.

Periodic Sentences. In periodic sentences you reserve the key word until the end of the sentence. In fact, the sentence is not grammatically complete until you say this last word. For example, in "Looking longingly into his eyes, the old woman fainted," the sentence doesn't make sense until the last word is spoken.

Summary of Concepts and Skills

In this chapter we looked at how language works and at how you can use language to better achieve your public speaking goals.

How Language Works

Language varies in several ways:

- ◆ Directness and indirectness
- ◆ Abstraction and specificity
- ◆ Objectivity and subjectivity
- ◆ Oral and written style
- ◆ Accuracy and inaccuracy (including errors such as polarization, fact–inference confusion, allness, static evaluation, and indiscrimination)

Choosing Words

In choosing your words to achieve an effective public speaking style, focus on the following qualities:

- ◆ Clarity: Be economical; be specific; use guide phrases; use short, familiar terms; use repetition and restatement; avoid clichés; avoid misusing commonly confused words.

- ◆ Vividness: Use active verbs; use strong verbs; use figures of speech; use imagery.
- ◆ Appropriateness: Speak on the appropriate level of formality; avoid unfamiliar terms; avoid slang and vulgar terms; avoid racist, sexist, ageist, and heterosexist expressions; avoid ethnic expressions (generally); use the preferred cultural identifiers.
- ◆ Personal style: Use personal pronouns; ask questions; create immediacy.

Phrasing Sentences

Construct your sentences to achieve clarity and forcefulness:

- ◆ Use short rather than long sentences.
- ◆ Use direct rather than indirect sentences.
- ◆ Use active rather than passive sentences.
- ◆ Use positive rather than negative sentences.
- ◆ Vary the types and lengths of sentences, making use of parallel, antithetical, and periodic sentences.

Vocabulary Quiz

Public Speaking Style

Match these terms about style with their definitions. Record the number of the definition next to the term.

_____ parallel structure

_____ idiom

_____ abstraction

_____ indiscrimination

_____ immediacy

_____ allness

_____ polarization

_____ denotation

_____ connotation

_____ imagery

1. A generalization.

2. Objective meaning; the meaning of a word in a dictionary.

3. Subjective meaning; the meaning that a person attaches to a word or phrase because of his or her unique experiences.

4. The tendency to see things in terms of extremes or opposites.

5. The failure to recognize the uniqueness of each person or event.

6. The misevaluation that occurs when you assume you know all or have said all about anything.

7. Descriptions that appeal to the visual, auditory, or tactile senses, for example.

8. A sense of connectedness or relatedness between speaker and listener.

9. Phrasings that are similar in style and grammatical structure.

10. Expressions that are unique to a specific language and whose meaning cannot be discovered from a simple analysis of the individual words.

Web Explorations

Companion Website

www.ablongman.com/devito

The Companion Website's Chapter 7 offers a variety of aids for improving your use of language and style in public speaking: an extended example of "Oral and Written Style," a self-test ("Can You Distinguish Facts from Inferences?"), a discussion of "Forcefulness and Power," suggestions for using "Humor In Public Speaking," and exercises on "Rephrasing Clichés"; "Metaphors, Similes, and Public Speaking"; and "Making Concepts Specific."

Public Speaking Exercises

7.1 Making Concepts Specific

One of the major skills in public speaking is learning to make your ideas specific so that your listeners will understand exactly what you want them to understand. Here are 12 sentences. Rewrite each of the sentences making the italicized terms more specific.

1. The *teacher* was *discussing economics*.
2. The *player scored*.
3. No one in the *city* thought the *mayor* was right.
4. The *girl* and the *boy* each received *lots* of *presents*.
5. I read the *review* of the *movie*.
6. The *couple* rented a *great car*.
7. The *detective* wasn't much help in solving the *crime*.
8. The *dinosaur approached* the *baby*.
9. He *walked* up the *steep hill*.
10. *They* played *games*.
11. The *cat climbed* the *fence*.
12. The *large house* is in the *valley*.

7.2 Talking about Cultural Identities

Anonymously, on an index card, each class member should write one of his or her cultural identities (race, religion, nationality) and three strengths that the person feels a significant number of members of this cultural group possess. The cards should be collected, randomized, and read aloud. This brief experience—along with any discussion it generates—should make the following clear:

1. Not only do people have diverse cultural identities, but each individual has several such identities.
2. Each identity has its own perceived strengths. Even the "strengths" themselves may not be recognized as "strengths" by members of other cultures.
3. The most effective individual is likely to be the one who recognizes and welcomes the strengths of different cultures.

7.3 Analyzing a Speech

MEDICAL MISCOMMUNICATION: IMPROVING THE DOCTOR–PATIENT INTERACTION

Steven N. Blivess

A week after graduation, Harvard Medical School student Jody Heymann woke up in a hospital emergency room. The doctors working on her didn't tell her where she was, how she'd gotten there, or what was wrong with her. Further, throughout her 18-month stay, no one explained to her why a 90-minute operation lasted 10 hours. And still later, because of her medication, she began vomiting a brilliant green fluid; the resident refused her request to change her medication. This lack of communication between Heymann and her physicians is a problem that continually plagues today's medical industry. And while communication may be at the heart of the practice of medicine, according to the May 1, 1995, *Hartford Courant*, miscommunication can cause a psychological barrier that will prevent people from getting the medical care they need. For us to see how both doctors and patients are responsible for miscommunications, we will first examine common communication problems that afflict physicians. Next, we will look at

How direct do you find the speaker's introduction to be? Can you identify specific examples of direct and indirect language?

how the patients' ineffective communication skills contribute to the problem. And finally, we will uncover solutions to help ourselves become better and more effective participants in our medical treatment.

Our first step towards rebuilding the bridge of doctor–patient communication begins with the physician. While doctors face a myriad of communication problems, we will focus on three of the more pressing issues: the power relationship, the doctor's rhetorical insensitivity, and communicating across a gender gap. The first major problem the doctor faces arises from their view of the so-called "power relationship." Because many doctors continue to harbor the archaic belief that the patient is subservient to them, according to the 1995 edition of the *Journal of Social Science & Medicine*, the questions that they ask "are mostly closed-ended: a yes or no answer is all that is expected." The effect of this often condescending attitude is that vital information can be lost. Take the case of Michael James, as chronicled in the February 26, 1995, *Pittsburgh Post Gazette*. Having entered the hospital with complaints of a debilitating headache, we must wonder why the doctors on duty never asked about the head injury he had suffered during a mugging the previous year. Perhaps a simple inquiry into his background could have prevented a barrage of tests he would later receive.

The second major problem facing today's medical practitioner, according to Dr. Gary Kreps, the foremost expert on health communication, lies in their rhetorical insensitivity. In a telephone interview on March 13, 1996, Dr. Kreps stated that doctors often offer explanations that are saturated with technical jargon that create a language barrier. Further, Dr. Dewitt Baldwin of the American Medical Association explained in a telephone interview that also took place on March 13, 1996, that by comparing patient satisfaction to the occurrence of malpractice cases he discovered that physicians who spend little time explaining technical language to their patients see an increased instance of dissatisfaction and malpractice suits. The March 1, 1995, *Journal of the American Medical Association* corroborates this assessment when it reports that "the result of language barriers is often poor compliance, inappropriate follow-up, and patient dissatisfaction."

A final problem facing physicians is related to gender differences. According to the 1995 edition of the *Journal of Woman and Health*, "medical discourse tends to marginalize" the information brought by women to the physicians, labeling it as trivial, troublesome, and irrelevant to diagnosis. This blatant disregard for what women are saying eliminates the opportunity for women to get comprehensive examinations or effective treatments. The April 11, 1995, *New York Times* reports that District Attorney Michael McCann has considered filing charges against a New York doctor for

How would you describe the language in terms of abstraction? Can you identify an example from the first paragraph of a high- and a low-level abstraction? Does this help gain and focus your attention on the topic?

Do you get the feeling that both you and the speaker share similar connotative meanings for such terms as power relationship, rhetorical insensitivity, *and* gender gap?

As you read this speech, do you find any instances of polarization, fact–inference confusion, allness, static evaluation, or indiscrimination?

How would you describe the speaker's style? Is it basically an oral style? Does it contain elements of written style?

misdiagnosing cervical cancer. Because the doctor failed to take the complaints of his patient seriously, her pap smear was misdiagnosed and the patient, ultimately, died.

While doctors may take the majority of the blame for miscommunication, we as patients are also at fault for the widening communication gap between ourselves and our doctors. The first problem we face as patients is that we acquiesce as passive consumers. We consciously don't take an active role as a participant in the medical give-and-take process. One factor, according to the April 14, 1995, *St. Louis Post-Dispatch*, is the stress of the situation. The anxiety of being confronted with an unfamiliar illness leads to details being lost. For an example, let's look, once again, at the Michael James case. Earlier, we bashed the doctors for not asking about his previous medical history. However, we must also note that James failed to volunteer his history to help doctors diagnose his symptoms.

Do you find the language clear? For example, is the language economical? Are specific rather than general terms used? Are guide phrases provided?

The second problem facing patients is that we haven't adequately prepared ourselves for the doctor–patient interaction. In many cases, we simply don't know the correct medical terminology. Take as a metaphor the auto repair industry. We have all at some point said that our car is making a pinging noise, yet we are unable to articulate further as to the specifics of the problem. The same holds true in the medical repair industry. We tell doctors our stomach is making gurgling sounds without clarity and expect instant diagnosis. Unfortunately, doctors can't check under the hood, or put us up on the rack. Both our passive nature and inadequate preparation can force doctors to make assumptions that lead down the wrong diagnostic path, or force the doctor to assume an over-authoritative role which just perpetuates the problematic cycle.

How vivid do you find the language? Are the verbs active and strong? Does the speaker use figures of speech and imagery? Is this level of vividness appropriate to the topic and the audience?

Having diagnosed the problems, it's time to prescribe some solutions for more effective doctor–patient communication. There are several steps we as patients can take. First, collaborate in the search for information. According to the 1995 article *Patients as Partners* by Carnegie Mellon University researcher Amanda Young, collaboration offers an additional strategy for care giving. By structuring the dialogue between the patient and the doctor towards working together, a partnership is formed in interpreting symptoms, recognizing their effects and planning an effective treatment plan. In addition, a collaborative effort includes being willing to ask for written material to accompany oral instruction. According to a personal correspondence with Lorraine Jackson, a professor at the California Polytechnical Institute, that took place on March 11, 1996, written material can be kept, reread and referred to, thus increasing the probability that information will be followed and treatment will be completed.

Does the speaker speak on the appropriate level of formality, given the topic and, let's assume, your public speaking class as the audience?

Second, select a doctor with whom you are comfortable. Although in the age of HMOs it may be hard—shop around. In his book *Communicating with Your Doctor*, Dr. Gary Kreps, the previously mentioned health communication expert, says that finding a doctor that suits your personality goes a long way towards good communication. One characteristic Dr. Kreps advises us to look for is what kind of approach does the doctor take towards medicine. Dr. Dewitt Baldwin also stated in the previously mentioned interview that a humanistic approach to medicine provides for increased interaction between the patient and the doctor. A humanistic approach means that the physician uses eye contact to establish trust, listens without interrupting to avoid pre-judging, and encourages the patient to open up. By looking for doctors who employ these few simple techniques, we vastly improve our ability to communicate with our physicians.

Do you find the language appropriately personal?

Finally, we need to be able to relate our symptoms, which means knowing the correct medical terminology. To this end the March, 1995, *American Health* reports that there are medical books that have been designed with the lay person in mind. One example would be the American Medical Association's *Home Medical Encyclopedia*. While purchasing one of these books is recommended, it should never be used to replace a visit to our doctor, but instead be used as a tool to supplement the visit. Ultimately, what each of these solutions boils down to is effective communication only becomes possible when both the doctor and the patient, can, and do, work together to find a cure for the patient's ailment.

Do you find the language appropriately forceful and powerful? Do you think a more forceful style would have been more effective? Might a less forceful style have been more effective?

How would you describe the sentence structure used in the speech?

Medical care isn't just a matter of diagnosis and prescription; it's also a matter of social relations finely adjusted by language. Without the ability to communicate, we as social animals would find ourselves lost in the barren wasteland that is silence. Yet, we, as patients, continue to hinder our ability to communicate with our doctors, and vice versa. Having looked at the problems from both perspectives, we have determined that miscommunications between doctors and patients, is, in fact, a significant problem in today's society. Fortunately, we have also learned some steps we can take as medical consumers to begin to re-establish the lines of communication between ourselves and our physicians. So as we move into the future secure in our ability to communicate, we can be sure that if we wake to find ourselves in the emergency room someday, we will be able to find out where we are, how we got there, and what was wrong with us.

Will you remember this speech? Will you remember the speaker's main points? What did the speaker do to make his speech easy to remember?

Blivess, S. N. (1996). Medical miscommunication: Improving the doctor–patient interaction. In L. Schnoor (Ed.), *Winning orations of the Interstate Oratorical Association* (pp. 87–89). Mankato, MN: Interstate Oratorical Association.

8 Delivering Your Speech

Why Read This Chapter?

It will enable you to deliver your speech with effective voice and action by helping you to:

❖ use your voice (volume, rate, pitch, and pauses, for example) to your best advantage

❖ use nonverbal communication (eyes, face, body posture, gestures, and movements) to aid your audience's understanding and to further your informative or persuasive purpose

❖ rehearse your speech efficiently and effectively to improve your delivery

> " I like people who refuse to speak until they are ready to speak.
>
> **—Lillian Hellman**

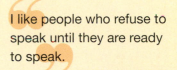

If you're like most students, your greatest concern is not with limiting the topic or writing the outline, it's with delivery, the topic of this chapter. Here we'll focus on delivery skills that will help you achieve your purpose. After all, the best organized and researched speech, if delivered poorly, is not going to have the effect you want it to have.

 # Methods of Delivery

Speakers vary widely in their methods of delivery. Some speak "off-the-cuff," with no apparent preparation; others read their speeches from manuscript. Some memorize their speeches word for word; others construct a detailed outline and create the speech itself at the moment of delivery. Speakers use all four of these general methods of delivery: impromptu, manuscript, memorized, and extemporaneous. Each has advantages and disadvantages.

Speaking Impromptu

When you give an **impromptu speech,** you speak without any specific preparation or advance thinking. You and the topic meet for the first time, and immediately the speech begins. On some occasions you will not be able to avoid speaking impromptu. In a classroom, after someone has spoken, you might comment on the speech you just heard in a brief impromptu speech of evaluation. In asking or answering questions in an interview situation, you're giving impromptu speeches, albeit extremely short ones. At meetings you may find yourself speaking impromptu as you explain a proposal or defend a plan of action; these, too, are impromptu speeches. The ability to speak impromptu effectively depends on your general public speaking ability. The more proficient a speaker you are, the better you'll be able to function impromptu. Suggestions unique for speaking impromptu are offered in Public Speaking Exercise 8.1 at the end of this chapter.

The impromptu experience provides excellent training in different aspects of public speaking, such as maintaining eye contact; responding to audience feedback; gesturing; organizing ideas; and developing examples, arguments, and appeals. The major disadvantage of speaking impromptu is that it does not permit attention to details of public speaking such as audience adaptation, research, and style.

Speaking from Manuscript

With a **manuscript speech,** you write out the entire speech, exactly as you want it to be heard by your audience, and read it to the audience. Because the manuscript method allows you to control exactly what you'll say, it may be the logical method to use in, say, politics, where an ambiguous phrase might prove insulting or belligerent and cause serious problems.

One of the major advantages of a manuscript speech is that you control the timing precisely. This is particularly important when you are delivering a speech that will be recorded (on television, for example). Also, there's no danger of forgetting an important point; everything is there for you on paper. Still another advantage is that the manuscript method allows you to use the exact wording you (or a team of speech writers) want. The most obvious disadvantage is that it's difficult to read a speech and sound natural and nonmechanical. Reading material from the printed page or a teleprompter with liveliness and naturalness is itself a skill that is difficult to achieve without considerable practice. Audiences don't like speakers to read their speeches. They prefer speakers who speak *with* them. Also, reading a manuscript makes it difficult to respond to feedback from your listeners. And when the manuscript is on a stationary lectern, as it most often is, it's impossible for you to move around. You have to stay in one place. The speech controls your movement or, rather, your lack of movement.

Speaking from Memory

As in the manuscript method, the memorizing approach involves writing out the speech word for word. Instead of reading it, however, you commit it to memory and recite it or "act it out."

The advantages of this method are the same as for the manuscript method, but speaking from memory also allows you freedom to move about and otherwise to concentrate on delivery. The major disadvantage, of course, is that you might forget your speech. In a memorized speech each sentence cues the recall of the following sentence. Thus, when you forget one sentence, you may forget the rest of the speech. Another disadvantage is that this method makes it difficult to adjust to audience feedback. And if you're not going to adjust to feedback, you lose the main advantage of face-to-face contact.

Speaking Extemporaneously

An **extemporaneous speech** involves thorough preparation and a commitment to memory of the main ideas and their order (and, if you wish, your introduction and conclusion). There is, however, no commitment to exact wording for the remaining parts of the speech.

Extemporaneous delivery is useful in most speaking situations. Good college lecturers use the extemporaneous method. They prepare thoroughly and know what they want to say and in what order they want to say it, but they have given no commitment to exact wording.

One advantage of this method is that it allows you to respond easily to feedback. Should audience feedback suggest that a point needs clarification, for example, you can rephrase the idea or give an example. Extemporaneous delivery is the method that comes closest to conversation, a kind of "enlarged conversation." With this method you can move about and interact with the audience.

Here are a few guidelines for using the extemporaneous method—the method recommended for your classroom speeches and for most of the speeches you'll deliver throughout your life.

◆ Memorize the opening and closing lines; this will help you focus your complete attention on the audience and will put you more at ease. Similarly, memorize the main points and the order in which you'll cover them; this will free you from relying on your notes and will make you feel more in control of the speech and of the entire speech-making situation.

◆ Speak naturally. Listeners will enjoy your speech and believe you more if you speak as if you were conversing with a small group of people. Don't allow

? DEVELOPING STRATEGIES

Dressing for a Speech. Pat has to give three speeches on the same topic—school hate speech codes—to (1) the faculty of an exclusive prep school, (2) your class, and (3) the city council. Pat wonders how to dress for these presentations. If you were an image consultant, what advice would you give for dressing in each of these three situations if Pat were a man? If Pat were a woman?

❖ **CONSIDER** the ideal delivery style of a college professor. What professorial delivery characteristics help you maintain interest and attention? Which characteristics contribute to your losing interest?

your delivery to call attention to itself. Your ultimate aim should be to deliver the speech so naturally that the audience won't even notice your delivery.

◆ Use delivery to reinforce your message. All aspects of your delivery—your voice, bodily action, and general appearance, for example—should work together to make your ideas instantly intelligible to your audience.

◆ Vary your delivery. Variety in voice and bodily action will help you maintain your listeners' attention. Vary your vocal volume and your rate of speaking. In a similar way, avoid standing in exactly the same position throughout the speech. Use your body to express your ideas, to communicate to the audience what is going on in your head.

◆ Create immediacy with delivery. Make your listeners feel that you're talking directly and individually to each of them: Maintain appropriate eye contact with the audience members, talk directly to your audience and not to your notes or to your visual aids, smile when it's appropriate and consistent with your speech purpose, and maintain a physical closeness that reinforces a psychological closeness (don't stand behind the desk or lectern).

◆ Be expressive. You can do this by allowing your facial muscles and your entire body to reflect and echo your inner involvement. Use gestures appropriately. Too few gestures may signal lack of involvement; too many may communicate uneasiness, awkwardness, or anxiety. Read carefully the feedback signals sent by your audience, and respond to these signals with verbal, vocal, and bodily adjustments.

The remaining sections of this chapter will explain how you can use your voice and your bodily action to most effectively communicate your thoughts and feelings.

Effective Vocal Delivery

You can achieve effective vocal delivery by mastering your volume, rate, pitch, articulation and pronunciation, and pauses. Let's look at each in turn.

Volume

The word **volume** refers to the relative intensity of the voice. (The word *loudness* refers to the hearer's perception of that relative intensity.) In an adequately controlled voice, volume will vary according to several factors. For example, the distance between you and your listeners, the competing noise, and the emphasis you wish to give an idea will all influence volume.

DEVELOPING STRATEGIES

Speaking Volume. After sitting through two rounds of speeches, George wonders if the class wouldn't be ready for a speech spoken at noticeably higher volume than normal—rather like television commercials, which are played at a greater volume than the regular broadcast. What would you advise George to do?

Problems with volume are easy to identify in others, though difficult to recognize in ourselves. One obvious problem is a voice that is too soft. When speech is so soft that listeners have to strain to hear, they'll soon tire of expending so much energy. On the other hand, a voice that is too loud will prove disturbing because it intrudes on listeners' psychological space; it also may communicate aggressiveness and give others the impression that you are difficult to get along with.

The most common problems are too little volume variation and variation that falls into an easily predictable pattern. If the audience can predict volume changes, they'll focus on that pattern and not on what you're saying.

Fading away at the end of sentences is particularly disturbing. Some speakers begin sentences in an appropriate volume but end them at an extremely low volume. Be careful to avoid this tendency; when finishing sentences, make sure the audience is able to hear at an appropriate volume.

Rate

Your speech **rate** is the speed at which you speak. About 150 words per minute seems average for speaking as well as for reading aloud. The problems with rate

CRITICAL LISTENING/THINKING *Link*

Listening to Emotional Appeals

Emotional appeals are all around you, urging you to do all sorts of things—usually to buy a product or to support a position or cause. As you listen to these inevitable appeals, consider the following:

- Emotional appeals do not constitute proof. No matter how passionate the speaker's voice or bodily movement, no matter how compelling the language, passion does not prove the case a speaker is presenting.
- You really can't tell with certainty what the speaker is feeling. The speaker may, in fact, be using facial management techniques or clever speechwriters to communicate emotions without actually feeling them.
- Speakers may use emotional appeals to divert attention from a lack of real evidence. If emotional appeals are being used to the exclusion of argument and evidence, or if you suspect that the

speaker seeks to arouse your emotions so you forget that there's no evidence, ask yourself why.
- Emotional appeals may be appeals to either high or low motives. A speaker can arouse feelings of love and peace but also feelings of hatred and war. In asking for charitable donations, an organization may appeal to high motives such as your desire to help those less fortunate than you, or to lower motives such as guilt. For example, an appeal may present images of children playing and learning as a result of your contributions, or it may present images of children eating garbage and dying of starvation as a result of your not contributing.
- Be especially on the lookout for what logicians call *argumentum ad misericordiam*—the appeal to pity, as in, "I really tried to write the speech, but I've been having terrible depression and find it difficult to concentrate."

Getting Critical. Examine one of the speeches in this book, on the book's Companion Website, or at one of the many Internet sources containing speeches (for example, the History Channel at www.historychannel.com, Northwestern University's Douglass site at http://douglassarchives.org/, or the Great Speeches site at www.pbs.org/greatspeeches) for emotional appeals. As a critical listener/thinker, how would you describe the use of these emotional appeals?

are speaking too fast or too slow, speaking with too little variation, or speaking with too predictable a pattern. If you talk too fast, you deprive your listeners of time they need to understand and digest what you're saying; they may simply decide not to spend the energy needed to understand your speech. If your rate is too slow, your listeners' attention may wander to matters unrelated to your speech. Speak at a pace that engages the listeners and allows them time for reflection without boring them.

Use variations in rate to call attention to certain points and to add variety. For example, if you speak of the dull routine of an assembly line worker at a rapid and varied pace, or of the wonder of a circus with no variation in rate, you're surely misusing this important vocal dimension. Again, if you're interested in and conscious of what you're saying, your rate variations should flow naturally and effectively.

Pitch

Pitch is the relative highness or lowness of your voice as perceived by your listener. More technically, pitch results from the rate at which your vocal cords vibrate. If they vibrate rapidly, listeners will perceive your voice as having a high pitch. If they vibrate slowly, they'll perceive it as having a low pitch.

Pitch changes often signal changes in the meanings of many sentences. The most obvious is the difference between a statement and a question. Thus, the difference between the declarative sentence "So this is the proposal you want me to support" and the question "So this is the proposal you want me to support?" is inflection or pitch. This, of course, is obvious. But note that depending on where the inflectional change is placed, the meaning of the sentence changes drastically. Note also that all of the following questions contain exactly the same words, but they each ask a different question when you emphasize different words:

- Is *this* the proposal you want me to support?
- Is this the proposal *you* want me to support?
- Is this the proposal you want *me* to support?
- Is this the proposal you want me to *support*?

The obvious problems with pitch are levels that are too high, too low, or too patterned. Neither of the first two problems is common in speakers with otherwise normal voices, and with practice you can correct a pitch pattern that is too predictable or monotonous. As you gain speaking experience, pitch changes will come naturally from the sense of what you're saying. Because each sentence is somewhat different from every other sentence, there should be a normal variation—a variation that results not from some predetermined pattern but rather from the meanings you wish to convey to the audience.

Articulation and Pronunciation

Articulation and pronunciation are similar in that they both refer to enunciation, the way in which we produce sounds and words. Technically, the two processes do differ. **Articulation** consists of the movements the speech organs make as they modify and interrupt the air stream you send from the lungs. Different movements of these speech organs (for example, the tongue, lips, teeth, palate, and vo-

USING TECHNOLOGY

Visit American Rhetoric at http://www.americanrhetoric.com/speechbank.htm for lots of links to Internet sites containing full text, audio, and video versions of public speeches. What vocal characteristics do the best speakers share?

cal cords) produce different sounds. **Pronunciation** is the production of syllables or words according to some accepted standard, as identified in any good dictionary. Our concern here is with identifying and correcting some of the most common problems associated with faulty articulation and pronunciation.

Articulation Problems

The three major articulation problems are omission, substitution, and addition of sounds or syllables. These problems occur both in native speakers of English and in speakers whose first language is not English. Fortunately, they can be easily corrected with informed practice.

Errors of Omission. Omitting sounds or even syllables is a major articulation problem but one easily overcome with concentration and practice. Here are some examples:

Not This	This
gov-a-ment	gov-ern-ment
hi-stry	hi-story
wanna	want to
studyin	studying
a-lum-num	a-lum-i-num
comp-ny	comp-a-ny

Errors of Substitution. Substituting an incorrect sound for the correct one is another easily corrected problem. Among the most common errors are substituting "d" for "t" and "d" for "th."

Not This	This
wader	waiter
dese	these
ax	ask
undoubtebly	undoubtedly
beder	better
ekcetera	etcetera

Errors of Addition. When there are errors of addition, sounds are added where they don't belong. Some examples include:

Not This	This
acrost	across
athalete	athlete
Americer	America
idear	idea
filim	film
lore	law

If you make any of these errors, you can easily correct them. First, become conscious of your own articulation patterns (and of any specific errors you may be making). Then listen carefully to the articulation of prominent speakers (for example, broadcasters), comparing their speech patterns with your own. Practice the correct patterns until they become part of your normal speech behavior.

Pronunciation Problems

Among the most widespread pronunciation problems are putting the **accent** (stress or emphasis) on the wrong syllable and pronouncing sounds that should remain silent. Both of these pronunciation problems may result from learning English as a second language. For example, a person may use the accent system of his or her first language to pronounce words in English that may have a different accent system. Similarly, in many languages, all letters that appear in a word are pronounced in speech, whereas in English some letters are silent.

Errors of Accent. Here are some common examples of words accented incorrectly:

Not This	This
New Orleáns	New Órleans
ínsurance	insúrance
orátor	órator

Errors of Pronouncing Silent Sounds. For some words correct pronunciation means not articulating certain sounds, as in the following examples:

Not This	This
often	offen
homage	omage
Illinois	Illinoi
evening	evning

The best way to deal with pronunciation problems is to look up in a good dictionary any words whose pronunciation you're not sure of. Learn to read the pronunciation key in your dictionary, and make it a practice to look up words you hear others use that seem to be pronounced incorrectly as well as words that you wish to use yourself but are not sure how to pronounce.

Pauses

Pauses come in two basic types: filled and unfilled. Filled pauses are pauses in the stream of speech that you fill with vocalizations such as *er, um, ah, well,* and *you know.* Filled pauses are ineffective and will make you appear hesitant, unprepared, and unsure of yourself.

Unfilled pauses, silences interjected into the normally fluent stream of speech, can be effective in public speaking if used correctly. Here are just a few examples of places where unfilled pauses—silences of a second or two—should prove effective.

❖ **CONSIDER** the suggestions for vocal effectiveness you might give the speaker pictured here. How would your suggestions differ for the speaker addressing a small group as opposed to a speaker addressing an audience of several hundred?

RESEARCH *Link*

Integrating Research into Your Speech

By integrating and acknowledging your sources of information in your speech, you'll give fair credit to those whose ideas and research findings you're using, and at the same time you'll help establish your own reputation as a responsible researcher. You'll also lessen the risk that anything you say can be interpreted as plagiarism (see pp. 100–101). Here are a few suggestions for integrating your research into your speech:

Mention the Sources in Your Speech. Cite at least the author; if appropriate, cite the publication and the date. Check out some of the speeches reprinted in this book and note especially how the speakers have integrated their sources in the speech. In your written preparation outline, give the complete bibliographical reference.

Here's an example of how you might cite your source and establish credibility at the same time.

> Don't expect an extremely effective drug to treat most cases of hepatitis C within the next two years. Dr. Howard J. Worman of New York Presbyterian Hospital, one of the leading scientists in the field of liver disease, the author of more than 70 medical and scientific papers and of *The Liver Disorders Sourcebook,* and the creator of the Diseases of the Liver website, expressed this opinion in his article *Hepatitis C: An Epidemic Ignored,* published on the healthology.com website, which I accessed this week.

Here's another example:

> My discussion of the symptoms of arrhythmia is based on the insights of Dr. Anthony R. Magnano (2001), a clinical fellow in cardiology at Columbia University College of Physicians and Surgeons. Magnano is an active researcher on arrhythmia

and has written widely on the topic. In a 2001 article on arrhythmias on the healthology.com website, which I last accessed on August 21, Magnano identifies three symptoms he sees most often in his patients: heart palpitations, lightheadedness, and fainting spells.

In the reference list following the preparation outline for the speech, this speaker would identify the author, the article title, the URL address, and the date the speaker accessed the site. The reference would look like this:

Magnano, Anthony R. (2001). Arrhythmias: An introduction. http://www.healthology.com/focus_article.asp?f=cardio&b=healthology&c=arrhythmias_intro (accessed August 21, 2001).

Although it's possible to overdo oral source citations—to give more information than listeners really need—there are even greater dangers in leaving out potentially useful source information. Because your speeches in this course are learning experiences, it will be better to err on the side of being more rather than less complete.

Avoid Useless Lead-In Expressions. Comments such as "I have a quote here" or "I want to quote an example" serve no purpose. Let the audience know that you're quoting by pausing before the quote, taking a step forward, or—to read an extended quotation—referring to your notes. If you want to state more directly that this is a quotation, you might do it this way:

> Recently, Mary Kay Ash put this in perspective: "A woman can no more duplicate the male style of leadership than an American businessman can exactly reproduce the Japanese style."

Research Activity. What kind of oral citations would you use in integrating one of your textbooks, a website, and a newsgroup post in your speech?

◆ Pause before beginning your speech. Don't start your speech as soon as you get to the front of the room; instead, position yourself so that you feel comfortable. Then scan the audience and begin your speech.

◆ Pause at transitional points to signal that you're moving from one part of the speech to another or from one idea to another.

◆ Pause at the end of an important assertion to give the audience time to think about the significance of what you're saying.

◆ Pause after asking a rhetorical question to let your listeners think about how they'd answer the question.

◆ Pause before an important idea. This will help signal that what comes next is especially significant.

◆ If there's a question period following your speech and you're in charge of it, pause after you've completed your conclusion and ask the audience if they have any questions. If there's a chairperson, pause after your conclusion, then nonverbally indicate to the chairperson that you're ready to entertain questions.

◆ If there's no period for questions and answers, pause after the last sentence of your conclusion, continue to maintain eye contact with the audience, and then walk, do not run, back to your seat. Once you are back in your seat, focus on the class activity taking place.

Effective Bodily Action

You speak with your body as well as with your mouth. The total effect of the speech depends not only on what you say but also on the way you present it. It depends on your movements, gestures, and facial expressions as well as on your words. Seven aspects of bodily action are especially important in public speaking: eye contact, facial expression, posture, gestures, movement, proxemics, and the use of notes.

Eye Contact

The most important single aspect of bodily communication is eye contact. The two major problems with eye contact are inappropriate eye contact and eye contact that does not cover the audience fairly. In much of the United States, listeners perceive speakers who don't maintain enough eye contact as distant, unconcerned, and less trustworthy than speakers who look directly at their audience. Consequently, it's generally best to maintain relatively focused eye contact with your audience. Use your eyes to communicate your concern for and interest in what you're saying and to convey your confidence and commitment. Avoid staring blankly through your audience or glancing over their heads, at the floor, or out the window. In other cultures—for example, in many Asian cultures—focused eye contact may prove embarrassing to audience members, so in such cultures, it's often best to politely scan the audience without locking eyes with specific listeners.

Involve all listeners in the public speaking transaction. Communicate equally with the members on the left and on the right, in both the back and the front. Eye contact will also enable you to secure audience feedback, to see if your listeners are interested or bored or puzzled. Use eye contact to gauge listeners' level of agreement and disagreement.

"He's energizing his base."

© The New Yorker Collection 2004 David Sipress from cartoonbank.com. All Rights Reserved.

Facial Expression

Facial expressions are especially important in communicating emotions—anger and fear, boredom and excitement, doubt and surprise. If you feel committed to and believe in your thesis, you'll probably display your meanings appropriately and effectively.

Nervousness and anxiety, however, may at times prevent you from relaxing enough so that your emotions come through. Fortunately, time and practice will allow you to relax, and the emotions you feel will reveal themselves appropriately and automatically.

Generally, members of one culture will be able to recognize the emotions displayed facially by members of other cultures. But there are differences in what each culture considers appropriate to display in public. As discussed in Chapter 4, each culture has its own "display rules" (Ekman, Friesen, & Ellsworth, 1972). For example, Japanese Americans watching a stress-inducing film spontaneously displayed the same facial emotions as did other Americans when they thought they were unobserved. But when an observer was present, the Japanese Americans masked (tried to hide) their emotional expressions more than did the other Americans (Gudykunst & Kim, 1992).

USING TECHNOLOGY

Visit an interesting website for public speakers at http://speeches.com/index.shtml. This site contains a variety of speeches and speaker resources. What advice on delivery can you find?

Posture

When delivering your speech, stand straight but not stiff. Try to communicate a command of the situation without communicating the discomfort that is actually quite common for beginning speakers.

Avoid the common mistakes of posture: Avoid putting your hands in your pockets or clasping them in front or behind your back; and avoid leaning on the desk, the lectern, or the chalkboard. With practice you'll come to feel more at ease and will communicate this by the way you stand before the audience.

Gestures

Gestures in public speaking help illustrate your verbal messages. We gesture for this purpose regularly in conversation. For example, when saying "Come here," you probably move your head, hands, arms, and perhaps your entire body to motion the listener in your direction. Your body as well as your verbal message say "Come here."

Avoid using your hands to preen, however. For example, avoid fixing your hair or adjusting your clothing; don't fidget with your watch, ring, or jewelry.

Effective bodily action is spontaneous and natural to you as the speaker, to your audience, and to your speech. If gestures seem planned or rehearsed, they'll appear phony and insincere. As a general rule, don't do anything with your hands that doesn't feel right for you; the audience will recognize it as unnatural. If you feel relaxed and comfortable with yourself and your audience, you'll generate natural bodily action without conscious or studied attention.

Movement

The word *movement* refers here to movements of your whole body. In public speaking it helps to move around a bit. Movement keeps both you and the audience more alert. Even when speaking behind a lectern, you can give the illusion of movement. You can step back or forward or flex your upper body so it appears that you're moving more than you are.

If you're using a lectern, you may wish to signal transitions by stepping to the side or in front of it and then behind it again as you move from one point to another. Generally, however, it's best to avoid too much or too little movement around the lectern. Too much movement may make you appear ill-at-ease, fidgety, or nervous, which in turn will detract from your credibility. Too little movement may make you appear frightened or uninvolved, which also will work against your establishing credibility. For example, you may wish to lean over the lectern when, say, posing a question to your listeners or advancing a particularly important argument. But never lean on the lectern; never use it as support.

Avoid the three problems of movement: too little, too much, and too patterned. Speakers who move too little often appear strapped to the podium, afraid of the audience, or too uncommitted to involve themselves fully. With too much movement the audience begins to concentrate on the movement itself, wondering where the speaker will wind up next. With movement that is too patterned, the audience may become bored—too steady and predictable a rhythm quickly becomes tiring. The audience will often view the speaker as nonspontaneous and uninvolved.

Use whole-body movements to emphasize transitions and to emphasize the introduction of a new and important assumption, bit of evidence, or closely reasoned argument. Thus, when making a transition, you might take a step forward to signal that something new is coming.

❖ **CONSIDER** the ways in which culture influences how a speaker delivers a speech. Can you identify characteristics of voice and bodily action that members of your culture would evaluate positively? What characteristics would they evaluate negatively?

Proxemics

Proxemics, or the way you use space in communication, can be a crucial factor in public speaking. Consider the spaces between you and your listeners and among the listeners themselves. If you stand too close to your listeners, they may feel uncomfortable, as if their personal space is being violated. If you stand too far away from your audience, you may be perceived as uninvolved, uninterested, or uncomfortable. Watch where your instructor and other speakers stand, and adjust your own position accordingly.

Using Notes

For some speeches it may be helpful for you to use notes. As one public speaking consultant put it, "By using notes you are demonstrating that you 'plan your work and work your plan.' You are a well-organized speaker. You have more sense than to spend valuable time memorizing an entire presentation" (Fensholt, 2003). To make the most effective use of notes, however, do keep in mind the following guidelines.

◆ **Keep notes to a minimum.** The fewer notes you take with you, the better off you'll be. One reason so many speakers bring notes with them is that

RESEARCH *Link*

Citing Research Sources

In citing references, first find out what style manual is used in your class or at your school. Generally, it will be a style manual developed by the American Psychological Association (APA), the Modern Language Association (MLA), or the University of Chicago (the *Chicago Manual of Style*). Different colleges and even different departments within a given school often rely on different formats for citing research, which, quite frankly, makes a tedious process even worse.

Fortunately, a variety of websites provide guides to the information you'll need to cite any reference in your speech. For example, Purdue University offers an excellent site that covers APA and MLA style formats and provides examples for citing books, articles, newspaper articles, websites, e-mail, online postings, electronic databases, and more (http://owl.english.purdue.edu/handouts/research). This site also provides extremely useful advice for searching the Web and evaluating website information. Another excellent website is Capital Community College's Guide for Writing Research Papers (http://ccc.commnet.edu/apa/apa_index.htm). Guidelines for using the *Chicago Manual of Style* may be found at Ohio State's website (http://www.lib.ohio-state.edu/). This site provides guidance for citing all types of print and electronic sources. Another valuable source is the Columbia Guide to Online Style (http://www.columbia.edu/cu/cup/cgos/idx_basic.html); the Columbia site provides detailed instructions and examples for citing e-mail, listserv, and newsgroup communications; and even software programs and video games. After reviewing these websites, print out the one or two that you find most useful so you can have them in easy reach.

Research Activity. If you have access, log on to Research Navigator (www.researchnavigator.com) and read the section on citing sources; or consult The Speech Writer's Workshop CD-ROM, Version 2 (see page xvi). Both of these resources allow you to insert the various source materials into a template and then rearrange them into proper citation form for a variety of formats.

they want to avoid the face-to-face interaction required. With experience, however, you should find this face-to-face interaction the best part of the public speaking experience.

Resist the normal temptation to bring with you the entire speech outline. You may rely on it too heavily and lose direct contact with the audience. Instead, compose a delivery outline (see pp. 162–163), using only key words. Bring this to the lectern with you—one side of an index card (5-by-8 cards work extremely well for most short speeches) or at most an 8½-by-11 page should be sufficient. This will relieve anxiety over the possibility of forgetting your speech but will not be extensive enough to interfere with direct contact with your audience.

◆ **Use notes with "open subtlety."** Don't make your notes more obvious than necessary. At the same time, don't try to hide them. Don't gesture with your notes and thus make them more obvious than they need be; at the same time, don't turn away from the audience to steal a glance at them either. Use them openly and honestly but gracefully, with "open subtlety." To do this effectively, you'll have to know your notes intimately. Rehearse at least twice with the same notes that you'll take with you to the speaker's stand.

◆ **Don't allow your notes to prevent directness.** When using your notes, pause to look at them. Then regain eye contact with the audience and continue your speech. Don't read from your notes; just take cues from them. The one exception to this is an extensive quotation or complex set of statistics that you have to read; read it and then, almost immediately, resume direct eye contact with the audience.

Your experience in delivering speeches will greatly influence the satisfaction you derive from the entire public speaking interaction. You may wish to pause at this point and examine your own public speaking satisfaction by taking the accompanying self-test, "How Satisfying Is Your Public Speaking Experience?"

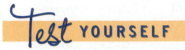 **YOURSELF**

How Satisfying Is Your Public Speaking Experience?

Respond to each of the following statements by recording the number best representing your feelings during your last speech, using this scale: Strongly agree = 1, moderately agree = 2, slightly agree = 3, neutral = 4, slightly disagree = 5, moderately disagree = 6, and strongly disagree = 7.

_____ **1.** The audience let me know that I was speaking effectively.

_____ **2.** My speech accomplished nothing.

_____ **3.** I would like to give another speech like this one.

_____ **4.** The audience genuinely wanted to get to know me.

Potus

(www.ipl.org/ref/POTUS)

This is one of many websites that provide access to the speeches of the presidents of the United States. Visit the POTUS site and listen to one of the speeches of a president in whom you're interested. How would you characterize the style of delivery?

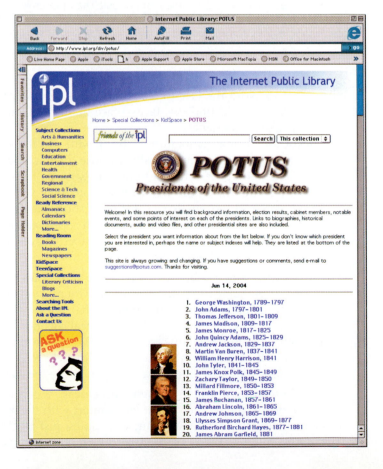

_____ **5.** I was very dissatisfied with my speech.

_____ **6.** I was very satisfied with my speech.

_____ **7.** The audience seemed very interested in what I had to say.

_____ **8.** I did not enjoy the public speaking experience.

_____ **9.** The audience did not seem supportive of what I was saying.

_____ **10.** The speech flowed smoothly.

❖ **HOW DID YOU DO?** To compute your score, follow these steps:

1. Add the scores for items 1, 3, 4, 6, 7, and 10.
2. Reverse the scores for items 2, 5, 8, and 9 so that 7 becomes 1, 6 becomes 2, 5 becomes 3, 4 remains 4, 3 becomes 5, 2 becomes 6, and 1 becomes 7.
3. Add the reversed scores for items 2, 5, 8, and 9.
4. Add the totals from steps 1 and 3 to yield your communication satisfaction score.

You may interpret your score along the following scale:

10	20	30	40	50	60	70
Extremely satisfying	Quite satisfying	Fairly satisfying	Average	Fairly unsatisfying	Quite unsatisfying	Extremely unsatisfying

How accurately do you think this scale captures the satisfaction you derive from public speaking?

❖ **WHAT WILL YOU DO?** As you become a more successful and effective public speaker, your satisfaction is likely to increase. What specific actions can you take to increase your satisfaction?

Adapted with permission from Hecht, M. (1978). The conceptualization and measurement of interpersonal communication satisfaction. *Human Communication Research, 4,* 253–264. This test was adapted for public speaking from the conversational satisfaction test and is used with the permission and suggestions of the author.

A CASE OF *Ethics*

Correcting Errors

During a speech on HIV infection, you mention that the rate of HIV infection in women has declined over the last several years. You meant to say that the rate had increased, but—probably because of nervousness—you say exactly the opposite of what you intended. Even though no one asks you about this during the question-and-answer session following your speech, you wonder if you should correct yourself. The problem, you feel, is that if you do correct yourself, the audience may question your entire speech; and this could undercut a message that you feel very strongly about—that all people must take precautions to prevent HIV infection.

What is your ethical obligation in this case? More generally, what ethical responsibility does a speaker have to correct her or his mistakes?

Rehearsal: Practicing and Improving Delivery

Through rehearsal you can develop delivery skills that will help you achieve the purposes of your speech. Rehearsal also will enable you to time your speech and to see how the speech will flow as a whole. Additionally, rehearsal will help you test out your presentation aids, detect any technological problems, and resolve them. And, of course, through rehearsal you'll learn your speech effectively and reduce your apprehension and gain greater confidence.

The following procedures should assist you in achieving these goals.

Rehearse the Speech as a Whole

Rehearse the speech from beginning to end. Don't rehearse the speech in parts. Rehearse it from getting out of your seat, through the introduction, body, and conclusion, to returning to your seat. Be sure to rehearse the speech with all the examples and illustrations (and audiovisual aids if any) included. This will enable you to connect the parts of the speech and to see how they interact with one another.

Time the Speech

Time the speech during each rehearsal. Make any necessary adjustments on the basis of this timing. If you're using computer presentation software, you'll be able to time your speech very precisely. Such software will also enable you to time the individual parts of your speech so you can achieve the balance you want—for example, you might want to spend twice as much time on the solutions as on the problems, or you might want to balance the introduction and conclusion so that each constitutes about 10 percent of your speech.

Approximate the Actual Speech Situation

Rehearse the speech under conditions as close as possible to those under which you'll deliver it. If possible, rehearse the speech in the same room in which you'll present it. If this is impossible, try to simulate the actual conditions as closely as you can—in your living room or even in a bathroom. If possible, rehearse the speech in front of a few supportive listeners. It's always helpful (especially for your beginning speeches) if your listeners are supportive rather than critical. Merely having listeners present during your rehearsal will further simulate the conditions under which you'll eventually speak. Get together with two or three other students in an empty classroom where you can each serve as speaker and listener.

Incorporate Changes and Delivery Notes

Don't interrupt your rehearsal to make notes or changes; if you do, you may never experience the entire speech from beginning to end. But do make any needed changes in the speech between rehearsals. While making these changes,

DEVELOPING STRATEGIES

Unexpected Feedback. Angie introduced her speech with a story she found extremely humorous and which made her laugh out loud as she relayed it to the audience. Unfortunately, the audience just didn't get it—not one smile in the entire audience. What might Angie do now (if anything)?

note any words whose pronunciation or articulation you wish to check. Also, insert pause notations, "slow down" warnings, and other delivery suggestions into your outline.

If possible, record your speech (ideally, on videotape) so you can hear exactly what your listeners will hear: your volume, rate, pitch, articulation and pronunciation, and pauses. You'll then be in a better position to improve these qualities.

Rehearse Often

Rehearse the speech as often as seems necessary. Two useful guides are: (1) Rehearse the speech at least three or four times; less than this is sure to be too little. And (2) rehearse the speech as long as your rehearsals continue to produce improvements in the speech or in your delivery.

? DEVELOPING STRATEGIES

Technical Problems. Carmen prepared a great slide show for her informative speech. Unfortunately, the projector that she needed to show the slides never arrived at the location of the speech. But she has to give the speech, and she has to (or must she?) explain something about what happened to her prepared slide show. What might Carmen say (if anything)?

Summary of Concepts and Skills

In this chapter we looked at ways you can make the delivery of your speech more effective.

Methods of Delivery

Four general methods of delivery are used in public speaking:

- Impromptu: speaking without preparation; useful in certain aspects of public speaking.
- Manuscript: reading from a written text; useful when exact timing and wording are essential.
- Memorized: acting out a memorized text; useful when exact timing and wording are required.
- Extemporaneous: speaking after thorough preparation and memorization of the main ideas; useful in most public speaking situations.

Effective Vocal Delivery

Several key qualities make for effective vocal delivery:

- Volume: overly soft, loud, or unvaried, and fading away at ends of sentences.
- Rate: too rapid, too slow, too little variation, and too predictable a pattern.

- Pitch: overly high, low, monotonous, or too predictable a pattern.
- Articulation and pronunciation; omission, substitution, and addition, using the wrong accent, and pronouncing silent sounds.
- Pauses: use pauses to signal transitions between parts of the speech, give the audience time to think, allow listeners to ponder rhetorical questions, and signal the approach of especially important ideas.

Effective Bodily Action

Seven aspects of bodily action are important:

- Maintain eye contact.
- Allow facial expressions to convey thoughts and feelings.
- Use posture to communicate command of the speech experience.
- Gesture naturally.
- Move around a bit.
- Position yourself neither too close nor too far from the audience.
- Use a few notes, but use them with "open subtlety" so that they don't prevent maintaining direct contact with your audience.

Rehearsal

Follow these rehearsal guidelines:

◆ Rehearse the speech as a whole.

◆ Time the speech.

◆ Approximate the actual speech situation.

◆ Incorporate changes and delivery notes.

◆ Rehearse often.

Vocabulary Quiz

Public Speaking Delivery

Match the terms dealing with delivery in public speaking with their definitions. Record the number of the definition next to the appropriate term.

_____ impromptu speech

_____ vocal volume

_____ pronunciation

_____ proxemics

_____ manuscript speech

_____ vocal rate

_____ articulation

_____ vocal pitch

_____ pause

_____ extemporaneous speech

1. A speech made without any prior preparation; off-the-cuff speaking.

2. A public speech that is written out and read aloud word for word.

3. Speech that involves thorough preparation but no commitment to memory of the exact wording.

4. The relative intensity of the voice.

5. The number of words you speak per minute.

6. The relative highness or lowness of your voice as perceived by listeners.

7. The movements your speech organs make as they modify and interrupt the air stream from your lungs.

8. The production of syllables or words according to some accepted standard.

9. An interruption in the stream of speech that may be filled with such expressions as *er* or *ah* or may be unfilled.

10. The way in which the speaker uses space in communicating.

Web Explorations

Companion Website

www.ablongman.com/devito

Chapter 8 of the Companion Website offers additional suggestions for improving your public speaking delivery and rehearsal in "Undertaking a Long-Term Delivery Program." Two exercises will give you opportunities to practice using nonverbal signals to communicate: "Communicating Vocally but Nonverbally" and "Communicating Emotions Nonverbally."

Public Speaking Exercises

8.1 Developing the Impromptu Speech

The following experience may prove useful as an exercise in delivery. Each student should take three index cards and write an impromptu speech topic on each of the cards. The topics to be used for impromptu speaking should be familiar (but not clichés) and should be worthwhile and substantive, not trivial. The cards should be collected and placed face down on a table. A speaker chosen through some random process selects two cards, reads the topics, selects one of them, and takes approximately one or two minutes to prepare a two- to three-minute impromptu speech. A few guidelines may prove helpful:

1. Don't apologize. Everyone will have difficulty with this assignment, so there's no need to emphasize any problems you may have.

2. Don't express verbally or nonverbally any displeasure or any negative responses to the experience, the topic, the audience, or even yourself. Approach the entire task with a positive attitude and a positive appearance. It will help make the experience more enjoyable for both you and your audience.

3. When you select your topic, jot down two or three subtopics that you'll cover and perhaps two or three bits of supporting material that you'll use in amplifying these two or three subtopics.

4. Develop your conclusion. It will probably be best to use a simple summary conclusion in which you restate your main topic and the subtopics that you discussed.

5. Develop an introduction. Here it will probably be best simply to identify your topic and orient the audience by telling them the two or three subtopics that you'll cover.

8.2 Communicating Vocally but Nonverbally

This exercise is designed to give you practice in communicating effectively with your voice and body. In this exercise a speaker recites the alphabet and attempts to communicate with each letter one of the following emotions: anger, nervousness, fear, pride, happiness, sadness, jealousy, satisfaction, love, or sympathy. The speaker should first number the emotions in random order so that he or she will have a set order to follow that is not known to the audience, whose task it will be to guess the emotions expressed.

As a variation, have the speaker go through the entire list of emotions twice: once facing the audience and employing any nonverbal signals desired, and once with his or her back to the audience and giving no nonverbal signals.

After the exercise is completed, consider some or all of the following questions:

1. What vocal cues help communicate the various emotions?

2. What bodily cues are useful in communicating these various emotions?

3. Are there gender display rules for effectively communicating some or all of these emotions? That is, are men and women expected to use different cues when communicating certain emotions?

9 Informing Your Audience

Why Read This Chapter?

It will enable you to convey information to an audience by helping you to:

❖ follow the principles for effectively informing an audience so that, for example, you don't overwhelm your listeners or tell them what they already know

❖ select organizing patterns and strategies for describing (a person, object, event, or process), defining (a concept or theory), or demonstrating (how to do something or how something operates)

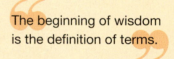

> " The beginning of wisdom is the definition of terms. "
> —**Socrates**

One of the most important types of speeches you'll be called upon to deliver is the informative speech, the subject of this chapter. Let's first consider some general guidelines for all informative speeches; then we'll focus on three types of informative speeches—speeches that describe, define, or demonstrate.

Guidelines for Informative Speaking

USING TECHNOLOGY

Many public speaking courses maintain websites to help students find topics and develop informative speeches. Search for "informative speeches" and similar phrases; or visit, for example, the Cincinnati State Technical and Community College website for public speaking ideas at http://faculty. cinstate.cc.oh.us/gesellsc/ publicspeaking/topics.html.

To communicate information is to tell your listeners something they don't know, something new. Inform your audience about a new way of looking at old things or an old way of looking at new things. You may discuss a theory not previously heard of or a familiar concept not fully understood. You may talk about events that the audience may be unaware of or explain happenings they may have misconceptions about. Regardless of what type of informative speech you intend to give, the following guidelines should help.

Limit the Amount of Information

There's a limit to the amount of information that a listener can take in at one time. Resist the temptation to overload your listeners with information. Instead of enlarging the breadth of information you communicate, expand its depth. It's better to present two new items of information and explain these in depth with examples, illustrations, and descriptions than to present five items without this needed amplification. The speaker who attempts to discuss the physiological, psychological, social, and linguistic differences between men and women, for example, is clearly trying to cover too much and is going to be forced to cover these areas only superficially, with the result that little new information will be communicated. Even covering *one* of these areas completely is likely to prove difficult. Instead, select one subdivision of one area—say, language development or differences in language problems—and develop that in depth.

Adjust the Level of Complexity

As you know from attending college classes, information can be presented in very simple or very complex form. The level of complexity on which you communicate your information should depend on the wide variety of factors considered throughout this book: the level of knowledge your audience has, the time you have available, the purpose you hope to achieve, the topic on which you're speaking, and so on. If you simplify a topic too much, you risk boring or, even worse, insulting your audience. On the other hand, if your talk is too complex, you risk confusing your audience and failing to communicate your message.

Generally, beginning speakers err by being too complex and not realizing that a 5- or 10-minute speech isn't long enough to make an audience understand sophisticated concepts or complicated processes. At least in your beginning speeches, try to keep it simple rather than complex. Make sure the words you use are familiar to your audience; alternatively, explain and define any unfamiliar terms as you use them. For example, remember that jargon and technical vocabulary familiar to the computer hacker may not be familiar to the person who still uses a typewriter. Always see your topic from the point of view of the audience; ask yourself how much they know about your topic and its particular terminology.

Stress Relevance and Usefulness

Listeners remember information best when they see it as relevant and useful to their own needs or goals. Notice that as a listener you yourself regularly demonstrate this principle. For example, in class you may attend to and remember the stages in the development of language in children simply because you'll be tested on the information and you want to earn a high grade. Or you may remember a given piece of information because it will help you make a better impression in your job interview, make you a better parent, or enable you to deal with relationship problems. Like you, listeners attend to information that will prove useful to them.

If you want the audience to listen to your speech, relate your information to their needs, wants, or goals. Throughout your speech, but especially in the beginning, make sure your audience knows that the information you're presenting is or will be relevant and useful to them now or in the immediate future. For example, you might say something like:

> We all want financial security. We all want to be able to buy those luxuries we read so much about in magazines and see every evening on television. Wouldn't it be nice to be able to buy a car without worrying about where you're going to get the down payment or how you'll be able to make the monthly payments? Actually, that is not an unrealistic goal, as I'll demonstrate in this speech. In fact, I'll show you several investment strategies that have enabled many people to increase their income by as much as 20 percent.

Relate New Information to Old

Listeners will learn information more easily and retain it longer when you relate it to what they already know. So, relate the new to the old, the unfamiliar to the familiar, the unseen to the seen, the untasted to the tasted. Here, for example, Betsy Heffernan, a student from the University of Wisconsin (Reynolds & Schnoor, 1991), relates the problem of sewage to a familiar historical event:

> During our nation's struggle for independence, the citizens of Boston were hailed as heroes for dumping tea into Boston Harbor. But not to be outdone, many modern day Bostonians are also dumping things into the harbor: five-thousand gallons of human waste every second. The New England Aquarium of Boston states that since 1900, Bostonians have dumped enough human sewage into the harbor to cover the entire state of Massachusetts chest deep in sludge. Unfortunately, Boston isn't alone. All over the country, bays, rivers, and lakes are literally becoming cesspools.

In this next example, Teresa Jacob, a student from Ohio State University (Schnoor, 1997, p. 97), relates the problems of drug interactions (the new) to mixing chemicals in the school lab (the old or familiar).

> During our high school years, most of us learned in a chemistry class the danger of mixing harmless chemicals in lab. Add one drop of the wrong compound and suddenly you've created a stink bomb, or worse, an explosion. Millions of Americans run the same risk inside their bodies each day by combining drugs that are supposed to help restore or maintain good health.

DEVELOPING STRATEGIES

Explaining Concepts. Elaine wants to give an informative speech on virtual reality simulation, but most of her audience members have never experienced it. How would you advise Elaine to communicate this concept and this experience to her audience?

A CASE OF *Ethics*

Using Another's Work

In an economics course you took at another school, you received a handout that very clearly explained the relationship of interest rates to stock prices. Now you are planning to give a speech on that very topic.

> *Would it be ethical to use the handout to support one of your points without saying where you got it or who prepared it—to allow your audience to draw the conclusion that you prepared it yourself? If not, how might you use this handout effectively and ethically? More generally, what ethical guidelines should govern materials a speaker distributes to listeners?*

Vary the Levels of Abstraction

You can talk about freedom of the press in the abstract by talking about the importance of getting information to the public, by referring to the Bill of Rights, and by relating a free press to the preservation of democracy. But you can also talk about freedom of the press on a low level of abstraction, a level that is specific and concrete; for example, you can describe how a local newspaper was prevented from running a story critical of the town council or how Lucy Rinaldo was fired from the *Accord Sentinel* after she wrote a story critical of the mayor.

Combining high abstraction (the very general) and low abstraction (the very specific) seems to work best. Too many generalizations without the specifics or too many specifics without the generalizations will prove less effective than the combination of abstract and specific.

Here, for example, is an excerpt from a speech on the homeless. Note that in the first paragraph we have a relatively abstract description of homelessness. In the second paragraph, we get into specifics. In the last paragraph the abstract and the concrete are connected.

[Here the speaker begins with relatively general or abstract statements.] Homelessness is a serious problem for all metropolitan areas throughout the country. It's currently estimated that there are now more than 200,000 homeless in New York City alone. But what is this really about? Let me tell you what it's about.

[Here the speaker gets to specifics.] It's about a young man. He must be about 25 or 30, although he looks a lot older. He lives in a cardboard box on the side of my apartment house. We call him Tom, although we really don't know his name. All his possessions are stored in this huge box. I think it was a box from a refrigerator. Actually, he doesn't have very much, and what he has easily fits in this box. There's a blanket my neighbor threw out, some plastic bottles Tom puts water in, and some Styrofoam

❖ **CONSIDER** the principles of public speaking that you often see violated or used effectively in the speeches of celebrities. What two or three suggestions would you offer celebrities giving public speeches?

containers he picked up from the garbage from Burger King. He uses these to store whatever food he finds.

[The conclusion combines the general and the specific.] What is homelessness about? It's about Tom and 200,000 other "Toms" in New York and thousands of others throughout the rest of the country. And not all of them even have boxes to live in.

Make Your Speech Easy to Remember

The principles of public speaking (principles governing use of language, delivery, and supporting materials, for example) will all help your listeners remember your speech. If, for example, you stress interest and relevance—as already noted—the audience is more likely to remember what you say because they see it as important and relevant to their own lives. But here are a few extra suggestions.

◆ *Repeat the points you want the audience to remember.* Help your audience to remember what you want them to remember by repeating your most important points.

◆ *Use guide phrases.* Guide your audience's attention to your most memorable points by saying, for example, "the first point to remember is that . . . ," "the argument I want you to remember when you enter that voting booth is . . . ."

◆ *Use internal summary transitions.* Internal summary transitions will remind the audience of what you have said and how it relates to what is to follow. This kind of repetition will reinforce your message and help your listeners remember your main points.

◆ *Pattern your messages.* If the audience can see the logic of your speech, they'll be better able to organize what you say in their own minds. If they can see that you're following a temporal pattern or a spatial pattern, for example, it will be easier for them to retain more of what you say, because they'll have a framework into which they can fit what you say.

◆ *Focus audience attention.* The best way to focus the listeners' attention is to tell them to focus their attention. Simply say, "I want you to focus on three points that I will make in this speech. First, . . . " or "What I want you to remember is simply this: . . . ."

Now that the principles of informative speaking have been identified, we'll turn to three types of informative speeches: description, definition, and demonstration. Be aware, however, that this three-part classification is only one way of looking at informative speeches. You may be interested in some alternative classifications of information speeches that other writers in public speaking have devised.

Stephen Lucas (2004) uses a four-part classification:

◆ Speeches about objects, persons, places, or things; for example, the contributions of a noted scientist or philosopher

◆ Speeches about processes or series of actions; for example, an explanation of how to do something

◆ Speeches about events or happenings; for example, the story of your first date

◆ Speeches about concepts, beliefs, or ideas; for example, a review of theories of economics

George Rodman and Ron Adler (1997) offer a four-part classification for classroom speeches:

◆ Introductions, whether of yourself or of objects, events, or concepts

◆ Instructions about how to do something; for example, how to use a scanner

◆ Demonstrations to show how something works; for example, how CPR works

◆ Explanations that clarify why something works; for example, why cocaine has the effects it does

George Grice and John Skinner (2004) offer an eight-part system:

◆ Speeches about people (Cesar Chavez, Margaret Mead)

◆ Speeches about objects (electric cars, the Great Wall of China)

◆ Speeches about places (Ellis Island, the Nile)

◆ Speeches about events (sinking of the *Titanic*, Woodstock festivals)

◆ Speeches about processes (cartooning, waterproofing)

◆ Speeches about concepts (liberty, nihilism)

◆ Speeches about conditions (McCarthyism, the civil rights movement)

◆ Speeches about issues (the use of polygraph tests, fetal tissue research)

USING TECHNOLOGY

Colorado State University maintains an excellent website on informative speaking, covering the purposes and types of informative speaking and offering lots of suggestions for developing and delivering informative speeches. Visit this site at http://writing.colostate.edu/references/speaking/infomod/index.cfm and read the material on topics about which you want more information.

Informative Speeches of Description

In a speech of **description,** you're concerned with explaining an object, person, event, or process. Here are a few examples:

Describing an Object or Person

◆ the structure of the brain

◆ the contributions of Thomas Edison

◆ the parts of a telephone

◆ the layout of Philadelphia

◆ the hierarchy of a corporation

◆ the components of a computer system

Describing an Event or Process

◆ the attacks of September 11, 2001

◆ the events leading to World War II

◆ organizing a body building contest

◆ how a newspaper is printed

◆ purchasing stock online

◆ how a child acquires language

Strategies for Describing

Here are some suggestions for describing objects, people, events, and processes.

RESEARCH *Link*

News Sources

Often you'll want to read reports on scientific breakthroughs, political speeches, congressional actions, obituaries, financial news, international developments, United Nations actions, or any of a host of other topics. Or you may wish to locate the time of a particular event and learn something about what else was going on in the world at that particular time. For this type of information you may want to consult a reliable newspaper. Especially relevant are newspaper indexes, newspaper databases, newspaper and newsmagazine websites, news wire services, and news networks.

- **Newspaper indexes.** One way to start a newspaper search is to consult one of the newspaper indexes, such as the *National Newspaper Index,* which covers 27 newspapers, including the *Christian Science Monitor,* the *Wall Street Journal,* the *Los Angeles Times,* and the *Washington Post.* Each of these newspapers also has its own index. The *New York Times* is available through Research Navigator.
- **Electronic newspaper databases.** Many newspapers can be accessed online or through CD-ROM databases to which your college library probably subscribes. The *New York Times* database, for example, contains complete editorial content of the paper, one of the world's most comprehensive newspapers. All aspects of news, sports, editorials, columns, obituaries, New York and regional news, and the *New York Times Book Review* and *Magazine* are included.
- **Newspaper and newsmagazine websites.** Most newspapers now maintain their own websites from which you can access current and past issues. Here are a few to get you started:

www.latimes.com/ (*Los Angeles Times*), www.usatoday.com/ (*USA Today*), www.wsj.com (*Wall Street Journal*), and www.nytimes.com (the *New York Times*). The *Washington Post* (www.washingtonpost.com) maintains an especially extensive website; the accompanying Web page visual will give you an idea of the enormous amount of information it provides. Two particularly useful websites are http://www.newslink.org/menu.html, which provides access to a variety of online newspapers and magazines, and Hotlinks to Newspapers Online, which provides links to more than 1,000 daily, more than 400 weekly, and more than 100 international newspapers (http://www.newspaperlinks.com).

- **News wire services.** Three wire services should prove helpful. The Associated Press can be accessed at http://www.ap.org/, Reuters at http://www.reuters.com/, and PR Newswire at http://www.prnewswire.com/. The advantage of getting your information from a news wire service is that it's more complete than you'd find in a newspaper; newspapers often must cut copy to fit space requirements and in some cases may put a politically or socially motivated spin on the news.
- **News networks online.** All of the television news stations maintain extremely useful websites. Here are some of the most useful: Access CNN at http://www.cnn.com/, ESPN at http://espn.sportszone.com/, ABC News at http://www.abcnews.com/newsflash, CBS News at http://www.cbs.com/news/, or MSNBC News at http://www.msnbc.com/news.

Research Activity. Using the *New York Times* or the newspaper database, both of which you may have access to via Research Navigator (www.researchnavigator.com), look up and read an article relevant to your next speech.

Select an Appropriate Organizational Pattern

Consider using a spatial or a topical organization when describing objects and people. Consider using a temporal pattern when describing events and processes. For example, if you were to describe the layout of Philadelphia, you might start from the north and work down to the south (using a spatial pattern). If you were to describe the contributions of Thomas Edison, you might select the three or four major contributions and discuss each of these equally (using a topical pattern).

The *St. Louis Post-Dispatch*
(www.stltoday.com)
Most of the world's major newspapers maintain extensive websites. Visit the *St. Louis Post-Dispatch* site or the websites of newspapers of other cities you're interested in. A website tour is not exactly a vacation, but it provides a change of scene as well as a wealth of current and generally reliable information you'll be able to use in your speeches.

If you were describing the events leading up to World War II, you might use a temporal pattern, starting with the earliest and working up to the latest. A temporal pattern would also be appropriate for describing how a hurricane develops or how a parade is put together.

Use a Variety of Descriptive Categories
Describe the object or event with lots of descriptive categories. With physical categories, for example, ask yourself questions such as these: What color is it? How big is it? What is it shaped like? How much does it weigh? What is its volume? How attractive/unattractive is it?

Also consider social, psychological, and economic categories. In describing a person, for example, consider such categories as friendly/unfriendly, warm/cold, rich/poor, aggressive/meek, and pleasant/unpleasant.

Consider Using Presentation Aids
Presentation aids such as those described in Chapter 5 will help you describe almost anything. Use aids if you possibly can. In describing an object or a person, show your listeners a picture; show them the inside of a telephone, pictures of the brain, the skeleton of the body. In describing an event or process, show them a diagram or flowchart to illustrate the stages or steps; for example, the steps involved in buying stock, in publishing a newspaper, in putting a parade together.

Consider *Who? What? Where? When?* and *Why?*
These journalistic categories are especially useful when you want to describe an event or a process. For example, if you're going to describe how to purchase a house, you might want to consider the people involved (who?), the steps you have to go through (what?), the places you'll have to go (where?), the time or sequence in which each of the steps have to take place (when?), and the advantages and disadvantages of buying the house (why?).

USING TECHNOLOGY

Compare the news available on one of the major newspapers' websites (for example, the *Washington Post* site or the *New York Times* site) with the news presented by a wire service such as the Associated Press (http://www.ap.org) or Reuters (http://www.reuters.com). Which do you prefer? Why?

Developing the Speech of Description

Here are two examples of how you might go about constructing a speech of description. In this first example, the speaker describes four suggestions for reducing energy bills.

General purpose: To inform.

Specific purpose: To describe how you can reduce energy bills.

Thesis: Energy bills can be reduced. (How can energy bills be reduced?)

    I. Caulk window and door seams.
   II. Apply weather stripping around windows and doors.
  III. Insulate walls.
  IV. Install storm windows and doors.

In this second example, the speaker describes the way in which fear works in intercultural communication.

General purpose: To inform.

Specific purpose: To describe the way fear works in intercultural communication.

Thesis: Fear influences intercultural communication. (How does fear influence intercultural communication?)

    I. We fear disapproval.
   II. We fear embarrassing ourselves.
  III. We fear being harmed.

In delivering such a speech a speaker might begin by saying:

Three major fears interfere with intercultural communication. First, we fear disapproval—from members of our own group as well as from members of the other person's group. Second, we fear embarrassing ourselves, even making fools of ourselves, by saying the wrong thing or appearing insensitive. And third, we may fear being harmed—our stereotypes of the other group may lead us to see its members as dangerous or potentially harmful to us.

Let's look at each of these fears in more detail. We'll be able to see clearly how they influence our own intercultural communication behavior.

Consider, first, the fear of disapproval.

USING TECHNOLOGY

The OneLook Dictionary Search website at http://www.onelook.com will enable you to search a wide variety of dictionaries at the same time. Visit this site and search for two or three words whose definitions may be important in one of your future speeches.

Informative Speeches of Definition

What is leadership? What is a born-again Christian? What is the difference between sociology and psychology? What is a cultural anthropologist? What is safe sex? These are all topics for informative speeches of definition.

A **definition** is a statement of the meaning or significance of a concept or term. Use definitions when you wish to explain difficult or unfamiliar concepts or when you wish to make a concept more vivid or forceful.

RESEARCH Link

Interviewing for Information

Here are a few suggestions to help you use interviewing to find needed information.

- **Select the person you wish to interview.** You might, for example, look through your college catalog for an instructor teaching a course that involves your topic. Or visit newsgroups and look for people who have posted articles on your topic. If you want to contact a book author, you can always write to the author in care of the publisher or editor (listed on the copyright page), though many authors are now including their e-mail address. You often can find the address and phone number of a professional person in the *Encyclopedia of Associations,* or you can write to the person via the association's website. Newsgroup and listserv writers are of course the easiest to contact, as their e-mail addresses are included with their posts. To find an expert, try *The Yearbook of Experts, Authorities, and Spokespersons* or any of a variety of websites, such as http://www.experts.com or http://uscnews3.usc.edu/experts/.

- **Secure an appointment.** Phone the person or send an e-mail requesting an interview. State the purpose of your request and say that you hope to conduct a brief interview by phone or that you'd like to send this person a series of questions by e-mail.

- **Develop your questions.** Generally, ask questions that provide the interviewee with room to discuss the issues you want to raise. Thus, asking, "Do you have formal training in the area of family therapy?" may elicit a simple yes or no, which will not be very informative. On the other hand, asking, "Can you tell me something of your background in this field?" is open-ended, allowing the interviewee to talk in some detail. Ask questions phrased in a neutral manner. Try not to lead the interviewee to give the answers you want.

- **Establish rapport with the interviewee.** Open the in-person, telephone, e-mail, or chat-group interview by thanking the person for making the time available and again stating your purpose. You might say something like this: "I really appreciate your making time for this interview. As I mentioned, I'm preparing a speech on XYZ, and your expertise and experience in this area will help a great deal."

- **Ask for permission to tape or print the interview.** It's a good idea to keep an accurate record of the interview, so ask permission to tape the interview if it's in person or by telephone. Taping will eliminate your worry about taking notes and having to ask the interviewee to slow down or repeat. It will also provide you with a much more accurate record of the interview than will handwritten notes. But always ask permission first. Similarly, if the interview is by e-mail or via chat group and you want to quote the interviewee's responses, ask permission first. An agreement to be interviewed does not include permission to print or distribute the interview or even parts of it.

- **Close with an expression of appreciation, and follow up with a thank-you note.** Thank the person for making the time available for the interview and for being informative, cooperative, helpful, or whatever. Follow up on the interview with a note of thanks. Or, perhaps you might send the person you interviewed a copy of your speech (e-mail would work well here), again with a note of thanks for the help.

Research Activity. With the topic of your next speech in mind, select a person you might interview. Compose an interview guide with specific questions to help you manage this potential interview.

In giving a speech of definition, you may focus on defining a term, defining a system or theory, or pinpointing the similarities and/or differences among terms or systems. A speech of definition may be on a subject new to the audience or may present a familiar topic in a new and different way. Here are some examples:

Defining a Term
- What is a smart card?
- What is machismo?
- What is creativity?
- What is affirmative action?
- What is multiculturalism?
- What is political correctness?

Defining a System or Theory
- What is the classical theory of public speaking?
- What are the parts of a generative grammar?
- Confucianism: its major beliefs
- What is expressionism?
- What is futurism?
- The "play theory" of mass communication

Defining Similar and Dissimilar Terms or Systems
- Football and soccer: What's the difference?
- What do Christians and Muslims have in common?
- Oedipus and Electra: How do they differ?
- Genetics and heredity
- Animal and human rights
- Key-word and directory searches

Strategies for Defining

Like all speeches, speeches of definition require research. Now that you've covered a significant part of this text's material or research, assess your research competencies by taking the following self-test. Several strategies will help you do an effective job of defining your topic. Let's look at some of these approaches.

Test YOURSELF

What Are Your Research Competencies?

Indicate your research competencies by responding to each of the 10 research tasks according to the following scale:

A = Finding this would be simple; I'd be able to find it with a relatively direct search.
B = Finding this would be possible, but would take some effort; I'd probably not be able to find it with a direct search but would make a few wrong turns before I eventually found it.
C = Finding this would be impossible without asking someone for help; I wouldn't even know where to begin.

_____ **1.** An article on India that appeared in the *New York Times* sometime in 1998

_____ **2.** Ten newsgroups dealing with the topic of computers

_____ **3.** Ten listservs dealing with topics relating to your professional goal

_____ **4.** The most recent stock quotation for IBM

_____ **5.** Ten abstracts of articles dealing with hepatitis

_____ **6.** The communication courses offered at Kansas State University

_____ **7.** The populations of Toronto and Tokyo

_____ **8.** The speeches given during the last session of Congress

_____ **9.** The biography of a state political figure

_____ **10.** Recent law cases dealing with sexual harassment

❖ **HOW DID YOU DO?** These 10 research tasks are typical of those you'll need to master as you prepare public speeches, term papers, reports, and the like. If you responded with a lot of A's (say 7 to 10), you probably have fairly sophisticated research skills. If you responded with a lot of C's (say 5 or more), then your research skills need work.

❖ **WHAT WILL YOU DO?** One way to improve your research skills is to read the various Research Links throughout this text very carefully and to access the websites mentioned. Another way is to access some of the general research websites mentioned in the early Research Links (for example, the Chapter 3 Research Links on "Libraries" and "Using and Evaluating Internet Resources") and study the suggestions offered there. Still another way is to share your responses with a small group of five or six others, learning from the strengths of others and teaching others your own strengths. As you discuss the various responses, also consider: Which avenues of research are the most efficient? Which are the most reliable? Which will prove the most credible with your peers?

Use a Variety of Definitions

When explaining a concept, it's helpful to define it in a number of different ways. Here are some of the most important ways to define a term.

Define by Etymology. One way to define a term is to trace its historical or linguistic development. In defining the word *communication,* for example, you might note that it comes from the Latin *communis,* meaning "common"; in "communicating" you seek to establish a commonness, a sameness, a similarity with another individual. And *woman* comes from the Anglo-Saxon *wifman,* which meant literally a "wife man," where the word *man* was applied to both sexes. Through phonetic change *wifman* became *woman.* Most larger dictionaries and, of course, etymological dictionaries will help you find useful etymological definitions.

Or you might define a term by noting not its linguistic etymology, but how it came to mean what it now means. For example, you might note that *spam* on the Net comes

"It all depends on how you define 'chop.'"

USING TECHNOLOGY

Visit the Eclectic Writer website at http://www.eclectics.com/writing/writing.html. What information on this website might prove useful to the public speaker?

from a Monty Python television skit in which every item on the menu contained the product Spam. And much as the diner was forced to get Spam, so the Net surfer gets spam—even when he or she wants something else.

Define by Authority. You can often clarify a term by explaining how a particular authority views it. You might, for example, define *lateral thinking* by authority and say that Edward deBono, who developed lateral thinking in 1966, has noted that "lateral thinking involves moving sideways to look at things in a different way. Instead of fixing on one particular approach and then working forward from that, the lateral thinker tries to find other approaches." Or you might use the authority of cynic and satirist Ambrose Bierce and define love as nothing but "a temporary insanity curable by marriage" and friendship as "a ship big enough to carry two in fair weather, but only one in foul."

Define by Negation. You also might define a term by noting what the term is not; that is, define it by negation. "A wife," you might say, "isn't a cook, a cleaning person, a babysitter, a seamstress, a sex partner. A wife is . . ." or "A teacher isn't someone who tells you what you should know but rather one who . . . ."

Here Michael Marien (1992) defines futurists first negatively and then positively:

> Futurists do not use crystal balls. Indeed, they're generally loath to make firm predictions of what will happen. Rather, they make forecasts of what is probable, sketch scenarios of what is possible, and/or point to desirable futures—what is preferable and what strategies we should pursue to get there.

Define by Direct Symbolization. You also might define a term by direct symbolization—by showing the actual thing or a picture or model of it. For example, a sales representative explaining a new computer keyboard would obviously use an actual keyboard in the speech. Similarly, a speech on magazine layout or types of fabrics would include actual layout pages and fabric samples.

Use Definitions to Add Clarity

If the purpose of the definition is to clarify, then it must do just that. This would be too obvious to mention except for the fact that so many speakers, perhaps for want of something to say, define terms that don't need extended definitions. Some speakers use definitions that don't clarify and that, in fact, complicate an already complex concept. Make sure your definitions define only what needs defining.

Use Credible Sources

When you use an authority to define a term, make sure the person is in fact an authority. Tell the audience who the authority is and state the basis for the individual's expertise. In the following excerpt, note how Russell Peterson (1985) uses the expertise of Robert McNamara in his definition:

> When Robert McNamara was president of the World Bank, he coined the term "absolute poverty" to characterize a condition of life so degraded by malnutrition, illiteracy, violence, disease and squalor, to be beneath any reasonable definition of human decency. In 1980, the World Bank estimated that 780 million persons in the developing countries lived in absolute poverty. That's about three times as many people as live in the entire United States.

Proceed from the Known to the Unknown

Start with what your audience knows and work up to what is new or unfamiliar. Let's say you want to explain the concept of phonemics (with which your audience is totally unfamiliar). The specific idea you wish to get across is that each phoneme stands for a unique sound. You might proceed from the known to the unknown and begin your definition with something like this:

> We all know that in the written language each letter of the alphabet stands for a unit of the written language. Each letter is different from every other letter. A *t* is different from a *g* and a *g* is different from a *b* and so on. Each letter is called a "grapheme." In English we know we have 26 such letters.
>
> We can look at the spoken language in much the same way. Each sound is different from every other sound. A *t* sound is different from a *d* and a *d* is different from a *k* and so on. Each individual sound is called a "phoneme."
>
> Now, let me explain in a little more detail what I mean by a "phoneme."

❖ **CONSIDER** the principles for defining a concept or system. What principles do you see followed and which do you see violated in the speeches of information you hear in your classes or in your community?

Developing the Speech of Definition

Here are two examples of how you might go about constructing a speech of definition. In this first example, the speaker explains the parts of a resume and follows a spatial order, going from the top to the bottom of the page.

General purpose: To inform.

Specific purpose: To define the essential parts of a resume.

Thesis: There are four major parts to a resume. (What are the four major parts of a resume?)

I. Identify your career goals.
II. Identify your educational background.
III. Identify your work experience.
IV. Identify your special competencies.

In this second example, the speaker selects three major types of lying for discussion and arranges these in a topical pattern.

General purpose: To inform.

Specific purpose: To define lying by explaining the major types of lying.

Thesis: There are three major kinds of lying. (What are the three major kinds of lying?)

I. Concealment is the process of hiding the truth.
II. Falsification is the process of presenting false information as if it were true.
III. Misdirection is the process of acknowledging a feeling but misidentifying its cause.

? DEVELOPING STRATEGIES

Defining. Simka wants to give a speech defining the basic tenets of her religion. Some members of her audience have a fairly negative view of the religion; others hold positive views. Simka wants to acknowledge her understanding of these diverse attitudes. What might Simka say?

CRITICAL LISTENING/THINKING *Link*

Listening to New Ideas

Ideally, informative speeches communicate information that is new and potentially useful to you as a listener. A useful technique in listening to new ideas is PIP'N, a technique that derives from the insights of Carl Rogers (1970) on paraphrase as a means for ensuring understanding and from Edward deBono's (1976) PMI (plus, minus, interesting) technique for critical thinking. In analyzing new ideas with the PIP'N technique, you follow four steps:

P = **Paraphrase**. State in your own words what you think the other person is saying.

Paraphrasing will help you understand and remember the idea.

I = **Interesting**. Consider why the idea is interesting.

P = **Positive**. Think about what's good about the idea; for example, might it solve a problem or improve a situation?

N = **Negative**. Think about any negatives that the idea might entail; for example, might it be expensive or difficult to implement?

Getting Critical. How might you use PIP'N to gain insight into, say, the cultural emphasis you find in your college textbooks or in a particular required course—or into the PIP'N technique itself?

In delivering such a speech, a speaker might begin the speech by saying:

A lie is a lie is a lie. True? Well, not exactly. Actually, there are a number of different ways we can lie. We can lie by concealing the truth. We can lie by falsification, by presenting false information as if it were true. And we can lie by misdirection, by acknowledging a feeling but misidentifying its cause.

Let's look at the first type of lie—the lie of concealment. Most lies are lies of concealment. Most of the time when we lie we simply conceal the truth. We don't actually make any false statements. Rather we simply don't reveal the truth. Let me give you some examples I overheard recently.

Informative Speeches of Demonstration

In using **demonstration** (or in a speech devoted entirely to demonstration), you show the audience how to do something or how something operates. Here are some examples:

Demonstrating How to Do Something

- how to give mouth-to-mouth resuscitation
- how to drive defensively
- how to mix colors
- how to ask for a raise
- how to burglarproof your house
- how to use PowerPoint in business meetings

Demonstrating How Something Operates

◆ how the body maintains homeostasis

◆ how perception works

◆ how divorce laws work

◆ how e-mail works

◆ how a hurricane develops

◆ how a heart bypass operation is performed

Strategies for Demonstrating

In demonstrating how to do something or how something operates, consider the following guidelines.

Use Temporal Organization

In most cases, a temporal pattern will work best in speeches of demonstration. Demonstrate each step in the sequence in which it's to be performed. In this way, you'll avoid one of the major difficulties in demonstrating a process—backtracking. Don't skip steps even if you think they're familiar to the audience. They may not be. Connect each step to the next with appropriate transitions. For example, in explaining the Heimlich maneuver, you might say,

> Now that you have your arms around the choking victim's chest, your next step is to . . . .

Assist your listeners by labeling the steps clearly, for example, "the first step," "the second step," and so on.

Begin with an Overview

It's often helpful when demonstrating to give a broad general picture and then present each step in turn. For example, suppose you were talking about how to prepare a wall for painting. You might begin with a general overview to give your listeners a general idea of the process, saying something like this:

> In preparing the wall for painting, you want to make sure that the wall is smoothly sanded, free of dust, and dry. Sanding a wall isn't like sanding a block of wood. So, let's look at the proper way to sand a wall.

Consider the Value of Presentation Aids

Presentation aids are especially helpful in speeches of demonstration. A good example of this is the signs in restaurants demonstrating the Heimlich maneuver. These signs demonstrate the sequence of steps with pictures as well as words. The combination of verbal and graphic information makes it easy to understand this important process. In a speech on this topic, however, it would be best to use only the pictures so that the written words would not distract your audience from your oral explanation.

❖ **CONSIDER** the similarities between a speech of demonstration and a sales pitch. In what ways are they similar? In what ways are they different?

DEVELOPING STRATEGIES

Informative Strategies. Alex is planning to give an informative speech on defensive driving and is considering the strategies he might use. How might he introduce his speech? What organizational pattern might he use? What types of presentation aids might he use?

Developing the Speech of Demonstration

Here are two examples of the speech of demonstration. In this first example, the speaker explains the proper way to paint a wall by rag rolling. As you can see, the speaker uses a temporal organizational pattern and covers three stages in the order in which they would be performed.

General purpose: To inform.

Specific purpose: To demonstrate how to rag roll.

Thesis: Rag rolling is performed in three steps. (What are the three steps of rag rolling?)

   I. Apply the base coat of paint.

  II. Apply the glaze coat.

 III. Roll a rag through the wet glaze.

In the next example, the speaker identifies and demonstrates how to listen actively.

General purpose: To inform.

Specific purpose: To demonstrate three techniques of active listening.

Thesis: We can learn active listening. (How can we learn active listening?)

   I. Paraphrase the speaker's meaning.

  II. Express understanding of the speaker's feelings.

 III. Ask questions.

In delivering the speech, the speaker might begin by saying:

Active listening is a special kind of listening. It's listening with total involvement, with a concern for the speaker. It's probably the most important type of listening you can engage in. Active listening consists of three steps: paraphrasing the speaker's meaning, expressing understanding of the speaker's feelings, and asking questions.

Your first step in active listening is to paraphrase the speaker's meaning. What is a paraphrase? A paraphrase is a restatement in your own words of the speaker's meaning. That is, you express in your own words what you think the speaker meant. For example, let's say that the speaker said . . .

DEVELOPING STRATEGIES

Demonstrating. Latka wants to demonstrate how e-mail works. The audience is probably mixed in terms of their knowledge of technology generally—some know a great deal and others know very little. How might Latka open his speech so that all audience members will want to listen?

Summary of Concepts and Skills

In this chapter we considered the informative speech, first surveying some general principles, then examining three main types of information speaking (description, definition, and demonstration).

Guidelines for Informative Speaking

Among the guidelines for informative speaking are these:

◆ Limit the amount of information you communicate.
◆ Adjust the level of complexity.
◆ Stress the relevance and the usefulness of the information to your audience.
◆ Relate new information to old.
◆ Vary the levels of abstraction.

Informative Speeches of Description

Informative speeches of description examine a process or procedure, an event, an object, or a person.

Informative Speeches of Definition

Speeches of definition define a term, system, or theory, or similarities and/or differences among terms.

Informative Speeches of Demonstration

Speeches of demonstration show how to do something or how something operates.

Vocabulary Quiz

The Informative Speech

Match the terms of informative speeches with their definitions. Record the number of the definition next to the appropriate term.

_____ informative speaking
_____ speeches of description
_____ definition
_____ speeches of demonstration
_____ adjusting the level of complexity
_____ stressing relevance and usefulness
_____ varying the levels of abstraction
_____ definition by etymology
_____ descriptive categories
_____ definition by direct symbolization

1. A type of speaking in which the speaker seeks to tell the audience something it doesn't know.
2. A speech that seeks to explain an object, person, event, or process.
3. Explanation of a term by tracing its historical or linguistic development.
4. A speech that seeks to explain how to do something or how something operates.
5. Combining the general and the specific.
6. Making your message appropriate to what your listeners already know so as not to bore them or confuse them.
7. A way of making the information in a speech meaningful to the listeners.
8. Physical, social, psychological, or economic characteristics that help explain objects or events.
9. A statement of the meaning or significance of a concept or term.
10. Explaining a term by showing the actual thing, a picture, or model.

Web Explorations

Companion Website
www.ablongman.com/devito

The Companion Website's Chapter 9 offers a brief discussion of "What Is Information?" to further clarify what is and what is not informative. In addition, there is an extended explanation of "Making Your Speech Easy to Remember."

Public Speaking Exercises

9.1 Defining Terms

Select one of the following terms and define it, using at least three of the different types of definition we've considered (etymology, authority, negation, or direct symbolism): *communication, love, friendship, conflict, leadership, audience.* You'll find it helpful to visit a few online dictionaries or thesauruses: http://c.gp.cs.cmu.edu: 5103/ prog/webster/; http://www.m-w.com/netdict.htm; http:// humanities.uchicago.edu/forms_unrest/ROGET.html. A useful website containing links to varied types of dictionaries is http://www.bucknell.edu/~rbeard/diction.html.

9.2 A Two-Minute Informative Speech

Prepare and deliver a two-minute informative speech in which you do one of the following:

◆ **Explain a card game:** Explain the way a card game such as solitaire, poker, gin rummy, bridge, canasta, or pinochle is played.

◆ **Explain a board game:** Explain the way a board game such as chess, backgammon, Chinese checkers, Go, Othello, Scrabble, Yahtzee, or Monopoly is played.

◆ **Explain food preparation:** Explain how to make a pie, a soup, a western omelet, a pizza, roast beef, a dip, or a casserole (any kind you'd like).

◆ **Explain a sport:** Explain the way a sport such as football, baseball, basketball, hockey, soccer, tennis, or golf is played.

9.3 Analyzing a Speech

This informative speech was delivered by Steve Zammit of Cornell University. In this speech, Zammit informs his listeners about the nature of the electric heart and claims that the electric heart will significantly influence the treatment of heart problems.

THE ELECTRIC HEART

Steve Zammit

On February 21, 2000, David Letterman returned to the *Late Show* after his quadruple bypass with a list of the "Top 10 Things You Don't Want to Hear When You Wake Up from Surgery." They include: Number 2— "Hello Mr. Letterman . . . or should I say Miss Letterman?" and Number 1—"We did what we could, Mr.

Letterman, but this is Jiffy Lube." But after the gags, Dave brought his doctors on stage and choked up as he thanked them for "saving my life."

One year later, the *New York Times* of February 1, 2001, announced conditional FDA approval for a medical device that will bring similar results to millions of heart patients. But rather than bypass a clogged artery, this revolutionary device bypasses the heart itself, thus fulfilling the life vision of 55-year-old scientist and heart surgeon Dr. David Lederman. Dr. David Lederman is the inventor of the [VA] Electric Heart.

The Electric Heart is a safe, battery-operated, permanent replacement that is directly implanted into the body. The February 12, 2001, *Telegram and Gazette* predicts that within one generation more than 10 million Americans will be living with terminal heart disease. For them, and for the 100,000 transplant candidates who pray for a new heart when only 2,000 are annually available, hope has been fleeting . . . until now.

So to learn why UCLA transplant surgeon Dr. Steven Marelli calls it the "Holy Grail of Heart Surgery," let's first plug into the heart's development and see how it works. Next, we'll flesh out its current status. So that finally we can see how the device's future impact will be heart-stopping.

In early 1982, Washington dentist Barney Clark's heart was stopping—literally. The world watched as Dr. Robert Jarvik implanted Clark with the first ever artificial heart. After 112 days marked by kidney failure, respiratory problems, and severe mental confusion, the heart stopped. It didn't take a rocket scientist to see that, as the *New York Times* of May 16, 1988, declared, artificial heart research was medical technology's version of Dracula. Basically, it sucked. Getting Dracula out of his coffin would require a little thinking outside the box. Enter Dr. David Lederman, who, in a happy coincidence, reported *Forbes* of April 17, 2000, is an actual rocket scientist. In fact, Lederman changed his career path in the early 1970s when he heard a lecture by a physicist who insisted artificial hearts would rise or fall based on fluid mechanics.

Lederman's design can be likened to space flight in that the concept is easy, but the tiniest problems can prevent a launch or cause an explosion. *What separates the Electric Heart from Jarvik's earlier model is the development and implementation of space-age technology.* In particular, the *Pittsburgh Post-Gazette* of January 28, 2001, explains that an artificial heart must simultaneously weigh two pounds, be flexible enough to expand and contract, and be tough enough to absorb 40 million beats a year. The solution is a proprietary titanium compound called Angioflex, the first man-made material on earth that fits the mold.

A typical heart pumps blood through constant muscular contractions regulated by the nervous system. [VA]

How effective was the introduction? What purposes did it accomplish? Would you have sought to accomplish any other purpose(s)? If so, what would you have said?

Note that the speech transcript shows the points at which visual aids are to be presented.

*Does the speaker **stress relevance and usefulness** to maintain your attention? How would you have stressed relevance and usefulness?*

What did you think of the way the speaker phrased the orientation to the major propositions of the speech? Did the orientation add clarity? Did it add humor?

What functions did the Dracula example serve? Do you feel this was too flippant for a speech on such a serious topic? Do you feel it added the right note of levity?

*How would you describe the **level of complexity** in this speech?*

Although you can't see the visual aids the speaker used, you can imagine what they were. If you were listening to this speech, what would you have liked to have seen in these visuals?

But Lederman's model propels blood using an internal motor regulated by a microprocessor embedded inside the abdomen. A small external belt transmits energy through the skin to a copper coil, allowing the entire system to be continuously stimulated.

When he returned last February, David Letterman was stimulated by a hospital gown–clad Robin Williams, who performed a zany strip tease. . . . I'll spare you the VA. But to see if Dr. Lederman is himself a tease, we must now evaluate his project's current status as well as the obstacles it faces.

Can you identify transitions the speaker used to connect the speech parts?

The *Houston Chronicle* of January 31, 2001, reveals that FDA approval of the Electric Heart was based on its wild success when implanted in animals. More than 100 cows have been recipients of the heart, and in Dr. Lederman's words, three hours after surgery, "I have seen the animals standing in their stalls munching hay, with their original hearts in a jar nearby." Sometime in early June, surgical teams will swap an Electric Heart for the failing one in five critically ill human patients, for what Dr. Lederman calls "the most public clinical trials in history." For those skeptics who argue it's a little early to break out the bubbly, Dr. Lederman adamantly agrees. He told the February 5, 2001, *Glasgow Herald*, "At first, you had the Wright brothers. Today, you can easily cross the Atlantic. Our heart is the equivalent of making the flight from Boston to New York," but the trip across the Atlantic is only a matter of time.

As you read the speech do you feel that the speaker successfully involved you in the speech? If not, what might the speaker have done to make you feel he was talking about you to you?

Despite the optimism, the beat will not go on until Dr. Lederman convincingly addresses two concerns about practicality. As the *British Medical Journal* of March 17, 2001, explains, organ transplant recipients must take expensive, nauseating drugs to prevent clotting and rejection. Fortunately, Angioflex's producer, Abiomed, revealed in a 2000 Securities and Exchange Commission filing that the material is perfectly seamless and can withstand over 20 years of abuse without cracking. No cracks, no place for clots to form. And since the Electric Heart is made of inert materials, UCLA transplant surgeon Dr. Steven Marelli told the February 7, 2001, *University Wire*, the body will not reject it, an observation confirmed by animal trials. Essentially, Electric Heart recipients will come back without expensive drug therapy.

How effectively did the speaker integrate research into the speech?

*Does the speaker **limit the amount of information** he communicates so that there is significant depth? Would you have done things differently?*

Speaking of comebacks, just as David Letterman's return culminated in an Emmy nomination, Dr. Lederman will soon be picking up some awards of his own, due to the Electric Heart's impact on individuals and society. As transplant pioneer Robert Jarvik once said, "the artificial heart must not only be dependable, but truly forgettable." But during periods of increased energy demand—including making love—Jarvik's model required a user to be tethered to a power unit in the wall. Lederman's model, in the words of the February 2001 *GQ*, is "The Love Machine." As *GQ* observes, the

*Does the speaker successfully **relate new information to old**?*

internal battery can allow "unassisted" exercise for 30 minutes—every man's dream. But the *Boston Globe* of February 1, 2001, reveals that advances in battery technology eventually will allow a sleeping user to be charged for a full day—allowing recipients to emulate the Energizer Bunny in more ways than one.

But by normalizing life for individuals, the Electric Heart will be revolutionizing medicine in society. The March 26, 2001, *Los Angeles Times* notes that 400,000 Americans are diagnosed with heart failure each year. Add the number of other failing internal organs, as well as a glut of aging baby boomers, and we are a generation away from a crisis. To cope, some researchers have famously approached organ shortages by genetically engineering them to grow in a lab, a process that will still take years. But the Electric Heart is both more immediate, and carries none of the ethical entanglements of manipulating the human genome. As Dr. Ed Berger, vice president of Abiomed, explained in an April 2, 2001, telephone interview, Angioflex is so versatile, it could eventually be used to construct artificial kidneys and lungs.

Unfortunately, the *American Journal of Medicine* of February 1, 2001, reports that heart disease disproportionately strikes those in lower socioeconomic brackets, a group that often lacks access to advanced technology. But the April 19, 2001, *Boston Herald* predicts the procedure will eventually retail for about $25,000, the same as a traditional heart bypass. Coupled with the cost savings on drug treatment, the procedure should be affordably covered by most insurance companies, including Medicare. So whether rich or poor, young or old, resting or energized, the Electric Heart will be an equal opportunity lifesaver.

Although you can never mend a broken heart, Dr. Lederman has done the next best thing. By reviewing the Electric Heart's unusual development and current testing, we have seen its future impact on viewers around the world. On the night of his comeback, David Letterman put a human face on heart disease. But for thousands who find themselves in the comedian's shoes, laughter—and everything else—is insufficient medicine. But soon, Dr. David Lederman will reach audiences with a message of hope. For them, the Electric Heart will not just make the Top 10 List. It will be number one.

Source: Stephen Zammit, Cornell University.

Of all the research cited in the speech, which did you think was the most effective? Which was the least effective? Why?

*Did the speaker **vary the levels of abstraction** effectively, or would you have wished to hear more high-level or more low-level abstractions?*

What influence did the research and its integration into the speech have on your image of the speaker's credibility?

How effective do you think the speech title, "The Electric Heart," was? What other titles might have worked?

What one thing will you remember most from this speech? Why will you remember this? That is, what did the speaker say that made this one thing most memorable?

How effective was the speaker's conclusion? What functions did the conclusion serve? What other functions might it have served?

Now that you've finished reading the speech (don't look back), what were the major propositions of the speech? What did you learn from this speech?

10 Persuading Your Audience

Why Read This Chapter?

It will enable you to influence an audience by helping you to:

❖ follow principles of persuasion that will enable you to exert influence fairly and ethically

❖ avoid fallacious reasoning in your own speaking—and recognize fallacies in the speeches of others so as not to get taken in by bogus argument

❖ select organizational patterns and strategies for speeches on facts, values, and policies in order to change your listeners' attitudes or move them to action

> I resent the idea that people would blame the messenger for the message, rather than looking at the content of the message itself.
>
> **—Anita Hill**

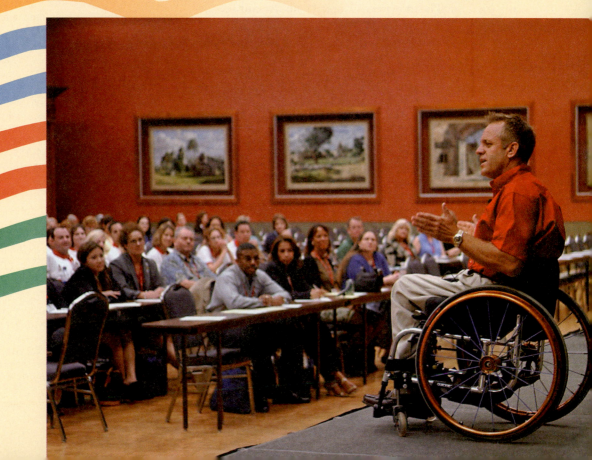

In Chapter 9 we focused on informative speaking, examining both guidelines for communicating information and varied types of informative speeches. This chapter will look at persuasive speaking. As in the previous chapter, we will consider important guidelines to follow in persuading an audience and then will explore varied types of persuasive speeches you might give. First, however, let's look at the goals of persuasion.

Goals of Persuasion

Generally, the word **persuasion** refers to the process of influencing another person's attitudes, beliefs, values, and/or behaviors. Briefly, an **attitude** is a tendency to behave in a certain way. For example, if you have a positive attitude toward science fiction, then you're likely to watch science fiction movies or read science fiction books; if you have a negative attitude, you'll be likely to avoid such movies and books. A **belief** is a conviction in the existence or reality of something or in the truth of some assertion. For example, some believe that God exists, that democracy is the best form of government, or that soft drugs lead to hard drugs. A **value** is an indicator of what you feel is good or bad, ethical or unethical, just or unjust. Many people in your audience will positively value "college education" or "free speech" and negatively value "discrimination" or "war." In the context of persuasion, the word *behavior* refers to overt, observable actions such as voting for a particular person, contributing money to the Red Cross, or buying a Dodge.

Your persuasive speeches may focus on your listeners' attitudes, beliefs, values, or behaviors. You may want to accomplish any one of the following three general goals of persuasive speaking:

◆ **To strengthen or weaken attitudes, beliefs, or values.** Persuasion often aims to strengthen audience views. For example, religious sermons usually seek to strengthen the existing beliefs of the audience. Similarly, many public service announcements try to strengthen existing beliefs about, say, recycling, smoking, or safe sex. At times, however, you may want to weaken the existing beliefs of the audience—to suggest that what they currently believe may not be entirely true. For example, you might want to weaken the favorable attitudes people might have toward a particular political party or policy. This type of speech is often used in combination with additional efforts designed to gradually weaken existing beliefs and ultimately to change them.

◆ **To change attitudes, beliefs, or values.** Sometimes you'll want to change your audience's thinking. You might want to change their attitudes to the college's no-smoking rules, to change their beliefs about television's influence on viewer violence, or to change their values about the efficacy of war.

◆ **To motivate to action.** Ultimately, your goal is to get people to do something—for example, to vote for one person rather than another, to donate money to a fund for the homeless, or to take a course in criminology.

It's useful to view the effects of persuasion as a continuum ranging from one extreme to another. Let's say, to take one issue currently in the news, that you want to give a persuasive speech on same-sex marriage. You might visualize

USING TECHNOLOGY

Visit the History Channel (www.historychannel.com/speeches), History and Politics Out Loud (http://www.hpol.org), or C-Span (http://www.c-span.org/classroom/lang/speeches.asp) and search for speeches you consider persuasive. How would you describe the purposes and theses of the speeches on these websites?

| Strongly in favor of same-sex marriage ___:___:___:___:___:___:___ | Strongly opposed to same-sex marriage |

❖ **FIGURE 10.1**

The Persuasion Continuum

Any movement along the continuum would be considered persuasion.

your audience as existing on a continuum ranging from strongly in favor to strongly opposed, as shown in Figure 10.1. Your task is to move your audience in the direction of your persuasive purpose. You can center your message on strengthening, weakening, or changing your listeners' attitudes, beliefs, or values about same-sex marriage; or you can center your message on moving the listeners to act—to protest, write letters, or sign a petition.

If your purpose is to persuade the audience to oppose same-sex marriage, then in Figure 10.1 any movement toward the right will be successful persuasion; if your purpose is to persuade listeners to support same-sex marriage, then any movement toward the left will be successful persuasion. Notice, however, that it's quite possible to give a speech in which you hope to move your listeners in one direction but actually to succeed in moving them in the other direction. This "negative persuasion" effect can occur, for example, when the audience perceives the speaker as dishonest or self-promoting.

Now that we've considered the general goals of persuasive speaking, let's turn to guidelines that can help you become an effective persuader.

Guidelines for Persuasive Speaking

You can become more successful in strengthening or changing attitudes or beliefs and in moving your listeners to action by following these guidelines for persuasive speaking.

Anticipate Selective Exposure

People listen in accordance with the principle of **selective exposure.** This principle or law has two parts: It states that (1) listeners actively seek out information that supports their opinions, beliefs, values, decisions, and behaviors; and (2) listeners actively avoid information that contradicts their existing opinions, beliefs, attitudes, values, decisions, and behaviors.

Of course, if you're very sure that your opinions and attitudes are logical and valid, then you may not bother to seek out supporting information. Similarly, you may not actively avoid contradictory messages. People exercise selective exposure most often when their confidence in their own opinions and beliefs is weak.

If you want to persuade an audience that holds attitudes different from your own, anticipate selective exposure operating and proceed inductively; that is, hold back on your thesis until you've given your evidence and argument. Only then relate this evidence and argument to your initially contrary thesis.

If you were to present them with your thesis first, your listeners might tune you out without giving your position a fair hearing. So become thoroughly familiar with the attitudes of your audience if you want to succeed in making these necessary adjustments and adaptations.

Let's say you're giving a speech on the need to reduce spending on college athletic programs. If your audience were composed of listeners who agreed with you and wanted to cut athletic spending, you might lead with your thesis. Your introduction might go something like this:

> Our college athletic program is absorbing money that we can more profitably use for the library, science labs, and language labs. Let me explain how the money now going to unnecessary athletic programs could be better spent in these other areas.

On the other hand, suppose you were addressing alumni who strongly favored the existing athletic programs. In this case, you might want to lead with your evidence and hold off stating your thesis until the end of your speech.

Ask for Reasonable Amounts of Change

The greater and more important the change you want to encourage in your audience, the more difficult your task will be. Put in terms of the continuum of persuasion introduced earlier, this principle suggests that you'll be more successful if you ask for small (rather than large) movements in the direction of your speech purpose. The reason is simple: As listeners we normally demand a greater number of reasons and a lot more evidence before we make important decisions—such as, say, changing careers, moving to another state, or investing in stocks.

On the other hand, we may be more easily persuaded (and demand less evidence) on relatively minor issues—whether to take a course in "Small Group Communication" rather than "Persuasion" or to give to the United Heart Fund instead of the American Heart Fund.

Generally, people change gradually, in small degrees over a long period of time. Persuasion, therefore, is most effective when it strives for small changes and works over a period of time. For example, a persuasive speech stands a better chance when it tries to get a drinker to attend just one AA meeting rather than advocating giving up alcohol for life. If you try to convince your audience to change their attitudes radically or to engage in behaviors to which they're initially opposed, your attempts may backfire. In this type of situation, the audience may tune you out, closing its ears to even the best and most logical arguments.

So in your classroom speeches, set reasonable goals for what you want the audience to do. Remember you have only perhaps 10 minutes, and in that time you cannot move the proverbial mountain. Instead, ask for small, easily performed behaviors. Encourage your listeners to visit a particular website (perhaps even one dedicated to beliefs or values that they do not currently share), to vote in the next election, or to buy the new virus protection software.

When you are addressing an audience that is opposed to your position and your goal is to change their attitudes and beliefs, be especially careful to seek change in small increments. Let's say, for example, that your ultimate goal is to get an antiabortion group to favor abortion on demand. Obviously, this goal is too great to achieve in one speech. Therefore, strive for small changes. Here, for example, is an excerpt in which the speaker attempts to get an audience that opposes legal abortion to agree that at least some abortions should be legal. The speaker begins as follows:

> One of the great lessons I learned in college was that most extreme positions are wrong. Most of the important truths lie somewhere between the extreme opposites. And today I want to talk with you about one of these truths. I want

? DEVELOPING STRATEGIES

Magnitude of Change. Luke wants to get his listeners to contribute four hours a week to the college's program in which volunteers help high school students prepare for college. How would you suggest that Luke use the foot-in-the-door technique? How might he use the door-in-the-face technique? Which strategy do you think would work best if your class were the audience?

"In the interest of streamlining the judicial process, we'll skip the evidence and go directly to sentencing."

to talk with you about rape and the problems faced by the mother carrying a child conceived in this most violent of all violent crimes we can imagine.

Notice that the speaker does not state a totally pro-choice position but instead focuses on one situation involving abortion and attempts to get the audience to agree that in some cases abortion should be legal.

When you have the opportunity to persuade your audience on several occasions (rather than simply delivering one speech), two strategies will prove helpful: the foot-in-the-door and door-in-the-face techniques.

Foot-in-the-Door Technique

As its name implies, the **foot-in-the-door technique** involves getting your foot in the door by requesting something small, something that your listeners will easily agree to. Once they agree to this small request, you then make your real request (Cialdini, 1984; Dejong, 1979; Freedman & Fraser, 1966; Pratkanis & Aronson, 1991). People are more apt to comply with a large request after they've complied with a similar but much smaller request. For example, in one study the objective was to get people to put a "Drive Carefully" sign on their lawn (a large request). When this (large) request was made first, only about 17 percent of the people were willing to agree. However, when this request was preceded by a much smaller request (to sign a petition), between 50 and 76 percent granted permission to install the sign. Agreement with the smaller request paves the way for the larger request and puts the audience into an agreeable mood.

Door-in-the-Face Technique

With the **door-in-the-face technique,** the opposite of foot-in-the-door, you first make a large request that you know will be refused and then follow it with a more moderate request. For example, your large request might be "We're asking people to donate $100 for new school computers." When this is refused, you make a more moderate request, the one you really want your listeners to comply with (for example, "Might you be willing to contribute $10?"). In changing from the large to the more moderate request, you demonstrate your willingness to compromise and your sensitivity to your listeners. The general idea here is that your listeners will feel that because you've made concessions, they should also make concessions and at least contribute something. Listeners will probably also feel that $10 is actually quite a small amount considering the initial request and are more likely to donate the $10 (Cialdini, 1984; Cialdini & Ascani, 1976).

Identify with Your Audience

If you can show your audience that you and they share important attitudes, beliefs, and values, you'll clearly advance your persuasive goal. Other similarities are also important. For example, in some cases similarity of cultural, educational, or social background may help you identify yourself with your audience. Be aware, however, that insincere or dishonest identification is likely to backfire and create problems. So avoid even implying similarities between yourself and your audience that don't exist.

As a general rule, never ask the audience to do what you have not done yourself; always demonstrate that you have done what you want the audience to do. If you don't, the audience will rightfully ask, "Why haven't you done it?" In addition, besides doing whatever it may be, show your listeners that you're pleased to have done it. For example, tell them of the satisfaction you derived from donating blood or from reading to blind students.

Use Logical Appeals

Logical, emotional, and credibility appeals all can be effective means to persuade an audience, and we'll look at all three. However, we'll start with the most effective: **logical appeals.** When a speaker persuades listeners with logical arguments—focusing on facts and evidence rather than on emotions or credibility claims—the listeners are more likely to remain persuaded over time and are more likely to resist counterarguments that may come up in the future (Petty & Wegener, 1998). There are three main categories of logical appeals.

❖ **CONSIDER** the persuasive appeals that have been used on you recently. Were any such appeals of the foot-in-the-door or the door-in-the-face type?

Reasoning from Specific Instances and Generalizations

In reasoning from **specific instances** (or examples), you examine several specific instances and then conclude something about the whole. This form of reasoning, known as induction, is useful when you want to develop a general principle or conclusion but cannot examine the whole. For example, you sample a few communication courses and conclude something about communication courses in general; you visit several Scandinavian cities and conclude something about the whole of Scandinavia. Critically analyze reasoning from specific instances by asking the following questions.

Were enough specific instances examined? Two general guidelines will help you determine how much is enough. First, the larger the group you wish covered by your conclusion, the greater the number of specific instances you should examine. If you wish to draw conclusions about members of an entire country or culture, you'll have to examine a considerable number of people before drawing even tentative conclusions. On the other hand, if you're attempting to draw a conclusion about a bushel of 100 apples, sampling a few is probably sufficient.

Second, the greater the diversity of items in the class, the more specific instances you will have to examine. Some classes or groups of items are relatively homogeneous, whereas others are more heterogeneous; this will influence how many specific instances constitute a sufficient number. Pieces of spaghetti in boiling water are all about the same; thus, sampling one usually tells you something about all the others. On the other hand, communication courses are probably very different from one another, so valid conclusions about the entire range of communication courses will require a much larger sample.

Are there significant exceptions? When you examine specific instances and attempt to draw a conclusion about the whole, take into consideration the exceptions. Thus, if you examine the GPA of computer science majors and

CRITICAL LISTENING/THINKING *Link*

Listening to Fallacies: Personal Attacks

Fallacies of argument are all around us; these are efforts at persuasion that may seem logical on the surface but when inspected more closely turn out to be illogical, irrelevant, and often unethical (Lee & Lee, 1972, 1995; Pratkanis & Aronson, 1991; Herrick, 2004). Here are a few such fallacies that focus on attacking the person. Be alert for fallacies like these in the speeches of others, and eliminate them from your own reasoning.

Personal Interest. Personal interest attacks may take either of two forms. In one form the speaker disqualifies someone from having a point of view because he or she isn't directly affected by an issue or proposal or doesn't have firsthand knowledge; for example, a speaker might dismiss an argument on abortion merely because it was made by a man. In another form the speaker disqualifies someone because he or she will benefit in some way from a proposal. For example, arguing that someone is rich, middle class, or poor and thus will benefit greatly from a proposed tax cut does not mean that the argument for the tax cut is invalid. The legitimacy of an argument can never depend on the gender (or culture) of the individual. Nor can it depend on the gain that a person may derive from the position advocated. The legitimacy of an argument can be judged only on the basis of the evidence and reasoning presented.

Character Attacks. Often referred to as *ad hominem* arguments, **character attacks** involve accusing another person (usually an opponent) of some wrongdoing or of some character flaw. The purpose is to discredit the person or to divert attention from the issue under discussion. Arguments such as "How can we support a candidate who has smoked pot [or avoided the military]?" or "Do you want to believe someone who has been unfaithful on more than one occasion?" are often heard in political discussions but probably have little to do with the logic of the argument.

Name-Calling. In **name-calling,** often referred to as "poisoning the well," the speaker gives an idea, a group of people, or a political philosophy a bad name ("atheist," "Neo-Nazi") to try to get listeners to condemn an idea without analyzing the argument and evidence. The opposite of name-calling is the use of "glittering generalities," in which the speaker tries to make you accept some idea by associating it with things you value highly ("democracy," "free speech," "academic freedom"). By using these "virtue words," the speaker tries to get you to ignore the evidence and simply approve of the idea.

Getting Critical.   Can you recall any examples of personal attack fallacies? What effect did they have on your feelings about the speaker? On your attitudes toward the position advocated?

discover that 70 percent have GPAs above 3.5, you may be tempted to draw the conclusion that computer science majors are especially bright. But what about the 30 percent who have lower GPAs? How much lower are these scores? This may be a significant exception that must be taken into account when you draw your conclusion and would require you to qualify your conclusion in significant ways. Exactly what kind of or how many exceptions will constitute "significant exceptions" will depend on the unique situation.

Reasoning from Causes and Effects

In reasoning from **causes and effects,** you may go in either of two directions. You may reason from cause to effect (from observed cause to unobserved effect) or from effect to cause (from observed effect to unobserved cause). In testing reasoning from cause to effect or from effect to cause, ask yourself the following questions.

Might other causes be producing the observed effect? If you observe a particular effect (say, high crime or student apathy), you need to ask if causes other than the one you're postulating might be producing these effects. Thus, you might postulate that poverty leads to high crime, but there might be other factors actually causing the high crime rate. Or poverty might be one cause but not the most important cause. Therefore, explore the possibility of other causes' producing the observed effects.

Is the causation in the direction postulated? If two things occur together, it's often difficult to determine which is the cause and which is the effect. For example, a lack of interpersonal intimacy and a lack of self-confidence often occur in the same person. The person who lacks self-confidence seldom has intimate relationships with others. But which is the cause and which is the effect? It might be that the lack of intimacy "causes" low self-confidence; it might also be, however, that low self-confidence "causes" a lack of intimacy. Of course, it might also be that some other previously unexamined cause (a history of negative criticism, for example) might be producing both the lack of intimacy and the low self-confidence.

Reasoning from Sign

Reasoning from **sign** involves drawing a conclusion on the basis of the presence of clues or symptoms that frequently occur together. Medical diagnosis is a good example of reasoning by sign. The general procedure is simple. If a sign and an object, event, or condition are frequently paired, the presence of the sign is taken as proof of the presence of the object, event, or condition. For example, fatigue, extreme thirst, and overeating serve as signs of hyperthyroidism, because they frequently accompany the condition. In reasoning from sign, ask yourself these questions.

Do the signs necessitate the conclusion drawn? Given extreme thirst, overeating, and the like, how certain may you be of the "hyperthyroid" conclusion? With most medical and legal matters we can never be absolutely certain, but we can be certain beyond a reasonable doubt.

Are there other signs that point to the same conclusion? In the thyroid example, extreme thirst could be brought on by any number of factors. Similarly, the fatigue and the overeating could be attributed to other causes. Yet taken together, the three signs seem to point to only one reasonable diagnosis. Generally, the more signs that point toward the conclusion, the more confidence you can have that it's valid.

Are there contradictory signs? Are there signs pointing toward contradictory conclusions? For example, if the butler had a motive and a history of violence (signs supporting the conclusion that the butler was the murderer) but also had an alibi (a sign pointing to the conclusion of innocence), then the conclusion of guilt would have to be reconsidered or discarded.

Use Emotional Appeals

Emotional appeals, or appeals to your listeners' feelings, needs, desires, and wants, also can be powerful means of persuasion (Wood, 2000). Specifically, when you use motivational appeals, you appeal to those forces that energize, move, or motivate people to develop, change, or strengthen their attitudes or ways of behaving. For example, one motive might be the desire for status. This

? DEVELOPING STRATEGIES

Negative Audience. Will is planning to give a speech in favor of the college's restricting access to certain lifestyle websites. Will knows that his audience is opposed to his position, so he wonders what types of arguments will work best. What advice would you give Will?

CRITICAL LISTENING/THINKING *Link*

Listening to Fallacies: Pseudo-Argument

In this box we continue the discussion of fallacies, this time concentrating on "arguments" that appear to address issues but really don't. Here are 10 such pseudo-arguments (Lee & Lee, 1972, 1995; Pratkanis & Aronson, 1991; Herrick, 2004). As with personal attack fallacies, learn to spot pseudo-arguments in the speeches of others, and avoid them in your own speeches.

Anecdotal Evidence. Often you'll hear people use **anecdotal evidence** to "prove" a point: "Women are like that; I know, because I have three sisters." "That's the way Japanese managers are; I've seen plenty of them." One reason this type of "evidence" is inadequate is that it relies on too few observations; it's usually a clear case of overgeneralizing on the basis of too little evidence. A second reason it's inadequate is that one person's observations may be unduly clouded by his or her own attitudes and beliefs; your personal attitudes toward women or the Japanese, for example, may influence your perception of their behaviors.

Straw Man. A **straw man** argument (like a man made of straw) is a contention that's easy to knock down. In this fallacy a speaker creates an easy-to-destroy simplification of an opposing position (that is, a straw man) and then proceeds to smash it. But, of course, if the opposing case were presented fairly and without bias, it wouldn't be so easy to demolish.

Appeal to Tradition. Often used to argue against change, the **appeal to tradition** simply claims that some proposed innovation is wrong or should not be adopted because it was never done before. This pseudo-argument is used repeatedly by those who don't want change. But, of course, the fact that something has not been done before says nothing about its value or whether or not it should be done now.

Bandwagon. In the **bandwagon** fallacy, often referred to as arguing *ad populum* (to the people), the speaker tries to persuade the audience to accept or reject an idea or proposal because "everybody's doing it" or because the "right" people are doing it. The speaker urges you to jump on this large and popular bandwagon—or be left out by yourself. This is a popular technique in political elections; campaigns trumpet the results of polls in an effort to get undecided voters to jump on the bandwagon of the leading candidate. After all, you don't want to vote for a loser.

Testimonial. The **testimonial** technique involves using the image associated with some person to secure your approval (if you respect the person) or your rejection (if you don't respect the person). This is the technique of advertisers who use people dressed up to look like doctors or plumbers or chefs to sell their products. Sometimes this technique takes the form of using only vague and general "authorities," as in "experts agree," "scientists say," "good cooks know," or "dentists advise."

Transfer. In **transfer** the speaker associates her or his idea with something you respect (to gain your approval) or with something you detest (to gain your rejection). For example, a speaker might portray a proposal for condom distribution in schools as a means for "saving our children from AIDS" (to encourage acceptance) or as a means for "promoting sexual promiscuity" (to encourage disapproval). Sports car manufacturers try to get you to buy their cars by associating them with high status and sex appeal; promoters of exercise clubs and diet plans attempt to associate them with health, self-confidence, and interpersonal appeal.

Plain Folks. Using the **plain folks** device, the speaker identifies himself or herself with the audience. The speaker is good—the "reasoning" goes—because he or she is one of the people, just plain folks like everyone else. Of course, the speaker who presents himself or herself as plain folks often is not. And even if he or she is plain folks, it has nothing to do with the issue under discussion.

Card-Stacking. In the pseudo-argument known as **card-stacking**, the speaker selects only evidence and arguments that support his or her case and may even falsify evidence or distort facts to better fit the case. Despite these misrepresentations, the speaker presents the supporting materials as "fair" and "impartial."

Thin Entering Wedge. In the **thin entering wedge** pseudo-argument, a speaker argues against a position on the grounds that as a "thin entering wedge" it will release the floodgates and lead to all sorts of catastrophes (Chase, 1956). Though often based on no evidence, this argument has been used throughout history to oppose change. Some examples are "wedge" claims that school integration and interracial marriage will bring the collapse of American education and society, same-sex unions will destroy the family, computers will lead to mass unemployment, and banning smoking in all public places will lead to the collapse of the restaurant industry.

Agenda-Setting. In **agenda-setting** a speaker contends that XYZ is the issue and that all others are unimportant and insignificant. This kind of fallacious appeal is heard frequently, as in "Balancing the budget is the key to the city's survival" or "There's only one issue confronting elementary education in our largest cities, and that is violence." In almost all situations, however, there are many issues and many sides to each issue. Often the person proclaiming that X is the issue really means, "I'll be able to persuade you if you focus solely on X and ignore the other issues."

Getting Critical. Can you recall a recent speech or college lecture in which any of these fallacies were used? Were you influenced by the pseudo-arguments? Were you persuaded?

desire might motivate someone to enter a high-status occupation or to dress a certain way.

Developed more than 30 years ago, one of the most useful analyses of human motives remains Abraham Maslow's fivefold **hierarchy of needs,** reproduced in Figure 10.2 on page 248 (Benson & Dundis, 2003; Hanley & Abell, 2002; Kiel, 1999; Maslow, 1970). One of the assumptions contained in this theory is that people seek to fulfill the needs at the lowest level first. Only when those needs are satisfied do the needs at the next level begin to influence behavior. For example, people would not concern themselves with the need for security or freedom from fear if they were starving (if their need for food had not been fulfilled). Similarly, they would not be concerned with friendship if their need for protection and security had not been fulfilled. The implication for you as a speaker is that you have to know what needs of your audience are unsatisfied. These are the needs you can appeal to in motivating them.

Here are several useful motivational appeals organized around Maslow's hierarchy. As you review these, try to visualize how you would use each one in your next speech.

Physiological Needs

In many parts of the world, and even in parts of the United States, the basic physiological needs of people are not fully met and thus, as you can appreciate, are powerful motivating forces. Lech Walesa, former leader of the Polish Solidarity Party, recognized this when he wrote: "He who gives food to the people will win." In many of the poorest countries of the world, the speaker who promises to meet fundamental physiological needs is the one the people will follow. Most college students in the United States, however, have their physiological needs for food, water, and air well satisfied; so these issues will not prove helpful in motivating and persuading them. In other words, if they already have sufficient food, they won't need it and therefore won't be motivated to get it.

Safety Needs

Those who do not have their basic safety and freedom-from-fear needs met will be motivated by appeals to security, protection, and freedom from physical harm and from psychological distress. You see appeals to this need in advertisements for burglar protection devices for home and car, in political speeches promising greater police protection on the streets and in schools, and in the

❖ **FIGURE 10.2**
Maslow's "Hierarchy of Needs"

How would you describe the satisfied and unsatisfied needs of members of your public speaking class? Which of these needs would, according to Maslow, be most motivating for your class?

Source: Based on Abraham Maslow, *Motivation and Personality*. New York: HarperCollins, 1970.

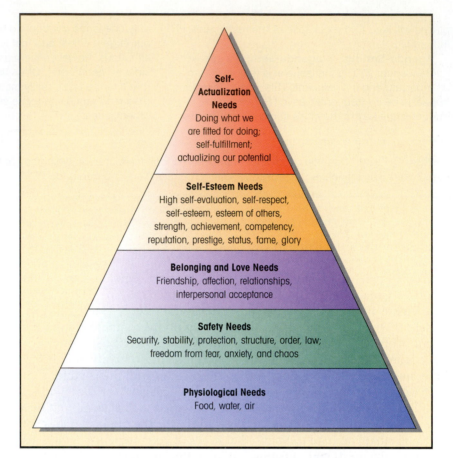

Self-Actualization Needs
Doing what we are fitted for doing; self-fulfillment; actualizing our potential

Self-Esteem Needs
High self-evaluation, self-respect, self-esteem, esteem of others, strength, achievement, competency, reputation, prestige, status, fame, glory

Belonging and Love Needs
Friendship, affection, relationships, interpersonal acceptance

Safety Needs
Security, stability, protection, structure, order, law; freedom from fear, anxiety, and chaos

Physiological Needs
Food, water, air

speeches of motivational gurus who promise psychological safety and freedom from anxiety. Freedom from anxiety also seems to be the motive many psychic services use in their ads, which promise that the services can tell you what is really going on (with, say, your romantic partner) as well as what will happen in the future. With this information, the ads imply, you'll be free of the anxiety that a lack of knowledge brings. You'll also learn what you should do—break off your relationship, move to the West Coast, or take that new job. The fact that this "information" is totally without any factual basis seems not to deter people from spending millions of dollars on psychics.

Sometimes the safety motive is seen in individuals' desire for order, structure, and organization—motives clearly appealed to in advertisements for personal data assistants like the Palm Pilot, cell phones, and information management software. Many people fear what is unknown, and order and structure seem to make things predictable and hence safe.

Belonging and Love Needs

Belonging and love needs are extremely powerful and comprise a variety of specific motives. For example, most people are motivated to love and be loved. For most persons, love and its pursuit occupy a considerable amount of time and energy. If you can teach your audience how to be loved and how to love, your audience will be not only attentive but also grateful.

As humans we also want affiliation—friendship and companionship. We want to be a part of a group, despite our equally potent desire for independence and individuality. Notice how advertisements for singles clubs, cruises, and dating services appeal to this need for affiliation. On this basis alone they successfully gain the attention, interest, and participation of thousands. Again, affiliation and group membership seem to assure us that we are in fact worthy creatures. If we have friends and companions, surely we are people of some merit.

USING TECHNOLOGY

Visit http://www.lawpublish.com/ or http://www.hg.org/advert.html and examine the laws that govern advertising. In what ways do the laws deal with the motivational appeals used in advertising?

Self-Esteem Needs

"In his private heart," wrote Mark Twain, "no man much respects himself." And perhaps because of this, we have a need for positive **self-esteem**: a favorable self-image, a view of ourselves that casts us in the best possible light. We want to see ourselves as self-confident, worthy, and contributing human beings. Inspirational speeches, speeches of the "you're the greatest" type, never seem to lack receptive and suggestive audiences.

Self-esteem derives, at least in part, from the approval of others (something that is important in all cultures but especially in collectivist cultures). Most people are concerned not only with peer approval but also with approval from family, teachers, elders, and even children. And beyond contributing to positive self-esteem, approval from others also promotes the attainment of related goals. For example, if you have peer approval, you probably also have influence. If you have approval, you're likely to have status. In addressing your audience's desire for approval, however, avoid being too obvious. Few people want to be told that they need or desire approval.

People also want power, control, and influence. First, they want to have power over themselves—to be in control of their own destiny, to be responsible for their own successes. As Ralph Waldo Emerson put it, "Can anything be so elegant as to have few wants, and to serve them one's self?"

Many people also want to have power over other persons, to be influential. Similarly, they may want to increase control over their environment and over events and things in the world. Because of this you'll motivate your listeners when you make them see that they can increase their power, control, and influence if they learn what you have to say or do as you suggest.

People want to achieve in whatever they do. You want to be a successful student. You also want to achieve as a friend, as a parent, as a lover. This is why books and speeches that purport to tell people how to be better achievers are so successful. At the same time, of course, you also want others to recognize your achievements as real and valuable. In using the achievement motive, be explicit in stating how your speech, ideas, and recommendations will contribute to the listeners' achievements. At the same time, recognize that different cultures will view achievement very differently. To some achievement may mean financial success, to others it may mean group popularity, to still others it may mean security. Show your listeners how what you have to say will help them achieve the goals they seek, and you'll likely have an active and receptive audience.

Although they often deny it, most people are motivated to some extent by the desire for financial gain—for what money can buy, for what it can do. Concern for lower taxes, for higher salaries, and for fringe benefits all are related to the money motive. Show the audience that what you're saying or advocating

? DEVELOPING STRATEGIES

Persuasive Appeals. Kevin wants to give a speech urging listeners to vote in favor of establishing a hate speech code at the college. He wants to use both logical and emotional appeals. If Kevin were speaking to your class, what logical and what emotional appeals would you advise him to use?

will make them money, and they'll listen with considerable interest—much as they read the get-rich-quick books that constantly flood the bookstores.

Self-Actualization Needs

At the top of Maslow's hierarchy is the self-actualization motive. According to Maslow (1970), this motive influences attitudes and behaviors only after all other needs are satisfied. Because these other needs are very rarely all satisfied, the time spent appealing to self-actualization needs might be better spent on other motives. And yet it seems that regardless of how satisfied or unsatisfied your other desires may be, you have a desire to self-actualize, to become what you feel you're fit for. If you see yourself as a poet, you must write poetry. If you see yourself as a teacher, you must teach. Even if you don't pursue these as occupations, you nevertheless have a desire to write poetry or to teach. Appeals to self-actualization

⦿ RESEARCH *Link*

Biographical Material

As a speaker you'll often need information about particular individuals. For example, you may want to look up authors of books or articles to find out something about their education, their training, or their other writings. Or you may wish to discover if there have been critical evaluations of their work such as, say, book reviews or articles about them or their writings. Knowing something about your sources enables you to more effectively evaluate their competence, convey their credibility to the audience, and answer audience questions about them.

First, consult the *Biography and Genealogy Master Index*. In print, on CD-ROM, or online, it indexes several hundred biographical indexes. This master index will send you to numerous specialized works, such as *The Dictionary of American Biography* (DAB), which contains articles on famous deceased Americans from all areas of accomplishment; *Current Biography,* which is the best single source for living individuals and includes both favorable and unfavorable comments on each individual; and *Who's Who in America,* which also covers living individuals.

In addition, there are a host of other more specialized works whose titles indicate their scope:

The Dictionary of Canadian Biography, The Dictionary of National Biography (British), *Directory of American Scholars, International Who's Who, Who Was Who in America, Who's Who* (primarily British), *American Men and Women of Science, Great Lives from History, Notable American Women, Who's Who in the Arab World, Who's Who in Finance and Industry, Who's Who in American Politics, Who's Who among Black Americans, Who's Who of American Women, Who's Who among Hispanic Americans,* and the *Biographical Directory of the American Congress.*

Not surprisingly, lots of Internet sources offer biographical information. For example, http://www.nobel.se/search/all_laureates_c.html supplies links to biographical information on Nobel Prize winners. If you want information on members of the House of Representatives, try http://www.house.gov. And http://www.biography.com/ will provide you with brief biographies of some 25,000 famous people, living and dead. Other excellent sources include Lives, the Biography Resource at http://amillionlives.com and the Biographical Dictionary at http://s9.com/biography, which covers over 28,000 men and women (see the Web page on page 251).

Research Activity. Conduct a biographical search for some famous person you're interested in by using one of the biographical dictionaries mentioned in this Research Link or by simply typing the person's name in the search box of your favorite search engine.

needs—to the yearning "to be the best you can be"—encourage listeners to strive for their highest ideals and are often welcomed by the audience.

Use Credibility Appeals

Your **credibility** is the degree to which your audience regards you as a believable spokesperson. If your listeners see you as competent and knowledgeable, of good character, and charismatic or dynamic, they will find you credible. As a result, you'll be more effective in changing their attitudes or in moving them to do something. Credibility is not something you have or don't have in any objective sense; rather, it's a function of what the audience thinks of you.

What makes a speaker credible will vary from one culture to another. In some cultures people would see competence as the most important factor in, say, their choice of a teacher for their preschool children. In other cultures the most important factor might be the goodness or morality of the teacher or perhaps the reputation of the teacher's family.

At the same time, each culture may define each of the factors in credibility differently. For example, "character" may mean following the rules of a specific religion in some cultures and following the individual conscience in others. To take another example, the Quran, the Torah, and the New Testament will be ascribed very different levels of credibility depending on the religious beliefs of the audience. And this will be true even when all three religious books say essentially the same thing on a given point.

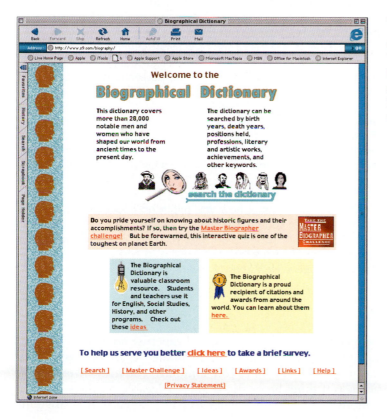

The Biographical Dictionary

(http://s9.com/biography/)
This is one of the many biographical websites. Browse the Biographical Dictionary site or similar others, making note of the kinds of information these sites contain and in what ways you might use them in your own research.

Before reading any farther about the ways to establish your credibility, you may wish to take the self-test "How Credible Are You?"

 **YOURSELF**

How Credible Are You?

Respond to each of the following phrases to indicate how you think members of your class see you when you deliver a public speech. Use the following scale: Definitely true = 5; probably true = 4; neither true nor untrue = 3; probably untrue = 2; and definitely untrue = 1.

_____ **1.** Knowledgeable about the subject matter

_____ **2.** Experienced

_____ **3.** Informed about the subject matter

_____ **4.** Fair in the presentation of material (evidence and argument)

_____ **5.** Concerned with the audience's needs

_____ **6.** Consistent over time on the issues addressed in the speech

_____ **7.** Assertive in personal style

_____ **8.** Enthusiastic about the topic and in general

_____ **9.** Active rather than passive

❖ **HOW DID YOU DO?** This test focuses on the three qualities of credibility—competence, character, and charisma—and is based on a large body of research (for example, McCroskey, 1997; Riggio, 1987). Items 1 to 3 refer to your perceived competence: How competent or capable do you seem to the audience when you give a public speech? Items 4 to 6 refer to your perceived character: Does the audience see you as a good and moral person? Items 7 to 9 refer to your perceived charisma: Does the audience see you as dynamic and active rather than as static and passive? Total scores will range from a high of 45 to a low of 9. If you scored relatively high (say around 32 or higher), then you feel your audience sees you as credible. If you scored relatively low (say below 27), then you feel your audience sees you as lacking in credibility.

❖ **WHAT WILL YOU DO?** Think about how you might go about increasing your credibility. What specific steps can you take to change any audience perception with which you may be unhappy? Are there specific things you can do to strengthen your competence, character, and/or charisma? A good source to consult is Ronald Riggio's (1987) *The Charisma Quotient* (New York: Dodd).

Competence

Your perceived **competence** is the knowledge and expertise an audience thinks you have. The more knowledge and expertise the audience sees you as having, the more likely the audience will believe you. Similarly, you're likely to believe a teacher or doctor if you think he or she is knowledgeable on the subject at hand. You can demonstrate your competence to your audience in a variety of ways.

Tell Listeners of Your Competence. Let the audience know of any special experience or training that qualifies you to speak on this specific topic. If you're speaking on communal living and you've lived on a commune yourself, then say so in your speech. Tell the audience of your unique personal experiences when these contribute to your credibility.

This recommendation to tell listeners of your competence generally applies to most audiences you'll encounter in the United States. But in some cultures—notably collectivist cultures such as those of Japan, China, and Korea, for example—to stress your own competence or that of your corporation may be taken as a suggestion that your audience members are inferior or that their corporations are not as good as yours. In other cultures—notably individualist cultures such as those of Scandinavia, the United States, and western Europe, for example—if you don't stress your competence, your listeners may assume it's because you don't have any.

Cite a Variety of Research Sources. Make it clear to your audience that you've thoroughly researched your topic. Do this by mentioning some of the books you've read, the persons you've interviewed, the articles you've consulted. Weave these references throughout your speech. Don't bunch them together at one time.

Stress the Competencies of Your Sources. If your audience isn't aware of them, then emphasize the particular competencies of your sources. In this way it becomes clear to the audience that you've chosen your sources carefully so as to provide the most authoritative sources possible. For example, saying simply, "Senator Cardova thinks . . . " does nothing to establish the senator's credibility. Instead, consider saying something like "Senator Cardova, who headed the finance committee for three years and was formerly a professor of economics at MIT, thinks . . . ."

Character

An audience will see you as credible if they perceive you as being someone of high moral **character,** someone who is honest, and someone they can trust. When an audience perceives your intentions as good for them (rather than for your own personal gain), they'll think you credible and they'll believe you. You can establish your high moral character in a number of ways.

Stress Fairness. If delivering a persuasive speech, stress that you've examined both sides of the issue (if indeed you have). If you're presenting both sides, then make it clear that your presentation is accurate and fair. Be particularly careful not to omit any argument the audience may already have thought of—this is a sure sign that your presentation isn't fair or balanced. Tell the audience that you would not advocate a position if you did not base it on a fair evaluation of the issues.

Stress Concern for Audience. Make it clear to the audience that you're interested in their welfare rather than seeking self-gain. If the audience feels that you are "out for yourself," they'll justifiably downgrade your

USING TECHNOLOGY

Visit a few college and university websites. For example, Harvard University is at www.harvard.edu; Dartmouth is at www.dartmouth.edu; any popular search engine or http://www.globalcomputing.com/university.html can give you links to the websites of more than 500 additional colleges and universities. What contributes to your impression of the credibility of each college?

❖ **CONSIDER** the obligations that religious speakers have to their audiences and the types of messages that audiences want to hear.

USING TECHNOLOGY

Visit a website devoted to a specific personality—for example, a movie star, musician, politician, sports figure, or film director—and examine it for references to credibility. How do these websites establish the competence, character, and charisma of the individuals? Could these techniques help you establish your own credibility?

credibility. Make it clear that the audience's interests are foremost in your mind. Tell your audience how the new legislation will reduce *their* taxes, how recycling will improve *their* community, how a knowledge of sexual harassment will make *their* workplace more comfortable and stress free.

Stress Concern for Enduring Values. We view speakers who are concerned with small and insignificant issues as less credible than speakers who demonstrate a concern for lasting truths and general principles. Thus, make it clear to the audience that your position—your thesis—is related to higher-order values; show them exactly how this is true.

Charisma

Charisma is a combination of your personality and dynamism as seen by the audience. An audience will perceive you as credible (and believable) if they like you and if they see you as friendly and pleasant rather than aloof and reserved. Similarly, audiences favor the dynamic speaker over the hesitant, nonassertive speaker. They'll perceive you as less credible if they see you as shy, introverted, and soft-spoken rather than as an extroverted and forceful individual. (Perhaps people feel that a dynamic speaker is open and honest in presenting herself or himself but that a shy, introverted individual may be hiding something.) As a speaker there's much that you can do to increase your charisma and hence your perceived credibility.

Demonstrate a Positive Outlook. Show the audience that you have a positive orientation to the public speaking situation and to the entire speaker–audience encounter. We see positive and forward-looking people as more credi-

TABLE 10.1	**The Motivated Sequence as a Persuasive Strategy**		
STEP	**PURPOSE**	**AUDIENCE QUESTION SPEAKER SHOULD ANSWER**	**AUDIENCE RESPONSE YOU WANT TO AVOID**
Attention	Focus listeners' attention on you and your message.	Why should I listen? Why should I use my time listening?	This is boring. This is irrelevant. This is of no interest to me.
Need	Demonstrate that there is a problem that affects them.	Why do I need to know or do anything?	I don't need to hear this. Things are fine now. This won't benefit me.
Satisfaction	Show listeners how they can satisfy the need.	How can I do anything about this?	I really can't do anything. It's beyond my control.
Visualization	Show listeners what their lives will be like with the need satisfied.	How would anything be different or improved?	I can't see how anything would be different. Nothing's going to change.
Action	Urge listeners to do something to solve the problem.	What can I do to effect this change?	I can't do anything. I'll be wasting my time and energy.

ble than negative and backward-looking people. Stress your pleasure at addressing the audience. Stress hope rather than despair; stress happiness rather than sadness.

Demonstrate Enthusiasm. The lethargic speaker, the speaker who somehow plods through the speech, is the very opposite of the charismatic speaker. Try viewing a film of Martin Luther King Jr. or Billy Graham speaking—they're totally absorbed with the speech and with the audience. They're excellent examples of the enthusiasm that makes a charismatic speaker.

Be Emphatic. Use language that is emphatic rather than colorless and indecisive. Use gestures that are clear and decisive rather than random and hesitant. Demonstrate a firm commitment to the position you're advocating; the audience will be much more likely to agree with a speaker who believes firmly in the thesis of the speech.

Motivate Your Listeners

If you want to persuade your listeners you have to motivate them to believe or to act in some way. One way to motivate, as explained in Chapter 6 (pp. 137–142), is to use the motivated sequence—the organizational structure in which you gain your listeners' attention, demonstrate that a need exists, demonstrate how that need can be satisfied by their believing or doing what you say, showing them what things will be like if the need is satisfied as you suggested, and urging them to do something to solve the problem.

? DEVELOPING STRATEGIES

Establishing Credibility. Joan is planning a speech on baseball. The problem is that simply because she's a woman, her audience is not going to perceive her as credible—even though she knows more about baseball than any other person in the room. What would you advise Joan to do to establish her credibility?

IDEAL AUDIENCE RESPONSE	SPEECH MATERIALS TO USE	CAUTIONS TO OBSERVE
This sounds interesting. Tell me more.	Attention-gaining materials, pp. 145–146.	Make attention relevant to speech topic.
Ok, I understand; there's a problem.	Supporting materials (examples, statistics, testimony), pp. 99–106.	Don't overdramatize the need.
I can change things.	Supporting materials, pp. 99–123; logical, motivational, and ethical appeals, pp. 243–255.	Answer any objections listeners might have to your plan.
Wow! Things look a lot better this way.	Motivational appeals, pp. 247–251; illustrations and language high in imagery (pp. 182–184).	Be realistic; don't visualize the world as perfect once your listeners do as you suggest.
Let me sign up. Here's my contribution. I'll participate in the campaign.	Motivational appeals, pp. 247–251; specific language, pp. 179–182.	Be specific. Ask for small attitude changes and easily performed behaviors.

Table 10.1 on pages 254–255 summarizes the motivated sequence as a persuasive strategy and will help you develop your speeches whether they deal with questions of fact, value, or policy—the topics to which we now turn.

Persuasive Speeches on Questions of Fact

Questions of fact concern what is or is not true, what does or does not exist, what did or did not happen. Some questions of fact are easily answered. These include many academic questions you're familiar with: What is philosophy? Who was Aristotle? When was the first satellite launched? Questions of fact also include more mundane questions like: What's on television? When is the meeting? What's Jenny's e-mail address? You can easily find answers to these questions by looking at some reference book, finding the relevant website, or asking someone who knows the answer.

The questions of fact that we deal with in persuasive speeches are a bit different. Although these questions also have answers, the answers are not that easy to find and in fact may never be found. The questions concern controversial issues for which different people have different answers. Daily newspapers abound in questions of fact. For example, the February 29, 2004, edition of the *New York Times* dealt with questions of fact that included such issues as these: Was Martha Stewart guilty of lying to government investigators about a stock sale? What was causing Zimbabwe's food shortage? How had the nurse who killed some 40 people continued to get hired, and who was responsible for allowing him to work for so long in so many hospitals? Did the British spy on UN Secretary General Kofi Annan? What was the N.F.L. doing to reduce steroid usage among athletes?

Thesis

For a persuasive speech on a question of fact, you'll formulate a thesis on the basis of a factual statement such as:

- This company has a glass ceiling for women.
- The plaintiff was slandered (or libeled or defamed).
- The death was a case of physician-assisted suicide.
- Gay men and lesbians make competent military personnel.
- Television violence leads to violent behavior in viewers.

If you were preparing a persuasive speech on, say, the first example given above, you might phrase your thesis as "This company discriminates against women." Whether or not the company does discriminate is a question of fact; clearly the company either does or does not discriminate. Whether you can prove it does or it doesn't, however, is another issue.

Main Points

Once you've formulated your thesis, you can generate your main points by asking the simple question "How do you know this?" or "Why would you believe

DEVELOPING STRATEGIES

Assessing Questions of Fact. Adam wants to give his persuasive speech on a question of fact and is thinking of developing one of the five theses suggested here. With which thesis would his task be easiest (assuming the audience was your public speaking class)? With which thesis would his task be the most difficult? On what basis do you make these assumptions?

this is true (factual)?" The answers to one of these questions will enable you to develop your main points. The bare bones of your speech might then look something like this:

General purpose: To persuade.

Specific purpose: To persuade my listeners that this company discriminates against women.

Thesis: This company discriminates against women. (How can we tell that this company discriminates against women?)

I. Women earn less than men.

II. Women are hired less often than men.

III. Women occupy fewer managerial positions than men.

Support

Having identified your main points, you would then begin searching for information to support them. Taking the first point, you might develop it something like this:

I. Women earn less than men.

   A. Over the past five years, the average salary for editorial assistants was $6,000 less for women than it was for men.

   B. Over the past five years, the entry-level salaries for women averaged $4,500 less than the entry-level salaries for men.

   C. Over the past five years, the bonuses earned by women were 20 percent below the bonuses earned by men.

The above speech focuses entirely on a question of fact; the thesis itself is a question of fact. In other speeches, however, you may want just one of your main points to center on a question of fact. So, for example, let's say you're giving a speech advocating that the military give gay men and lesbians full equality. In this case, one of your points might focus on a question of fact: You might seek to establish that gay men and lesbians make competent military personnel. Once that was established, you'd then be in a better position to argue for equality in military policy.

Developing Speeches on Questions of Fact

In developing a persuasive speech on a question of fact, consider the following suggestions.

   1. Emphasize logical proof. Facts are your best support. The more facts you have, the more persuasive you'll be in dealing with questions of fact. For example, the more evidence you can find that women earn less than men, the

"When I think of the as yet undreamed-of loopholes that are going to be available to you guys!"

A CASE OF *Ethics*

Omitting the Negative

You're preparing a persuasive speech in which you will ask students to sign up to record textbooks so visually impaired students will be able to listen to the books on tape. You've developed a wide variety of reasons why students should do this—it's a learning experience for the reader, it's socially responsible, and it pays reasonably well. But there's also a negative side. For example, you have to travel at your own expense to the recording studio; you have to do the recording when the studio is available, which is often on weekends; and if your recording is not adequate, you have to rerecord it with no further payment. You're thinking of omitting these negatives; after all, you don't have the time to include everything, even the arguments that support your position. You also figure that it's the listeners' responsibility to ask about the negatives and not necessarily your job to tell them.

What would you do in this situation? More generally, what is a speaker's responsibility in regard to revealing evidence and arguments against the position she or he is advocating?

more convincing you will be in proving that women do in fact earn less and, ultimately, that women are discriminated against.

2. Use the most recent materials possible. The more recent your materials, the more relevant they will be to the present time and the more persuasive they're likely to be. Notice in our example, if you said that in 1980 women earned on average $10,000 less than men, it would be meaningless in proving that the company discriminates against women *now.*

3. Use highly competent sources. When you use the testimony of others or you cite research, establish the competence of the source. Let the audience see that the people you're citing know what is going on and have the competence to speak authoritatively.

4. Clearly connect your main points to your thesis in your introduction, when introducing each of the points, and again in your summary. Don't allow the audience to forget that the lower salaries that women earn directly supports the thesis that this company discriminates against women.

Persuasive Speeches on Questions of Value

Questions of value concern what people consider good or bad, moral or immoral, just or unjust. In the *New York Times* of February 29, 2004, there are a lot of questions of value debated. For example, should marriage be restricted to opposite-sex couples? Should Israel have a right to build walls in the West Bank? Should Lebanon have reinstituted the death penalty? Should additional public lands throughout the United States be opened for logging? Should creationism and evolution both be taught in schools? Should Social Security benefits be cut?

Often, speeches on questions of value will seek to strengthen audiences' existing attitudes, beliefs, or values. This is true of much religious and political speaking; for example, people who listen to religious speeches usually are already believers, so these speeches strive to strengthen the beliefs and values the people already hold. In a religious setting the listeners already share the speaker's values and are willing to listen. Speeches that seek to change audience values are much more difficult to construct. Most people resist change. When you try to get people to change their values or beliefs, you're fighting an uphill (though not necessarily impossible) battle.

Thesis

Theses devoted to questions of value might look something like this:

- ◆ The death penalty is unjustifiable.
- ◆ Bullfighting is inhumane.
- ◆ Discrimination on the basis of affectional orientation is wrong.
- ◆ Chemical weapons are immoral.
- ◆ Human cloning is morally justified.
- ◆ College athletics minimize the importance of academics.

Main Points

As with speeches on questions of fact, you can generate the main points for a speech on a question of value by asking a strategic question of your thesis, such as "Why is this good?" or "Why is this immoral?" For example, you can take the first thesis given above and ask, "Why is the death penalty unjustifiable?" The answers to this question will give you the speech's main points. The body of your speech might then look something like this:

General purpose: To persuade.

Specific purpose: To persuade my listeners that the death penalty is unjustifiable.

Thesis: The death penalty is unjustifiable. (Why is the death penalty unjustifiable?)

I. The criminal justice system can make mistakes.

II. The death penalty constitutes cruel and unusual punishment.

III. No one has the moral right to take another's life.

Support

To support your main points, you would then begin to search for evidence. For example, to show that mistakes have been made, you might itemize three or four high-profile cases in which people were put to death and later, through DNA, found to have been innocent.

At times, and with certain topics, it may be useful to identify the standards you would use to judge something moral or justified or fair or good. For example,

? DEVELOPING STRATEGIES

Developing Main Points for a Speech of Value. Grace wants to develop her persuasive speech on one of the theses identified above. Following a pattern such as that illustrated for the first thesis (under the discussion of "main points") what main points would be appropriate for any one of the other five theses (assuming the audience was your public speaking class)?

in the "bullfighting is inhumane" speech, you might devote your first main point to defining when an action can be considered inhumane. In this case the body of your speech might look like this:

I. An inhumane act has two qualities.

   A. It is cruel and painful.

   B. It serves no human necessity.

II. Bullfighting is inhumane.

   A. It is cruel and painful.

   B. It serves no necessary function.

Notice that in the example of capital punishment, the speaker aims to strengthen or change the listeners' beliefs about the death penalty. The speaker is not asking the audience to do anything about capital punishment but merely to believe that it's not justified. However, you might also use a question of value as a first step toward persuading your audience to take some action. For example, once you got your listeners to see the death penalty as unjustified, you might then ask them to take certain actions—perhaps in your next speech—to support an anti–death penalty politician, to vote for or against a particular proposition, or to join an organization fighting against the death penalty.

Developing Speeches on Questions of Value

In constructing your persuasive speech on a question of value, consider these suggestions:

1. Define clearly the specific value on which you're focusing. For example, let's say that you're developing a speech to persuade high school students to attend college. You want to stress that college is of value, but what type of value do you focus on? The financial value (college graduates earn more money than nongraduates)? The social value (college is a lot of fun and a great place to make friends)? The intellectual value (college will broaden your view of the world, make you a more critical and creative thinker)? Once you clarify the type of value on which you'll focus, you'll find it easier to develop the relevant points. You'll also find it easier to locate appropriate supporting materials.

2. Begin with shared assumptions and beliefs, then progress gradually to areas of disagreement. For example, in the death penalty speech, it's likely that even those in favor of the death penalty would agree that mistakes can be made; and they probably would be willing to accept evidence that mistakes have in fact been made, especially if you cite reliable statistical evidence and expert testimony. By starting with this issue, you secure initial agreement and can use that as a basis for approaching areas where you and the audience see things differently.

3. Use sources that the audience values highly. For example, if you were addressing an audience of devout Catholics who were active participants in their church, the testimony of the pope or a cardinal would likely be influential. But if your audience were composed of Muslims, Jews, Buddhists, or atheists, then it's unlikely that these sources would be as influential. To some listeners, these sources might even have a negative effect. So do a thorough audience analysis before you select your testimonials.

Persuasive Speeches on Questions of Policy

When you move beyond a focus on value to urging your audience to do something about an issue, you're then into a question of policy. For example, in a speech designed to convince your listeners that bullfighting is inhumane, you'd be focusing on a question of value. If you were to urge that bullfighting should therefore be declared illegal, you'd be urging the adoption of a particular policy. Items that focused on questions of policy in the February 29, 2004, *New York Times* included, for example, these issues: Should the United States enact a constitutional amendment to limit marriage to opposite-sex couples? Should same-sex couples have a legal right to marry? How can hunger in Zimbabwe be alleviated? What should the United States do in regard to the Haitian rebellion? What should Iraq's constitution look like? Who should police financial institutions holding pension funds?

Questions of policy concern what should be done, what procedures should be adopted, what laws should be changed; in short, what policy should be followed. In some speeches you may want to defend a specific policy, whereas in others you may wish to argue that a current policy should be discontinued.

Thesis

Persuasive speeches frequently revolve around questions of policy and may use theses such as the following:

◆ Hate speech should be banned in colleges.
◆ Our community should adopt a zero tolerance policy for guns in schools.
◆ Abortion should be available on demand.
◆ Music CDs should be rated for violence and profanity.
◆ Medical marijuana should be legalized.
◆ Smoking should be banned from all public buildings and parks.

As you can tell from these examples, questions of policy almost invariably involve questions of values. To argue, for example, that hate speech should be banned in colleges is based on the value judgment that hate speech is wrong. To argue for a zero tolerance policy on guns in schools implies that you think it's wrong for students and faculty to carry guns to school.

Main Points

You can develop your speech on a question of policy by asking a strategic question of your thesis. With policy issues the question will be "Why should the policy be adopted?" or "Why is the policy desirable?" or "Why is this policy better than what we now have?" Taking our first example, we might ask, "Why should hate speech be banned on campus?" From the answers to this

❖ **CONSIDER** the kinds of questions (fact, value, or policy) that a presidential press secretary deals with most often.

question, you would develop your main points, which might look something like this:

I. Hate speech encourages violence against women and minorities.

II. Hate speech denigrates women and minorities.

III. Hate speech teaches hate instead of tolerance.

Support

You would then support each main point with a variety of supporting materials that would convince your audience that, for example, hate speech should be banned from college campuses. For example, you might cite the websites put up by certain groups that advocate violence against women and minority members or quote from the lyrics of performers who came to campus. Or you might cite examples of actual violence that had been accompanied by hate speech or hate literature.

In some speeches on questions of policy, you might simply want your listeners to agree that the policy you're advocating is a good one. In other cases you might want them to do something about the policy—to vote for a particular candidate, to take vitamin C, to diet, to write to their elected officials, to participate in the walkathon, to wear an AIDS awareness ribbon, and so on.

Generally, questions of policy are used as theses more often than as main points. Still, in some instances, you might phrase a main point around a policy issue. For example, in a speech designed to get a client off on a driving-while-intoxicated charge, a lawyer might want to argue that the blood alcohol level used to define "drunk driving" should be much higher than it currently is.

Developing Speeches on Questions of Policy

In developing your speech on a question of policy, consider the following suggestions:

1. Prove that the policy is needed. You might, for example, show that a health care plan is needed because currently workers have no health care coverage. Or you might show that a particular policy is needed because the current policy is inadequate.

2. Emphasize that the policy you're supporting is practical and reasonable. If possible, show that the policy you're advocating has been successfully put into operation elsewhere.

3. Show your listeners how the policy will benefit them directly. Generally, listeners want to know that changes will prove beneficial to them on a personal level. The more personally relevant you can make a policy, the better it will be received.

4. When asking for action, ask for small, easily performed, and very specific behaviors. For example, it will generally be easier to get listeners to sign a

DEVELOPING STRATEGIES

Selecting Arguments. Helen is preparing a persuasive speech on a question of policy arguing that owners of phone-in psychic advice services should be prosecuted for fraud. What types of arguments would Helen need if she were presenting this speech to your class?

petition than to donate their Saturday afternoon to a walkathon. Similarly, it's likely to be easier to get listeners to contribute $1 to the athletic fund than $20.

5. Use an organizational pattern that best fits your topic. For example, in the speech on zero tolerance for guns in school, you might consider using a problem–solution pattern in which your speech would be divided into two basic parts:

> I. Guns are destroying our high schools. (problem)
>
> II. We must adopt a zero tolerance policy. (solution)

Organizational Examples

Questions of policy are especially well suited to organization with the motivated sequence and comparison-and-contrast patterns.

The Motivated Sequence

To use the motivated sequence in the hate speech example, you might develop the speech somewhat as follows:

Attention

I. Here are just a few examples of the hate speech I collected right here on campus.

[Show slides 1–7]

Need

II. Hate speech creates all sorts of problems.
   A. Hate speech encourages violence.
   B. Hate speech denigrates women and minorities.
   C. Hate speech teaches intolerance.

Satisfaction

III. If we're to build an effective learning environment, hate speech must go.

Visualization

IV. Banning hate speech will help us build an environment conducive to learning.
   A. Students will not fear violence.
   B. Women and minorities will not feel as if they are second-class citizens.
   C. Tolerance can replace intolerance.

Action

V. Sign my petition urging the administration to take action, to ban hate speech.

Comparison and Contrast

If you're persuading your listeners that one policy will be more effective than another (say the present policy), then a comparison-and-contrast organization might work best. Here you might divide each of your main points into two parts—the present plan and the proposed plan—so as to effectively compare

RESEARCH *Link*

Academic Research Articles

Academic research forms the core of what we know about people and the world; it is the most valid and the most reliable source of information you're likely to find. Academic research articles are reports of studies conducted by academicians around the world. For the most part, these articles are conducted by unbiased researchers using the best research methods available. Further, this research is subjected to careful critical review by experts in the specific field of the research.

Each college library subscribes to a somewhat different package of CD-ROM and online databases of scholarly articles. These databases contain information on the nature and scope of the database and user-friendly directions for searching, displaying, printing, and saving retrieved information to disk. In addition, you may have access to Research Navigator (see Chapter 1), which you will have been using throughout the course. Research Navigator makes searching for these articles extremely easy.

Research Activity. If you have access, log on to www.researchnavigator.com and to your own college library's database of academic research articles, and examine the many databases available. Research Navigator organizes the databases by academic discipline, but don't let academic boundaries prevent you from examining research in related fields of study.

and contrast them on each issue. For example, the body of a speech urging a new health care plan might look something like this:

I. The plans are different in their coverage for psychiatric problems.

A. The present plan offers nothing for such problems.

B. The proposed plan treats psychiatric problems with the same coverage as physical problems.

II. The plans differ in their deductibles.

A. The present plan has a $2,000 deductible.

B. The proposed plan has a $500 deductible.

III. The plans differ in the hospitalization allowances.

A. In the present plan two days are allowed for childbirth; in the proposed plan four days are allowed.

B. In the present plan all patients are assigned to large wards; in the proposed plan all patients are assigned to semiprivate rooms.

Summary of Concepts and Skills

In this chapter we looked at the persuasive speech, first covering several guidelines for persuasion and then discussing three main types of persuasive speeches.

Goals of Persuasion

Persuasive speaking has three general goals:

- To strengthen or weaken attitudes, beliefs, or values
- To change attitudes, beliefs, or values
- To motivate to action

Guidelines for Persuasive Speaking

Among the important guidelines for persuasive speaking are:

- Anticipate selective exposure.
- Ask for reasonable amounts of change.
- Identify with your audience.
- Use logical appeals.
- Use emotional appeals.
- Use credibility appeals.
- Motivate your listeners.

Persuasive Speeches on Questions of Fact

Persuasive speeches on questions of fact focus on what is or is not true. In a speech on a question of fact:

- Emphasize logical proof.
- Use the most recent materials possible.
- Use highly competent sources.
- Clearly connect your main points to your thesis.

Persuasive Speeches on Questions of Value

Speeches on questions of value focus on issues of good and bad, justice or injustice. In designing speeches to strengthen or change attitudes, beliefs, or values:

- Define clearly the specific value on which you're focusing.
- Begin with shared assumptions and beliefs, then progress gradually to areas of disagreement.
- Use sources that the audience values highly.

Persuasive Speeches on Questions of Policy

Speeches on questions of policy focus on what should or should not be done, what procedures should or should not be adopted. In designing speeches to move listeners to action:

- Prove that the policy is needed.
- Emphasize that the policy you're supporting is practical and reasonable.
- Show your listeners how the policy will benefit them directly.
- When asking for action, ask for small, easily performed, and very specific behaviors.
- Use an organizational pattern that best fits your topic.

Vocabulary Quiz

The Persuasive Speech

Match the terms dealing with the persuasive speech with their definitions. Record the number of the definition next to the appropriate term.

_____ competence

_____ motives

_____ reasoning from sign

_____ charisma

_____ foot-in-the-door technique

_____ identification

_____ character

_____ door-in-the-face technique

_____ speaker credibility

_____ hierarchy of needs

1. A persuasive strategy in which the speaker stresses his or her similarity with the audience.

2. A persuasive technique whereby you make a large request that you know will be refused and follow it with a more modest request.

3. A persuasive technique whereby you request some small compliance and then follow it with a more extensive request.

4. Needs or desires that lead people to act in hopes of fulfilling these needs or desires.

5. A view of motives holding that certain motives are more basic than others and that before higher-order needs can motivate behavior, more basic needs must be met.

6. The persuasiveness of a person, apart from anything the person says or does.

7. The knowledge and expertise that an audience believes a speaker possesses.

8. The integrity and good morals that an audience feels a speaker possesses.

9. A speaker's personality or dynamism as perceived by an audience.

10. Drawing a conclusion on the basis of the presence of clues or symptoms that frequently occur together.

Web Explorations

Companion Website

www.ablongman.com/devito

The Companion Website's Chapter 10 offers additional insights into the nature of persuasion and into the strategies of persuasive speaking: "Principles of Motivation"; "Additional Motivational Appeals"; "How You Form Credibility Impressions"; "General Guidelines for Communicating Credibility"; "Thinking Critically about Persuasive Speaking"; "Evaluating the Adequacy of Reasoning"; "Analyzing Arguments: The Toulmin Model";

"Comparative Credibility Judgments"; and "Gender, Credibility, and the Topics of Public Speaking." A self-test on the ethics of persuasion is presented in "When Is Persuasion Unethical?" An excellent persuasive speech by Upendri Gunasekera, "The Perils of Philanthropy," also appears here along with annotations and questions for analysis.

Public Speaking Exercises

10.1 Developing Persuasive Strategies

The objective of this exercise is to stimulate the discussion of persuasive strategies on a variety of contemporary cultural issues. The exercise may be completed individually, in small groups, or with the entire class.

What persuasive strategies would you use to convince your class of the validity of either side in any of the following points of view? For example, what persuasive strategies would you use to persuade your class members that interracial adoption should be encouraged or discouraged? These points of view are simplified for purposes of this exercise and shouldn't be taken to suggest that the viewpoints given here are complete descriptions of these complex issues.

Point of View: Interracial Adoption. Those in favor of interracial adoption argue that the welfare of the child—who might not get adopted if made to wait for someone of the same race—must be considered first. Adoption (regardless of race) is good for the child and therefore is a positive social process. Those opposed to interracial adoption argue that children need to be raised by those of the same race if they are to develop self-esteem and become functioning members of their own ethnic group. Interracial adoption is therefore a negative social process.

Point of View: Gay Men and Lesbians in the Military. Those in favor argue that gay men and lesbians should be accorded exactly the same rights and privileges as heterosexuals—no more, no less; equality means equality for all. Those opposed argue that gay men and lesbians will undermine the image of the military and will make heterosexuals uncomfortable.

Point of View: Affirmative Action. Those in favor of affirmative action argue that because of the injustices in the way certain groups (racial, national, gender) were treated, they should now be given preferential treatment to correct the imbalance caused by social injustices. Those opposed to affirmative action argue that merit must be the sole criterion for promotion, jobs, entrance to graduate schools, and so on, and that affirmative action is just reverse racism; one form of injustice cannot correct another form of injustice.

10.2 Analyzing a Speech

Here is an excellent persuasive speech, "The Home of the Slaves," given by Jayme Meyer of the University of Texas at Austin at the American Forensic Association's National Individual Events tournament in 2004. The speech is used here with the permission of Jayme Meyer.

THE HOME OF THE SLAVES

Jayme Meyer

History books tell us that slavery ended after the Civil War. Try telling that to Andrea. At the age of 4, she was sold by her mother and enslaved for 12 years. Locked in a basement with 16 other children, the *New York Times Magazine* of January 25, 2004, explains, Andrea was raped almost every night while her owner got rich. Tragically, Andrea and her companions were not victims of an inadequate Third World government, but, according to the September 2003 *National Geographic*, they are among the almost 150,000 slaves currently held here in the United States.

Unlike the slaves of our early history, these slaves are lured to America with false promises of a better life through well-paying jobs or marriage. But as the *Boston Globe* of April 17, 2003, elaborates, once they arrive, these immigrants are forced to work in "brothels, sweatshops, fields, or private homes." And the terror doesn't

This is a particularly dramatic story designed to gain attention and to suggest the topic of the speech. Did it gain your attention? If not, what else might the speaker have done?

Is 150,000 people a lot? How might the speaker have dramatized this number and made it more significant to an audience of college students?

stop there. The *San Antonio Express News* of April 3, 2003, reveals that slavery is now the third-largest source of money for organized crime, generating $19 billion annually, money that is often used for other criminal activity, including drug trafficking and arms smuggling, producing more crime for all of us to deal with here at home.

So in order to break this cycle of slavery, we must first, explore the extent of slavery in the United States; next, understand why this problem keeps us in chains; and finally, implement some solutions to what John Miller of the U.S. State Department calls in the *Washington Post* of January 1, 2004, "the emerging human rights issue of the 21st century."

The 13th Amendment was supposed to end slavery in December 1865, but even today slaves are forced into the U.S. and slavery fosters additional crime. Kristiina Kangaspunta of the United Nations tells the Associated Press of May 13, 2003, that the United States is now one of the top three human trafficking destinations in the world, with most slaves originating from Thailand, Russia, or the Ukraine. The January 25, 2004, *New York Times Magazine* explains that traffickers promise slaves better lives in the U.S. as waiters, actors, models or nannies. But after tricking them into paying their own way into Mexico, the traffickers smuggle them across the border and force them into a nightmare world of brutality. According to the U.S. Department of State's *Trafficking in Persons Report* of June 11, 2003, slaves are exposed to appalling working conditions, sexually transmitted diseases from rape and forced prostitution, poor nutrition, and even torture. For instance, four girls between the ages of 14 and 17 were recently discovered working in an underground brothel in Plainfield, New Jersey. The same *New York Times Magazine* described the conditions when the police found them: the emaciated girls slept on rotting mattresses, used a doorless, filthy bathroom, and were surrounded by morning-after pills and abortion-inducing medications.

Although we may not personally be enslaved, all of us are affected by America's slave trade. According to the summer/fall 2003 *Brown Journal of World Affairs*, the profits made from slavery are often invested in the mainstream economy, giving criminal networks more power because of their immense wealth. And the more they make, the more we're affected. As M2 Presswire of October 14, 2003, explains, crime syndicates use the billions of dollars generated by slavery to fund other criminal activities, including drug trafficking, arms smuggling, and money laundering. While 150,000 slaves suffer the immediate evils of slavery, all of us are endangered by its long-term implications.

This elaboration continues to dramatize the situation of modern slavery and presents it as a problem for the listeners. Was the speaker successful in convincing you that this is a problem for society and for you? If not, what else might the speaker have done to convince you that this problem really affected you personally?

Here the speaker provides an excellent orientation to the speech and identifies the three major sections of the speech: (1) the present state of slavery in the United States, (2) the reasons this is a problem, and (3) ways of solving the problem.

The organizational pattern is also identified; the first two sections present the problem and the third presents the solution. In what other ways could this speech have been organized?

Here the speaker begins to explain the current state of slavery and makes us see it as a horrendous crime.

The speaker continues to introduce current material from reliable sources and makes us feel he is well prepared and knowledgeable, which adds to his credibility.

The speaker makes a great effort to make the topic of these enslaved individuals significant for a group of listeners who are probably quite comfortable and secure. Did the speaker succeed in making you feel that this problem affects you? If not, what else might the speaker have done?

Here the speaker moves from general statements about slavery to a specific case of four girls. Moving from the abstract to the specific is a useful technique for making your listeners understand and feel the problem.

The speaker cleverly answers the potential audience question ("Why should this concern me?") by relating the problem to one that creates additional crime from which we all suffer. Was the speaker successful in getting you to feel that this is important to you? How much do you care about these other problems—drug trafficking, arms smuggling, and money laundering? If you don't care very much, what might the speaker have done to make you care?

We pride ourselves on our freedoms, but 150,000 people within our borders are denied theirs because of slavery's lucrative nature and ineffective legislation. The *Agence France Presse* of August 1, 2003, reports the results of an International Labour Organization study: modern-day slavery is "more lucrative . . . than drug trafficking." As the aforementioned *Trafficking in Persons Report* reveals, slave owners make up to thousands of dollars for each child laborer and tens of thousands for each brothel worker. And, as a February 24, 2004, article on the Florida State University Web page notes, "unlike drugs, humans can be recycled . . . so it's a better investment for the traffickers." And according to the *National Geographic* of September 2003, countless people take advantage of its lucrative nature: Juan, Ramiro, and Jose Ramos forced men and women from Mexico to pick fruit in Florida. Sardar and Nadira Gasanov made women from Uzbekistan work in strip clubs in West Texas. Louisa Satia and Kevin Nanji tricked a 14-year-old girl from Cameroon into working as their private servant in Maryland after raping her and imprisoning her in their house—and the list goes on.

And unfortunately, current laws are simply not strong enough. The Trafficking Victims Protection Act of 2000 has done a good job of protecting some victims, giving former slaves temporary U.S. visas and offering protection from their traffickers. But helping victims after they are discovered doesn't get to the root of the problem; getting traffickers off the streets would. The *San Antonio Express News* of April 3, 2003, states that while $60 million per year is spent on the cause, only 75 traffickers were actually prosecuted in 2000, simply not enough for the problem that Assistant Secretary of State Richard Armitage tells the *Weekly Standard* of October 6, 2003, will "outstrip the illicit trade in guns and narcotics within a decade."

We thought we abolished slavery in 1865, but the fight obviously is not over. Action from the UN and the United States government, as well as our own attention, can help protect those who have lost all freedom. The United Nations needs to follow through with its international database of human trafficking. As a UN press release of May 16, 2003, states, the database, now consisting of about 3,000 cases, tracks the "countries of origin, transit and destination of trafficked persons." This database needs to be continuously updated in order to give governments accurate information to prosecute those who traffic human beings. The U.S. government needs to work in conjunction with the UN to help populate the database, and then must utilize the information once it is available. This database will help us find a way to stop the flow of slaves into the United States, allowing us to get to the root of the problem.

What has the speaker done throughout this speech to identify with the audience? What else might the speaker have done?

Would selective exposure play a role in this speech? If so, what could the speaker do to anticipate selective exposure?

What kinds of logical appeals does the speaker use in this speech? How effective are they?

Again, the speaker cleverly weaves in specific examples along with the generalizations and gives the problem a human face.

What types of emotional appeals can you find throughout this speech? How effective are they? How might they have been made even more effective?

This first sentence is an interesting but subtle transition between the problem, already discussed, with the solution which is about to be discussed. Would you have preferred a more obvious and direct transition?

Does the speaker convince you that the United Nations can help in combating this problem?

Once this information is acquired, United States law-makers must also take swift action. The Trafficking Victims Protection Act of 2000 was definitely a good first step. However, it needs to refocus its funding on the prosecution of traffickers. To reach this goal, more money obviously needs to be spent. According to Mohamed Matted, codirector of the Protection Project at Johns Hopkins University, in his testimony to the House Committee on International Relations on June 24, 2003, this can be done by confiscating traffickers' assets. This money could be used to fund prosecution of other traffickers as well as provide restitution for the victims.

Finally, you and I easily can play our part in abolishing slavery by going to the American Anti-Slavery Group's website at iAbolish.com. Next time you are online, become an e-abolitionist by signing antislavery petitions and joining the site's Freedom Action Network. The Network will send you weekly e-mail newsletters to keep you informed and to alert you to antislavery events in your area. We have condemned past slavery and those who allowed it to persist. But now it's our turn to stand up for what we know is right and help abolish the slavery that plagues our time.

Even though Andrea has been free for about 5 years, so are those who tortured her for 12. Fearing retribution, she's in constant hiding, dealing with the daily trauma from her years of forced servitude. But after understanding the extent of modern-day slavery and discussing how it came about, we can implement solutions to help people like Andrea see for themselves that we do live in the land of the free, not the home of the slave.

The second part of the solution concerns lawmakers. Does the speaker make an effective case for the role that laws and lawmakers must play in human trafficking?

*What types of **credibility appeals** can you identify throughout this speech? Would you have used credibility appeals differently? What would you have said?*

The third part of the solution is to act on a personal level, specifically to participate in a particular Internet group devoted to the speech's ultimate aim—the elimination of human slavery. Is this something you might do after reading this speech? If not, what might the speaker have said to move you to action?

*Is the speaker asking for **reasonable amounts of change?** If not, what correction would you suggest?*

Here the speaker returns to the introduction, and you know that he is nearing the end of his speech.

The speaker here summarizes the main points that were introduced in the introduction and developed throughout the speech.

Now that you've read the entire speech, what would you have titled it if it had been prepared for presentation in your public speaking class?

11 Speaking on Special Occasions

Why Read This Chapter?

It will enable you to develop additional types of public speeches by helping you to:

❖ prepare and deliver a variety of special occasion speeches, including speeches designed to secure goodwill, to praise another person, to present or accept an award, or to honor or celebrate some occasion

❖ apply these special occasion insights and guidelines to all kinds of informative and persuasive speeches

> "Never rise to speak unless you have something to say; and when you have said it, cease."
>
> **—John Witherspoon**

In addition to the many varieties of informative and persuasive speeches, there are several types of speeches usually called "special occasion speeches," with which you'll want to achieve some familiarity. In this chapter we'll consider speeches to introduce someone, to present or accept an award, to secure goodwill or apologize, to dedicate something, to congratulate a graduating class (the commencement speech), to eulogize someone, to bid farewell, or to toast. We'll conclude the chapter with a look at the role of culture in the special occasion speech.

The Speech of Introduction

Chapter 1 (see Public Speaking Exercise 1.2) illustrated the speech designed to introduce you or another person to an audience. The aim of that speech is to help listeners learn something about you or another person. The **speech of introduction** considered here is a bit different and is usually designed to introduce a speaker or a topic area which a series of speakers will address. For example, before a speaker addresses an audience, another speaker often sets the stage by introducing both the speaker and the topic. At conventions, where a series of speakers address an audience, a speech of introduction might introduce the general topic on which the speakers will focus and perhaps provide connecting links among the several presentations.

In a speech of introduction, your main purpose is to gain the attention and arouse the interest of the audience. Your speech should pave the way for favorable and attentive listening. The speech of introduction is basically informative and follows the general patterns already discussed for the informative speech. The main difference is that instead of discussing a topic's issues, you discuss who the speaker is and what the speaker will talk about. In your speeches of introduction, follow these general principles:

◆ Establish the significance of the speech. Focus the audience's attention and interest on the main speaker and on the importance of what the speaker will say.

◆ Establish relevant connections among the speaker, the topic, and the audience and answer your listeners' inevitable question: Why should we listen to this speaker on this topic?

◆ Stress the speaker's credibility (see Chapter 10) by telling the audience what has earned this speaker the right to speak on this topic to this audience.

◆ Speak in a style and manner that is consistent with the main speech. Introduce the speaker with the same degree of formality that will prevail during the actual speech. Otherwise, the speaker will have to counteract an inappropriate atmosphere created by the speech of introduction.

◆ Be brief (relative to the length of the main speech). If the main speech is to be brief—say, 10 to 20 minutes—your introduction should be no longer than 1 or 2 minutes. If, on the other hand, the main speech is to be an hour long, then your introduction might last 5 to 10 minutes or even longer.

◆ Don't cover the substance of the topic the speaker will discuss. Also remember that clever stories, jokes, startling statistics, or historical analogies, which are often effective in speeches of introduction, will prove a liability if the main speaker intended to use this same material.

◆ Don't oversell the speaker or topic. Present the speaker in a positive light, but don't create an image that the speaker will find impossible to live up to.

Here is a sample speech of introduction, given by Jack Shea, introducing the 1998 John Huston Awards.

Good evening, and welcome to the fifth annual John Huston Award Dinner, tonight honoring Tom Cruise. At past events, we've honored such staunch advocates of artists' rights as Fred Zinnemann, Steven Spielberg, Martin Scorsese, and Milŏs Forman. Each evening has turned out to be celebratory, informative and entertaining—as well as inspiring—and tonight will be no exception. Now, helping to make this evening possible are our very generous sponsors: Sprint, Tiffen Manufacturing, DTS, and the Bandai Foundation. We also want to acknowledge United Airlines and Ray Ban Sunglasses for their support and contribution tonight. And, finally, we thank the Huston family and Robert Graham who has designed and created the John Huston Award.

In keeping with the spirit of the event, we've taken into consideration that one of the basic rights of the artist is to not have to work on an empty stomach. So, we've opted to serve the dinner before the testimonials. While you're digesting, we've prepared a short film about who we are, why we are, and what we are, and where we would be probably if we weren't who, why, and what we are. Enjoy the film, enjoy the evening, and thank you all for coming.[1]

The Speech of Presentation or Acceptance

We'll consider speeches of presentation and speeches of acceptance together, both because they're frequently paired and because the same general principles govern both types of speeches. In a **presentation speech** you seek to (1) place an award or honor in some kind of context and (2) give the award an extra air of dignity or status. A speech of presentation may focus on rewarding a colleague for an important accomplishment (being named Teacher of the Year) or on recognizing a particularly impressive performance (winning an Academy Award). It may honor an employee's service to a company or a student's outstanding grades or athletic abilities.

The **acceptance speech** is the other side of this honoring ceremony. Here the recipient accepts the award and attempts to place the award in some kind of context. At times the presentation and the acceptance speeches are rather informal and amount to a simple "You really deserve this" and an equally simple "Thank you." At other times—for example, in the presentation and acceptance of a Nobel Prize—the speeches are formal and are prepared in great detail and with great care. Such speeches are frequently reprinted in newspapers throughout the world. Somewhere between these two extremes lie average speeches of presentation and acceptance.

? DEVELOPING STRATEGIES

Presenting an Award. Adrian has been asked to present the award for Recording Artist of the Year (select your own favorite). The speech is to last no longer than one minute (approximately 150 words). What would you advise Adrian to say?

---

[1]Sample speech of introduction by Jack Shea at the 1998 John Huston Awards. Reprinted with permission from Director's Guild of America.

RESEARCH Link

General Research and Opinion Posts

In preparing a special occasion speech—or any speech—you'll find magazines a useful source. Articles in magazines differ greatly from those in professional journals. They're most often written by professional writers rather than by researchers. Magazine articles may be summaries of research by others or may be largely in the nature of opinion. Often they're simplified accounts of rather complex issues, written for the general public rather than for an audience of professional researchers. Further, they seldom undergo the rigorous review process that accompanies publication in a professional academic journal. As a result, articles appearing in popular magazines are much less reliable than those appearing in such professional research journals as, say, *Communication Monographs, Journal of Experimental Psychology,* or *The New England Journal of Medicine.* Nevertheless, magazine articles and general posts are often very helpful for speakers. Here are a few suggestions for finding the information you want.

Indexes. The *Readers' Guide to Periodical Literature,* available in print and electronic formats, covers magazine articles for the period from 1900 to the present. This guide indexes by subject and by author (in one convenient alphabetical index) articles published in about 180 different magazines. *Readers' Guide* is valuable for its broad coverage, but it's limited in that it covers mostly general publications and only a few of the more specialized ones. The *Alternative Press Index* (also available on CD-ROM, to which your library might subscribe) indexes approximately 250 "alternative, radical, and left publications." This index is valuable for speakers dealing with such issues as the Third World, minority rights, socialism, and the like. The National Institutes of Health maintain the National Library of Medicine at www.nlm.nih.gov/, an essential source for any topic dealing with health and medicine. A similar general index for legal issues from FindLaw is available at www.findlaw.com, and an index for financial issues from Goinvest at www.financialfind.com.

Listservs, Usenet groups, and the World Wide Web. Listservs, newsgroups, and the World Wide Web contain a wide variety of articles, many more than you could possibly use in any one speech or even in many speeches. Explore relevant listservs through Topica (www.topica.com), newsgroups through Google (http://groups.google.com/) and the vast array of World Wide Web documents with the help of your favorite search engines.

Research Activity. Consult one of the general indexes related to your speech topic, and in a two-minute speech explain why this index might also be of value to others in the class.

In your speeches of presentation, follow these two principles:

◆ State the reason for the presentation. Make clear why this particular award is being given to this particular person.

◆ State the importance of the award. The audience (as well as the group authorizing or sponsoring the award) will no doubt want to hear something about this. You might point out the importance of the award by referring to the previous recipients (assuming they're well known to the audience), emphasizing the status of the award (assuming that it's a prestigious award), or describing the award's influence on previous recipients.

Here is a sample speech of presentation given by Michael Greene as president of the National Academy of Recording Arts & Sciences. In this relatively short speech Greene presents five Life Achievement awards and succeeds in highlighting the careers and contributions of five outstanding recording artists.

Just as the Grammy Awards represent the best in today's music, our Life Achievement and Trustees Awards recognize individuals whose careers and cumulative contributions have had a profound effect on our culture. This year's five recipients, through their artistry and vision, have both enriched and advanced the recording medium.

Our first recipient is Barbra Streisand. She recorded her first album in 1962 and since then 50 albums have borne her artistic stamp, earning her eight Grammy Awards and a worldwide audience. A singer at heart, she's achieved unprecedented success as an actress, director, and producer as well. She is also a spokesperson for many humanitarian causes.

Henry Mancini. A twenty-time Grammy winner, redefined the art of composing for film while carving out an equally enviable career as a conductor, instrumentalist, songwriter, and arranger. A tireless supporter of arts education, the recording industry and the academy are deeply in the debt of this extraordinary gentleman.

Patsy Cline. The female country star who crossed over to pop and to timeless ballads. We lost Patsy far too soon, but her music continues to exert a powerful influence on several generations of country and pop artists.

Curtis Mayfield. Singer, songwriter, producer, guitarist, and record executive. The Chicago-born pioneer of the soul era influenced attitudes and opinions around the world with his socially relevant songs. A Grammy Legend Award winner last year, his energy and creativity continue to inspire us all.

And Miss Peggy Lee. "Why Don't You Do Right" was the title of her first hit with Benny Goodman and she's been doing right ever since—as a jazz and pop vocalist and song writer. Forever identified with such classics as "Mañana," "Fever," and "Is That All There Is," Peggy was the embodiment of coolness, hipness, and sophistication.

With us in the house this evening are two of our Life Achievement honorees. Please help me acknowledge Curtis Mayfield and Peggy Lee.[2]

In preparing and presenting your speech of acceptance, follow these three principles:

◆ Thank the people responsible for giving you the award—the academy members, the board of directors, the student body, your teammates.

◆ Acknowledge those who helped you achieve the award. Be specific without being overly detailed.

◆ Put the award into personal perspective by telling the audience what the award means to you right now and perhaps what it will mean to you in the future.

Here is an exceptionally moving and provocative acceptance speech that clearly illustrates how closely tied together are the speaker, audience, and occasion. The speech was given by Elizabeth Taylor in acceptance of the Jean Hersholt Humanitarian Award, given for her humanitarian work on behalf of people with AIDS. The speech was transcribed from television.

I have been on this stage many times as a presenter. I have sat in the audience as a loser. And I've had the thrill and the honor of standing here as a winner. But, I never, ever thought I would come out here to receive this award.

---

[2]Reprinted by permission of Michael Greene. Copyright © 1995 by Michael Greene.

USING TECHNOLOGY

For fun and insight into the acceptance speech, log on to the Academy Award Acceptance Speech Generator (http://www.chickenhead.com/stuff/oscar/index.asp). What can you learn from such automatic speech generators?

❖ **CONSIDER** what you'd say in accepting an award such as that pictured here. What would you want to be sure to include? Are there things that you would want to be sure to avoid saying?

It is the highest possible accolade I could receive from my peers. And for doing something I just have to do, that my passion must do.

I am filled with pride and humility. I accept this award in honor of all the men, women, and children with AIDS who are waging incredibly valiant battles for their lives—those to whom I have given my commitment, the real heroes of the pandemic of AIDS.

I am so proud of the work that people in Hollywood have done to help so many others, like dearest, gentle Audrey.[3] And while she is, I know, in heaven, forever guarding her beloved children, I will remain here as rowdy an activist as I have to be and, God willing, for as long as I have to be. [Applause]

Tonight I am asking for your help. I call upon you to draw from the depths of your being, to prove that we are a human race, to prove that our love outweighs our need to hate, that our compassion is more compelling than our need to blame, that our sensitivity to those in need is stronger than our greed, that our ability to reason overcomes our fear, and that at the end of each of our lives we can look back and be proud that we have treated others with the kindness, dignity, and respect that every human being deserves.

Thank you and God bless.[4]

Here is another speech of acceptance, this one written for the scene depicting John Nash's acceptance of the 1994 Nobel Prize in Economic Sciences in the 2002 movie *A Beautiful Mind* (http://www.americanrhetoric.com/MovieSpeeches/moviespeechabeautifulmind.html, accessed February 6, 2004):

Thank you. I've always believed in numbers and the equations and logics that lead to reason. But after a lifetime of such pursuits, I ask, "What truly is logic? Who decides reason?" My quest has taken me through the physical, the meta-physical, the delusional—and back. And I have made the most important discovery of my career, the most important discovery of my life: It is only in the mysterious equations of love that any logic or reasons can be found. I'm only here tonight because of you [his wife, Alicia]. You are the reason I am. You are all my reasons.

The Speech to Secure Goodwill

The **goodwill speech** is part information and part persuasion. On the surface, the speech informs the audience about a product, company, profession, institution, or person. Beneath this surface, however, lies a more persuasive purpose:

---

[3]Audrey Hepburn, who had been presented with a posthumous award for her humanitarian work, especially for UNICEF.

[4]Acceptance Speech for the Jean Hersholt Humanitarian Award by Elizabeth Taylor.

to heighten the image of a person, product, or company—to create a more positive attitude toward this person or thing. Many speeches of goodwill have a further persuasive purpose: to get the audience ultimately to change their behavior toward the person, product, or company.

A special type of goodwill speech is the speech of self-justification, in which the speaker seeks to justify his or her actions to the audience. Political figures do this frequently. Richard Nixon's "Checkers Speech," his Cambodia-bombing speeches, and, of course, his Watergate speeches are clear examples of speeches of self-justification. Edward Kennedy's Chappaquiddick speech, in which he attempted to justify what happened when Mary Jo Kopechne drowned, is another example. In securing goodwill, whether for another person or for yourself, consider the following suggestions:

"No, I haven't performed the procedure myself, but I've seen it done successfully on 'E.R.' and 'Chicago Hope.'"

◆ Demonstrate the contributions that deserve goodwill. Show how the audience may benefit from this company, product, or person. Or at least—in the speech of self-justification—show that the listeners have not been hurt; or, if they have been hurt, that the injury was unintentional.

◆ Stress uniqueness. In a world dominated by competition, the speech to secure goodwill must stress the uniqueness of the specific company, person, profession, situation, and so on. Distinguish it clearly from all others, otherwise, any goodwill you secure will be spread over the entire field.

◆ Establish credibility. Speeches to secure goodwill must also establish credibility, thereby securing goodwill for the individual or commodity. To do so, concentrate on those dimensions of credibility discussed in Chapter 10. Demonstrate that the person is competent, of good intention, and of high moral character.

◆ Don't be obvious. The effective goodwill speech looks, on the surface, very much like an objective informative speech. It will not appear to ask for goodwill, except on close analysis.

A particularly effective example of the speech to secure goodwill—perhaps *the* classic in the world of business—is the following speech by Lee Iacocca, former CEO of Chrysler Corporation. Iacocca was presented with a particularly difficult problem: Chrysler was accused of disconnecting odometers so that cars would appear to be new despite 40 miles of road testing. This was not a particularly horrible offense; most car buyers know that their cars are put through various tests. Yet it presented Iacocca with a credibility problem. He met this head on with a series of print and television advertisements in which he admitted the error of judgment and spelled out what he would do to correct it.

Testing cars is a good idea. Disconnecting odometers is a lousy idea. That's a mistake we won't make again at Chrysler. Period.

—Lee Iacocca

DEVELOPING STRATEGIES

Securing Goodwill. Natalie has been asked by her catering firm—which was cited by the Board of Health for several health violations a year ago—to present to the local Board of Education the firm's case for the catering contract for the entire elementary school district. The board members agree to hear Natalie but are generally reluctant to hire her firm because of its history of unsafe practices. What advice would you give Natalie for her speech, in which she'll try to secure goodwill (and another chance)?

Let me set the record straight.

1. For years, spot checking and road testing new cars and trucks that come off the assembly line with the odometers disengaged was standard industry practice. In our case, the average test mileage was 40 miles.
2. Even though the practice wasn't illegal, some companies began connecting their odometers. We didn't. In retrospect, that was dumb. Since October 1986, however, the odometer of every car and truck we've built has been connected, including those in the test program.
3. A few cars—and I mean a few—were damaged in testing badly enough that they should not have been fixed and sold as new. That was a mistake in an otherwise valid quality assurance program. And now we have to make it right.

What we're doing to make things right.

1. In all instances where our records show a vehicle was damaged in the test program and repaired and sold, we will offer to replace that vehicle with a brand new 1987 Chrysler Corporation model of comparable value. No ifs, ands, or buts.
2. We are sending letters to everyone our records show bought a vehicle that was in the test program and offering a free inspection. If anything is wrong because of a product deficiency, we will make it right.
3. Along with free inspection, we are extending their present 5-year or 50,000-mile protection plan on engine and powertrain to 7 years or 70,000 miles.
4. And to put their minds completely at ease, we are extending the 7-year or 70,000-mile protection to all major systems: brakes, suspension, air conditioning, electrical, and steering.

The quality testing program is a good program. But there were mistakes and we were too slow in stopping them. Now they're stopped. Done. Finished. Over.

Personally, I'm proud of our products. Proud of the quality improvements we've made. So we're going to keep right on testing. Because without it we couldn't have given America 5-year, 50,000-mile protection five years ahead of everyone else. Or maintained our warranty leadership with 7-year, 70,000 mile protection. I'm proud, too, of our leadership in safety-related recalls.

But I'm not proud of this episode. Not at all.

As Harry Truman once said, "The buck stops here." It just stopped. Period.[5]

DEVELOPING STRATEGIES

Speech of Apology. If you had been CEO of Ford Motors when the company was confronted with the evidence of defective tires on certain SUVs, what kind of announcement would you have issued? What strategies might you have taken from Iacocca?

Another type of goodwill speech is the speech of **apology,** a speech in which the speaker apologizes for some transgression and tries to restore his or her credibility. A particularly dramatic example of this type of speech, given by President William Jefferson Clinton, is presented here. The speech was given to the nation on August 17, 1998, after Clinton testified to a grand jury about a variety of issues. The issue that the nation and the media focused on, however, was the president's affair with a White House intern, Monica Lewinsky, including the extent to which he misled the country and the question of whether he obstructed justice. This speech was almost universally criticized for not expressing enough of an apology, for not asking for forgiveness, and for attacking the opposition rather than taking responsibility. (If you wish to learn more about this speech and some of the critical reactions to it, visit *The American Communication Journal* online at http://www.uark.edu/~aca and go to Volume Two, Issue Two [February, 1999].)

---

[5]*Testing Cars* by Lee Iacocca.

Good evening. This afternoon in this room, from this chair, I testified before the Office of Independent Counsel and a grand jury. I answered their questions truthfully, including questions about my private life, questions no American citizen would ever want to answer.

Still I must take complete responsibility for all my actions, both public and private. And that is why I am speaking to you tonight.

As you know, in a deposition in January, I was asked questions about my relationship with Monica Lewinsky. While my answers were legally accurate, I did not volunteer information. Indeed I did have a relationship with Miss Lewinsky that was not appropriate. In fact, it was wrong.

It constituted a critical lapse in judgment and a personal failure on my part for which I am solely and completely responsible.

But I told the grand jury today, and I say to you now, that at no time did I ask anyone to lie, to hide or destroy evidence, or to take any other unlawful action.

I know that my public comments and my silence about this matter gave a false impression. I misled people. Including even my wife. I deeply regret that.

I can only tell you I was motivated by many factors. First, by a desire to protect myself from the embarrassment of my own conduct. I was also very concerned about protecting my family. The fact that these questions were being asked in a politically inspired lawsuit which has since been dismissed was a consideration too.

In addition, I had real and serious concerns about an independent counsel investigation that began with private business dealings 20 years ago—dealings, I might add, about which an independent Federal agency found no evidence of any wrongdoing by me or my wife over two years ago.

The independent counsel investigation moved on to my staff and friends. Then into my private life. And now the investigation itself is under investigation. This has gone on too long, cost too much, and hurt too many innocent people.

Now this matter is between me, the two people I love most—my wife and our daughter—and our God. I must put it right. And I am prepared to do whatever it takes to do so.

Nothing is more important to me personally, but it is private. And I intend to reclaim my family life for my family. It's nobody's business but ours. Even Presidents have private lives. It is time to stop the pursuit of personal destruction and the prying into private lives and get on with our national life.

Our country has been distracted by this matter for too long, and I take my responsibility for my part in all of this. That is all I can do. Now it is time, in fact it is past time, to move on. We have important work to do, real opportunities to seize, real problems to solve, real security matters to face.

And so tonight I ask you to turn away from the spectacle of the past seven months, to repair the fabric of our national discourse and to return our attention to all the challenges and all the promise of the next American century.

Thank you for watching and good night.

USING TECHNOLOGY

Visit the POTUS (Presidents of the United States) website at www.ipl.org/ref/POTUS, which contains, among many other things, the inaugural addresses of the presidents. Select one address and identify its thesis and its major propositions. What do you think might be a likely thesis for the next presidential inaugural address?

The Speech of Dedication

The **dedication speech** is designed to give some specific meaning to, say, a new research lab, a store opening, or the start of the building of a bridge. This speech is usually given at a rather formal occasion. You'll need to do some research on exactly what it is that is being dedicated. For example, if it's a bridge, then you'll want to learn something about why the bridge was built, when it was

A CASE OF *Ethics*

Using Fear Appeals

You're an elementary school teacher and are required to teach your eighth-grade class the unit on sex education. Your objective, which is mandated by the state syllabus but also is consistent with your own feeling, is to get students to avoid sexual relationships until they are much older. But you know from talking with students that many of them intend to have sexual relationships at the earliest opportunity; in fact, some are currently sexually active. You wonder if it would be ethical to use fear appeals to scare the students about the potential dangers of sex. For example, you could show them photos of people with advanced cases of sexually transmitted diseases, youngsters living in poverty because they now have children to support, and so on. Your purpose, you feel, is a noble one; but you wonder if the means to achieve that end are ethical.

What would you do in this situation as you tried to balance accuracy with advocacy of ideas that you believed would benefit your audience? More generally, what ethical guidelines should govern the use of appeals to fear? Would you advocate different guidelines for audiences composed of adults and audiences composed of children?

constructed, and who designed it. In preparing a dedication speech, consider the following suggestions:

◆ State the reason you're giving the dedication; for example, identify the connection you have to the project.

◆ Explain exactly what is being dedicated; for example, the opening of the bridge linking Roosevelt Island to Manhattan.

◆ Tell the audience who is responsible for the project; for example, who designed the bridge, who constructed it, who paid for it.

◆ Explain why this project is significant—what advantages it will create. For example, describe the relevance the bridge has to your audience; for example, what changes will occur as a result of this bridge and how the bridge will benefit your listeners.

? DEVELOPING STRATEGIES

Commencement Speech.
Leland will be delivering the commencement speech to your graduating class. He wants to criticize the poor educational (especially computer) facilities the college has provided students over the last four years as well as the college's lack of placement services to help secure jobs for the students. Given that a commencement speech is usually a positive, congratulatory exercise, what would you advise Leland to do?

The Commencement Speech

The **commencement speech** recognizes and celebrates the end of some training period, such as the listeners' school or college years. The commencement speech is designed to congratulate and inspire the recent graduates and is often intended to mark the transition from school to the next stage in life. Usually the person asked to give a commencement speech is a well-known personality. The speakers at college graduations—depending on the prestige of the institution—are often important men and women in the world: presidents, senators, religious leaders, Nobel Prize winners, famous scientists, and people of similar accomplishment. Or a commencement speech may be given by a student who has achieved some exceptional goal; for example, the student with the highest grade point average or the winner of a prestigious award. In giving a commencement speech, consider the following:

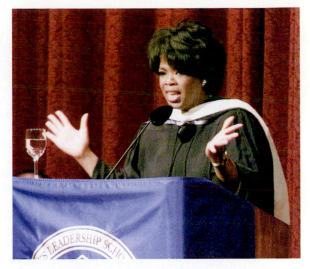

- Organize the speech in a temporal pattern, beginning with the past, commenting on the present, and projecting into the future.
- Do your research. Learn something about the school, the student body, the goals and ambitions of the graduates, and integrate these into your speech.
- Be brief. Recognize that your audience has other things on their minds—the graduation party, for example—and may become restless if your speech is too long.
- Congratulate the graduates—but also congratulate the parents, friends, and instructors who also contributed to this day.
- Offer the graduates some kind of motivational message, some guidance, some suggestions for taking their education and using it in their lives.
- Offer your own good wishes to the graduates.

❖ **CONSIDER** the types of messages that graduating classes hear from commencement speakers. What types of messages would you want to hear? What would you not want to hear?

The Eulogy

The **eulogy** is a speech of tribute in which you seek to praise someone who has died. In the eulogy you attempt to put the person's life and contributions in perspective and show them in a positive light. This type of speech is often given at a funeral or at the anniversary of the person's birth or death. This is not the time for a balanced appraisal of the individual's life. Rather, it's a time for praise. In developing the eulogy, consider the following:

- Relate the person whose life you're celebrating to yourself, to those in the audience—and, if appropriate, to the larger audience—for example, the scientific community, the world of book lovers, or those who have devoted their lives to peace.
- Be specific; show that you really knew the person or know a great deal about the person and the best way to do that is to give specific examples from the person's life. Then combine the specifics with the more general so that the audience can see these specifics as being a part of some larger whole—for example, after you mention the several books that the author wrote, frame the author's contribution in a more general way within the mystery genre or contemporary poetry genre.
- Make the audience see that this person is deserving of the praise you are bestowing on him or her by explaining what this person accomplished and how this person influenced—for example—the world of patient care, the design of safer cars, and so on.
- Show the audience what they can learn from this individual.

USING TECHNOLOGY

To locate information about someone who is deceased and whom you admire, visit the *New York Times* website (you can access this through Research Navigator at www. researchnavigator.com) or http://www.rootsweb.com/~obituary/ (see the accompanying website on p. 283). Write a brief two-minute eulogy for this person.

Here is a brief version of an especially moving eulogy, written and delivered by Bernard Brommel, a professor of communication and family therapist, at the funeral of his sister. The complete text of this eulogy is available at www.ablongman.com/devito; see "Example of a Eulogy."

Today we gather to honor the memory of Florence who is at rest from her labors and we rejoice in knowing her love and good deeds remain with us, the living. It's an honor to speak on behalf of her family, especially seven wonderful sons, her husband Bill, my siblings, and our Aunt/Stepmother, Florence, who was her namesake.

Florence set an example for courage, drive, responsibility, patience, honesty, tolerance, and countless other virtues. Most of all, she set for us an example of how to love, both as a giver and a receiver of it. It took so little to please her and evoke that quiet smile of appreciation. Gentle and kind, never loud or outspoken, she supported each of us by her nurturing nature and that rare ability, seldom found in many humans, to listen without judging. It's easy to understand why it was her heart that kept her alive in the last weeks. Everything in her system failed, but not her heart! Her physical heart was symbolic of her loving heart that reached each of us and was the last to go.

As the oldest of nine, she grew up with far more responsibility than most children. She grew up at the side of her mother as a constant helper. I remember her stirring cakes at five or six; there were no mixes then! She churned butter by hand, washed thousands of dishes, milk pails, diapers, and scrubbed those splintered floors. Mama was frequently ill or having difficult pregnancies. Florence took over! No wonder Florence could later in life manage a bank.

CRITICAL LISTENING/THINKING *Link*

Listening to Credibility Appeals

Credibility appeals are especially relevant to the special occasion speech. When you listen to credibility appeals, evaluate them critically. Here are three questions that you'll find helpful:

- *Is the dimension of credibility used relevant to the issue at hand?* For example, are the politician's family members (nice though they may be) relevant to his or her position on gun control or social security or immigration? Is the politician's former military service (or the lack of it) relevant to the issue being discussed?
- *Are credibility appeals being used instead of argument and evidence?* In typical examples of invalid credibility appeals, speakers may emphasize their educational background (to establish "competence"), appear at religious rituals (to establish "moral character"), or endeavor to present themselves as take-charge, alpha-type individuals (to demonstrate "charisma"). When done to divert attention from the issues or to mask the absence of evidence, such appeals are meaningless.
- *Are the credibility appeals true?* The actor who advertises toothpaste dressed as a dentist is still an actor doing a modeling job, not a dentist. Too often people unconsciously attribute credibility to a performance because of a uniform. Even when the endorser is a real dentist, remember that this dentist is getting paid for the endorsement. Although this doesn't necessarily make the endorsement false, it does (or should) make you wonder.

Getting Critical. How many credibility appeals can you find in an evening of television viewing? Do such appeals influence you, or do you easily dismiss them?

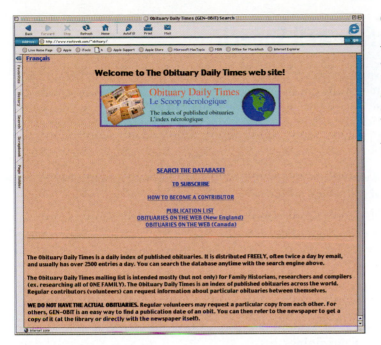

Obituary Index

(http://www.rootsweb.com/~obituary)
This is one of the many popular obituary websites. Obituaries provide a wealth of information on people who died recently as well as on those long gone. Obituary websites are excellent adjuncts to biography websites. Together, these resources should help you find just about any information you want on an individual.

Three years ago this week we buried Dad. Two themes characterized his life: one, that it was a hard life but it got easier, and a second one, work—work—work. Florence's life experiences were similar. In our time Florence represented what has happened to women in transition—a transition for women from a domestic life to combining a professional life with raising a large family. She married at 18. She never planned a career; it just evolved out of necessity! Like her mother, or favorite aunt, Dolly, she might have preferred staying home with her sons. There were no maternity leaves; she saved her two-week vacations to coincide with delivery dates, and then back to work to keep the groceries on the table.

For us, the living, that have loved Florence, it's so hard to accept her death from cancer. Sixty-one years isn't long enough for this gentle soul, but God has called her and we have to accept His decision.

To each of her sons, I express my admiration for the way you helped look after your mom, not only in illness but throughout the years. You stayed out of trouble and made life easier for her because you did. In the hospital, Louie, you rubbed her feet and talked to her about her fears. Greg and Mike, each of you stopped by at noon hour or after work. David—you probably knew your mother best and always brought a special smile to her parched lips. To Will, the farmer, who she said was the loudest of her quiet boys. You could tell that he loved his mom whenever their eyes met. To John and Bob, identical twins who only their mother knew from day one the differences between the two of you. You knew how special you were to her. Finally to my siblings—the time has come for us to say farewell to Florence. Weren't we blessed with a great sister who left us with so much joy to remember? Thanks, Bill, for your love for our sister. Florence will have the last words. I asked her what she wanted me to say on this occasion and she, through tears, said, "Tell each of those at my funeral, 'I love you and I'll miss you, but I'm OK!'"[6]

---

[6]Reprinted by permission.

The Farewell Speech

In the **farewell speech** you say goodbye to an organization or to colleagues and signal that you're moving on. In this speech you'll want to express your positive feelings to those you're leaving. Generally, the farewell speech is given after you've achieved some level of distinction within a company or other group or organization that you're now leaving. In developing a farewell speech, consider the following:

◆ Thank those who made life interesting, helped you in your position, taught you essential principles, and so on.

◆ Set your achievements in a positive light, but do it modestly.

◆ Express your enjoyment of the experience. This is a time for positive reflection, not for critical evaluation, so put aside the negative memories, at least for this speech.

◆ If appropriate, state your reason for leaving and your plans for the future.

◆ Express good wishes to those who remain.

◆ Offer some words of wisdom that you learned and that you now want to pass on to those remaining.

Here is an example of a farewell speech, delivered by Cal Ripken Jr. on his retirement from baseball (http://www.americanrhetoric.com/speeches/calripkenjr. htm, accessed February 6, 2004):

As a kid, I had this dream.

And I had the parents that helped me shape that dream.

Then, I became part of an organization, the Baltimore Orioles—the Baltimore Orioles, to help me grow that dream. Imagine playing for my hometown team for my whole career.

And I have a wife and children to help me share and save the fruits of that dream.

And I've had teammates who filled my career with unbelievable moments.

And you fans, who have loved the game, and have shared your love with me.

Tonight, we close a chapter of this dream—my playing career.

But I have other dreams.

You know, I might have some white hair on top of this head—well, maybe on the sides of this head. But I'm really not that old.

My dreams for the future include pursuing my passion for baseball. Hopefully, I will be able to share what I have learned. And, I would be happy if that sharing would lead to something as simple as a smile on the face of others.

One question I've been repeatedly asked these past few weeks is, "How do I want to be remembered?" My answer has been simple: to be remembered at all is pretty special.

I might also add that if, if I am remembered, I hope it's because, by living my dream, I was able to make a difference.

Thank you.

RESEARCH *Link*

Book Sources

Books will provide you with especially detailed information.

Each library catalogs its books, journals, and government documents in its own particular way, depending on its size and the needs of its users. Every library, however, makes use of some form of computerized catalog. These catalogs are uniformly easy and efficient to use. The catalog is the best place to find out what books are in your college library or in a library whose books you can secure on interlibrary loan.

Generally, you access material by looking up your major subject heading(s). A good way to do this is to make a list of the five or six major concepts that appear in your speech and look each of these up in the library catalog. Create a reasonably complete bibliography of available sources and examine each one. Sometimes you may want to locate works by or about a particular person. In this case you'd look up the author's name much as you would a concept.

Browsing through any large brick-and-mortar bookstore is almost sure to give you insights into your topic. If you're talking about something that people are interested in today, there's likely to be a book dealing with the subject on the shelves of most bookstores. Also visit some of the online bookstores, such as Amazon (www.amazon.com), Barnes & Noble (www.bn.com), or Borders (www.Borders.com). In addition, other useful sites include: http://aaupnet.org/ (the Association of American University Presses) and http://www.cs.cmu.edu/Web/People/spok/banned-books.html (contains links to texts of books that have been banned in the United States and elsewhere). Some online bookstores now enable you to search some of their books for specific topics and read a paragraph or so on each topic reference.

Research Activity. What are the advantages and disadvantages of browsing through an online versus a brick-and-mortar bookstore?

The Toast

The **toast** is a brief speech designed to celebrate a person or an occasion. You might, for example, toast the next CEO of your company, a friend who just got admitted to a prestigious graduate program, or a colleague on the occasion of a promotion. Often toasts are given at weddings or at the start of a new venture. The toast is designed to say hello or good luck in a relatively formal sense. In developing your toast consider the following:

◆ Be brief; realize that people want to get on with the festivities and don't want to listen to an overly long speech.

◆ Focus attention on the person or persons you're toasting, not on yourself.

◆ Avoid inside jokes that only you and the person you're toasting understand; remember that the toast is not only for the benefit of the person you're toasting but for the audience as well.

USING TECHNOLOGY

Using one of the popular search engines, look for one of the types of special occasion speeches discussed here. Or take a look at http://www.blissweddings.com/library/toasts.asp for a wide variety of toasts, including poems, vows, and ideas for speeches. How might these websites help you prepare special occasion speeches?

◆ When you raise your glass in the toast—an almost obligatory part of toasting—make the audience realize that they should drink and that your speech is at an end.

The Special Occasion Speech in Cultural Perspective

Like all forms of communication, the special occasion speech must be developed with a clear understanding of the influence of culture. For example, the discussion of the speech of introduction suggested that you not oversell the speaker; excessive exaggeration is generally evaluated negatively in much of the United States. On the other hand, exaggerated praise often is expected in some Latin cultures.

Similarly, the discussion of the speech of goodwill suggested that you present yourself as being worthy of the goodwill rather than as a supplicant begging for it. In some cultures, however, this attitude might be seen as arrogant and disrespectful to the audience. In some Asian cultures, for example, pleading for goodwill would be seen as suitably modest and respectful of the audience.

In introducing or in paying tribute to someone, consider the extent to which you wish to focus on the person's contribution to the group or to individual achievement. An audience with a predominantly collectivist orientation will expect to hear group-centered achievements, whereas an audience of predominantly individualist orientation will expect to hear more individually focused achievements.

❖ **CONSIDER** the influence that culture has on special occasion speeches. What does your culture say about the toast? The eulogy? The speech of dedication?

Culture also will influence the way in which an acceptance should be framed. Not surprisingly, collectivist cultures would suggest that you give a lot of credit to the group, whereas individualist cultures would suggest that taking self-credit is appropriate when it's due. Thus, if you were accepting an award for a performance in a movie, an extreme collectivist orientation would lead you to give great praise to others and to claim that without others you never could have accomplished what you did. An extreme individualist orientation would lead you to accept the award and the praise for yourself; after all, you did it! In the media business, as you see from the numerous televised award shows, everyone gives thanks to almost everyone connected with the project. That's the custom; the collectivist form of expression has become the norm, at least in the context of show business. To examine your own tendencies toward an individual or collectivist orientation, take the accompanying self-test.

USING TECHNOLOGY

Visit one or several of the presidential libraries (see the National Archives and Records Administration's website hotlinks to these libraries at http://www.archives.gov/). What kinds of special occasion speeches can you find in these libraries? What other types of information are archived in these libraries?

Test YOURSELF

How Individualistic Are You?

Indicate how true or false the following statements are of you. Use the following scale: Almost always true = 1; more often true than false = 2; true about half the time and false about half the time = 3; more often false than true = 4; and almost always false = 5.

_____ **1.** My own goals rather than the goals of my group (for example, my extended family, my organization) are the more important.

_____ **2.** I feel responsible for myself and to my own conscience rather than for the entire group and to the group's values and rules.

_____ **3.** Success to me depends on my contribution to the group effort and the group's success rather than on my own individual success or on surpassing others.

_____ **4.** Being kind and polite is usually more important than telling the truth, so I might say things that are not true in a literal sense if they allow the other person to appear in a positive light.

_____ **5.** In my communications I prefer a direct and explicit communication style; I believe in "telling it like it is," even if it hurts.

❖ **HOW DID YOU DO?** To compute your individualist–collectivist score, follow these steps:

1. Reverse the scores for items 3 and 4: If your response was 1, reverse it to a 5; if your response was 2, reverse it to a 4; if your response was 3, keep it as 3; if your response was 4, reverse it to a 2; and if your response was 5, reverse it to a 1.
2. Add your scores for all 5 items, being sure to use the reverse scores for items 3 and 4 in your calculations. Your score should be between 5 (indicating a highly individualist orientation) and 25 (indicating a highly collectivist orientation).
3. Position your score on the following scale:

5 _____ 12/13 _____ 25
highly individualist   about equally individualist   highly collectivist
                            and collectivist

❖ **WHAT WILL YOU DO?** Do your score and your position on the scale accurately measure the way in which you see yourself on this dimension? Is this orientation going to help you achieve your personal and professional goals? Might it hinder you? What can you do to make your individualist and collectivist attitudes more productive?

Summary of Concepts and Skills

In this chapter we discussed special occasion speeches, highlighting a variety of specific types, and placed special occasion speeches in a cultural context.

The Speech of Introduction

The speech of introduction introduces another speaker or series of speakers. In this speech: Establish a connection among speaker, topic, and audience; establish the speaker's credibility; be consistent in style and manner with the major speech; be brief; avoid covering what the speaker intends to discuss; and avoid overselling the speaker.

The Speech of Presentation of Acceptance

The speech of presentation explains why the presentation is being made, and the speech of acceptance expresses thanks for the award. In the speech of presentation, state the reason for the presentation and state the importance of the award. In the speech of acceptance, thank those who gave the award, thank those who helped, and state the meaning of the award to you.

The Speech to Secure Goodwill

The speech to secure goodwill attempts to secure or, more often, regain, the listeners' good graces. In this speech: Stress benefits the audience may derive; stress uniqueness; establish your credibility and the credibility of the subject; avoid being obvious in securing goodwill; and avoid pleading for goodwill.

The Speech of Dedication

The speech of dedication gives specific meaning to some event or object. In this speech: Explain why you're giving the speech; explain what is being dedicated; state who is responsible for the event or object; and say why this is significant, especially to your specific listeners.

The Commencement Speech

The commencement speech celebrates the end of some training period. In this speech: Consider the values of a temporal organizational pattern; learn something about the training organization and demonstrate this knowledge in your speech; be brief; congratulate the larger audience, not only those who went through the training; offer some motivational message; and offer your own good wishes.

The Eulogy

The eulogy seeks to praise someone who has died. In this speech: Show the connection between yourself and the person you're eulogizing; be specific; combine specifics with the general; stress that the person is deserving of your praise; and show your listeners what they can learn from this person.

The Farewell Speech

The farewell speech signals a transition between what was and what will be. In this speech: Thank those who helped you; portray the positives of the past; explain your reasons for making the transition; and offer some words of wisdom, some motivational message.

The Toast

The toast celebrates a person or an occasion. In the toast: Be brief; focus attention on the person or event you're toasting; avoid references that listeners may not understand; and make it clear that this is the end of your speech when you raise your glass.

The Special Occasion Speech in Cultural Perspective

The special occasion speech needs to be developed with an awareness of the cultural norms and rules specific to the occasion and to the audience members. Especially relevant here is the distinction between individualist and collectivist cultures.

Vocabulary Quiz

The Special Occasion Speech

Match the terms dealing with the special occasion speech with their definitions. Record the number of the definition next to the term.

_____ speech of acceptance

_____ toast

_____ commencement speech

_____ farewell speech

_____ eulogy

_____ speech of apology

_____ speech of presentation

_____ speech of self-justification

_____ speech of introduction

_____ speech to secure goodwill

1. Introduces another speaker or general topic area of, say, a series of speeches.
2. The counterpart or response to the speech of presentation.
3. A speech given with an award or honor.
4. A speech designed to improve or rehabilitate the image of the speaker.
5. A speech in which the speaker asks forgiveness for some transgression.
6. A speech designed to increase positive regard for a person, product, or idea.
7. A speech in praise of a dead person.
8. A speech designed to say goodbye.
9. A speech designed to congratulate and inspire graduates.
10. A short speech designed to say good luck or express honor for some person.

Web Explorations

Companion Website

www.ablongman.com/devito

Chapter 11 of the Companion Website provides an extended example of a eulogy, President William Clinton's farewell address, Martin Scorsese's acceptance speech for the John Huston Award for Artists Rights, and an exercise, "Developing the Speech of Tribute."

Public Speaking Exercises

11.1 Developing the Speech of Introduction

Prepare a speech of introduction approximately two minutes in length. For this experience you may assume that the speaker you introduce will speak on any topic you wish. Do, however, assume a topic appropriate to the speaker and to your audience—your class. You may wish to select your introduction from one of the following suggestions:

1. Introduce a historical figure to the class.
2. Introduce a contemporary religious, political, or social leader.
3. Prepare a speech of introduction that someone might give to introduce you to your class.
4. Introduce a famous media (film, television, radio, recording, writing) personality—alive or dead.
5. Introduce a series of speeches debating the pros and cons of a cultural emphasis in college courses.

11.2 Developing the Speech of Presentation/Acceptance

Form pairs. One person should serve as the presenter and one as the recipient of a particular award or honor. These two people can select a situation from the list presented below or make one up themselves. The presenter should prepare and present a two-minute speech in which she or he presents one of the awards to the other person. The recipient should prepare and present a two-minute speech of acceptance.

1. Academy Award for best performance.
2. Gold watch for service to the company.
3. Ms. or Mr. America.
4. Five million dollars for the college library.
5. Award for contributions to intercultural understanding.
6. Book of the Year award.
7. Mother (Father) of the Year award.
8. Honorary Ph.D. in communication for outstanding contributions to the art.
9. Award for outstanding achievement in architecture.
10. Award for raising a prize hog.

11.3 Developing the Speech to Secure Goodwill

Prepare a speech approximately three to five minutes in length in which you attempt to secure the goodwill of your audience toward one of the following:

1. Your college (visualize your audience as high school seniors).
2. A particular profession or way of life (teaching, religious life, nursing, law, medicine, bricklaying, truck driving, etc.).
3. This course (visualize your audience as college students who have not yet taken this course).
4. The policies of a particular foreign country now in the news.
5. A specific multinational corporation.

12 Speaking in Small Groups

Why Read This Chapter?

It will enable you to function more effectively in small groups by helping you to:

❖ solve problems effectively in a variety of small groups, including groups widely used in business and the professions such as nominal groups, Delphi groups, and quality circles

❖ function as an effective member or leader in a small group setting

❖ present the group's thinking in a wide variety of public speaking situations

> Do not wait for leaders, do it alone, person to person.
>
> **—Mother Teresa**

You'll often find yourself in small group situations—especially in the workplace—in which the principles of public speaking will have considerable relevance. In this chapter we'll look at the small group experience and particularly at speaking in small groups.

Small Groups

A **small group** is a relatively small collection of individuals (usually around 5 to 12) who are related to one another by some common purpose and have some degree of organization among them. People on a bus do not constitute a group, because they're not working toward some common purpose. Should the bus get stuck in a ditch, however, the riders may quickly become a group and work together to get the bus back on the road.

Culture, Gender, and the Small Group

Many groups—especially long-standing work groups—develop into small cultures with their own norms. These **group norms** are rules or standards that say which behaviors are appropriate (for example, being willing to take on added tasks or directing conflict toward issues rather than toward people) and which

"I won it for being the most noncompetitive in preschool."

are inappropriate (for example, coming late or failing to contribute actively). Sometimes these rules for appropriate behavior are explicitly stated in a company contract or policy: "All members must attend department meetings." Sometimes rules are implicit: "Members should be well groomed." Regardless of whether norms are spelled out or not, they're powerful regulators of group members' behaviors.

Norms may apply to individual members as well as to the group as a whole and, of course, will differ from one group to another (Axtell, 1990, 1993). For example, in Japan and in many Arab countries, it's customary to begin meetings with what many Americans would see as unnecessary socializing. Many Americans prefer to get right down to business, but the Japanese prefer rather elaborate socializing before getting to the business at hand. They want to first experience confidence and trust (DeVries, 1994).

In the United States men and women in business are expected to interact when making business decisions as well as when socializing. In Muslim and Buddhist societies, however, religious restrictions prevent mixing the sexes. In many societies—those of the United States, Bangladesh, Australia, Germany, Finland, and Hong Kong, for example—punctuality for business meetings is very important. But in countries like Morocco, Italy,

Brazil, Zambia, Ireland, and Panama, time is less highly regarded; being late is no great insult and is even expected. In the United States and much of Asia and Europe, meetings are held between two individuals or groups. In many Persian Gulf nations, however, the business executive is likely to conduct meetings with several different people—sometimes dealing with totally different issues—at the same time. In such a situation you have to expect to share what in the United States would be "your time" with these other parties. In the United States very little interpersonal touching goes on during business meetings; in Arab countries, however, touching (for example, hand holding) is common and is a gesture of friendship.

Cross-cultural studies show that members of different cultures have different tendencies to conform to group norms—even when these norms conflict with their own perceptions. For example, in a classic study, a participant is seated with confederates of the experimenter who misjudge the length of a line shown on a screen (Asch, 1946). Does the subject report what he or she really sees or go along with the majority? The answer is that many people do contradict their own perceptions to go along with the group, but the degree of "going along" varies with the culture. For example (and contrary to popular stereotypes), German and Japanese respondents are less conformist than North Americans or Chinese participants (Moghaddam, Taylor, & Wright, 1993). It's also interesting to note that people are showing less conformity to group norms today than they did when the original studies were conducted in the 1950s (Moghaddam, Taylor, & Wright, 1993).

USING TECHNOLOGY

Visit http://www.aol.com/netfind/scoop/newsgroup_etiquette.html which provides information on how to politely post a message to a newsgroup. What small group communication norms can you detect from these suggestions? After you read the information, visit one or a few newsgroups. Can you see these communication norms manifested in the messages posted?

Problem Solving in Groups

Although groups can serve any number of functions, their role as vehicles of problem solving is central, so we will concentrate on that function here. A **problem-solving group** is a collection of individuals who meet to solve a problem or to reach a decision. Group problem solving requires not only knowledge of small group communication techniques but also a thorough knowledge of the particular problem.

Generally, problem-solving groups follow a pattern that philosopher John Dewey (1910) identified in his six steps in reflective thinking. Following this **problem-solving sequence** will make the process of problem solving more efficient and more effective.

Step 1. Define and Analyze the Problem. Define the problem as an open-ended question ("How can we improve the student newspaper?") rather than as a statement ("The student newspaper needs to be improved") or a yes/no question ("Does the student newspaper need improvement?"). The open-ended question allows for greater freedom of exploration.

Limit the problem so that it identifies a manageable area for discussion. A question such as "How can we improve the university?" is too broad and general. Rather, identify one subdivision of the university on which the group might focus, such as the student newspaper, student–faculty relationships, or registration.

Step 2. Establish Criteria for Evaluating Solutions. Before any solutions are proposed, identify the standards or criteria that you'll use in evaluating the solutions or in selecting one solution over another. For example, you might decide that ideas for improving the student newspaper must not increase the budget, must lead to a higher number of advertisers, must increase the readership by at least 10 percent, and so on.

Step 3. Identify Possible Solutions. Identify as many solutions as possible, focusing on quantity rather than quality. Brainstorming may be particularly useful at this point (see discussion of idea-generation groups on page 297). Solutions to the student newspaper problem might include initiating reviews of faculty publications, adding student evaluations of specific courses, or incorporating employment information in the paper.

Step 4. Evaluate Solutions. Evaluate each solution according to the standards already identified. For example, to what extent would incorporating employment information meet the criteria for evaluating solutions? Would this move increase the budget? Would it lead to an increase in advertising revenue?

Step 5. Select the Best Solution(s). Select the best solution or solutions. Thus, for example, if "reviews of faculty publications" and "course evaluations" best met the criteria for evaluating solutions, the group might then decide to select these as the solutions to the problem.

Step 6. Test Selected Solution(s). After selecting one or more solutions, put them into operation to test their effectiveness. For example, you might decide to run the two new features in the paper for several months. Then you might poll students about the new features or examine the number of copies purchased. Or you might analyze the advertising revenue or see if readership has increased. If you found positive results, you'd then recommend these solutions as permanent changes.

If, on the other hand, the selected solutions proved ineffective, you'd go back to one of the previous stages and repeat part of the process. Often this step takes the form of selecting other solutions to test. But it also may involve going farther back—to, for example, reanalysis of the problem, identification of other solutions, or restatement of the criteria for evaluating solutions.

Here are five types of problem-solving groups that are popular in the workplace and that will give you an overview of the way in which the small group can be used to solve problems.

The Nominal Group

The **nominal group** is a method of problem solving that uses limited discussion and confidential voting to obtain a group decision. It's especially helpful when some members may be reluctant to voice their opinions in a regular problem-solving group or when the issue is controversial or sensitive. With this technique, each member contributes equally and each contribution is treated equally. Another advantage of this technique is that it can be accomplished in a

DEVELOPING STRATEGIES

Group Techniques. Lilly wants to explore ways to increase alumni financial support for the college where she works as a development officer. How might Lilly use small group formats (for example, focus groups, nominal groups, and quality circles) to develop strategies to move alumni to make the largest possible contributions?

Library of Congress
(www.loc.gov)
As you can see from its home page, the Library of Congress website contains a wealth of information and should be useful to you in your speeches as well as in just about any research task you can imagine.

relatively short period of time. The nominal group technique can be divided into seven steps (Kelly, 1994):

1. The problem is defined and clarified for all members.
2. Each member writes down (without discussion or consultation with others) his or her ideas on or possible solutions to the problem.
3. Each member—in sequence—states one idea from his or her list, which is recorded on a board or flip chart so everyone can see it. This process is repeated until all suggestions are stated and recorded. Duplicates are then eliminated. Group agreement is secured before ideas are combined.
4. Each suggestion is clarified without debate. Ideally, each suggestion should be given equal time.
5. Each member rank orders the suggestions.
6. The rankings of the members are combined to get a group ranking which is then written on the board.
7. Clarification, discussion, and possible reordering may follow.

The highest-ranking solution may then be selected to be tested, or perhaps several high-ranking solutions may be put into operation.

The Delphi Group

In the **Delphi method,** a group of "experts" communicate by repeatedly responding to questionnaires (Kelly, 1994; Tersine & Riggs, 1980). This method is especially useful when you want to involve people who are geographically distant from one another; for example, when your sales staff is distributed throughout the United States and Asia and management is in San Francisco. The Delphi method also is useful when you want all members to be a part of the solution and to uphold it, and when you want to minimize the effects of dominant members or peer pressure. This method is best explained as a series of steps (Kelly, 1994):

1. The problem is defined (for example, "We need to improve intradepartmental communication"). The responsibilities of members are specified (for example, "Each member should contribute five ideas on this specific question").

2. Each member then anonymously contributes five ideas in writing. Formerly completed through questionnaires sent through traditional mail, this stage is now more frequently done through e-mail, greatly increasing the speed with which the Delphi process can be accomplished.

3. The ideas of all members are combined, written up, and distributed to all members who may be asked to select the three or four best ideas from this composite list.

4. From these responses another list is produced and distributed to all members who may be asked to select the one or two best ideas.

5. From these responses another list is produced and distributed to all members. The process may be repeated any number of times, but usually three rounds are sufficient for achieving a fair amount of agreement.

6. The "final" solutions are identified and are communicated to all members.

The Quality Circle Group

In **quality circles,** groups of workers (usually about 6 to 12) investigate and make recommendations for improving the quality of some organizational function. The members are drawn from the workers whose area is being studied. Thus, for example, if the problem is to improve advertising on the Internet, then the quality circle membership would be drawn from the advertising and computer departments. Generally, the motivation for establishing quality circles is economic; the company's aim is to improve quality and profitability.

RESEARCH Link

U.S. Government Publications

The U.S. Government Printing Office (GPO) is the largest publisher in the world. GPO publications originate in the various divisions of the federal government's 13 departments, each of which is a prolific publisher. The Departments of Agriculture, Commerce, Defense, Education, Energy, Health and Human Services, Housing and Urban Development, Interior, Justice, Labor, State, Treasury, and Transportation issue reports, pamphlets, books, and assorted documents dealing with their various concerns. Because of the wealth of published material, it would be best to first consult one of the guides to government publications. A few useful guides that should be in your college library include *Government Reference Books* (1968 to date), *A Bibliography of United States Government Bibliographies,* and *U.S. Government Books: Recent Releases* (published quarterly). The *Congressional Record* (1873 to date) is issued daily when Congress is in session.

Research Activity. Take a look at the Library of Congress website at www.loc.gov (see p. 295); visit the website for the Government Printing Office (www.access.gup.gov), which publishes much of its material on the Web); or see the Thomas website (http://thomas.loc.gov), which contains the *Congressional Record* as well as much legislative information. What kind of information here might be of value to you in your speeches? In your future profession?

❖ **CONSIDER** how you might set up a quality circle group to investigate the college experience. What specific questions would you want the group to address?

Another related goal is to improve worker morale; because quality circles involve workers in decision making, workers may feel empowered and more essential to the organization. The basic assumption of quality circle groups is that the people who work on tasks will be those best able to improve their results—by pooling their insights and working through problems they share (Gorden & Nevins, 1993).

Quality circle members investigate problems using any method they feel might be helpful; for example, they may use face-to-face problem-solving groups, nominal groups, or Delphi methods. The group then reports its findings and its suggestions to those with the authority to make changes. Or, in some cases, quality circle members may implement the solutions themselves.

The Idea-Generation Group

Many small groups exist solely to generate ideas. **Idea-generation groups** often follow the process called brainstorming (see Chapter 3)—a technique for bombarding a problem and generating as many ideas as possible (Osborn, 1957). Advertisers faced with the problem of developing an advertising campaign or creating a slogan, Jay Leno's writing team trying to come up with an effective monologue, and an electronics firm trying to find ways to cut costs would all make use of some form of brainstorming.

Brainstorming occurs in two phases. The first is the brainstorming period proper; the second is the evaluation period. In the brainstorming period, a problem is selected that is amenable to many possible solutions or ideas. Group members are informed of the problem to be brainstormed before the actual session, so they can think about it. When the group meets, each person contributes as many ideas as possible. All ideas are recorded either in writing or on tape. During this idea-generating session, the group follows four general rules:

◆ *Don't criticize.* No criticism is allowed. All ideas are recorded. They're not evaluated nor even discussed. Any negative criticism—whether verbal or nonverbal—is itself criticized by the leader or the members.

DEVELOPING STRATEGIES

Brainstorming. Danny is scheduled to lead a group of analysts in brainstorming ways to get new clients for his firm. In the past there's been very little enthusiasm for such sessions, and the groups' actual contributions have been only mediocre. Danny wants to change this. Any suggestions?

◆ *Work for quantity.* The more ideas the better. Somewhere in a large pile of ideas will be one or two good ones. The more ideas generated, the more effective the brainstorming session.

◆ *Combine and extend ideas.* Although you may not criticize a particular idea, you may extend it or combine it in some way. The value of a particular idea may well be in the way it stimulates someone to combine or extend it.

◆ *Think wild.* The wilder the idea the better. It's easier to tone an idea down than to spice it up. A wild idea can easily be tempered, but it's not so easy to elaborate on a simple or conservative idea.

After all the ideas are generated—a period lasting no longer than 15 or 20 minutes—they're evaluated. The ones that are unworkable are thrown out; the ones that show promise are retained and discussed. During this phase negative criticism is allowed.

The Focus Group

A different type of problem-solving group is the **focus group,** a kind of depth interview of a small group. The aim here is to discover what people think about an issue or a product. For example: What do men between 18 and 25 think of

CRITICAL LISTENING/THINKING *Link*

Listening to Solutions

A useful procedure in critically analyzing group solutions is provided by critical thinking pioneer Edward deBono (1987). The **critical thinking hats technique** suggests that in analyzing solutions you use six "thinking hats." With each hat you look at the solution from a different perspective and ask different questions.

1. The **fact hat** focuses on the data, the facts and figures. What are the relevant data? How can you get more information? How much will the proposal cost? How much profit can you get?
2. The **feeling hat** focuses on your feelings, emotions, and intuitions. How do you feel about the proposed solution?
3. The **negative argument hat** focuses on the downside outcomes that might result if the solution were accepted. Why might this proposal fail? What are the possible problems with this solution? What is the worst-case scenario?

4. The **positive benefits hat** focuses on the upside outcomes that might result if the solution were accepted. What are the opportunities that this new format would open up? What benefits would the solution provide? What's the best-case scenario?
5. The **creative new idea hat** focuses on new ways of looking at the solution and can easily be combined with the brainstorming techniques discussed in this chapter. In what other ways can you look at this solution? What other functions might this solution serve? Can you apply this solution to your other problems?
6. The **control of thinking hat** asks that you reflect on your own thinking. Have you adequately analyzed the solution? Are you focusing too much on insignificant issues? Have you given enough attention to possible negative effects?

Getting Critical. Develop one question for each thinking hat for any one of the following solutions: Tuition should be raised to save endangered academic programs. Elementary and high schools should use a 12-month calendar. The draft should be reinstituted to include men and women equally.

the new aftershave lotion and its packaging? What do young executives earning more than $100,000 think of buying a foreign luxury car? Ultimately, the aim of convening a focus group is to solve a problem; for example, to create new packaging for the aftershave lotion or to design advertisements for luxury cars.

Generally, a leader, who usually is a professional focus group facilitator rather than a member of the organization itself, assembles approximately 12 people. The leader explains the process, the time limits, and the general goal of the group—let's say, for example, to discover why these 12 members requested information on the XYZ health plan but then purchased a plan from another company. The idea is that these 12 members represent the general population. In this example, the leader will ask a variety of questions, such as: How did you hear about the XYZ health plan? What other health plans did you consider before making your actual purchase? What influenced you to buy the plan you eventually bought? Were any other people influential in helping you make your decision? Through the exploration of these and similar questions, the facilitator and the relevant organizational members (who may be seated behind a one-way mirror, watching the discussion) may put together a more effective health plan or a more effective advertising campaign.

Members and Leaders in Small Groups

By gaining insight into the roles of both members and leaders, you'll be in a better position to analyze your own small group behavior and to modify it as you wish.

Members in Small Groups

Understanding the major roles that members serve in small group communication and some of the guidelines that effective members follow will help you become a more effective participant.

Member Roles

Member roles can be divided into three general classes (Benne & Sheats, 1948). These roles are, of course, frequently served by leaders as well.

Group task roles help the group focus more specifically on achieving its goals. For example, one person may almost always seek the opinions of others, another may concentrate on elaborating details, another on evaluating suggestions, and still another on stimulating the group to greater activity. Usually, it's better for the roles to be spread about evenly among the members so that each may serve many group task roles.

Group building and maintenance roles focus not only on the task to be performed but on interpersonal relationships among members; for example, members may positively reinforce others, try to resolve conflict, keep the channels of communication open, or mediate differences between group members.

Individual roles are counterproductive. They hinder the group's achieving its goal and are individual rather than group oriented. Such roles, often termed dysfunctional, hinder the group's productivity and member satisfaction. People playing individual roles may, for example, express negative evaluations, try to

CRITICAL LISTENING/THINKING *Link*

Listening for Groupthink

Listen carefully for **groupthink,** an attitude that develops when members are more concerned with agreeing with one another than with carefully analyzing a problem (Janis, 1983; Schafer & Crichlow, 1996). The following symptoms should help you listen critically with an ear for groupthink:

- Group members think the group and its members are invulnerable and even create rationalizations to avoid dealing with warnings or threats.
- Members are overly selective in the information they consider seriously. They accept facts and opinions that support the group's position and ignore those that are contrary to the group's position.
- Members believe their group is moral.
- Members perceive people who are opposed to the group in simplistic, stereotyped ways.
- Members censor their own doubts and apply pressure to any member who expresses doubts or questions the group's proposals.
- Group members believe that all are in unanimous agreement, whether this is stated or not.

If you identify groupthink in a group you are participating in or leading, consider these suggestions for combating it:

1. When too-simple solutions are offered to problems, try to illustrate for the group (with specific examples, if possible) why the complexity of the problem is not going to yield to the solutions offered.
2. When you feel that members are not expressing their doubts about the group or its decisions, encourage members to voice disagreement. Ask members to play devil's advocate, to test the adequacy of the solution. Or, if members resist, do it yourself.
3. If you feel there is unexpressed disagreement, ask directly if anyone disagrees. If you still get no response, it may be helpful if you ask members to write their comments anonymously and then read them to the group.
4. To combat group pressure toward agreement, reward members who do voice disagreement. Say, for example, "That's a good argument; we need to hear more about the potential problems of this proposal. Does anyone else see any problems?"

Getting Critical. Have you ever been a member or a leader of a group in which groupthink operated? What form did it take? What effects did this attitude have on the group's critical thinking?

focus attention on themselves, try to dominate the group, or plead the cases of special groups or interests.

Member Participation

To gain another perspective on group membership, consider the recommendations for effective participation in small group communication:

- *Be group oriented.* In the small group you're a member of a team, a larger whole. Your participation is of value to the extent that it advances the goals of the group and promotes member satisfaction. Your task is to pool your talents, knowledge, and insight so that the group may arrive at a better solution than any one person could have developed.

- *Center conflict on issues.* Conflict is a natural part of the small group process. It's particularly important in the small group to center conflict on issues rather than on personalities. When you disagree, make it clear that your disagreement is with the solution suggested or the ideas expressed, not with the person or persons who expressed them.

◆ *Be critically open-minded.* Come to the group with a mind open to alternatives. Don't come with your mind already made up. When this happens, the small group process degenerates into a series of individual debates in which each person argues for his or her own position.

◆ *Ensure understanding.* Make sure that your ideas are understood by all participants. If something is worth saying, it's worth saying clearly. Don't hesitate to ask whether something you said was clear.

Leaders in Small Groups

In many small groups one person serves as leader. In others several persons may share leadership. In some groups a person may be appointed the leader or may serve as leader because of her or his position within the company or hierarchy. In other groups the leader may emerge as the group proceeds in fulfilling its functions or may be voted in as leader by the group members. In all cases, however, the effectiveness of **leadership** is vital to the well-being and effectiveness of the group.

Before examining the functions of leadership, analyze your own leadership qualities in the accompanying self-test, "Are You Leader Material?"

 **YOURSELF**

Are You Leader Material?

This self-test will help you think about yourself in the role of leader. Respond to the following statements in terms of how you perceive yourself and how you think your peers perceive you, using a 10-point scale on which 10 = extremely true and 1 = extremely false.

Others see me as	I see myself as	Perceptions
____ 1.	____ 1.	Popular with group members
____ 2.	____ 2.	Knowledgeable about the topics discussed
____ 3.	____ 3.	Dependable
____ 4.	____ 4.	Effective in establishing group goals
____ 5.	____ 5.	Competent in giving directions
____ 6.	____ 6.	Capable of energizing group members
____ 7.	____ 7.	Charismatic (dynamic, engaging, powerful)
____ 8.	____ 8.	Empowering of group members
____ 9.	____ 9.	Moral and honest
____ 10.	____ 10.	Skilled in satisfying both task and relationship needs
____ 11.	____ 11.	Flexible in adjusting leadership style on the basis of the situation
____ 12.	____ 12.	Able to delegate responsibility

❖ **HOW DID YOU DO?** This test was designed to encourage you to look at yourself in terms of four popular approaches to leadership. For each group of scores, the maximum (i.e., best) score will be 30. To compute your scores:

- Add your scores for statements 1–3: _____. This will give you an idea of how you and others see you in terms of the leadership qualities identified by the *trait approach,* which defines the leader in terms of specific personal traits or characteristics—for example, intelligence, self-confidence, determination, integrity, and sociability (Northouse, 1997).
- Add your scores for statements 4–6: _____. This will give you an idea of how you and others see you in relation to the varied leadership functions considered in the *functional approach,* which defines the leader as the person who performs such leadership functions as setting group goals, giving directions, and summarizing.
- Add your scores for statements 7–9: _____. This will give you an idea of the degree to which you and others see you as a *transformational leader*—a leader with the ability to elevate the group's members, enabling them to accomplish the group task and also to emerge as more empowered individuals.
- Add your scores for statements 10–12: _____. This will give you an idea of the degree to which you and others see you as a *situational leader*—a leader who balances the need to the task accomplished against a concern for the personal satisfaction of the group members and adjusts this balance depending on the situation.

❖ **WHAT WILL YOU DO?** As you read the remainder of this chapter, try to identify specific skills and competencies you might learn that would enable you to increase your scores on all four approaches to leadership. Also, try searching the Web for information on "leadership" as well as on variations on the leadership theme such as "business leadership" or "political leaders."

As noted in the self-test, leaders need to be concerned with both tasks and people, though each situation will call for a somewhat different combination of task and people concerns (Hersey & Blanchard, 1988). For example, a group of scientists working on AIDS research would probably need a leader who would provide them with the needed information to accomplish their task. They would be self-motivating and would probably need little in the way of social and emotional encouragement. On the other hand, a group of recovering alcoholics might require leadership that emphasized understanding of the social and emotional needs of the members.

In sum, leadership effectiveness depends on addressing the concerns for task and people according to the specifics of the situation. With this "situational view" of leadership, we can look at some of the major functions leaders serve. These functions are not the exclusive property of the leader; members may perform them as well. Nevertheless, when there's a specific leader, he or she is expected to perform them.

◆ *Activate group interaction.* Perhaps the group is newly formed and the members feel a bit uneasy with one another. As the group's leader, don't expect diverse members to sit down and discuss a problem without becoming familiar with one another. Instead, stimulate the members to interact. This leadership function also is important when members act as individuals rather than as a group.

USING TECHNOLOGY

Visit an Internet chat room and lurk for a time before writing anything yourself. What principles of group communication can you detect in this group? Is there an obvious leader? Do certain members play certain roles—roles similar to those discussed here?

◆ *Maintain effective interaction.* Even after the group is stimulated to group interaction, see that members maintain effective interaction and that all members have an opportunity to express themselves. If the discussion begins to drag, prod the group to effective interaction: "Do we have any additional comments on the proposal?" "Would anyone like to add anything?"

◆ *Keep members on track.* As the leader keep all members reasonably on track by asking questions, interjecting internal summaries as the group goes along, or providing transitions so that the relationship between the issue just discussed and the question about to be considered is clear.

◆ *Ensure member satisfaction.* If a group is to be effective, it must meet not only the surface purposes of the group but also the underlying or interpersonal purposes that motivated many of the members to come together in the first place.

◆ *Encourage ongoing evaluation and improvement.* Most groups encounter obstacles as they try to solve a problem, reach a decision, or generate ideas. Most groups could use some improvement. If the group is to improve, it must focus on itself. That is, along with trying to solve some external problem, the group must try to solve its own internal problems as well—for example, personal conflicts, failures to meet on time, or the tendency of members to come unprepared. As the leader, try to identify any such difficulties and encourage and help the group to resolve them.

❖ **CONSIDER** how you respond generally to three types of leadership styles: *laissez-faire* (the leader lets the group members do as they wish and offers information or opinions only when asked); *democratic* (the leader provides direction but allows the group to make its own decisions and to progress the way its members wish); and *authoritarian* (the leader dominates the group and makes the decisions regardless of what the group members may want). With which type of leader would you work best? With which would you have the most difficulty?

RESEARCH *Link*

Museum Collections and Exhibits

Not too long ago, museums weren't even included in research discussions; good museums were so far away from most people that the possibility of visiting any given museum was remote. Now, however, you have the world of museums literally at your fingertips. Every museum collects all sorts of information pertaining to its major focus; for example, to natural history, science, or art (see, for example, the website for one of the world's greatest art museums, the Metropolitan Museum of Art, at www.metmuseum.org/home.asp). Visiting a few museum websites will be time well spent. A few exceptionally good sites are those of the Franklin Institute Science Museum at http://sln.fi.edu/, London's Museum of Natural History at http://www.nhm.ac.uk, and the Smithsonian Institution at http://www.si.edu/ (see the accompanying website). An especially good site if you don't know what museum you'd like to visit is http://www.comlab.ox.ac.uk/archive/other/museums/usa.html, where you will find links to museums, archives, and galleries throughout the United States.

Research Activity. Take a break and visit the Smithsonian or any of the numerous art, science, or history online museums. Have fun.

The Smithsonian Institution
(http://www.si.edu/)
The Smithsonian Institution is one of the world's greatest museums, and you can access it anytime. The website will provide guidance for visiting the Smithsonian's 16 museums, the *Smithsonian Encyclopedia*, and lots more.

◆ *Prepare members for the discussion.* Preparing members may involve preparing them for the small group interaction as well as for the discussion of a specific issue or problem. If members are to discuss a specific problem, it may be necessary to brief them. Or perhaps you will need to distribute certain materials before the actual discussion or tell members to read certain materials or view a particular film or television show. Whatever the preparations, it is the leader's job to organize and coordinate them.

Presenting the Group's Thinking

The purpose of small group interaction isn't completed when the group has reached its decision. Rather, the group's decisions (findings, conclusions, recommendations) need to be presented to some larger group—the entire union membership, your class as a whole, the board of directors. There are a lot of ways in which these decisions may be presented. Let's begin by looking at some general guidelines and then examine some more specific suggestions for various group formats.

General Speaking Guidelines

If a group develops a solution to a problem, it will generally seek in some way to put this solution into operation. Often it's necessary to convince others that the solution is workable and cost effective. Try these suggestions:

◆ Attach the proposed solution to what people are already used to, if possible. People are more apt to understand and accept new solutions when the new ideas somehow resemble old and more comfortable approaches.

◆ Present the solution in a nonthreatening manner. New solutions often frighten people. For example, if your solution might lead people to feel insecure about their jobs, then alleviate these worries before you try to explain the solution in any detail. As a general rule it's best to proceed slowly, especially if you anticipate objections or hostility from your listeners.

◆ Present new solutions tentatively. In the excitement of inspiration, you may not have thought through all of the practical implications of your proposed solution. If you present your ideas tentatively and they're shown to be impractical or unworkable, you will be less hurt psychologically and—most important—more willing to present new solutions again.

❖ **CONSIDER** the role of power in a small group (e.g., among a film director, cast, and crew) and why some group members have power and others don't. What kinds of power are you regularly seen to possess? How can you tell that group members attribute these kinds of power to you?

◆ In many instances it will prove helpful to link changes to well-known problems in the organization. For example, if you're going to ask employees to complete extensive surveys, then show them how this extra work will correct a long-standing problem and benefit them and the organization.

◆ Say why you think the solution will work. Give the advantages of your plan over the existing situation and explain why you think your solution should be implemented. The patterns for organizing a public speech (see Chapter 6) will prove helpful in accomplishing this.

◆ State the negatives (there usually are some with most ideas) as you understand them—and, of course, explain why you think the positives outweigh them.

A CASE OF *Ethics*

Lying for the Good of the Group

You're leading a small group discussion among a group of high school freshmen you're mentoring. The discussion centers on marijuana use, and your objective is to get the students to avoid trying pot—or, if they have tried smoking already, to stop. During the discussion students ask you if you smoke pot. The truth is that on occasion you do, although it's a very controlled use. You feel that it would only destroy your credibility and encourage the students to experiment with pot or to continue smoking if they knew you used marijuana. At the same time, however, you wonder if you can ethically lie to them and tell them that you never smoke.

What would you do in this situation? More generally, what is the speaker's ethical responsibility when it comes to answering audience questions?

◆ Show how your solution is directly related to the needs and interests of those whom the solution will impact. Show others how your solution will benefit them.

Speaking in the Panel Group

In the **panel,** the group members are cast in the role of "experts" and participate informally and without any set pattern of who speaks when. The procedure is similar to that of any small group interaction, except that the panel is discussing the issue before an audience that is present but does not participate in the actual discussion. Normally a moderator guides the discussion.

A variation is the two-panel format, with an expert panel and a lay panel. The expert panel consists of the members who participated in the group and who ideally are more knowledgeable than the lay panel members. The topic is then discussed as the lay and the expert panel members interact. This is the format followed by many talk shows, such as those featuring Jerry Springer and Oprah Winfrey. On these shows the moderator is the host (Springer, Winfrey). The "expert panel" is the group of guests (the dysfunctional family, the gossip columnists, the political activists). And the lay panel consists of the members of the studio audience who ask questions or offer comments.

Here are a few suggestions for making the panel format more effective:

◆ Always treat panel members and their questions with respect. You'll notice this on the popular talk shows: No matter how stupid the question may be, the moderator treats it as serious, though often restructuring it just a bit so that it makes more sense. Treat the questions objectively; don't try to bias the question or the answer through your verbal or nonverbal responses.

◆ Speak in short turns. The group's interaction should resemble a conversation, rather than individual public speeches. Resist the temptation to tell long stories or go into too much detail.

◆ Try to spread the conversation around the group. Generally, try to give each member the same opportunity to speak.

Speaking in the Symposium and Team Presentations

In the **symposium,** each member delivers a prepared presentation, a public speech. All speeches are addressed to different aspects of a single topic. The symposium leader introduces the speakers, provides transitions from one speaker to another, and may provide periodic summaries.

In the team presentation, popular in business settings, two or three members of a group will report the group's findings to a larger group. In some situations team presentations may amount to "position papers" and may include both majority and minority reports, as at the Supreme Court. Or if, say, a group considered new scheduling systems, members of a team might each present one of the proposed systems and the advantages and disadvantages of each.

Here are a few suggestions for making symposia and team presentations more effective:

◆ Coordinate your presentations very carefully. Team presentations and symposia are extremely difficult to synchronize. Make sure that everyone knows exactly what he or she is responsible for. Make sure there's no (or very little) overlap among the presentations.

◆ Much as you would rehearse a public speech, try to rehearse these presentations and their coordination. This is rarely possible to do in actual practice, but it is very helpful to "rehearse" mentally or imaginatively, going through the proceedings in your mind in advance.

◆ Select a strong leader to introduce the presentations and manage audience questions.

◆ Keep last-minute changes to a minimum. When such changes are unavoidable, make sure that all members know about them.

◆ Adhere carefully to time limits. If you speak for more time than allotted, that time will be deducted from the minutes available to a later speaker. As you can appreciate, violating time limits will severely damage the entire group's presentation.

◆ Provide clear transitions between the presentations. Internal summaries work especially well as connectives between one speech and the next: "Now that Judy has explained the general proposal, Peter and Margarita will explain some of the advantages and disadvantages of the proposal. First, we'll hear from Peter with the advantages and then from Margarita with the disadvantages."

The Symposium–Forum Presentation

The symposium–forum presentation consists of two parts: a symposium, with prepared speeches (as just explained), and a **forum,** with questions from the audience and responses by the speakers. The leader introduces the speakers and moderates the question-and-answer session. The suggestions for making these presentations more effective are essentially the same as for the panel and the symposium.

Oral and Written Reports

In many cases the group leader will make a presentation of the group's findings, recommendations, or decisions to some other group—for example, to the class as a whole, the entire student body, the board of directors, the union membership, or the heads of departments.

Depending on the specific situation, these reports may be similar to speeches of information or speeches of persuasion. For example, if you are the group leader, your task may be simply to inform the other group of the findings or recommendations of your committee—the recommended ways to increase morale, the new pension proposals, the new developments in competing organizations. In other cases your report will be largely persuasive; for example, you'll need to convince the larger group to give you increased funding so that your group's decisions can be implemented.

In some situations both a brief oral report and a more extensive written report are required. A good example is the press conference. At a press conference you deliver an oral report to members of the press, who also receive a written

USING TECHNOLOGY

Visit some newsgroups; find them through your browser, which likely has links to newsgroups, or through your favorite search engine. In what ways are these newsgroups like the face-to-face groups discussed in this chapter? How are they different?

report. The press will then question you for further details. In some cases you may want to use a computer-assisted presentation and prepare handouts of your slides, your speaker's notes, or selected slides with space for your listeners to write notes (see Chapter 5). Here are a few suggestions for more effective oral and written reports.

◆ Write the written report as you would a term paper, and from that develop a summary of the report in the form of a public speech, following the 10 steps explained in Chapter 1 and elaborated throughout this text.

◆ Don't read the written report. Even though the oral and the written report may cover essentially the same content, they're totally different in development and presentation. The written report is meant to be read; the oral report is meant to be listened to.

◆ In some instances it's helpful to distribute the written report and to use your oral presentation to highlight the most essential aspects of the report. Listeners may then refer to the report as you speak—a situation not recommended for most public speeches.

◆ In very rare instances you may choose to distribute the written report only after you have completed your oral report. Generally, however, people don't like this procedure; they prefer the option of thumbing through the report as they listen or reserving reading until after they've heard the oral report.

Summary of Concepts and Skills

In this chapter we looked at the nature of the small group, the various types of small groups, the roles of group members and leaders, and aspects of public speaking in small group contexts.

Small Groups

The small group is a collection of individuals that is small enough for all members to communicate with relative ease as both senders and receivers. The members are related to each other by some common purpose. Most small groups develop norms identifying what is considered appropriate.

Problem Solving in Groups

Several types of problem-solving groups are especially important:

◆ The nominal group uses limited discussion and confidential voting to obtain a group decision.

◆ The Delphi method relies on a group of experts who communicate by repeatedly responding to questionnaires.

◆ The quality circle group consists of workers who make recommendations for improving the quality of some organizational function.

◆ The idea-generation group tries to generate as many ideas as possible.

◆ The focus group tries to solve problems by assessing people's feelings and thinking about decisions that an organization may have to make.

Members and Leaders in Small Groups

In small groups, members and leaders work together to accomplish a common goal.

◆ Members should be group-oriented, center conflict on issues, be critically open-minded, and ensure understanding.

◆ Leaders should seek to address both the task and the interpersonal needs of members, activate the group interaction, maintain effective interaction, keep members on track, ensure member satisfaction, encourage ongoing evaluation, and prepare members for discussion.

Presenting the Group's Thinking

Four general formats typically characterize presentations of group conclusions or proposals:

◆ The panel
◆ The symposium and team presentations
◆ The symposium–forum presentation
◆ Oral and written reports

Vocabulary Quiz

Speaking in Small Groups

Match the terms dealing with small group communication with their definitions. Record the number of the definition next to the appropriate term.

_____ Delphi group
_____ symposium
_____ forum
_____ focus group
_____ brainstorming
_____ individual roles
_____ small group norms
_____ nominal group
_____ problem-solving group
_____ small group

1. A relatively small collection of individuals who are related to one another by some common purpose.
2. Rules or standards of behavior that group members are expected to follow.
3. A group that comes together to reach a decision or solve a problem.
4. A collection of individuals who participate by responding to a series of questionnaires.
5. A group of individuals who interact not so much by talking with one another as by voting on a series of decisions.
6. A group meeting in which members each deliver a public speech all on a similar topic.
7. A meeting in which members of the audience question the speakers.
8. Counterproductive roles that hinder the group's achieving its goals.
9. An in-depth interview of group members whose aim is to discover what the members really think.
10. A group session whose goal is to develop as many ideas as possible.

Web Explorations

Companion Website

www.ablongman.com/devito

The Companion Website's Chapter 12 provides extensive additional coverage of the small group, including the interview. See "The Interview," "Accepting Group Norms," "Small Group Phases," "Personal Growth Groups," "Educational or Learning Groups," "Decision-Making Methods," "Empowering Group Members," "Combating Idea Killers," "How Apprehensive Are You in Group Discussions and Meetings?" (self-test), "Inter-

action Process Analysis," "Managing Conflict," "Approaches to Leadership," "Styles of Leadership," "What Kind of Leader Are You?" (self-test), "Qualities of Leadership," "'The Leader' from Attila the Hun," "The Agenda," "Steps in Problem Solving" (figure), "Power in the Small Group," "How Powerful Are You?" (self-test), "Communicating Power in the Small Group," and "The Distribution of Power in the Small Group." In addition, a speech by Michael Greene introducing a series of speeches is presented.

Public Speaking Exercises

12.1 Solving Problems in Groups

Divide up into problem-solving groups of five to seven people. Each group should discuss one of the following questions:

- ◆ What should we do about the homeless?
- ◆ What should we do to improve student morale?
- ◆ What should we do to better prepare ourselves for the job market?
- ◆ What should we do to improve student–faculty communication?
- ◆ What should be the college's responsibility concerning AIDS?

Before the groups meet, each member should prepare a discussion outline on his or her group's topic, answering the following questions:

- ◆ What is the problem? How long has it existed? What caused it? What are the effects of the problem?
- ◆ What criteria should be used to evaluate possible solutions?

- ◆ What are some possible solutions?
- ◆ What are the advantages and disadvantages of each of these possible solutions?
- ◆ What solution seems best (in light of the advantages and disadvantages)?
- ◆ How might we put this solution to a test?

After the group discussions, the findings of each group should be presented. Use one of the following methods or some combination of them:

a. a panel discussion

b. a symposium

c. a two- or three-person team presentation

d. a symposium–forum

e. a simulated press conference

f. an oral report

12.2 Responding to Individual Roles

For each of the three dysfunctional individual roles identified in the left column, write a response or two that you might make as a leader in trying to deal with this dysfunctional role playing. Be careful that your responses don't alienate the individual or the group.

Individual roles	Responses to individual roles
The *aggressor* expresses negative evaluations of the group and its members.	
The *blocker* is disagreeable, opposing other members and their ideas regardless of their merit.	
The *self-confessor* personalizes everything instead of focusing on the group.	

12.3 Combating Groupthink

Imagine that you are a member or a leader of a problem-solving group. You see the signs of groupthink noted in the left column, and you wish to accomplish the goal noted in the center column. Develop specific messages that you might use to fulfill your goal.

Suspected problem	Combat goal	Messages to accomplish your combat goal
Too-simple solutions are offered to problems.	Illustrate how the complexity of the problem is not going to yield to the solutions offered.	
Members are not expressing their doubts about the group or its decisions.	Encourage members to voice disagreement, or ask if anyone disagrees.	
There's lots of group pressure toward agreement.	Reward members who voice disagreement, or voice it yourself.	

References

Albright, M. K. (1998, June 15). *Vital Speeches of the Day, 64,* 518–520.

Alessandra, T. (1986). How to listen effectively. *Speaking of success* [videotape series]. San Diego, CA: Levitz Sommer Productions.

Allen, R. L. (1997, Octobar 6). People—the single point of difference—listening to them. *Nation's Restaurant News, 31,* 130.

Archambault, D. (1992, June 1). Columbus plus 500 years. *Vital Speeches of the Day, 58,* 491–493.

Arliss, Laurie P. (1991). *Gender communication.* Englewood Cliffs, NJ: Prentice-Hall.

Asch, S. (1946). Forming impressions of personality. *Journal of Abnormal and Social Psychology, 41,* 258–290.

Axtell, R. E. (1990). *Do's and taboos of hosting international visitors.* New York: Wiley.

Axtell, R. E. (1993). *Do's and taboos around the world* (3rd ed.). New York: Wiley.

Ayres, J. (1986). Perceptions of speaking ability: An explanation for stage fright. *Communication Education, 35,* 275–287.

Ayres, J., & Hopf, T. S. (1992). Visualization: Reducing speech anxiety and enhancing performance. *Communication Reports, 5,* 1–10.

Ayres, J., & Hopf, T. S. (1993). *Coping with speech anxiety.* Norwood, NJ: Ablex.

Ayres, J., Hopf, T., & Ayres, D. M. (1994, July). An examination of whether imaging ability enhances the effectiveness of an intervention designed to reduce speech anxiety. *Communication Education, 43,* 252–258.

Barker, L. L. (1990). *Communication* (5th ed.). Englewood Cliffs, NJ: Prentice-Hall.

Barker, L. L., Edwards, R., Gaines, C., Gladney, K., & Holley, F. (1980). An investigation of proportional time spent in various communication activities by college students. *Journal of Applied Communication Research, 8,* 101–109.

Bates, D. G., & Fratkin, E. M. (1999). *Cultural anthropology* (2nd ed.). Boston: Allyn & Bacon.

Beatty, M. J. (1988). Situational and predispositional correlates of public speaking anxiety. *Communication Education, 37,* 28–39.

Benne, K. D., & Sheats, P. (1948). Functional roles of group members. *Journal of Social Issues, 4,* 41–49.

Benson, S. G., & Dundis, S. P. (2003, September). Understanding and motivating health care employees: Integrating Maslow's hierarchy of needs, training and technology. *Journal of Nursing Management, 11,* 315–320.

Bok, S. (1978). *Lying: Moral choice in public and private life.* New York: Pantheon.

Boutras-Ghali, B. (1994, December 15). Transnational crime. *Vital Speeches of the Day, 60,* 130–132.

Brownback, S. (1998, May 15). Free speech: Lyrics, liberty and license. *Vital Speeches of the Day, 64,* 454–456.

Brownell, J. (1987). Listening: The toughest management skill. *Cornell Hotel and Restaurant Administration Quarterly, 27,* 64–71.

Burgoon, J. K., & Bacue, A. E. (2003). Nonverbal communication skills. In J. O. Greene & B. R. Burleson (Eds.), *Handbook of communication and social interaction skills* (pp. 179–220). Mahwah, NJ: Lawrence Erlbaum.

Burgoon, J. K., Buller, D. B., & Woodall, W. G. (1996). *Nonverbal communication: The unspoken dialogue* (2nd ed.). New York: McGraw-Hill.

Burke, K. (1950). *A rhetoric of motives.* New York: Prentice-Hall.

Carr, H. (1987, February 1). Communicating during a "crisis." *Vital Speeches of the Day, 53,* 248–250.

Chang, H. C., & Holt, G. R. (1996, Winter). The changing Chinese interpersonal world: Popular themes in interpersonal communication books in modern Taiwan. *Communication Quarterly, 44,* 85–106.

Chase, S. (1956). *Guides to straight thinking, with 13 common fallacies.* New York: HarperCollins.

Cialdini, R. T. (1984). *Influence: How and why people agree to things.* New York: Morrow.

Cialdini, R. T., & Ascani, K. (1976). Test of a concession procedure for inducing verbal, behavioral, and further compliance with a request to give blood. *Journal of Applied Psychology, 61,* 295–300.

Coates, J., & Cameron, D. (1989). *Women, men, and language: Studies in language and linguistics.* London: Longman.

Colino, R. (1986, June 1). Intelsat. *Vital Speeches of the Day, 52,* 492–496.

Collier, M. J., & Powell, R. (1990). Ethnicity, instructional communication and classroom systems. *Communication Quarterly, 38,* 334–349.

Culick, S. (1962). *The East and West: A study of their psychic and cultural characteristics.* Ruthland, UT: Charles E. Tuttle.

Dalton, J. (1994, March 1). The character of readiness. *Vital Speeches of the Day, 60,* 296–299.

deBono, E. (1976). *Teaching thinking.* New York: Penguin.

deBono, E. (1987). *The six thinking hats.* New York: Penguin.

Dejong, W. (1979). An examination of self perception mediation of the foot in the door effect. *Journal of Personality and Social Psychology, 37,* 2221–2239.

DeVito, J. A. (1974). *General Semantics: Guide and workbook* (Rev. ed.). DeLand, FL: Everett/Edwards.

DeVito, J. A. (1996). *Brainstorms: How to think more creatively about communication (or about anything else).* Boston: Allyn & Bacon.

DeVries, M. A. (1994). *Internationally yours: Writing and communicating successfully in today's global marketplace.* Boston: Houghton Mifflin.

Dewey, J. (1910). *How we think.* Boston: Heath.

Dillard, J. P., & Marshall, L. J. (2003). Persuasion as a social skill. In J. O. Greene & B. R. Burleson (Eds.), *Handbook of communication and social interaction skills* (pp. 479–514). Mahwah, NJ: Lawrence Erlbaum.

Eisenberg, N., & Strayer, J. (1987). *Empathy and its development.* New York: Cambridge University Press.

Ekman, P., Friesen, W. V., & Ellsworth, P. (1972). *Emotion in the human face: Guidelines for research and an integration of findings.* New York: Pergamon Press.

Fensholt, M. (2003, June). There's nothing wrong with taking written notes to the podium. *Presentations, 17,* 66.

Floyd, J. J. (1985). *Listening: A practical approach.* Boston: Allyn & Bacon.

Fraser, B. (1990, April). Perspectives on politeness. *Journal of Pragmatics, 14,* 219–236.

Freedman, J., & Fraser, S. (1966). Compliance without pressure: The foot-in-the-door technique. *Journal of Personality and Social Psychology, 4,* 195–202.

Frey, K. J., & Eagly, A. H. (1993, July). Vividness can undermine the persuasiveness of messages. *Journal of Personality and Social Psychology, 65,* 32–44.

Glucksberg, S., & Danks, J. H. (1975). *Experimental psycholinguistics: An introduction.* Hillsdale, NJ: Erlbaum.

Gorden, W. I., & Nevins, R. J. (1993). *We mean business: Building communication competence in business and professions.* New York: Allyn & Bacon.

Goss, B., Thompson, M., & Olds, S. (1978). Behavioral support for systematic desensitization for communication apprehension. *Human Communication Research, 4,* 158–163.

Grice, G. L., & Skinner, J. F. (2004). *Mastering public speaking* (5th ed.). Boston: Allyn & Bacon.

Gudykunst, W. B., & Kim, Y. Y. (Eds.). (1992). *Readings on communication with strangers: An approach to intercultural communication.* New York: McGraw-Hill.

Gudykunst, W., & Nishida, T. (1984). Individual and cultural influence on uncertainty reduction. *Communication Monographs, 51,* 23–36.

Gudykunst, W., Yang, S., & Nishida, T. (1985). A cross-cultural test of uncertainty reduction theory: Comparisons of acquaintance, friend, and dating relationships in Japan, Korea, and the United States. *Human Communication Research, 11,* 407–454.

Hall, E. T., & Hall, M. R. (1987). *Hidden differences: Doing business with the Japanese.* New York: Doubleday.

Han, S., & Shavitt, S. (1994). Persuasion and culture: Advertising appeals in individualistic and collectivistic societies. *Journal of Experimental Social Psychology, 30,* 326–350.

Hanley, S. J., & Abell, S. C. (2002, Fall). Maslow and relatedness: Creating an interpersonal model of self-actualization. *Journal of Humanistic Psychology, 42,* 37–56.

Harris, M., & Johnson, O. (2000). *Cultural anthropology* (5th ed.). Boston: Allyn & Bacon.

Hayakawa, S. I., & Hayakawa, A. R. (1990). *Language in thought and action* (5th ed.). New York: Harcourt Brace Jovanovich.

Hecht, M. L., Collier, M. J., & Ribeau, S. (1993). *African American communication: Ethnic identity and cultural interpretation.* Thousand Oaks, CA: Sage.

Hensley, C. W. (1994, March 1). Divorce—the sensible approach. *Vital Speeches of the Day, 60*, 317–319.

Henslin, J. M. (2000). *Essentials of sociology: A down-to-earth approach* (3rd ed.). Boston: Allyn & Bacon.

Herrick, J. A. (2004). *Argumentation: Understanding and shaping arguments*. State College, PA: Strata Publishing.

Hersey, P., & Blanchard, K. (1988). *Management of organizational behavior: Utilizing human resources*. Englewood Cliffs, NJ: Prentice-Hall.

Higgins, J. M. (1994). *101 creative problem solving techniques*. New York: New Management Publishing.

Himle, J. A., Abelson, J. L., & Haghightgou, H. (1999, August). Effect of alcohol on social phobic anxiety. *American Journal of Psychiatry, 156*, 1237–1243.

Holmes, J. (1995). *Women, men and politeness*. New York: Longman.

Jacobs, J. E. (1997, May 15). Rethinking the basics. *Vital Speeches of the Day, 63*, 461–464.

Jaffe, C. (2001). *Public speaking: Concepts and skills for a diverse society* (4th ed.). Belmont, CA: Wadsworth.

Jaksa, J. A., & Pritchard, M. S. (1994). *Communication ethics: Methods of analysis*, (2nd ed.). Belmont, CA: Wadsworth.

James, D. L. (1995). *The executive guide to Asia–Pacific communications*. New York: Kodansha International.

Jandt, F. E. (2000). *Intercultural communication* (3rd ed.). Thousand Oaks, CA: Sage.

Janis, I. (1983). *Victims of group thinking: A psychological study of foreign policy decisions and fiascoes* (2nd ed.). Boston: Houghton Mifflin.

Johannesen, R. L. (1996). *Ethics in human communication* (5th ed.). Prospect Heights, IL: Waveland Press.

Johnson, K. G. (Ed.). (1991). *Thinking creatically: thinking creatively, thinking critically*. Concord, CA: International Society for General Semantics.

Kelly, P. K. (1994). *Team decision-making techniques*. Irvine, CA: Richard Chang Associates.

Kiel, J. M. (1999, September). Reshaping Maslow's hierarchy of needs to reflect today's educational and managerial philosophies. *Journal of Instructional Psychology, 26*, 167–168.

Korzybski, A. (1933). *Science and sanity: An introduction to non-Aristotelian systems and General Semantics*. Concord, CA: International Society for General Semantics.

Kramarae, C. (1981). *Women and men speaking*. Rowley, MA: Newbury House.

Lee, A. M., & Lee, E. B. (1972). *The fine art of propaganda*. San Francisco: International Society for General Semantics.

Lee, A. M., & Lee, E. B. (1995, Spring). The iconography of propaganda analysis. *ETC.: A Review of General Semantics, 52*, 13–17.

Lucas, S. E. (2004). *The art of public speaking* (8th ed.) New York: McGraw-Hill.

Lustig, M. W., & Koester, J. (1999). *Intercultural competence: Interpersonal communication across cultures* (3rd ed.). New York: Allyn & Bacon.

Mackay, H. B. (1991, August 15). How to get a job. *Vital Speeches of the Day, 57*, 656–659.

Maggio, R. (1997). *Talking about people: A guide to fair and accurate language*. Phoenix, AZ: Oryx Press.

Marien, M. (1992, March 15). Education and learning in the 21st century. *Vital Speeches of the Day, 58*, 340–344.

Martin, M. M., & Rubin, R. B. (1994, Winter). Development of a communication flexibility measure. *The Southern Communication Journal, 59*, 171–178.

Martin, M. M., & Rubin, R. B. (1995). A new measure of cognitive flexibility. *Psychological Reports, 76*, 623–626.

Maslow, A. (1970). *Motivation and personality*. New York: HarperCollins.

Matsuyama, Y. (1992, May 15). Japan's role in the new world order. *Vital Speeches of the Day, 58*, 461–466.

Maxwell, J. (1987, September 1). Economic forecasting. *Vital Speeches of the Day, 53*, 685–686.

McCroskey, J. C. (1997). *An introduction to rhetorical communication* (7th ed.). Boston: Allyn & Bacon.

McCroskey, J. C. (2001). *An introduction to rhetorical communication* (8th ed.). Boston: Allyn & Bacon.

McKerrow, R. E., Gronbeck, B. E., Ehninger, D., & Monroe, A. H. (2000). *Principles and types of speech communication* (14th ed.). Boston: Allyn & Bacon.

Meade, C. H. (2000). The misunderstood vividness effect: Roles in which vividness can enhance persuasion (Doctoral dissertation, University of Georgia, 2000). *Dissertation Abstracts International: B. The Physical Sciences and Engineering, 61*, (January):3323.

Midooka, K. (1990, October). Characteristics of Japanese style communication. *Media, Culture and Society, 12*, 477–489.

Moghaddam, F. M., Taylor, D. M., & Wright, S. C. (1993). *Social psychology in cross-cultural perspective*. New York: W. H. Freeman.

Nelson, A. (1986, June 1). The sanctuary movement. *Vital Speeches of the Day, 52*, 482–485.

Northouse, P. G. (1997). *Leadership: Theory and practice*. Thousand Oaks, CA: Sage.

Osborn, A. (1957). *Applied imagination* (Rev. ed.). New York: Scribners.

Payan, J. (1990, September 1). Opportunities for Hispanic women. *Vital Speeches of the Day, 56*, 697–700.

Pearson, J. C., West, R., & Turner, L. H. (1995). *Gender and communication* (3rd ed.). Dubuque, IA: William C. Brown.

Pei, M. (1956). *Language for everybody*. New York: Pocket Books.

Peterson, H. (Ed.). (1965). *A treasury of the world's great speeches*. New York: Simon & Schuster.

Peterson, R. W. (1985, July 1). Global issues. *Vital Speeches of the Day, 51*, 548–551.

Petty, R. E., & Wegener, D. T. (1998). Attitude change: Multiple roles for persuasion variables. In D. T. Gilbert, S. T. Fiske, & G. Lindzey (Eds.), *The handbook of social psychology* (4th ed., Vol. 1, pp. 323–390). New York: McGraw-Hill.

Pratkanis, A., & Aronson, E. (1991). *Age of propaganda: The everyday use and abuse of persuasion*. New York: W. H. Freeman.

Rankin, P. (1929). Listening ability. *Proceedings of the Ohio State Educational Conference's Ninth Annual Session*.

Reynolds, C. L., & Schnoor, L. G. (Eds.). (1991). *1989 championship debates and speeches*. Normal, IL: American Forensic Association.

Richardson, M. M. (1995, January 15). Taxation with representation. *Vital Speeches of the Day, 61*, 201–203.

Richmond, V. P., & McCroskey, J. C. (1998). *Communication: Apprehension, avoidance, and effectiveness* (5th ed.). Boston: Allyn & Bacon.

Riggio, R. E. (1987). *The charisma quotient*. New York: Dodd, Mead.

Rodman, G. (2001). *Making sense of media: An introduction to mass communication*. Boston: Allyn & Bacon.

Rodman, G., & Adler, R. B. (1997). *The new public speaking*. Fort Worth, TX: Harcourt Brace.

Rogers, C. (1970). *Carl Rogers on encounter groups*. New York: Harrow Books.

Rogers, L. (2001). *Sexing the brain*. New York: Columbia University Press.

Salopek, J. (1999, September). Is anyone listening? *Training and Development, 53*, 58.

Samovar, L. A., & Porter, R. E. (1991). *Communication between cultures*. Belmont, CA: Wadsworth.

Schafer, M., & Crichlow, S. (1996, September). Antecedents of groupthink. *Journal of Conflict Resolution, 40*, 415–435.

Schnoor, L. G. (Ed.). (1994). *1991 and 1992 championship debates and speeches*. River Falls, WI: American Forensic Association.

Schnoor, L. G. (Ed.). (1997). *Winning orations of the interstate oratorical association*. Mankato, MN: Interstate Oratorical Association.

Schnoor, L. G. (Ed.). (2000). *Winning orations of the interstate oratorical association*. Mankato, MN: Interstate Oratorical Association.

Schwartz, M., and the Task Force on Bias-Free Language of the Association of American University Presses (1995). *Guidelines for bias-free writing*. Bloomington: Indiana University Press.

Sojourner, R. J., & Wogalter, M. S. (1998). The influence of pictorials on the comprehension and recall of pharmaceutical safety and warning information. *International Journal of Cognitive Ergonomics, 2*, 93–106.

Sprague, J., & Stuart, D. (1996). *The speaker's handbook* (4th ed.). San Diego, CA: Harcourt Brace Jovanovich.

Steil, L. K., Barker, L. L., & Watson, K. W. (1983). *Effective listening: Key to your success*. Reading, MA: Addison Wesley.

Stephan, W. G., & Stephan, C. W. (1992). *Improving intergroup relations*. Thousand Oaks, CA: Sage.

Tannen, D. (1990). *You just don't understand: Women and men in conversation*. New York: Morrow.

Tersine, R. J., & Riggs, W. E. (1980). The Delphi technique: A long-range planning tool. In S. Ferguson & S. D. Ferguson (Eds.), *Intercom: Readings in organizational communication* (pp. 366–373). Rochelle Park, NJ: Hayden Books.

Thompson, M. (2000). *Ethics*. New York: Teach Yourself.

von Oech, R. (1990). *A whack on the side of the head: How you can be more creative* (Rev. ed.). New York: Warner.

Watzlawick, P. (1978). *The language of change: Elements of therapeutic communication*. New York: Basic Books.

Watzlawick, P., Beavin, J., & Jackson, D. D. (1967). *Pragmatics of human communication: A study of interactional patterns, pathologies, and paradoxes*. New York: Norton.

Weinstein, F. (1995, April). Professionally speaking. *Profiles: The Magazine of Continental Airlines, 8*, 50–55.

Werner, E. K. (1975). *A study of communication time*. M.A. Thesis, University of Maryland, College Park. Cited in A. Wolvin and C. Coakley (1988), *Listening* (3rd ed.). Dubuque, IA: William C. Brown.

Wolpe, J. (1957). *Psychotherapy by reciprocal inhibition*. Stanford, CA: Stanford University Press.

Wolvin, A. D., & Coakley, C. G. (1996). *Listening*. Dubuque, IA: William C. Brown.

Wood, W. (2000). Attitude change: Persuasion and social influence. *Annual Review of Psychology, 51*, 539–570.

Wright, W. (1999). *Born that way: Genes–behavior–personality*. New York: Knopf.

Index

Page numbers followed by *t* or *f* indicate tables and figures, respectively.

Credits

Text and Illustrations

Page 4: Companion Website reprinted by permission of Allyn & Bacon.

Page 6: Research Navigator website reprinted by permission of Allyn & Bacon.

Page 30: Public Speaking website reprinted by permission of Allyn & Bacon.

Page 56: By kind permission of Virtual Library, http:vlib.org.

Page 75: From the Gallup Poll website, www.gallup.com. Reprinted by permission.

Page 148: From speech by Bill Gates at United Nations Media Leaders Summit, January 15, 2004, www.gatesfoundation.org, Bill & Melinda Gates Foundation. Reprinted by permission.

Page 137: From Google website, www.google.com. Reprinted by permission.

Page 175: From Vivisimo website, www.vivisimo.com. Courtesy of Vivisimo, Inc.

Page 177: From the Institute of General Semantics, Fort Worth, Texas, website,www.general-semantics.org, March 12, 2004. Reprinted by permission.

Page 210: Home Page "IPL POTUS" by The Internet Public Library at website www.potus.com. Reprinted by permission of Robert S. Summers.

Page 223: Home Page from St. Louis Post-Dispatch website, www.stltoday.com. Courtesy STLtoday.com/St. Louis Post-Dispatch.

Page 251: "Welcome to the Biographical Dictionary" as appeared on website, www.s9.com/biography.

Page 276: Excerpt from *A Beautiful Mind* by Sylvia Nasar, 1994.

Pages 277–278: "Testing Cars" by Lee Iacocca.

Page 283: "Welcome to The Obituary Daily Times website" at www.rootsweb.com~obituary.

Page 284: From Cal Ripken's Farewell Speech, delivered September 9, 2001. Reprinted by permission of the Ripken Baseball Group.

Page 304: From Smithsonian website, www.si.edu. © 2004 Smithsonian Institution. Reprinted with permission.

Figures 1.2, 2.1, 3.1, and 5.3 used by permission of Allyn & Bacon.

Photos

Page 1: Charles Gupton/Corbis; **5:** Tom McCarthy/PhotoEdit, Inc.; **12:** Halebran/Liaison/Getty Images; **21:** David J. Sams/Stock Boston; **29:** Mark Joseph/The Image Bank/Getty Images; **32:** Bonnie Kamin/PhotoEdit, Inc.; **36:** ChitoseSuzuki/Index Stock Imagery; **44:** AP/Wide World Photos; **51:** Michael Newman/PhotoEdit, Inc.; **54:** The Everett Collection; **60:** Susan Van Etten/PhotoEdit, Inc.; **66:** Syracuse Newspapers/David Lassman/The Image Works; **72:** Ed Kashi/Corbis; **80:** Gary Hershorn/Reuters; **84:** David Young-Wolff/PhotoEdit, Inc.; **90:** Gary Conner/PhotoEdit, Inc.; **98:** Bob Mahoney/The Image Works; **104:** Harriet Gans/The Image Works; **111:** Gazin/The Image Works; **122:** Bob Mahoney/The Image Works; **130:** Michael Newman/PhotoEdit, Inc.; **142:** David Young-Wolff/PhotoEdit, Inc.; **148:** Bob Daemmrich/Stock Boston; **152:** Charles Gupton/Stock Boston; **171:** Suzanne Dunn/Syracuse Newspapers/The Image Works; **180:** Fotocronache Olympia/PhotoEdit, Inc.; **183:** David Young-Wolff/PhotoEdit, Inc.; **185:** Michael Newman/PhotoEdit, Inc.; **197:** Kathy McLaughlin/The Image Works; **200:** Bob Krist/Corbis; **204:** Mark Richards/PhotoEdit, Inc.; **208:** Consolidated/Archive PhotosGetty Images; **216:** Mark Richards/PhotoEdit, Inc.; **219:** Bary King/Liaison/Getty Images; **229:** David Young-Wolff/PhotoEdit, Inc.; **231:** Mark Richards/PhotoEdit, Inc.; **238:** Bob Daemmrich/The Image Works; **243:** Myrleen Ferguson Cate/PhotoEdit, Inc.; **253:** Randi Anglin/The Image Works; **262:** © 2001 Warner Bros. All Rights Reserved; **271:** PA/Topham/The Image Works; **276:** AP/Wide World Photos; **281:** Robert Mecca/Getty Images; **286:** Skjold Photographs/The Image Works; **291:** Paula Lerner/Index Stock Imagery; **297:** Photodisc Green/Getty Images; **303:** Ryanstock/TaxiGetty Images; **305:** The Everett Collection